"Silent No More"

Modern Jewish History

Henry L. Feingold, *Series Editor*

"Silent No More"

Saving the Jews of Russia,
The American Jewish Effort, 1967–1989

Henry L. Feingold

Syracuse University Press

ISBN-13: 978-0-8156-3101-9
ISBN-10: 0-8156-3101-4

Library of Congress Cataloging-in-Publication Data

Feingold, Henry L., 1931–
Silent no more : saving the Jews of Russia, the American Jewish
effort, 1967–1989 / Henry L. Feingold.—1st ed.
p. cm.—(Modern Jewish History)
Includes bibliographical references and index.
ISBN 0–8156–3101–4 (cloth : alk. paper)
1. Jews—Persecutions—Soviet Union.
2. Jews—Migrations—Government policy—Soviet Union. 3. Jews—
United States—Politics and government—20th century.
4. Soviet Union—Emigration and immigration—
Government policy. 5. Soviet Union—Ethnic relations.
6. National Conference on Soviet Jewry (U.S.) I. Title.
DS135.R92F45 2006
323.1192'404709045—dc22   2006023418

Manufactured in the United States of America

This book is dedicated to the hundreds of courageous Soviet refuseniks and the activists who took up their cause. It was their courage and fortitude that sustained the Soviet Jewry movement for over a quarter of a century.

Henry L. Feingold is professor of history emeritus, formerly at Baruch College and the Graduate Center of the City University of New York. Among other works, he is author of *Bearing Witness: How America and Its Jews Responded to the Holocaust* and *A Time for Searching: Entering the Mainstream, 1920–1945,* a volume in his highly acclaimed series, *The Jewish People in America.*

Contents ■

Illustrations ■

Preface ■

On the face of it the subject of this study is the story of a comparatively small population movement, barely a blip on the monitor of historical events. The Jewish historical experience is full of such emigrations but this one is unusual. It occurred in a closed society that required its citizens to carry an internal passport. There were many regulations but no single immigration law that governed the entering and leaving of Soviet space. Yet during a period of two decades thousands of Soviet Jews broke out from this virtual "prison house of nations." How that was achieved and its impact on world affairs is the story this book seeks to tell.

The insistence on the freedom of movement by Soviet activists challenged the control of a tyrannical state more directly than any other freedom. A totalitarian system cannot survive when its subjects can vote with their feet. In 1989, the year this study ends, thousands of East Germans, following the refusenik model, circumvented the Berlin Wall to make their way to the West through Hungary and Austria to the German Federal Republic, a breakout that marked the end of the Cold War. Though seldom mentioned among the noteworthy events of that war, the Soviet Jewish emigration movement acted like a slow leak in a tire, one of several silent catalysts that brought the eventual disintegration of the Soviet empire.

The Soviet Jewish emigration problem is the visible part of a historical knot that joins three streams of history. Its Soviet strand furnishes the actors in the historical drama. They are a remarkable group of activists, sometimes called "refuseniks" or "prisoners of conscience," who tested and defied the Soviet control system. In the early years and continuing through the 1980s their courage and persistence made them the prime movers in the historical drama. Their desire to emigrate and group cohesiveness are in turn tied to a historical strand that forms part of the immigration history of Israel. It was Israel's government that established a secret liaison bureau and furnished consular officials who built a network within the Soviet Union reestablishing a link to the forbidden outside world. Finally, there is American Jewry, whose contribution was enabled by its fortunate location that allowed it to play its familiar role of advocate before the American seat of power. It was its hesitant but also imaginative exercise of that power that brought Soviet Jewry's quest to emigrate to a high place on the Cold War agenda.

This study deals with all three strands, as it must, but its center of gravity is the last-mentioned stream. The problem is viewed in the context of American Jewish and Cold War history. The intertwining of different streams of history, each with its own players and motives, would be difficult to write under any circumstances. Imagine then the challenge faced by the historian in understanding the motivations of a foreign minority that seeks to be released from the grip of a powerful secretive government and looks upon a related American ethnic group to intercede through its government. To this day there are those who insist that the Jewish emigration problem was a Cold War contrivance of certain anti-détente "elements" in the United States. There may be some truth in that but the problems related to the emigration of Russian Jewry actually go back to the turn of the century, long before the years encompassed in this study. In reading the early chapters of this book that examine the early activities of the American government and the role played by Jacob Schiff and others on behalf of Russian Jewry, it becomes clear that in the relationship between Russian and American Jewry the notion "the more things change, the more they remain the same" is especially true.

In the Jewish Diaspora Russian Jewry ranks as one of the most productive though also one of its most beleaguered of communities. Yet for the historian the problem of defining the actual threat it faced during the years of this study is a real one. To some extent the Soviet system was an "equal opportunity" tyranny. Jews were after all not kulaks or "class enemies" earmarked for destruction. Some trot out statistics indicating that Soviet Jewry, especially its educated urban element, despite persistent discrimination, went further in achieving the Soviet version of the good life than other ethnic groups. There is some truth in that yet there was and always has been a Jewish problem in Russia that differentiates it from other victimized groups. But it is possible to misperceive the threat faced by Soviet Jewry. In the American movement, especially, the calibration of danger faced and miseries endured were bedeviled by the Holocaust, which haunts the imagination of all Jewish communities. There were activists who were convinced that Soviet Jewry needed to be rescued, the way the Jews of Europe were not during World War II.

That a prior searing historic experience such as the Holocaust would color the perception of subsequent events was predictable. But the impact of the Holocaust analogy makes the rendering of the Soviet Jewry story especially challenging. Unlike the Nazis, the Soviet regime sought to retain its Jews, not to make Russia *Judenrein*. The historian needs to be clear about it. After Stalin's death in 1953 the threat of physical destruction can be discounted, but the existential threat to Jewish communal and cultural life based on government policy and fueled by a generic anti-Semitism at the grass roots persisted.

Unless they openly challenged the system, as did the refuseniks, it was possible for a Soviet Jew to endure life despite open discrimination. Thousands, perhaps a majority, of Soviet Jews chose the path of accommodation. That has a great deal to do with the "dropout," problem that serves as an intriguing aspect of this study. The post-1975 wave of Soviet Jewish emigrants simply desired to leave a failing system, which, when combined with the specific denial of access, made the conception of a future for their children difficult. Each potential emigrant had to make a judgment on whether it was worth risking the social and economic limbo status that the Soviet bureaucracy reserved for those applying for a visa for the promise of life elsewhere. As the risk decreased after 1985 the number joining the emigrant stream increased. As that occurred the researcher increasingly has to re-examine the relevance of the rescue motif that so aroused the passions of adherents of the Soviet Jewry movement. If the movement, which had become worldwide by 1972, was not primarily about rescuing Soviet Jewry per se, then what was it about? It is the search for an answer to that question that fuels this study.

Approach and Sources

The archival mainstay of this work are the papers of the National Conference on Soviet Jewry housed in the archives of the American Jewish Historical Society located in the Center of Jewish History in New York, where much of the available archival material for researching the Soviet Jewry episode will eventually be centrally located. Because the redemption of Soviet Jewry that serves as the historic context of this work is in fact the most recent episode in a more than a century-long history of American Jewish relations with Russian Jewry, the papers of Louis Marshall and Jacob Schiff, housed in the National Jewish Archives on the campus of the Hebrew Union College in Cincinnati, proved particularly useful for the first chapter of this book.

This study seeks to contextualize the Soviet Jewish experience within the stream of American Jewry's extensive relations with related Jewish communities abroad. Use has been made of government documents generated by congressional hearings and State Department publications relating to the Soviet Jewry issue. The State Department's *Foreign Relations of the United States* series was also useful for the early chapters. Additional government-generated sources are listed below. Also extensively used are relevant monographs and monographic articles, memoirs relating to the emigration of Soviet Jewry. Extensive use was made of the Anglo-Jewish press and the publications of the organizations and agencies directly involved in the campaign to "free" Soviet Jewry. Especially useful was the *Daily Bulletin of the Jewish Telegraph Agency,* which serves as a kind of newspaper of record. For the way the story played in the American press I have used primarily the *New York Times* and the *Washington Post* and such other newspapers and magazines that occasionally featured a story or an article. Particularly useful has been the collection of more than one hundred interviews of activists involved with the Soviet Jewry movement now housed in the Dorot division of the New York Public Library and formerly part of the Wiener Oral History project of the American Jewish Committee. Use is also made of relevant doctoral dissertations.

An increasing number of sources are now available through specific Web sites on the internet. For example, "Googling" "Soviet emigrants" or some variation thereof yields documents and secondary material from agencies and organizations involved in the Soviet Jewry movement. Similarly "Googling" U.S. Department of State Office of Research yields a wealth of material on research conducted by the department regarding Soviet Jewry generally and specific matters such as changing Soviet emigration regulations. This research focuses on the American aspect of the Soviet Jewry movement, but one soon discovers that the story is interwoven with the Soviet and Israeli branches of the movement. I rely on the abundant published secondary sources. Particularly worthy of mention is a translation of heretofore secret documents of the Soviet KGB archives, Boris Morozov's *Documents on Soviet Jewish Emigration* (London: Frank Cass, 2001).

Finally, I am especially grateful to the Baruch College Library and its well-trained staff that assured me access to its interlibrary loan program and data banks, which proved especially useful for accessing newspapers and journals.

I have tried to keep the research apparatus as simple as possible while satisfying the standards of modern scholarship. Footnotes are confined to direct quotations or paraphrasing and useful information, especially statistics, that would interfere with the flow of the narrative and background information that clarifies or furnishes background for a point made in the narrative. A modified *Chicago* style format for citations is employed. There is a first full citation and thereafter "ibid." is used for citations in direct sequence. A shortened version of the full citation is used for additional citations not in direct sequence.

Acknowledgments ■

This research project was conceived and organized by the late Dr. Murray Friedman, founder and director of the Myer and Rosaline Feinstein Center for American Jewish History of Temple University in Philadelphia. Two activists, Connie and Joseph Smukler, who played leading roles in the movement, provided a generous grant administered by the Feinstein Center, which gave me a free hand to delve into all corners of this complex, passion-ridden subject. They have my gratitude for their support and patience. I am also grateful to the archivists, librarians, and sundry helpers associated with the third floor reading room of the Center for Jewish History in New York City and the Dorot Center for Jewish History of the New York Public Library, where much of the research was undertaken. The major archival collection on which this work rests, the papers of the National Conference on Soviet Jewry (NCSJ), is part of the archives of the American Jewish Historical Society. I learned the intricate details of how things were done "on the ground" from this collection, which went far to shape my image of the movement. Finally, I need to thank Veronica Manlow, who administers Baruch College's Jewish Resource Center under my direction. There were others who helped by reading and informing me where I might be out of bounds. They know who they are. Errors of fact and syntax that are bound to occur in such a broad study are my own as is overall conception of how the Soviet Jewry issue is approached.

"Silent No More"

ONE Historic Seeds

The desire of Jews to leave Russia was not a new aspiration in Russian history nor was the American Jewish concern about the treatment of Russian Jewry. In the discussion that follows episodes are drawn from the century-long history of American Jewish involvement with the travails of Russian Jewry and its government. The episodes are not chosen arbitrarily. Each casts light on an analogous situation between 1967 and 1989, the years on which this study focuses. We learn that whether we speak of the campaign to abrogate the Commercial Treaty of 1832, the private efforts of Jacob Schiff to deny the American bond market to Moscow, or the campaign to add the Jackson-Vanik Amendment to the Russo-American treaty of 1974, the ingredients of this historic stew remain remarkably constant. There are the hapless Jewish victims, and there is a quest from American Jewry for succor and diplomatic intercession. There are the vexing problems posed by resettlement. Sometimes the glance backward reveals a startling similarity to the rationale of a contemporary problem. Our probe of the Crimean resettlement project of the 1920s shows that the question of whether Soviet Jewry can be best helped in place or through mass emigration is not new and neither is American Jewry's conflict with the world Zionist movement about the disposition of the emigrants.

The assumption that we can learn directly from history by simply finding a like incident from the past requires a note of caution. It is true that the American Jewish mobilization to "rescue" Russian Jewry had historic precedents that give it its shape. These similarities are not examples of history repeating itself. They speak, rather, to the continuity of the flow of historical events. We also need to be aware of one difference that makes the emigration of Soviet Jewry unprecedented. It concerns the amplification of a seemingly minor problem on the international relations agenda into an important one. At the turn of the century the question of Russian Jewish emigration remained primarily a communal concern. We want to know more about the historical circumstances and the strategies that made possible the elevation of Soviet Jewish emigration into an international concern.

■ From the perspective of history the emigration of Soviet Jewry was part of the latest phase of an East-West Jewish migration that began in earnest in the last third of the nineteenth century and that brought millions of Jewish immigrants to American shores. Between 1875 and 1914 about 2.4 million Jews from eastern Europe immigrated to the United States, about 1.5 million from Tsarist Russia.[1] That by itself tells a good deal about the reason for American Jewry's interest in the condition of the Jews of Russia. They were more than merely coreligionists, a term frequently used in the diplomatic correspondence. American Jewry became a derivative east European Jewry that had Russian Jewry at its core. The Soviet emigrants American Jewry sought to "rescue" were culturally and sometimes somatically connected to them. That sense of kinship adds dimension to the notion of family reunification that became Moscow's rationale for allowing some to emigrate. It was the grandchildren and great-grandchildren of these eastern immigrants who took up the cudgels for their "kin" in the Soviet Union. Yet by 1967 that sense of personal kinship after many generations was remote, so one needs to wonder whether the passion to "rescue" Soviet Jewry among American activists had something to do with a search for their own Jewish identities.

Family ties also played a crucial role in the confrontation with the Tsarist regime regarding the rights of American passport holders. A lively commerce that involved primarily visits of earlier Jewish immigrants to the families left behind developed. When Bernard Bernstein, a Russian immigrant holding American citizenship, returned to his native town to visit his parents, he was arrested and imprisoned for draft evasion. In 1864 the State Department, under Secretary William Seward, intervened in 1864 and won Bernstein's release. It was the first of innumerable cases concerning the validity of the American passport and the rights of American citizens abroad.[2]

The passport problem was but one of several clashes with the Kremlin involving the rights of naturalized American Jewish citizens in Russia. Jewish communal leaders requested diplomatic intercession for their religious brethren abroad in the Damascus blood libel case in 1840 and for the infamous kidnapping of Edgar Mortara (1858), a Jewish child whom the church claimed as its own after baptism. It was the two days of mob violence in Kishinev in April 1903 that more than other events fixed the focus of American Jewry on Russian depredations. According to one observer it was "the last pogrom of the Middle ages and the first atrocity of the twentieth century."[3] The birth of American Jewish activism that we later witness in protests against incidents such as the Leningrad hijacking trial began with the reaction to Kishinev.

Then, as today, American Jewish leaders appealed to the government in Washington for intercession. A kind of ritual developed whereby upon request the State Department would have such a note penned by the department's master of penmanship and humanitarian sentiments, Alvey Adee. For Jews the idea of asking for diplomatic intercession was based on the notion that a "spirit of civilization" could be mobilized to protect their brethren. Though there was ample evidence after the Holocaust that Jews were not considered part of such a "universe of obligation," the assumption that there existed such a spirit of concern of "civilization" remained very much part of Jewish political culture during the struggle to "free" Soviet Jewry.

The diplomatic notes could be passionate in their quest for redress. One of the earliest notes concerning the removal of twenty thousand Jews from southwest Russia was sent by the Grant administration in 1867. Another noteworthy for its philosemitism was composed for Secretary of State James Blaine to the British Foreign Office inquiring about the possibility of joint protest action after the punishing May Laws of 1881. The British rejected the idea. As the Russian crisis intensified the number of requests for diplomatic intercession increased. As early as 1891 Benjamin Harrison created a commission that furnished a national interest rationale for American concern about how Tsarist Russia treated its Jews. The Weber commission pointed out that the massive influx of penniless Russian Jews was so straining facilities that the United States was inevitably involved in a problem that affected the welfare of its citizens.[4]

The State Department's complaint to the Kremlin was not an exaggeration. So dire had the situation become for Russian Jewry that according to one historian, "Emigration became one of [its] characteristic phenomena."[5] The note and Harrison's mention of the Russian Jewish immigration problem in his third annual address to Congress in December 1891 won the plaudits of the growing number of restrictionists but did little to ameliorate the miserable condition of Russian Jewry. In December 1905, a particularly bad year for the Jews of Russia, Jacob H. Schiff, the leading American Jewish philanthropist who had become obsessed with Russia's mistreatment of its Jews, requested yet another note: "If the United States was justified in 1898. . . . to intercede in Cuba," he argued in a letter to Theodore Roosevelt, "is it not in the face of the horrors now occurring in Russia . . . the duty of the civilized world to intercede [in Russia]. . . . ?"[6] But Schiff's assumption that the welfare of a distant Jewish population could generate the same kind of interest as the invasion of Cuba and the Philippines was naïve. Though rhetoric of human rights and humanitarian aspiration was often infused in Roosevelt's explanation of

"Big Stick" diplomacy, he abhorred moralistic dispatches when there was no intent to back them up with force. Six decades later Jewish leaders depended on a similar rationale of human rights in its public relations concerning Soviet Jewry. The Soviet Jewry movement would have experienced difficulty sustaining itself without such an assumption. It was assumed that humanitarianism was part of the intent of American foreign relations.

During these early years of the twentieth century the request for diplomatic intercession became an integral part of ethnic politics. After Romania passed its infamous Artisan Law (1902) restricting Jews from learning and practicing certain crafts, the State Department, upon request of Jewish leaders, responded by characterizing the law as "repugnant to the moral sense of liberal modern peoples." It was the kind of rhetoric that spoke to American Jewry. John Hay's note triggered an outburst of gratitude, and he was invited to campaign on Manhattan's Lower East Side for Roosevelt, who had become American Jewry's favorite political leader. Teddy's name, after all, appeared on their treasured citizenship papers. On 20 August 1902, Hay wrote a thank you note to Adee, with the admonition "please burn promptly." The note informed Adee that "the President is greatly pleased and the Hebrews . . . poor dears! all over the country think we are bully boys." Later when the now shrewder *American Hebrew* began castigating the administration for its indifference to the Russian depredations, Hay instructed Adee to pen yet another note: "Even if Russia does nothing," he observed, "we shall have a good note to print next winter."[7]

Much like the practitioners of realpolitik in Kissinger's State Department, the department policy makers at the turn of the century had little faith that moralistic dispatches could generate moral behavior. As in the later period, those in the department were aware that immigration policy was an internal matter, but they were also anxious to avoid losing Jewish political support. That was clearly the case of the massive petition collected by B'nai B'rith to be transmitted to the Kremlin after the Kishinev pogrom. Wanting to forestall a humiliating incident for the American government, Hay pointed out to the three prominent Jewish organizers of the mass petition addressed to the Tsarist government, Leo Levi, Simon Wolf, and Oscar Straus, that despite their heroic efforts to attract names of important people, the Russian government would probably not accept the petition. The petition organizers were nonplussed. The idea of a petition to the Tsarist government had been thought up by the leaders to help assuage the growing pressure for action emanating from the "noisy quarter," the "uptown" appellative for the Jews of the Lower East Side, many of whose inhabitants had but a few years previously suffered the outrages of the Russian pogroms. There was talk of organizing an international conference on the Kishinev pogrom.[8] Eventually Hay convinced the leaders that the wisest course would be to place the petition in the department's archives without ever delivering it. Adee outdid himself in praise of this futile action. "It is a valuable addition to public literature, and it will be sacredly cherished among the treasures of this Department," he wrote. The petition was never delivered.

It was Roosevelt's aversion to such diplomatic gestures that brought the matter of Jewish requests for intercession and the State Department's response with a "politics of gestures" to a head.[9] He thought that Jacob Schiff's insistence on such intercessions was "hysterical." His response was not unlike the reaction of many in the first Bush administration who came to believe that the "Jewish thing" interfered with the policy of détente. But in 1903, after the pogrom in Kishinev, the cry for action from the Jewish immigrant community reached a crescendo and again compelled Jewish leaders to turn to the government. In the face of pressure that followed even Roosevelt, who had informed Oscar Straus that the posing of empty threats made the United States appear ridiculous, had to step back. When news was received before Easter of 1905 that a new wave of pogroms was imminent, the State Department responded with the usual notes of concern and received in response news from its consuls that depredations were exaggerated and no pogroms were expected. As was the case in later years, State Department officials in the Nixon and Ford administrations and Jewish leaders such as Nahum Goldmann preferred to address such problems through "quiet" diplomacy.

Adee's eloquent notes may not have had serious intent behind them, but when they were examined six decades later, it was noticed that many of the human rights principles then cited have reappeared in diplomatic correspondence. American delegates such as Morris Abram and Rita Hauser at the United Nations Commission on Human Rights drew upon a precedent of U.S. concern that was established in the nineteenth century and early decades of the twentieth. Well before 1967, because there always seemed to be some beleaguered Jewish community on the horizon, there was already in place a ritual of petitioning the American government for intercession and redress. In turn, the government response brought dozens of demarches and notes of concern, oral inquiries, and congressional resolutions addressed to the tyranny of the moment. The notes were not expected to change behavior and were meant primarily as a gesture that cost the administration nothing but earned political points.

American Jews were not alone in requesting government intercession on their behalf. Poles, Greeks, Irish, and other American ethnics have tried to project such influence on the making of foreign policy.[10] But the Jewish Diaspora communities were more vulnerable. Even after formal emancipation they continued to be viewed as "guests," as was the case in some Rhineland communities where they had settled before the native population. American Jewish leaders had a greater need to seek the intercession of the American government and became practiced at it. The projection of such influence was not without danger. In later years the late chairman of the Senate Foreign Relations Committee, Sen. J. William Fulbright, felt that the so-called Jewish lobby projected too much influence on American foreign policy.[11] The Jewish response to such charges emphasized the confluence between the American and Jewish interest bound together by common Judeo-Christian standards of moral behavior. Whatever the case, the patterns of request and response had become so stylized by the Cold War period that they are almost instantly recognizable by the researcher.

These analogous patterns are especially apparent in the effort of Jewish leaders to wring better treatment for Russian Jewry by abrogating the Commercial Treaty of 1832 that governed Russian exports to the American market at the turn of the century. There is a remarkable resemblance in strategy to the Jackson-Vanik Amendment a half century later but the parallels should not conceal the fact that although the strategy used seem the same they were in fact quite different episodes. At the turn of the century America was wracked by racial and ethnic tensions, and support for mass immigration was on the wane. Between 1894 and 1914 the nation witnessed about 3,600 lynchings, the Chinese Exclusion Act (1882) and the Gentleman's Agreement (1907–8) were passed, and a movement to set higher medical and literacy standards for immigrants was well underway. The passion for what the *American Hebrew* called "nordomania," the preference of the blond and blue-eyed immigrant from northern and western Europe, would become the basis of the quota system of the Immigration Act of 1924. To the noted Yiddish journalist Gedaliah Bublick, testifying before a congressional hearing, the law seemed to be aimed specifically at restricting Russian Jewish immigrants.[12] The act contrasts sharply with the generous refugee law in effect in 1972, which made America an ideal, if still far removed from being fully accessible.

The most startling contrast between the two episodes is that the Tsarist regime wanted to rid itself of the Jews, at least one-third of them, through emigration, whereas Soviet policy could not abide anyone wanting to leave the Socialist paradise and in effect prohibited free immigration.[13] The originating circumstances of the two episodes are also quite different. The initiative for the

Jackson-Vanik Amendment that sought to link Soviet behavior toward Jewish emigration with most-favored-nation status, which was customarily accompanied by favorable credit arrangements, emanated from Congress. In contrast, the movement to abrogate the commercial treaty with Russia started as a strategy of the leadership of the American Jewish Committee (AJC) and was implemented by Louis Marshall, its first president.

The roots of the earlier conflict are again found in Moscow's refusal to honor the reciprocal rights clause of the commercial treaty that gave citizens of the treaty the right to "sojourn and trade" in each domain. In the last quarter of the nineteenth century Moscow began routinely to restrict most Jewish returnees by refusing to visa their passports. The American government was requested to separate visa applications of Jewish returnees. When American officials complied with the Russian request, the government became in effect an instrument to extend an anti-Semitic Tsarist policy. By discriminating against its own citizens it violated the equal rights provisions of the Constitution as well as the sanctity of the American passport.

Both these points were endlessly pressed by Louis Marshall and other Jewish leaders, but neither the Roosevelt nor Taft administration, the latter in the throes of "dollar diplomacy," were anxious to disrupt trade with Russia for the sake of a few thousand persecuted Jews. It was only when these tactics were exhausted that the campaign to use the commercial treaty was initiated. Triggered by the horrendous Beilis blood libel trial and foreseeing that the troubled campaign of 1912 would furnish a good political moment, Jewish leaders, much like the anti-détente faction around Sen. Jackson, sensed that the time was ripe to use a new tactic to wring concessions from the Kremlin. The termination or abrogation issue was now placed in the forefront of American Jewish concerns, and the pressure was switched from the executive branch, which opposed tampering with Russian trade, to Congress. Clause twelve of the treaty permitted Congress to request the president for termination. It became a political issue.

◼ After the democratization movement of Jewish communal life initiated by the Congress movement in the first decade of the century, it became rare to find a leader such as Schiff who possessed the financial estate, personal influence, and total immersion in Jewish affairs. In posture and political bent Max Fisher bore some resemblance to Schiff. He had similar affiliation with the Republican Party and total involvement with Jewish politics, but he did not have the resources of a powerful banking house at his command. In the years before the abrogation campaign Schiff used his economic power to deny a credit-starved Russia loans. Though aware that using his economic leverage ran the risk of reinforcing the prevalent anti-Semitic image of a Jewish money conspiracy, Schiff nevertheless wielded this economic tool without hesitation. It was a private instrument with only a fraction of the denial power of the Jackson-Vanik Amendment. His conviction that Russia would only respond to relentless pressure bears an uncanny resemblance to the Soviet activists and leadership of the Union of Councils for Soviet Jewry (UCSJ) who came to the same conclusion five decades later.

Like Max Fisher in the later period, Schiff and Marshall were actively involved in the Republican Party and maintained good relations with President Roosevelt. A heavy German accent and a hearing problem were not allowed to interfere with his strong advocacy of the rights of Jews as Americans. Serge Witte, the Russian foreign minister, who negotiated several times with Schiff on the Russian Jewish issue once declared, "I have never met such a Jew as Schiff. Proud, dignified, conscious of his power, he declared to me solemnly that as long as the Tsar's government would continue its anti-Jewish policy he would exert every effort to make it impossible for Russia to get a copeck in the U.S."[14] There are some like Nahum Goldmann who aspired to a similar role later in the century but no one like Schiff ever developed. The democratization of Jewish communal governance no longer allowed for it.

Virtually every instrument and tactic used between 1967 and 1989 was developed during the period in which Marshall and Schiff were leaders. Our interest lies primarily in understanding how Schiff deployed the resources and instruments available to him to influence public policy. He led the Jewish effort to have the newly created investigative Weber commission report accurately on the Russian Jewish condition to the Harrison administration. He had become convinced that an enlightened public could move mountains, and the road to such enlightenment was through public relations and a free press. To ensure that information was available and accurate, he went one step further in trying to get Andrew White, former president of Cornell University and known for his sympathy for the Jewish plight, posted as ambassador to Russia. After his appointment, White kept Schiff informed of developments in Russia so that Schiff maintained his own private information pipeline. No effort was spared to get the story of Russian Jewry out. The later Soviet Jewry movement's efforts to "let my people know" find their precedent in Schiff's earlier effort. Schiff alerted the liberal press—Oswald Garrison Villard, editor of the *Nation,* George Jonas of the *New York Times,* and Horace White, editor of the *New York Evening Post*—to the Russian problem and then actually underwrote a reporting trip to Russia by a well-known journalist, Harold Frederic of the *New York Times*. Single handedly he arranged for publications of scholarly books on the Russian situation and became fast friends with George Kennan, the first scholar and diplomat to expose the Tsarist Gulag. He even thought of sponsoring a pro-Jewish press in Russia. Schiff's anti-Russian campaign became a personal fixation. He was a kind of Moshe Decter, with money.[15]

In one respect Schiff's approach stands in sharp contrast to the contemporary Soviet Jewry movement. He feared unleashing the "masses" to exert pressure and would have been especially uncomfortable with some of the public relations tactics later deployed to win public attention. Predictably, he faced staunch opposition from the members of the Congress movement who sought democracy in Jewish communal governance. Abraham Cahan, the editor of the popular *Forward*, condemned him as a shtadlan, a court Jew who acts for rather than with his Jewish constituency. The Socialist Cahan, foreseeing the later conflict between Soviet activists who favored the democratization of the Soviet Union in place and those Jews who simply wanted to emigrate, believed, incorrectly as it developed, that only the overthrow of the Tsarist regime would bring the complete liberation of Russian Jewry, which faced oppression under the Communist regime as well. Yet without Schiff's financial support, the first centralized body dealing specifically with Russian Jewry, the National Committee for Relief of Sufferers by Russian Massacre, founded after the pogroms of 1905 and a kind of historic precursor to the National Conference on Soviet Jewry (NCSJ), would never have seen the light of day.

His primary effort to convince the Kremlin to ameliorate the oppressive conditions under which Russian Jews lived was made after the Kishinev pogrom. Schiff then abandoned the idea that the "good will" of the Russian authorities could be won by normal petitioning. He became an "active adversary."[16] He maximized efforts to deny Russia credit on the American bond market. He assumed that the ability of Kuhn-Loeb to do so would be strengthened by the European Jewish banking nexus and by his friendship with Ernest Cassel and J. P. Morgan. The Rothschilds and other English banking houses had in any case ceased doing business with Russia. He was disappointed when the German Jewish banking houses did not follow his lead. When the National City Bank planned to float a Russian loan he threatened to resign from its board after failing to convince J. P. Morgan that the loan was morally as well as financially unsound. Schiff correctly predicted that they would suffer the financial consequences of Russia's default. But his failure to mobilize the banking community had a benevolent impact as well. Those who imagined a Jewish conspiracy to control the world's money supply were sadly disappointed when the Jewish banking families would not follow Schiff's anti-Russian plan to withhold credit. Charles Eliot, who became president of Harvard and imposed a policy of limiting Jewish enrollment, wondered why Jewish bankers did not act together to alleviate the distress of their religious brethren. Outsiders understood little of the fractiousness of Jewish organizational life.

Schiff's role is particularly relevant for this study because he attempted to achieve privately what the Jackson-Vanik Amendment later tried to do through public policy. His effort was not complicated by democratic politics, and his attempt to boycott credit was not completely successful. But it proved sufficiently effective to keep Japan in the field long enough to witness the collapse of a financially bankrupt Russia. Adolf Kraus, president of B'nai B'rith, arranged for the Russian negotiator Serge Witte to meet with five Jewish leaders at the peace negotiations in Portsmouth. Schiff reluctantly joined the group. The delegation, composed of Oscar Straus, Isaac Seligman, and Adolph Lewisohn as well as Kraus, thought they heard that finally the Russian government was prepared gradually to ameliorate the situation of its Jews. Witte argued that their help was necessary to keep Russia out of the revolutionary camp. But Schiff had heard it before and remained adamant in his opposition. He announced to his partners at Kuhn-Loeb that the house would resist Russian access to the bond market even after his death. He believed that a lessening of pressure on the Kremlin would worsen the condition of Russian Jewry. It was a situation that bears an uncanny resemblance to the split in the Jewish community in 1987 when Gorbachev's liberalization promised the fulfillment of aspirations for Soviet Jewry. His doubts about Moscow's intentions resemble those of the UCSJ in 1989. But Schiff's projections were more accurate. After the lost war with Japan the bloody pogroms actually intensified.

Moscow ultimately secured loans elsewhere, and Schiff's distrust was deepened by the Mendel Beilis blood libel trial that began in 1911. It was more evidence that Moscow had not changed its ways. But the trial posed a problem for Louis Marshall, who feared that the public agitation would muddy the waters because Beilis was not a citizen of the United States.[17] Realistic enough to realize that his efforts had brought little improvement for Russian Jewry, Schiff turned to a new strategy offered by the passport question. Perhaps a government-to-government approach might be more effective than one wealthy patrician trying to change government policy. Unlike the movement to terminate the Commercial Treaty of 1832 with Russia, when Jewish activists could not count on much support for a linkage between the lure of trade and better treatment from the Russian government, the movement to alter the Russo-American trade agreement of 1974 eventually gained the support of Congress.[18] In 1911 America was not yet an economic superpower, and trade was the lifeblood of economic development. The Taft administration was guided in its foreign relations by the policy of dollar diplomacy. As outlined by one of its major advocates, Secretary of State Philander Knox, the dollar would enhance American power and play the same role for the nation as other nations projected power through their military forces. In contrast, by the 1970s America's role in the world economy had become supreme and in a sense its prevailing Cold War sensibility bore a striking resemblance to the way Jacob Schiff viewed Moscow. That change made all the difference.

The influential role of corporations and agricultural interests involved in Russo-American trade in balancing the Jewish interest is instructive. In the Jackson-Vanik Amendment and in the abrogation campaign, business leaders mounted a strong campaign against the Jewish effort to use trade as a lever to obtain better behavior from Moscow. During the Carter and Reagan administrations, business leaders argued that the amendment would hurt the economy, the same note sounded in the congressional testimony presented by the Singer Sewing Machine Company, International Harvester Corporation, the Chattanooga Plow Company, and dozens of other firms in 1912. Statistics were deployed to show an enormous profit loss. It was suggested that competitors such as Germany and France stood ready to fill the vacuum and that Russia would retaliate against American exports. But Marshall, who directed the abrogation campaign, chose to not respond to these pocketbook arguments directly. Instead, he urged his testifiers to speak exclusively in terms of the rights of American citizens and the challenge Moscow presented to constitutional rights. In the first decade of the twentieth century no Cold War existed that would allow the Soviet Jewish emigration issue to become an instrument to win concessions. Jewish leadership was virtually alone in pressing the point that discrimination against Jewish passport holders challenged the integrity of American law and therefore required a response by the American government. Like the Nixon and Ford administration, Roosevelt and his successor Taft resisted, allowing the fate of a foreign minority to determine the shape of the nation's Russian policy. American Jewish political leadership had not yet been tested but one contrast is discernible. Unlike the hesitant and disunited posture of Jewish leadership during the Holocaust and to a lesser extent during the Soviet Jewry crisis, the leadership group led by Louis Marshall and the newly organized AJC never wavered from its primary objective. The more democratically governed community generated more energy and activism but also brought disunity and lack of coherence. Both forms of organization ultimately proved too weak to modify the behavior of a powerful foreign state. But American Jewry in the period after 1967 was less isolated and closer to those who controlled the levers of power and therefore more effective.

■   The strategies of coalition politics and the reliance on public relations first developed by Louis Marshall during the struggle for abrogation also called for enlisting prominent non-Jewish leaders to spearhead the movement. Largely financed by Jacob Schiff, the movement gained momentum in 1911 through a remarkable public relations effort. Marshall and Cyrus Adler, who in his long public career headed virtually every Jewish defense agency including the AJC, acted as the field commanders, and Schiff ran a kind of independent campaign. He encouraged Rep. Parsons, a Christian, rather than Rep. Goldfogle, representing a Jewish district, from introducing the final abrogation resolution.[19] A National Citizens Committee, organized to support the campaign, was headed by Andrew White and William McAdoo, two prominent Christian leaders. They testified at the congressional hearings, frequently mentioning that the Tsarist government also discriminated against Protestant and Catholic clergy as well as Christian missionaries. Finally, Marshall attached the abrogation movement to a group headed by George Kennan and John Bassett Moore, both friends of Schiff, who exposed the Tsarist "gulag" and advocated the abrogation of the Russian Extradition Treaty of 1887. The strategy was to project the campaign for abrogation as not a Jewish fight but an American one. The argument for the Jackson-Vanik Amendment was similarly couched in terms of human rights rather than wrongs committed exclusively against Soviet Jews.

In some ways Marshall's campaign was more innovative than the one sponsored by the American Soviet Jewry movement decades later. The basic theme was that discrimination against Jewish passport holders was an American and not merely a Jewish question. Two joint congressional resolutions calling for termination of the treaty, the first introduced by Rep. William Sulzer on 11 November 1911 and the second a month later, brought congressional hearings where the "termination" could be articulated and publicized. In recognition for his efforts Schiff later generously supported Sulzer's campaign for the governorship of New York. The Taft administration, in a desperate move to forestall the momentum building for abrogation, suggested to Moscow that they take advantage of article 12 of the treaty and that both parties call for the negotiation of a new treaty. But in a response not unlike that given by Moscow during the later Leningrad hijacking trial and its education tax debacle, the Kremlin rejected Knox's proposal. It eventually became clear that the Taft administration could not be moved on the passport issue. At the same time, and with the Beilis case acting as a stimulant, the determination to somehow make the Kremlin accountable for its behavior intensified. The congressional approval of the abrogation resolution in December 1911 signaled a victory in the campaign. Convinced that it would bear great consequence, Marshall expressed personal satisfaction at what had been achieved. For the stewards, such as Schiff and Marshall, it had become a personal matter. When a pro-termination plank found its way into the platform of both parties and Roosevelt's rump Progressive Party in the Bull Moose campaign of 1912, Jewish dominance of the issue seemed complete. Taft lost the election and his opponent Woodrow Wilson favored abrogation. In 1913, Russia's main exports to the United States, wood pulp and paper, ceased to be admitted under the minimum tariff rates of the treaty. Russian adamancy on the passport question actually hardened in 1912, and no new treaty was signed.

The Tsarist regime continued its passport discrimination against American Jews until 1917 when it was overthrown by revolution. Schiff tried to reconcile his relations with Taft and eventually switched allegiance to the Democratic Party but to no avail. To the end of his life Taft was convinced that Schiff was determined to ruin his career. He could not understand how such a shrewd businessman as Schiff could succumb to tribal emotionalism when profit and trade were involved. But strangely, after war broke out in August 1914, Schiff, aware that the consensus in the State Department held that aid to Russia would help Russian Jewry and stave off the revolution, sought to soften his credit boycott. In 1914 he offered the Kremlin a last opportunity to modify its anti-Jewish policy, again to no avail. He generously joined in efforts to extend philanthropic help to Russian Jewry but like many other Jews of his background he found it impossible to support "a war to make the world safe for democracy" when an anti-Semitic tyranny was on the Allied side. He joined fifty others to organize the New York branch of the American Neutral Conference Committee. As soon as the Tsarist regime was toppled in March 1917 he generously subscribed to the Russian Liberty Loan and moved to make Kuhn-Loeb's resources available to the provisional government that had at one stroke removed all legal disabilities from Russian Jews. That was what he had been fighting for.

The Jackson-Vanik Amendment was not the first time that a Jewish issue had occupied center stage in the nation's foreign relations. That honor belongs to the campaign to terminate the treaty of 1832. One historian calls it "a significant first in the annals of America Jewish stewardship."[20] Perhaps the most significant lesson to be learned from these tandem events is that the key argument—that nothing could be done because immigration policy is an internal matter, an argument often used by Kissinger—is true only in a restricted formal sense. Once American interest becomes convinced that its own interest is involved and throws its economic weight behind change, the impingement of immigration on both the sending and receiving nations makes it an international issue.

In both cases the improvement of the Jewish condition in Russia awaited a cataclysmic change in its governance. In 1917 it was the Russian Revolution; in 1989 it was the impending collapse of the Soviet empire. In both cases it was the movement of Russian Jews to and from Russia that was at issue. The question of freedom of movement that is at the heart of this study did not suddenly make its debut on the stage of history in 1967. It was present in some form decades before the Russian Revolution. The protection and extrication of Soviet Jewry are really the last episode in a historical stream whose principle players are the American and Russian governments and the relationship of American and Russian Jewry.

■ We come next to the impact of the revolution in Russia on the relationship between the two Jewries. This is not the place to examine each step of the perilous journey upon which Russian Jewry embarked after November 1917. The change of name from Russian to Soviet Jewry only hints at the enormous changes experienced by Jews as a result of the Communist seizure of power. The desire of Russian Jewry to leave Russia and the close link of that movement to American Jewry is not new. But under Communist governance an additional set of ideological strictures played an important role in the development of the emigration movement.

In America the outbreak of war posed problems not only for "uptown" Jewish stewards such as Jacob Schiff but also for the thousands of immigrants who had fled Russia, often leaving family behind. Schiff's hatred of Tsarist Russia had become a passion that involved not only his public life but his private fortune. But for the immigrants the question of support of the war effort was overshadowed by the news of the suffering of their kin in the battle zone. The outbreak of war in 1914 brought a momentary end to the massive immigration movement that linked Russian and American Jewry. In these early years family ties were still strongly felt. There was a sense that the days of mass immigration to the United States were about to end but no hint that under Communist rule the Jews of Russia would be cut off and subject to a massive effort to reshape their identity. For many Russian Jewish immigrants the problem of whether America should become involved on the same side with the most tyrannical power was resolved by the revolution itself. By the time America entered the war in April 1917 the Tsarist government had been overthrown, and one of its first acts of the provisional government was to revoke all anti-Jewish laws and decrees. When the Bolsheviks assumed power in November they issued their Declaration of the Rights of Peoples that included rights for Jews. Gorbachev's reforms after 1985 on the Jewish question were reminiscent of those proposed in this declaration.

The reforms of the provisional government spurred support of the formidable American Jewish volunteer network that now swung into action. The Joint Distribution Committee founded in 1914 and led by the same leadership group as the AJC made funds available for immediate relief. The most heralded project was a plan by the American Jewish Relief Committee to send an all Jewish hospital unit replete with the latest equipment and thirty Jewish doctors to show the appreciation for the abolition of all discriminatory decrees against the Jews.[21] At the same time a "freedom loan" in which Jacob Schiff and his circle of wealthy Jews participated was floated for the new government. Consideration was also given to revisiting the question of a new commercial treaty with Russia. But the satisfaction with the new course of events was short lived. There were rumors that Jewish organizations such as the Russian Jewish Bund were advocating a separate peace between Russia and Germany. The rumors proved to be untrue and Marshall requested the *New York Times* to print a correction lest Jewish patriotism be impugned.[22] A year later, to the chagrin of the patriotic patricians, the Bolshevik regime did negotiate a separate peace at Brest-Litovsk. What made the event painful were the reports in the press that most in the Soviet peace delegation were Jews. That rumor circulated simultaneously with another that Russian Jewish traders were supplying food and oil to the German army in southern Russia. The inability of Kerensky to hold off the Bolsheviks, who under the cry of "peace, bread, and land" were able to take advantage of the war fatigue and bring themselves to power, frightened many Americans, perhaps none more than the leadership group of the AJC. Their fear related to frequent images projected in the media of a Jewry conspiring to impose a Communist regime on the Russian people. Marshall tried his utmost to squelch such stories. The image based on an imagined connection between Communism and Judaism became a new mainstay of the rhetoric of anti-Semitism.[23] Predictably, when the Bolsheviks toppled the Kerensky government in November, the support of Schiff and that of Jews of a Social Democratic persuasion for the revolution diminished. The purchase of Liberty bonds ceased and the underwriting of a loan was stricken from the books of Kuhn-Loeb.[24]

The notion of a "Judeobolshevik" conspiracy went on to become a major currency of the anti-Semitic imagination and has ever since posed a serious threat to Jewish well-being. It persisted long after the Jews mobilized to "rescue" their brethren in the Soviet Union. Its relationship to the events inside the Soviet Union is a crucial part of our story. It became a major rationale for the anti-Jewish depredations during the civil war and the ideological rationale for Hitler's Final Solution. The newly established Jewish defense agencies such as the AJC were hard pressed to find some way to counteract the baneful effects of the linkage. By 1919 the "Red Scare" had taken hold of the nation and Attorney General Palmer, disregarding constitutional safeguards, deported hundreds of "Reds" to Russia. Again, a disproportionate number were rumored to be Jews. Louis Marshall, fearing that the charge of Judeobolshevism would conceal Jewry's contribution to the war effort and raise the question of Jewish loyalty, sponsored a special research study that showed that the Bolshevik faction that had seized power was not disproportionately Jewish, and Jews who were involved were precisely those who had renounced their Judaism. "Why should their shortcomings be charged to the Jewish people?" he wrote to the editor of a small New Jersey newspaper.[25] But it proved nigh impossible in the period before World War II to counteract the Judeobolshevik image. In a peculiar way a concealed dividend of the campaign to "free" Soviet Jewry may be the dissipation of the Judeobolshevik myth. Nothing could be more effective in doing that than the photos of thousands of Jews arriving in Israel and their total disaffection from anything that smacked of Socialism.

▪ These amazing historical parallels should not be allowed to conceal the fact that the American Jewry that encountered its "Russian" problem in 1967 was far removed from its predecessors at the turn of the twentieth century. The dominance of the German Jewish elite declined after the war.[26] Marshall had done yeomen's work in determining the Jewish future at Versailles. He placed a great deal of faith in the new minority rights clauses the newly emerging governments were compelled to include in their constitutions. Attention momentarily switched to events in Poland where the fear that a flood of Jewish immigrants would come to American shores as a result of the depredations. Marshall insisted that "most of the Jews of Poland desire to remain there. . . . They love the country."[27] But that perception was not shared by American lawmakers. The Emergency Immigration Act of 1921 was triggered partly by a fear that millions of Polish Jews were poised to emigrate from Poland. The restrictionist sentiment of the twenties prevailed in the period after World War II but an exception developed concerning refugees from behind the iron curtain. American generosity in the treatment of refugees figures prominently in the complex "dropout" problem that developed in the seventies.

For our purpose the work the "Joint," as the American Jewish Joint Distribution Committee (JDC) was often called, did in Poland and the Ukraine during the civil war period is particularly significant. Its training schools and soup kitchens earned the plaudits of Herbert Hoover with whose American Relief Administration the JDC cooperated. It came at a price that included the assassination of Israel Friedlander on 11 July 1920 while on a fact-finding mission to the Ukraine.[28] The JDC's operations in the Ukraine demonstrate that the philanthropic bridge from American Jewry on which the later Soviet emigration movement depended was already in place during the early twenties. It may have been the activity of Jewish relief agencies in Eastern Europe that came to include several resettlement programs that aroused Stalin's suspicion and led to Moscow's indictment of the JDC as a Central Intelligence Agency operation during the Slansky trial in 1952.

It was, however, the Zionist thrust with its cry of democracy in Jewish life that posed the real threat to the continued dominance of the "uptown" stewards. Led by Louis Brandeis, Zionist leaders had successfully won the support of the Wilson administration for the Balfour Declaration, much to the chagrin of Louis Marshall. Key political differences between the two groups surfaced during the election of 1912. As the "downtown Jews" came into their own there was a loss of communal coherence. "Marshall Law," the comical appellative that referred to Marshall's ability to dictate to Jewish leaders, was broken by 1919. Most important were the demographic changes. By 1920 the overwhelmingly eastern European character of American Jewry had become manifest. It was reflected in a new pattern of leadership where a single person like Marshall or Schiff could no longer determine communal priorities. It would be that broader diverse pattern of governance in which the Soviet Jewry movement would later be incubated.

For Russian Jewry, now become Soviet Jewry, the changes were more far reaching. They would be reshaped from basically a religious community to an ethnic one with a new sovietized culture using elements of the old, especially the Yiddish language. Once that change is understood the question of the Jewishness of the Soviet emigrants that later concerned the receiving communities can be answered. In the name of integration into a Socialist society, Soviet Jewry underwent an organizational religious and cultural decapitation process during the twenties. Its communal and rabbinic leadership was removed. The pain of that change was partly concealed by the fact that its urban base and relatively high level of literacy allowed Jews to be recruited for the new technical and bureaucratic elites that would manage the new society.[29] The result was that at the same moment that Jews were being culturally and religiously denuded they were also experiencing very rapid social mobility, probably more rapid than American Jews. The Socialist *gleichhaltung* of the regime also affected other religious denominations that underwent a similar crucible; their houses of worship and their seminaries were closed, and their spiritual and cultural leaders were often shipped off, never to be heard from again. The sting of the process of destroying all cultural and religious institutions was softened by the sense that the government's target was all institutionalized religion, not merely Judaism. The Russian Orthodox Church also turned to Washington in a desperate plea for help before it was diminished and turned into an agency of the state. But the more severe enforcement of the antireligious policy against Jewish communal groups seemed as though motivated by a special animus.

Like the provisional government, the Bolshevik regime had proclaimed its own policy of revoking Tsarist anti-Semitic laws. But that did not count for much at the grass roots where Jewish life became increasingly insecure. According to one estimate 10 percent of Ukrainian Jewry was slaughtered before the defeat of the Whites during the Russian Civil War.[30] Small wonder that many Jews came to view the Red Army as their savior. Lenin opposed a separate Jewish culture in Russia but he had spoken out against anti-Semitism, and after the civil war Communists associated anti-Semitism with the "reactionary" forces of the counterrevolution. In the comparatively liberal, experimental, and romantic cultural atmosphere that characterized the first flush of enthusiasm for the revolution in the twenties, Jews often welcomed the revolutionary changes. They thought of them as part of the long sought for emancipation. But before 1917 few actually joined the party, and leaders of Jewish origin such as Leon Trotsky, Grigori Zinoviev, Lev Kamenev, and Lazer Kaganovich had abandoned any sense of being Jewish. Three years later Lenin and other Bolshevik leaders were impressed with the large number of Jews flocking to join the party. Yet the Communist Party Census of 1922 revealed that fewer than 1,000 Jews had actually joined the party before 1917. By 1927, however, as many as 50,000 Jews, 4.1 percent of the total party membership, were Jewish.[31] It was not until several decades of experience with Stalinism and the destruction of the petit bourgeois merchant economy through which most Jews eked out a living that there grew a realization that their individual, political, and cultural aspirations could never be realized in the Soviet Union. In the first years after the revolution there was little thought of immigration. The promise of the revolution actually drew Jewish and Armenian immigrants to the Soviet Union.

The movement to reshape the Jews of Soviet Russia can serve as a good example of effective social engineering. For the most part it was not coerced from a community reluctant to give up its old ways. Many Jews had been attracted to Socialism and the revolution before 1917. The Jewish Workers Bund was the first organized labor movement in Russia and had a pervasive influence on Jewish communal life. When Count Witte informed Herzl in 1903 that 50 percent of all Russian revolutionaries were Jews, he was no doubt exaggerating. But that Jews felt disaffected from a regime that encouraged their persecution and welcomed the advent of Kerensky regime with enthusiasm there could be no doubt.[32] In a sense Jews were ready to be reshaped, they wanted to belong. Immigration to America was in any case no longer an option. But the program to refashion Jewish life on an ethnic basis, as initiated by the Jewish section of the Communist Party of the Soviet Union (CPSU) may actually have created a basis for continuing that culture in other terms. The notion that government-sponsored social engineering could overnight radically reshape a culture that had been developed over centuries was an illusion. It is mentioned here as a partial explanation of the origin of the Soviet activists and refuseniks who later challenged the Soviet control system. Many had rebuilt their identity from the shards of the pre-Revolutionary Jewish culture.

The history of Soviet Jewry might have been far different had it been granted a viable autonomous republic in the early years after the revolution. But Soviet planners were convinced that Soviet Jewry was too scattered to people such an enterprise. Of course modern Hebrew, which was in the process of being reborn under Zionist auspices, could not be an instrument in such a rebuilding. Instead, Yiddish, which was the language used by the majority of Jews in the Ukraine, Belarus, and Russia was made an official language. By the late twenties and the early pre-purge thirties, a rich Yiddish-speaking culture had been established. The Soviet Union had more Yiddish theaters, published more Yiddish books and newspapers, and generally possessed more of the accoutrements of culture than any other Jewish community, including the United States, where the Yiddish press and Yiddish theater showed signs of decline by the late twenties. The Soviet Union was well on the way to becoming the cultural center of the Yiddish-speaking world during the twenties.[33] But it was a fettered culture devoted to propagating the Communist message. That was done in every way possible. Yiddish folk songs now were likely to have their words changed to sing the praises of collectivization or of Stalin himself. The books and articles also sang the praises of Communism or the latest twist of the party line. The only thing Jewish about it was the language and the use of familiar Jewish folk tales and tunes. Like all Soviet agitprop it was strongly antireligious. There were free Yom Kippur dinners, anti-Passover events. But somehow even without the Judaic religious element and purged of "bourgeois nationalistic" content, a facsimile of Jewish culture survived.[34] Unforeseen by Soviet social engineers and members of Yevsektsiya, the Jewish branch of the CPSU, was that Jews were being encouraged to come together to celebrate the new culture so that even without synagogues and the myriad practices that compose the faith, the groupiness remained and found other reasons to cohere. That proved sufficient to maintain a separate Jewish consciousness at least for the moment, and it was that residual consciousness that the early Israeli consular staffs later encountered when seeking out Soviet Jews. The new songs and values were simply imposed on the old cultural base. The result was high-speed acculturation with little evidence of acceptance in the majority culture and a residual memory of what was abandoned. This phenomenon goes far to explain the puzzling nature of Soviet Jewish identity encountered during the years of Soviet Jewish emigration movement. The emigrants professed to be Jewish but had almost no knowledge of the content of Judaism. The initial wave of refuseniks who heroically challenged the system in the early seventies were Soviet Jews who had somehow avoided the new acculturation or had somehow picked up enough of what remained to form a Jewish identity. They were Zionists who had been able to retain that quest for a Jewish homeland from before the revolution when Russia was the home of Zionism, or they were new devotees of Zionism who brought to it the fervor of the convert after the June 1967 war. Learning Hebrew became a popular activity among Soviet Jewish activists.

Only a small minority of Soviet Jews sought to retrieve the abandoned and mostly destroyed Jewish culture of Russia. During the seventies more Jews were lost by rejecting the possibility of identifying themselves as Jews to the census takers than those who chose to emigrate. Those in the emigration wave of the late eighties and early nineties, including the many thousands who dropped out in Vienna or Rome, were descendants of those who underwent sovietization. They still considered themselves Jewish and so stated it on the internal passport carried by each Soviet citizen. Undoubtedly many had experienced the special restrictions and humiliations the government bureaucracy and the Soviet people reserved for Jews. Some even recalled the old songs and perhaps a Soviet Seder or Yiddish song with special words. But they were antireligious and anti—or non-Zionist; that much the forced acculturation had achieved. The reshaping of Russian Jewry had not been able to erase all traces of Jewishness, embedded in the Soviet yiddishist culture of their parents or in random memories of a once lively communal culture. That is the seedbed of the emigration movement.

■ Central to achieving an understanding of the Soviet response to the emigration movement is how the Soviets imagined the Jewish presence in the world and its link to Soviet Jewry. The three incidents that follow concern the Communist effort to exploit what they imagined to be a worldwide Jewish power nexus. The first concerned the Comintern's attempt to use the American Jewish labor movement to bring American organized labor into the Communist fold. The second concerned the mobilization of American Jewish resources for the resettlement and "productivization" of Jewry in the Crimea and Birobidzhan. The third concerned the wartime attempt to exploit the influence of American Jewry to open a second front and extend aid to the Soviet Union through the creation of the Anti-Fascist Committee (AFC) in 1943.

In its political culture American Jewry follows the pattern of other Jewish communities in the Western democracies by situating itself slightly to the left of center on the political spectrum. They were Social Democrats or some American equivalent of that. The east European immigrants that changed the face of American Jewry in the early decades of the twentieth century followed the more passionate east European variety of that pattern. They were usually closer to the revolutionary sensibility that dominated the forces of reform in the east. The fall of the Tsar and first phase of the Russian Revolution in March 1917 was celebrated among these Jews. In November 1917, when the Bolsheviks seized power, the momentum of support remained strong at least for the time being. Lenin's Bolsheviks had, after all, confirmed the revocation of the anti-Semitic laws and decrees implemented by the provisional government. Though not itself free from anti-Semitic excesses, during the three-year civil war, the Red Army fought against the bloody pogrom makers and generally acted to protect the Jews. But much of the remaining sympathy for the Bolsheviks was dissipated after their antireligious bent with its accompanying policy of community dismantling was revealed. After the Soviet government's assault on Jewish cultural and religious institutions, the split within the Jewish left grew deeper. In the United States the center of gravity of Jewish political culture remained with the social democrats, but the community now faced a challenge by its strengthened Communist wing that was gradually brought under total control of Moscow. The prize was control of the Jewish labor movement that the third congress of the Comintern meeting in 1921 chose as an instrument to help bring the entire American labor movement into the Communist fold.[35]

The Jewish labor movement was composed of an organizational triad: *Forward,* the Socialist-oriented Yiddish daily with the largest circulation in the nation; United Hebrew Trades, an umbrella organization for Jewish locals associated with the Jewish ethnic economy; and the fraternal order, Workmen's Circle. The Communist strategy called for boring from within, using locals already under their control and the newly created Trade Union Educational League. The result was a virtual civil war within the Jewish left with uncharacteristic physical violence. Commenting on a brutal attack by Communist activists on a member of the Workmen's Circle and former Bundist from Lodz, the *Forward* condemned Communist "hooliganism" and welcomed the arrest and high bail set for the attackers. Only the internal strife and change within the party line enabled the Jewish labor movement to withstand the Communist takeover attempt, but the ten-year struggle and a catastrophic strike called by the Communists in 1926 left the movement much weakened.

The intense politicization and the ideological conflicts were barely understood by the surviving "uptown" establishment. The *American Hebrew,* the Anglo Jewish journal that often spoke for this declining wing of the Jewish polity, condemned the resort to physical violence. If the political theories were simply eliminated from the conflict, they counseled, "bases for adjusting the economic difficulties could speedily be reached." [36] The older Jewish establishment had little sense of the political passions that motivated Jewish immigrant politics. Its lack of awareness came to the surface in its confrontation with Zionism over investing money for settlement of Jews in the Ukraine.

The reshaping of the contours of the American Jewish left by the struggle with the Communists have a direct bearing on the development of the Soviet Jewry movement in America. The defeat of the Communists, who remained slavishly under Moscow's control, led to the formation of the Jewish Labor Committee in 1934. Aside from its important role as a rescue agent of Jewish labor leaders during the Holocaust, it became one of the first American Jewish groups to sound the alarm about the depredations committed against Jews in the Soviet Union. It is possible to conceive that the genesis of the Soviet Jewry movement in America was the Jewish Labor Committee's effort to alert the organized Jewish community that something needed to be done to "rescue" the Jews of Russia. Predictably, American Jewish Communist Party members vehemently denied that Soviet anti-Semitism had assumed a virulent form under Stalin and had in fact become life-threatening by 1948.

The attempt by the Moscow-dominated Jewish Communist movement to penetrate the Jewish labor movement also suggests something about Communist thinking on the Jewish issue. The actual influence of the Jews, whether Bundist or Zionist, was consistently overestimated by the Communist movement. That influence led first to the possibility of instrumentalization of what they imagine to be a formidable Jewish power for the realization of their objectives. That influence was seen in the JDC's Crimean resettlement venture and the establishment of the AFC in 1943. The imagination of a vast Jewish conspiracy, this time often bearing the Zionist label, plays an important role in explaining the overreaction of the Soviet leadership during the years of this study.

Of special relevance is the American Jewish involvement with the Soviet re-settlement experiment of impoverished Jews in the Crimea and later in Biro-bidzhan. The possibility of rehabilitating Soviet Jewry in place and finding some way to ensure its security haunts the Soviet Jewry movement, which never developed a full consensus regarding the precise nature of the threat faced by Soviet Jewry. It also serves as an entrée for one of the most vexing aspects of the movement, the role of Zionism and Israel as crystallized in the dropout problem that brought American Jewish and Israeli movement into confrontation. Viewed through the Zionist lens the issue of investment of the philanthropic dollar for "rescue in place" in Crimea or Birobidzhan and subsidizing "dropouts" to settle outside of Israel is cut from the same cloth. They are considered here for the light they shed on the later conflict concerning "freedom of choice" for the Soviet emigrants.

The idea of resettlement as a solution for the problem of Soviet Jewry in which American Jewry would deal directly with the Soviet government was not new. There had been dozens of attempts to bring Jews to the land in nineteenth-century America, including many sponsored by the Am Olam movement. Proponents were convinced that a primeval reconnection with the soil such as preached by the Russian *Narodniks* was the key to Jewish rebirth. The kibbutz movement and the agricultural colonies in Argentina and the United States were based on the same principle. Indeed, before the Crimean resettlement project it was estimated that in the Ukraine alone there were already 76,000 Jewish farmers.

The origins of the idea of resettlement in the Crimea are not fully clear, but its historical context was the sense that something had to be done quickly for the impoverished Jews of the Ukraine.[37] Jews had suffered heavy losses during the civil war, and the economic base in crafts and merchandising was destroyed during the period of war Communism. The relief effort of the "Joint" helped stave off famine faced by a quarter million Ukrainian Jews. It was this endangered group that became the subject of a social engineering "productivization" scheme by Marxist-oriented social engineers. They were convinced that by changing the Jewish class structure from petty merchants and craftsmen to noble tillers of the soil, the "parasitic" element in Jewish economic life could be converted to a productive one. Clearly the rehabilitation impulse was strong on both sides of the Atlantic.

An elaborate partnership between the Soviet government acting through KOMZET, an acronym for a specialized resettlement agency, and the JDC, which had established Agro-Joint to act in its name, was agreed to in 1924. For Soviet leadership the idea was not merely to collect American dollars but to "normalize" and concentrate the Jewish population. Mikhail Kalinin, president of the USSR, disregarded warnings that the Jews of Russia were unsuited for agriculture.[38] The Soviet government would supply the land and the settlers; Agro-Joint would supply all else to build viable agricultural settlements. By May 1925 the first contingent of 4,000 of the 231,000 to be resettled by 1930 came to the land.[39]

The partnership with the Kremlin for resettlement in place won considerable communal support in the United States. It came from two distinct segments of American Jewry between whom there was little love lost. The American Jewish Communists predictably waxed enthusiastic about the scheme, and some returned to the Soviet Union to become personally involved. In 1925, 100 "returnees" from the United States organized a communal farm called the Herald thirty miles from Moscow. Later, at least 1,000 similarly oriented foreign Jews settled in Birobidzhan, paying KOMZET $200 per head for the privilege. In 1920 the Association for Jewish Colonization in the Soviet Union was established. Its magazine *ICOR,* which featured smiling Jewish peasants threshing wheat, circulated in many Jewish communities together with Zionist magazines featuring the same faces doing the same thing in the Emek region of Palestine. ICOR, which had 100 local committees and more than 10,000 dues-paying members, became KOMZET's recruiting and fund-raising arm. By the 1930s it was able to allocate thousands of dollars for the purchase of farm equipment and cultural activity, including the publication of several newspapers.

The extreme Jewish left that supported the Crimean project formed a small section of the Jewish polity but generated a resonance beyond its numbers. The more substantial support for Crimean settlement came from the stewards whose hold on Jewish communal life was loosening in the twenties. Altogether the JDC invested about $16 million in the project by 1933, most of which, as predicted by the Zionist leadership, was lost. The motivation of the stewards in supporting the resettlement scheme and actually entering into a partnership with the Soviet government is not as puzzling as may seem. Some harbored an adamant anti-Zionism behind which was a fear of dual loyalty represented by the Zionist venture in Palestine. That conflict between the Zionist-oriented immigrant community and the so-called uptowners had made the crucial annual fund-raising campaign into a battleground. Zionists, appalled by the granting of funds to a Soviet government agency, spoke of an unholy alliance between Wall Street and the Kremlin. Zionist leaders threatened to restart their own fund-raising campaign. A compromise that would have given the Zionists one-third of the funds raised in the campaign between 1924 and 1926 was proposed to mute Zionist fury. But for men such as Louis Marshall, who harbored a love of the Yiddish language and respect for Yiddish culture, and Julius Rosenwald, who invested millions in the Crimean project, something more than anti-Zionism was involved. They did not believe that Soviet Jews were ready to resettle in Palestine, and they were certain that resettlement in place was cheaper, more practical, and timely. "In Russia it is a matter of saving Jews for the present," observed one Jewish journalist, "in Palestine the task is to preserve Jews for the Future."[40] Rosenwald denied being anti-Zionist and pointed out that for many years he had generously supported resettlement efforts in Palestine. But, he added, "I have never been a believer in subsidizing immigration to the extent of moving people in masses from one country to another."[41] Zionists pointed out that the millions being invested in resettlement in the Crimea could not be secured by the Soviet regime's property laws and that the United States maintained no relations with the Soviet Union. Diplomatic relations might at least offer some protection against a regime that avowed its antipathy toward private property. In turn, supporters argued that the State Department at the behest of the AJC had approved of the project and that large American corporations such as Ford and McCormick Reaper were also heavily invested in the Soviet Union. Thousands of Jews had come to depend on the "Joint" for their survival during the years of the civil war. Their support for Crimean resettlement was merely an extension of that ameliorative program with an addition of a social engineering aspect. There was the feeling that one could do business with the Soviets and the hope that once settled on the land Soviet Jewish dependence on philanthropy would come to an end.

As in the later dropout phenomenon, the Zionist-oriented opponents of Crimea made an emotional appeal based on the Jewish national interest. Jewish communal life, they argued, could never be secure in Russia, whose soil was "soaked in Jewish blood." It was not only that Russian anti-Semitism was endemic but also that the current regime was devastating Jewish communal life. The Russian Zionist movement experienced a spurt of growth after the revolution only to see hundreds of its leaders imprisoned.[42] How could one contemplate working hand in hand with a regime that considered Judaism a backward religion that must be eliminated? For committed Zionists the answer was to develop a haven for Jews where they could freely uphold the tenets of their faith and realize their talents. From the Zionist perspective in the long run the investment in the *Yishuv* would better serve the Jewish interest. That thought was the rationale behind a resolution passed at the convention of the Zionist Organization of America convened in Buffalo in 1926. Faced with relentless Zionist attacks the JDC attempted to build a less direct connection with the project by dropping the name "colonization" in favor of "settlement." Agro-Joint would be replaced by the American Society for Jewish Farm Settlements. It would ostensibly be funded independently. But rumors that a Soviet default was imminent were already rife in 1928.

The conflict was resolved by developments on the ground. By 1929 there were signs that yet another twist in Soviet policy would cause the loss of government support for resettlement. All Soviet agriculture would be collectivized. By the late twenties both the Zionist and JDC resettlement endeavors were threatened. In the Ukraine some successful Jewish settlers were arrested and charged with being kulaks. There was opposition to the resettlement from the Crimean Tartars and signs that Moscow was dejudaizing the enterprise by recruiting a growing number of non-Jews for the colonies. At the same time the Zionists were confronted by bloody riots in Palestine in 1929 that put the future of its 100,000 settlers in jeopardy.

By 1929, the year of the market crash, much of the hope that was present at the birth of the resettlement idea had dissipated. The two staunchest supporters of the project, Louis Marshall and Julius Rosenwald, had died. Some settlement continued to 1935 but the project had lost momentum and no longer seemed to be a solution for the Soviet Jewish problem. The restrictive Immigration Act of 1924 ruled out the possibility of a solution by emigration to the United States. Settlement and amelioration in the Crimea was not fulfilling its promise, and even the Crimean project, it was argued, was too small to solve the problems caused by the impoverishment of Ukrainian Jewry. Something on a grander scale was needed. That idea was part of the thinking that led to the Stalin-supported effort in Birobidzhan that again attracted American Jews of the left and had the backing of the militantly anti-Zionist Yevsektsiya, the soon to be disbanded Jewish section of the CPSU.

The hope was that if sufficient number of Jews could be drawn to Birobidzhan a Jewish Soviet Autonomous Republic with full representation rights in Soviet governance could eventually be established. Again there was much hope at the outset, though some realized that the remote territory near the Chinese border was unsuitable for Jewish settlement. But Cyrus Adler, now president of the Jewish Theological Seminary, had become skeptical about the project and its supporting organization. He characterized the area as a "dreary waste" and feared that it would feed the charge of linkage between Jews and Communists.[43] The Jewish press also was outspoken in its opposition to the Birobidzhan project. For the Soviet regime the hopes of amelioration of the Jewish condition were now overshadowed by an obsessive need to offer an alternative to the Zionist settlement in Palestine. That ideological purpose was joined to a strategic one that developed after a brief border war with China in 1929. There was a need to fill this virtually empty area with settlers who could defend it in case of war. But the granting of an autonomous administrative status in 1934, a step before making it a Jewish autonomous region, and enthroning Yiddish as the "official" language to be taught in its schools and published in its newspapers in 1935, could not overcome the difficulty of everyday life in this remote mosquito-infested area. By 1939 despite the great interest Birobidzhan had created among Communist-affiliated American Jews who exerted great effort to support the enterprise, it too showed signs of failure. When World War II broke out, only 18,000 Jews remained.

An attempt to revive the enterprise after the war with 10,000 new settlers was promoted by the AFC, which had assumed some aspects of communal government for Soviet Jewry. A new fund-raising campaign in America proved equally unsuccessful. It made the error of persistently denouncing Zionism, which had become the reining ideology of American Jewry. During the "Black Years" of Soviet Jewry between 1948 and 1953, the leadership of Birobidzhan was again purged, its cultural institutions were closed down, its press muted and Yiddish books burnt. In the end the pervasive anti-Semitism of the Soviet state proved far more enduring than the ameliorative approach to the Jewish problem. It is a truth that we will observe again in the years between 1967 and 1989.

What can be gleaned from these early contacts between the American and Russian interests on the Jewish question? The American Jewish response to the tribulations of Soviet Jewry in the years of this study can best be viewed as the latest link in a historical chain that goes back to the late nineteenth century. That is especially apparent in its relationship to the Zionist movement. That resettlement in Israel should thrive while Crimea and Birobidzhan, which in numbers overshadowed the kibbutz movement, were failures, could not be easily reconciled. Moscow's opposition to emigration was not merely rooted in a fear of "brain drain," as some later maintained. We shall note later that, despite Israel's warning regarding the misuse of the visa by the dropouts, Moscow displayed little concern about the abuse of its visa procedure to leave the country. That mysterious indifference is best understood when projected against the long-standing competition for the heart and mind of Soviet Jewry between Zionism—and the idea of a national Jewish homeland it proffered—and loyalty to the Soviet Union. What could be more heartening to the men in the Kremlin than the emigrant's rejection of the Jewish homeland.

The effort to penetrate the American Jewish labor movement presents a clue regarding the vastly exaggerated image of Jewish power that prevailed among Communist leaders. Not uncommon in the mind-set of anti-Semites, that exaggerated notion of an all-powerful world Jewry is at the heart of their response to their efforts to enlist Jewish resources, real and imagined, for the fulfillment of their goals. At several junctures during the interwar period Soviet leaders sought to enlist Jewish influence and financial resources to fulfill their worldwide goals. Soviet strategy toward its Jews was based on a felt need to destroy what they imagined to be an all-powerful competing social structure, at the same time using its connection with world Jewry to help attain its goals. That much can be observed in the attempt to penetrate the Jewish labor movement. We again note its play in enlisting the JDC to finance the Crimean resettlement scheme and later in the establishment of the Jewish AFC.

■   One of the surprises of this study is that the American Jewish Communist left that played an important role in these efforts is nowhere to be found in the Soviet Jewry movement during the sixties, seventies, and eighties. One reason for that absence is American Jewry's growing disenchantment with Moscow. It was not only the growing awareness of the Soviet mistreatment of Jews but the startling twists and turns of the party line that undermined its credibility even for those who wanted to believe that a "new day" was dawning. During the United Front period of the early thirties it was still possible for some American Jews to view the Soviet experiment favorably. Many Jews reacted to the depression by staunchly supporting Roosevelt's welfare state that in the popular imagination seemed to be moving in the direction of Socialism. For some the total collapse of the capitalist system marked by the depression could only mean that the Marxist analysis that capitalism was doomed was correct. When the beloved Roosevelt extended diplomatic recognition to the Soviet regime in 1933, this act went far to legitimize the "Socialist experiment" for these Jews. Jews especially felt that Fascism was the enemy and flocked to defend the loyalist regime against Franco in Spain.[44] More important, after the invasion of the Soviet Union in June 1941, many Jews, anxious to forget the Russo-German Nonaggression Pact, became convinced that the Soviet Union was the only state willing and able to stand up to Hitler's racial machinations.

The political tension within the community between the Social Democratic and Communist left sharpened during the thirties. Mordecai Kaplan, the founder of the Reconstructionist movement, often sermonized about the need for economic justice for the poor. "Whenever I spoke that way," he complained, "I was accused of being a Bolshevik."[45] The Communists endlessly pointed out that there was no unemployment in Russia and anti-Semitism was outlawed. Nevertheless, in the second half of the decade several developments continued to undermine the attraction the Soviet regime held out for Jews. The purge trials with their abject confessions of betrayal by leaders who had been associated with the regime for their entire lives undermined confidence even among true believers. Many were "old" party members associated with the party before Stalin's control and a disproportionate number were of Jewish origin. Though Jewish in name only it seemed after the anti-Trotsky campaign that even such affiliated Jews were targeted for elimination. The Jewish section of the CPSU was disbanded, together with other ethnic sections, in December 1932. At the same time the dismantling of Jewish communal life continued. Party loyalists assumed that it was not especially Jews that were being targeted because churches and religious institutions were also being closed. But the discerning observer could note that the NKVD came down particularly hard on Jews who did not have the rudimentary protection of belonging to a Jewish Autonomous Republic. The little control of their culture and local politics Soviet Jews might have mustered in the autonomous region of Birobidzhan was quickly taken away, and the Jewish leadership there was purged. By the thirties the laws against anti-Semitism had become dead letters, and the educational campaign to counteract its baneful effects could no longer be heard. Instead, the festering campaign against Trotsky took on anti-Semitic tone. The declining quality and security of Soviet Jewish life in the thirties gave ample indication of the danger that lie ahead, but precious few read the signals.

Their vision was blocked by the ominous news in the international arena where the accession of Hitler to power in January 1933 threatened to overturn the power arrangements negotiated at Versailles. After the signing of the treaty of Brest-Litovsk that took Russia out of World War I, the Soviet Union remained diplomatically isolated. There were no Soviet diplomats at Versailles and none to settle a nettlesome war with Poland that brought additional casualties. Its isolation was an opening for another pariah state, defeated Germany, to seek ties. The diplomatic transaction was simple; Germany would open its market to Soviet wheat and would make its superior technology available. In turn the Kremlin would allow Russia to be used to circumvent the arms limitations imposed on it by the

Treaty of Versailles. The new German air force that would later wreak havoc on the Soviet people would receive it earliest training in Russia.

For many American Jewish leftists who understood that Nazi Germany posed a mortal threat to Jewish well-being, the Nonaggression Pact of August 1939 was a moment of truth. Some broke with the party but others, unaware of the treaty's secret clause dividing Poland in case of war, convinced themselves that the treaty was a brilliant strategic stroke that prevented the western democracies from turning Germany eastward and thereby gave Stalin, who had purged the officer corps of the Red Army, more time to prepare for war. The pact triggered intense conflict within American Jewry. Earl Browder, who had become secretary of the Communist Party of the United States after a bitter internecine struggle within the party, pictured Soviet Jewry "building a happy prosperous life in the new socialist society," but warned that support of a "second imperialist war" would bring "calamity" to the Jewish people.[46] Sidney Hook, the noted political thinker, cautioned Jews not to be taken in by the argument that the anti-Fascism preached by the Communists meant that they were immune from the disease of anti-Semitism. For Jews danger lurked at extremes, the left and right.[47] But it was more the unpalatable twists of the party line that led to such steps as the support of a "supreme" capitalist, Wendell Willkie, the Republican candidate in the presidential campaign of 1940, which helped break the party's hold on the Jewish left. Unlike other hyphenate voters, Jews increased their support of Roosevelt for a third term in 1940. The American Jewry that witnessed Pearl Harbor was far more centrist than in 1933. Its disenchantment with the Soviet Union grew apace during the Cold War. The Doctor's plot, the Slansky trial, and other manifestations of Stalin's paranoia during the Black Years did the rest. When our story begins the once powerful Communist left had little influence in the American Jewish community and played no role in the Soviet Jewry movement.

■ Paradoxically, the secret protocol of the Nonaggression Pact with Berlin became a lifesaver for Jews once the war began in September. In occupying its assigned part of Poland the area's 1.8 million Jews were able to escape the Final Solution behind Soviet lines. It was a record far superior to Britain or the United States and allowed the Soviets to project an image as rescuers of Jews during the Holocaust. Together with the Jewish population of the Baltic States, which Moscow occupied in 1940, the Jewish population under Soviet control was now greater than 5 million, more than that of American Jewry. But the real story that bears on the later development of the Soviet emigration movement challenges the

Soviet Holocaust rescue role. It is true that about 1.5 million Jewish workers were among those evacuated behind the Urals together with Soviet heavy industry. Thousands more were able to find a precarious haven in the Soviet Asian republics. But Moscow had no rescue plan for Jews and in fact preferred, as a matter of policy, not to recognize the Holocaust at all. Little warning was given to Jews of the special fate that awaited them under German occupation. The rescue role of the Soviet government and the postwar slander against the Jewish contribution to winning the "great patriotic" war figures prominently in the disaffection of many Soviet Jews who later chose to leave the Soviet Union.[48]

It is in the Soviet Union, where as many as one of every three Jews killed in the Holocaust was lost, that the impact of the Holocaust was most direct. The Einzatsgruppen and the Ordnungsdienst, operating with the collaboration of local paramilitary organizations, killed as many as 1.5 to 1.6 million Jews that considered together with wartime casualties may come to as high as 50 percent of the prewar Jewish population. There are few Soviet Jewish families that did not lose someone in the war. That loss serves as one of the most significant historic factors that binds Soviet Jewry together.[49] The famous Commissar Order, which mandated the summary execution of *politrukniks,* the Red Army's political officer at the battalion level, and Jews, is the only written order extant for the mass killing of Jews.

The war brought a momentary change in the Soviet government-sponsored policy of religious and cultural suppression. The antireligious strictures against Judaism and other religions were relaxed during the war as part of Stalin's effort to win the loyalty of the Russian people. But the virulent anti-Semitism at the folk level could not be so easily countermanded. It emerged in slander regarding the avoidance of combat that came out in wartime folk humor despite the fact that Jewish losses were four times as heavy as that of the general population. When a seventeen-year-old Jewish partisan, Masha Bruskina, was publicly hanged and later identified only as an "unknown partisan," a highly decorated Jewish veteran later observed that this "was the reason why Jews. . . . In this country feel the only correct decision is to leave."[50] For Soviet Jews the slander against them crystallized in the memorialization of Babi Yar, where thirty thousand of Kiev's Jews were slaughtered. The official memorial plaque honored 100,000 citizens of Kiev, without mentioning Jews. They became in death what they were not allowed to be in life, honored citizens of the Soviet Union. Predictably the official omission of the Jewish role, not merely as victims but contributors to victory, left deep wounds in the Jewish psyche and for many dissipated the remaining hope of the possibility of living as an identified Jew in the Soviet Union. It is the loss of that hope that partially explains the risks taken by the early petitioners for exit visas, most of whom became the refuseniks who sparked the movement in the Soviet Union.

The first signs of the seething discontent of many Soviet Jews during the fifties and sixties came in annual memorial meetings near killing grounds such as Babi Yar. The meeting of younger Jews, often traveling long distances to redeem the memory of Jewish blood shed, for a host nation who despised them, created lasting ties requisite for forming the networks that composed the movement. The Soviet Union sustained enormous casualties that are acknowledged in memorials all over the Soviet Union, but mention of the Jews being selected for a special crucible was muted as a matter of government policy.[51]

Ironically, even while denying the Jewish contribution to the war effort, Communist Party leaders had not forgotten their exaggerated vision of Jewish world power that they now sought to mobilize. The approach behind the recruitment of prominent Jews for the AFC in April 1942 was motivated by the same assumption of the mysterious existence of Jewish influence witnessed in the penetration of the Jewish labor movement and the Crimean resettlement project. This time its mission was to mobilize domestic and foreign Jewry in the fight against fascism. The idea probably originated in the inner recesses of the NKVD, perhaps with Lavrenti Beria, the infamous Minister of State Security. Earlier, Beria had recruited Henryk Erlich and Viktor Alter, two Bundist leaders who had found shelter in the Soviet Union, to help mobilize Jews abroad. But Stalin recalled that they were Mencheviks and ordered their execution. In August 1941 Solomon Mikhoels, a renowned actor and head of the Moscow State Theater, was recruited to address Jewish communities on the facilities of Radio Moscow, which beamed internationally.

Within a matter of months the AFC was formally established and fully functional. A well-promoted visit to Britain was followed by dispatch of a delegation to the United States where Mikhoels and Itzak Feffer, a poet who may have also doubled as Beria's agent, riding on the back of the Soviet victory at Stalingrad, were everywhere received with enthusiasm. The warnings of those who had firsthand knowledge of the Kremlin's machinations were disregarded. At a festive reception for the AFC delegation held at New York's Hotel Astor on 1 July 1943, James Rosenberg, chairman of the JDC and Agro-Joint, spoke enthusiastically about the success of the work in Crimea. He saw not the pallid ghetto types in the settlements but cavalry composed of "bronzed, strong lads galloping over the steppes." Soviet policy, on which the JDC had lost millions, was characterized as "humane, wise and far seeing. . . . not a mere scrap of paper." [52] The fate of the Crimean settlements was left unmentioned. Unwarned of the pending danger, what remained of the colonies was overrun in the first year of the war, and the remaining Jews in the settlements were never heard from again.

The AFC's postwar operation casts some light on the surviving communal cohesiveness of Soviet Jewry. Before the fourteen members of the group were tried and liquidated in 1952, the AFC developed into a kind of clearinghouse to assist Jews in locating missing relatives and then into a national Jewish governance agency that administered to the needs of Soviet Jewry including cultural and activities. The popularity of the Soviet Union in the postwar period was based on its crucial role in defeating the Nazi menace. But among Jewish survivors, that usually did not translate into choosing to make their lives there. Rather, the movement of displaced persons everywhere was from east Europe to the American zone in the West. After May 1948 it was Israel, not the alternative Socialist Zion in Birobidzhan, that became the centerpiece of Jewish interest. It may be that it was the Kremlin's perception of a Jewish drift to the West in Israel and among its own Jews that served as a trigger of Stalin's paranoia that culminated in the terrible Black Years of Soviet Jewry between 1948 and 1953.

The history of the AFC indicates that there existed a worldwide Jewish interest in the fate of Soviet Jewry as the war came to a close. More important, the postwar activities of the AFC present some evidence that despite the communal dismantling that had begun in the twenties and the radical losses suffered during the Holocaust, Soviet Jewish consciousness of belonging to a separate and distinct people had not been totally eliminated. A momentum for rebuilding a Soviet Jewish community existed in the immediate postwar years. But whether it could survive the onslaught after the founding of Israel was uncertain.

■   The historical seeds of the Soviet Jewry movement were planted throughout the last quarter of the nineteenth and the first six decades of the twentieth century. That included patterns of advocacy by Jewish leaders before the American government as well as the cosmetic government response. Both were in place before World War I as were the strategies employed to generate pressure through public relations and protest. Surprisingly, these instruments were frequently more effectively wielded by the predemocratic stewards such as Louis Marshall and Jacob Schiff than they were by the later leadership of the American Soviet Jewry movement.

Both leadership groups were primarily concerned with the mistreatment of

Russian Jewry, whose linkage to American Jewry was forged through immigration. Though the diplomatic dispatches exchanged between Washington and Moscow during both time periods seem almost interchangeable, there were significant differences in the two situations. Tsarist Russia wanted to rid itself of Jews; the Soviet Union did not want to let them go. The turn-of-the-century incidents involved the treatment of returnees who held an American passport, not potential emigrants. We note that the politics to terminate the Commercial Treaty of 1832 through which the stewards tried to wring better treatment by withholding trade and credit are virtually replayed in the politics involved in the later Jackson-Vanik Amendment that sought to withhold most-favored-nation status. But the wielding of the economic weapon used in both cases was different. In the earlier case it was wielded by one Jewish banker, Jacob Schiff, who was able through his control of Kuhn-Loeb to attract other banking houses to his effort to deny the American bond market to Russia. In the period of this study the control of credit to a hard-pressed Soviet government was achieved through congressional action embodied in the Jackson and Stevenson amendments. An evaluation of the effectiveness of this strategy in ameliorating the condition of Russian Jewry remains for later consideration.

These similarities should not come as a surprise. The Soviet Jewry problem on which we focus is the latest episode in a historical stream that stretches back to the late nineteenth century. Some elements remain constant while others change. For example, the communal stewards who were the first to take up the cudgels for Russian Jewry at the turn of the twentieth century had passed from the scene by 1930, but the agencies they established, the JDC and the closely related AJC, played a crucial role in both periods. At the same time conflict between the Jewish organizations, each representing a different constituency and possessing a different style and program, is a constant that plagues the effort in both periods. What is remarkable is that the axis of conflict, the issues on which they differed, is remarkably similar. The tensions between the passionately committed grass roots UCSJ and the more political NCSJ bear a strong resemblance to the tensions between the "downtown" "noisy quarter" who agitated for immediate action and who spoke not of their brethren but of their kin and the stewards, disciplined by "Marshall Law," who were no less dedicated but cooler in their approach. When activists of the UCSJ later refer to the NCSJ as the "establishment" it has the ring of historic but not actual truth. The establishment ceased dominating Jewish life decades before. Activists were in fact dealing with a federated leadership that came to their positions through democratic instruments unknown in the earlier Jewish community and not yet in possession of other American ethnic groups.

One American Jewish political group that cast a long shadow between 1917 and 1939 and whose interest in the Soviet Union was all consuming is conspicuous by its absence from the later historic scene. After allowing themselves to be ill used to infiltrate Jewish labor in the twenties and becoming the staunchest supporters of the Crimean and Birobidzhan colonization schemes, the Jewish Communists, having lost all credibility, simply vanish from the historical stage. Matters might have gone in a different direction had the Kremlin been able to use such an instrument between 1967 and 1989.

One element in the American Soviet Jewish historic relationship requires our special attention because it casts a historic light on the important dropout problem. It concerns the role of the "Joint" in supporting the Crimean resettlement scheme. It has been misperceived as a strange "alliance between Wall Street and the Kremlin" on the assumption that it was rooted in the visceral anti-Zionism of leaders such as Louis Marshall and financiers such as Julius Rosenwald and James Rosenberg. There may have been an element of truth in that assumption, but the enterprise was primarily based on a conviction that resettlement in place was more doable than mass immigration and resettlement in undeveloped areas such as Palestine. They shared with industrialists such as Ford the feeling that the Soviets could be worked with. But the investment of JDC's millions brought with it a monumental fracas with the American Zionist movement. For the first time we see the players that are central to our story on the stage of history. The scene is again reminiscent of the later conflict about the dropouts in which the JDC and Hebrew Immigrant Aid Society stood accused of seducing the Soviet emigrants away from settling in Israel.

Finally, there are the Russian Jews whose fate and disposition is at the heart of the problem we examine. Whether we focus on pre-Revolutionary Russia or the Russia of Gorbachev's perestroika, any study of the Soviet Jewry problem begins and ends with the pervasiveness of anti-Semitism on the folk and government level. It is a constant without which the desire to emigrate might have been far less intense. It is something of a paradox that Soviet Jewry, like the Jews of Germany, felt a special affinity for the culture of the society in which they lived, even while they received signals of unwelcome. Government or political anti-Semitism plays a central role because it directly shapes the public policy of the Soviet government from access to higher education to the granting of exit visas. Some of the Kremlin's strategic plans relating to American Jewry are based on a vision that sees an all-powerful Jewish influence at work in the world. For example, the Comintern decision to bore from within to gain control of the American Jewish labor movement is rooted in a fantastic overestimation of the power and size of that movement in relation to American organized labor. We again witness that characteristic instrumentalism in the Soviet enlistment of JDC financial support for Crimean resettlement and the alternate Socialist Zion in Birobidzhan. It again becomes discernable in the establishment the AFC and the Mikhoels mission to American Jewry in 1943. Behind the effort to raise American Jewish money for the Soviet war effort and to mobilize Jewish political influence for the opening of the Second Front was a notion of an all-powerful Jewish presence in the world that could be mobilized for its own purposes. It is that assumption, rooted in the idea of a satanic Jewish power at play in world affairs, that is later resonated in its irrational policy toward Israel with which it maintained no diplomatic ties for most of the years on which this study focuses.

The Soviet government's muting of the impact of the Holocaust and the omission of the contribution of Soviet Jewry to victory is yet another brand of anti-Semitism drawn from Russia's abundant arsenal, the impact of which has much relevance to this study. Their radical wartime losses that were denied recognition and slandered by the host nation are important in understanding the disaffection of many Soviet Jews. It led to a loss of hope that something might yet be achieved to make possible living at least secular Jewish life in the Soviet Union and helps explain the feeling in the first wave of refuseniks that democratization of the system will not work for Jews. Their response was emigration.

That sensibility that held sway among a minority of Jews was broadened by Stalin's Black Years and the virtual screening out of Jews from Soviet operational elites under Khrushchev and Brezhnev. Soviet Jewry, which had lost heavily during the Holocaust, was given no respite to lick its bloody wounds. That American Jewry, perhaps the most fortunate yet to appear in Jewish history, felt an urgency to come to their rescue should not come as a surprise. The need to do so was deeply embedded in the history of the relationship of the two communities.

TWO Setting the Stage

For the Soviet Union and its Jews the *Vernichtungskrieg* waged by the Germans on the eastern front was far bloodier than the war fought in the West, so much so that for some historians it is the war in the East that is the context in which the Holocaust is best understood.[1] But the reality of the massive Jewish losses was underplayed by Soviet authorities who feared that the coupling of Judaism and Bolshevism would strengthen its hold in the popular mind. The defeat of Germany yielded little respite for the surviving Jews. In the Soviet Union awareness of the precariousness of their position grew first among a small segment of urbanized Soviet Jews. Their sense of approaching danger was shared by a small group of Israelis whose interest in Soviet Jewry was often both ideological and nostalgic. Some were former inhabitants of the Soviet Union who still spoke Russian and appreciated its culture. In those postwar years the emigration idea was largely confined to that minority in the Soviet Union and Israel. Some hope of extricating Soviet Jewry existed since the revolution but it was only during the postwar years, fueled by the deterioration of conditions, that the desire to get out began to develop into a full-blown sentiment.

The idea that emigration was the answer coincided with early evidence that the "strange alliance" between the United States and the Soviet Union would not endure beyond the war. The tensions that marked the final wartime conferences in Yalta and Potsdam were partly a reflection of the changing flow of power from West to East as a result of Soviet victories on the field of battle. Soviet leaders were convinced, and many in the West agreed, that the defeat of the formidable Nazi war machine was in large measure attributable to the Red Army. Despite enormous losses, the Soviet Union ended the war on a note of triumph.

The war was followed by a series of crises between the USSR and the United States that was soon dubbed as a Cold War, a condition of deep mutual hostility that had all the characteristics of war except for actual fighting. Its benchmarks became familiar: the failure to conduct elections in Poland, the question of German reparations, the Berlin question. With the development of its own atomic bomb in

1948, the victory of Communism in China (1949) and the establishment of a series of client states in East Europe, the Socialist camp formed a formidable counter-force to balance that of America and its allies, which soon included the newborn Jewish state of Israel. The outbreak of war on the Korean peninsula in 1950 demonstrated how unstable the power balance actually was. It is against this Cold War background that the issue of Soviet Jewish emigration would be played out.

In simplest terms, the growing desire of some Soviet Jews to emigrate and the mobilization of Jewish activists and agencies abroad coalesced to form the world-wide Soviet Jewry movement. The agitation for emigration and the campaign to make it happen among Jewish communities in the West constituted a minor Cold War front. The mistreatment of Soviet Jewry became a Cold War weapon in the American arsenal, part of an indictment that drew attention to Soviet shortcomings on the human rights front. With the Helsinki Accords (1975) and the built-in follow-up conferences, the human rights agenda, which contained the freedom of movement idea, percolated beneath the surface of the emigration issue.

■ Despite radical losses and the persistence of negative stereotypes regarding Jewish valor on the field of battle, the three years following the war were comparatively good ones for Soviet Jewry, at least in the economic sense.[2] The spirit of triumph that swept the Russian people after the defeat of German arms had a special resonance for Jews who understood that they would not have survived had the victory gone the other way. Jewish veterans wore their medals with a special pride. They indicated that the bearer helped defeat an enemy of the motherland and of the Jewish people and, of course, it also gave the lie to those who denied the Jewish contribution to victory. There were other reasons for a sense of well-being. For the moment Jewish representation in the operational elite that managed the Soviet economy, in which Jews were disproportionately represented, was secure. The war and the expansion that followed increased the demand for people with formal education and training, which Jews consistently maintained at the highest level. Politically, too, things seemed stable. Anti-Semitism remained virulent, especially on the lower levels of Soviet society, but in May 1948 the Soviet Union extended full de jure recognition to Israel, just hours after the United States. Regaled for decades with anti-Zionist polemics and having staunchly supported Arab nationalistic anti-British movements, the Kremlin's astonishing reversal caught many Soviet Jews by surprise. There was speculation that Stalin probably held out the hopes that the anti-British stand of the *Yishuv* would help break Britain's imperialistic grip on the Middle East.[3] There was even some hope that, given the Socialist proclivities of Mapam, one of its major parties, Israel might yet join the Socialist camp to compensate for the defection of Tito's Yugoslavia. Czechoslovakia was encouraged to help the new state break the American arms embargo by selling it surplus Messerschmitt 109s and other military hardware left by the German *Wehrmacht*.[4] Most important in supporting Israel's application for UN membership, the usually tight-lipped Soviet delegate, Andrei Gromyko, took the rostrum on May 14, shortly before the final vote for Israel's independence, to speak eloquently of the special losses suffered by Jews during the Holocaust.[5] It was a rare exception to the customary silence maintained regarding the Holocaust. There was one note in Soviet public policy that was worrisome. The campaign to weed "rootless cosmopolitanism" out of Soviet life had been mounted with all the regime's propaganda resources. It was a portent of danger ahead, for who was more "rootless" than the urbanized Soviet Jew.

From the outset, Israel's leaders understood that establishing its demographic viability through immigration was crucial and that the Soviet Union, with its estimated three million Jews, held one of the keys to its security. Hopes were raised when in February 1941, Ivan Maysky, the Soviet ambassador to Britain, assured Chaim Weizmann, then Chairman of the Jewish Agency, that after the war Moscow would support the emigration of Jews who desired to leave.[6] There were some signs that Soviet leaders, perhaps convinced that Soviet Jewry was not interested in settling in Israel, would cooperate, if not with emigrants from the Soviet Union proper, then from satellites such as Romania, Hungary, and Poland. A trickle of ransomed Jews began the massive emigration from Romania, and the repatriation treaty with Poland in 1956 brought 200,000 back to that country by March 1959, about 18,000 of whom were Jews who, with full knowledge of Moscow, ultimately made their way to Israel, together with other Jews who were no longer welcome in Gomulka's Poland.[7] There was a glimmer of hope that the "iron curtain" that had descended across Europe could be circumvented. Based on that slim chance, Israel began to build a human network within the Soviet Union to generate aliyah.

But the new Cold War power balance arrangement proved insufficiently stable for such long-range planning. The difficulty of determining when power was actually balanced led to an expensive and dangerous arms race. In the early years of the 1950s it was still possible to settle the Arab-Israel conflict and the war in Korea without resort to the new weapons of mass destruction. There were ominous signs within the Soviet bloc that the system of repressive domestic controls did not yield the desired political stability. There was seething discontent in the satellites.

In June 1953 unrest broke out on the streets of East Berlin, and in 1956 an open rebellion was mounted in Hungary that was almost coincident with the June war in
the Middle East. Both the Soviet and American governments experienced serious
internal crisis. During the sixties the civil rights struggle followed by a growingly
unpopular war in Vietnam brought an almost continuous round of often violent
urban protest. Compared to the riots occurring in American cities, the Soviet
world looked like a model of tranquility. But that was an illusion. The unresolved
nationality problem, of which the Jewish problem was part, was an explosion waiting to happen. Soviet society was ruled on the assumption that the combination of
state police power and a massive propaganda apparatus to engineer consensus
would ensure stability. By establishing an outside connection with Jewish communities, Soviet Jewry became the first of its discontented minorities to seriously test
that assumption. It was surely the fear of that outside connection that played a role
in Moscow's harsh policy against Jewish applicants for emigration.

For Soviet Jews who sought change, the precariousness of the situation in the
international arena posed a problem. The need to maintain international peace
through a series of arrangements and disarmaments overshadowed the injustices
of the Soviet system that cried out for change. When an abusive regime has the
power to destroy civilization, the arguments favoring "peace" by almost any
means were difficult to overcome. That dilemma was one of the factors in the
early decision that the aim of the movement within the Soviet Union was not to
change the internal governance of the Soviet Union but to emigrate.

There is little agreement on the precise causes of the sharp deterioration of
the Soviet Jewish condition after the supportive role Moscow played in the creation of Israel in 1948. We have noted that there were worrisome signs in the anti-
cosmopolitanism campaign that all was not well concerning the Jewish question in
the new Soviet empire. Soon after hostilities ceased, Andrei Zhdanov, the party's
official caretaker for ideological purity, initiated this campaign with suspicious
anti-Semitic overtones. In the throes of a "struggle" with an invisible enemy thousands of returning Soviet war prisoners such as Aleksandr Solzhenitsyn were sent
to the Gulag on the suspicion that they had been contaminated by contact with the
West. In 1947 a disproportionate number of Jews were given severe sentences for
economic crimes and interned in the Gulag where some became Hebrew speakers
and Zionists. The cultural decapitation policy to prepare Jews for assimilation on
the basis of a Yiddish-speaking culture continued unabated. The policy of reopening of synagogues and religious schools, encouraged during the war, was discontinued. But at the same time a trickle of Jews from the newly incorporated Baltic

states were permitted to emigrate to join their families in Israel. The files of the Jewish Anti-Fascist Committee are filled with requests for help to leave the Soviet Union. The official advice given to such applicants for visas was to settle in the autonomous oblast of Birobidzhan, which was again on the growth list as a counterbalance to the momentum building in the *Yishuv* to declare a Jewish state.

The Soviet Jewish condition yielded a mixed picture. A historian peering into the future in 1946 would probably not have been able to foresee the radical turn of events of the Slansky trial in Prague in November 1952, the Ana Pauker case in Bucharest, and the machinations behind the Doctors' Plot. After 1948 there occurred an almost total shutdown of all Jewish cultural activities, including newspapers, theaters, and schools, and hundreds of Jewish actors, writers, painters, and other culture carriers disappeared into the Gulag. The Jewish chief of staff of the Red Army was replaced. The "homeless cosmopolitan" campaign, a thinly disguised euphemism for Jews, was intensified.[8] Collectively these events revealed that the mentality in the Soviet leadership from Stalin downward was possessed by a pathological anti-Semitic animus that had come to pose a life-threatening danger to Soviet Jews. The foundation of the Soviet Jewry movement, which begins and ends with its most militant component, the activists within the Soviet Union, was anchored in this perception.

It is still difficult to find one's way through the welter of contradictory steps in Soviet foreign and domestic policy during these early postwar years. The Kremlin began the postwar era with support for Israel but within the year converted to adamant opposition to the Jewish state, which persisted after Stalin's death in 1953. Was it Stalin's personal paranoia, fed by evidence that years of efforts to create the conditions for Jewish assimilation had failed, compounded by the defection of Tito's Yugoslavia, that caused the sharp change? To Moscow's chagrin the proclivities of the Israeli electorate were clearly not pro-Soviet. The only Communist in Ben-Gurion's provisional government, Shmuel Mikunis, secretary of the Communist Party of Israel, was not reelected in Israel's first election in January 1949.[9] In the hope that an opportunity for emigration of some Soviet Jews could still be arranged, Ben-Gurion held off entering a formal alliance with the United States. But now it was clear that Israel would eventually become part of the Western camp. The jubilant reception of Golda Meir by Soviet Jewry at New Year services in Moscow's synagogue may have been the event that confirmed Stalin's sense of the disloyalty of the Jews.[10] Just two days before Meir's synagogue visit, Ilya Ehrenburg, the well-known Jewish journalist with special connections to the inner party circle, cautioned in a concealed message in a long *Pravda* article against an overenthusiastic display of affection for Israel.[11] His warning was born out in the months that followed. "Within five months," Meir wrote, "there was practically no single Jewish organization left in Russia and the Jews kept their distance from us."[12] There is a direct line between these events and the breaking of diplomatic relations in 1956 and again after the war in 1967. Whether it stemmed from Stalin's personal suspicion, which he confided to his daughter Svetlana, or the decades-long ideological conflict begun by Lenin with both Jewish separatist political movements, the Jewish Labor Bund and the Zionist movement, was difficult to determine. No matter how many concessions Israel offered after 1967 to restore diplomatic ties, Moscow remained adamant in its rejection. The absence of diplomatic contact between Israel and the Soviet Union went on to become an important element in the emigration story.

With Stalin's death in March 1953 rumors of an impending mass deportation ceased and the remaining indicted Jewish doctors were released.[13] There was, however, no explanation and no apology under Khrushchev, who became Stalin's permanent successor. If anything, the exclusion of Jews from prized schools and institutions continued at a more rapid pace. Khrushchev's confessional about the excesses of Stalin and the "cult of personality" delivered to a thunderstruck members at the Twentieth Party Congress did not mention what had befallen Jews in the last three years of Stalin's reign. The military and diplomatic support of the Arab world in its relentless war against Israel continued unabated. That support undoubtedly strengthened Nasser's hand and encouraged his daring gamble to nationalize the Suez Canal with the probable intention of closing it to Israeli shipping. The nationalization set the stage for the Sinai war in June 1956 that was a battlefield tour de force for Israel but in the end a diplomatic victory for the Soviet Union and its Egyptian client.

◼   The form the policy of exclusion took during the Khrushchev-Brezhnev years was not new, but now it was implemented more intensively. Jewish representation in the nation's institutions of learning and party training schools declined. When faced with the charge of discrimination Soviet officials were able to point out that the Jewish representation in the professions, intelligentsia, and upper levels of the state civil service remained disproportionately high and that some thinning out was inevitable as new educated "cadres" made their debut.[14] Sometimes the defense against the charge of anti-Semitism brought a comical response, as in the case of the official who in defense enumerated the members of the Politburo who had Jewish wives only to elicit a comment that undoubtedly he could not comprehend: "Some of your best wives are Jewish."

The systematic exclusion of Jews is of paramount importance for this study because it suggests that by the mid-sixties it was becoming clear even to highly assimilated Jews who had little interest in retaining a Jewish identity that their station in life was not secure. The hope that their children would be able to rise higher or at least maintain their current status and the living standard that came with it became uncertain.[15] That factor played only a negligible role in the Zionized early emigration push of the late sixties and early seventies. The refuseniks were aware of the travail that the emigration quest posed for their economic security. But for the post-1975 emigrants who were increasingly choosing to drop out, it became an important ingredient behind the decision to leave the Soviet Union.

The purging of Jews from Soviet industry, science, and politics and the growth of Soviet Jewish consciousness led to an unforeseen response from abroad. That Soviet domestic trespasses had an international resonance, especially when it involved Jews, had already become apparent during the Slansky trial in Prague and the Doctors' Plot. In Jerusalem the response was direct and violent. On 9 February 1953 a bomb was planted in the courtyard of the building that housed the Soviet legation.[16] Western diplomats judged the "plot" as part of the accumulating evidence of a streak of madness in Soviet leadership. The progress of the plot was also carefully monitored by the Central Intelligence Agency and the State Department. President Eisenhower took to the airwaves to deny American government involvement, and Winston Churchill did the same in Britain. There was the usual congressional resolution condemning Soviet anti-Semitism. Protest marches before Soviet embassies and professional organizations of scientists and doctors demanding impartial investigations were organized. After the madness of the Slansky trial and the Doctors' Plot, the interest of the foreign press in Soviet machinations became more newsworthy. Khrushchev's revelation at the Twentieth Party Congress did not put a brake on the arrest of Jews for economic and cultural "crimes" and the closing of religious and cultural institutions continued.[17] But abetted by a growing information network the attention it brought abroad came at a historical juncture when Soviet leaders were increasingly sensitive to world opinion. When the Soviet minister of culture, Yekaterina Furtseva, was asked about the future of Yiddish culture at a news conference in February 1961, she frankly admitted that the program continued, not for domestic reasons, but only "to please our friends abroad."[18] Particularly noteworthy were the inquiries and protests of the Communist parties in Western Europe and America who had to respond directly about the clownish goings on in Moscow. Khrushchev's revelations concerning Stalin were particularly hard to bear for comrades who looked to Moscow as their

Mecca. Such intercessions from comradely sources carried weight in Moscow and were welcomed by activists in their protest during the seventies.[19]

Even the most practiced public relations enterprise could not put a good face on some of the more aberrant activities of the Kremlin. Moscow's heavy handedness had already become apparent during the Berlin airlift and the Slansky trial. The Sinyavsky-Daniel trial (1966), which was opened to foreign observers to demonstrate the fairness of the Soviet justice system, proved particularly vexing to Communists abroad. The defendants were allowed to plead innocent and speak in their own defense and did so eloquently. The Soviets had miscalculated and the effect abroad was electrifying, particularly among Communists.[20] The international protest over the publication of Trofim Kitchko's anti-Semitic tract, *Judaism Without Embellishments* (1963) was so intense that the book was withdrawn from publication at the party's behest.

But it was Babi Yar that provided the formidable public relations weapons in the hands of the growingly sophisticated Soviet Jewry movement. Between the Doctors' Plot in 1953 and the Leningrad hijacking trial in 1972 it was the event that contributed most to put the Soviet Jewry issue on the map. By its very nature the Babi Yar memorial question fed into the Jewish cause. Its resonance continued for virtually the life-span of the movement and made Babi Yar a name recognized the world over. Strangely, it did not concern unjust imprisonment or restriction and harassment faced by the growing number of refuseniks, but a continuation of a wartime slander concerning Jewish contribution to the Soviet war effort. The affair began innocently enough when the City Council of Kiev decided to build a park and stadium on one of several Jewish killing grounds that dot the Soviet map. The worldwide protest must have taken the authorities by surprise because they had little idea that a purely local matter could now be observed and commented upon from abroad. Under pressure the original plan was abandoned, and a memorial obelisk for "soviet citizens" was built. Jews were not specifically mentioned since they were supposedly included in the 100,000 Soviet dead to be memorialized. Rather than mute the protest Babi Yar became the source of a continuous cacophony of protest that poets such as Yevgeni Yevtushenko and composers such as Dimitri Shostakovich helped amplify.

Compounding the damage to their image in the West was the crushing of the Hungarian uprising in 1956 and the Warsaw Pact invasion to end the Prague Spring in August 1968. The Warsaw Pact invasion of Czechoslovakia helped focus the interest of the broader community of reformers and democratizers abroad. Strangely, despite public relations missteps such as the memorial at Babi Yar, the

Soviet leadership was growing increasingly sensitive to world public opinion. That sensitivity may partly account for the surprising answer by Aleksey Kosygin, chairman of the Council of Ministers, when questioned about the Jewish emigration at a news conference on 3 December 1966: "If there are some families divided by the war who want to meet their relatives outside the USSR, or even leave the USSR, we shall do all in our power to help them. The way is open to them and there is no problem." [21] These were not words mouthed by a mid-level official. Kosygin was at the top of the inner circle leadership, and the statement not only affirmed the possibility of emigration but proposed a strategy, family reunion, that would allow the Soviet Union to image itself as a humanitarian nation.

Kosygin's response went far to awaken an interest in the possibility of emigration. Many Soviet Jews found themselves out of step with the government position on the 1967 war and secretly rejoiced at the performance of Israel's army. The admiration of things Israeli, songs and books, began to grow enhanced by the informal network created by Israel. When it was learned that an Israeli delegation was present in Moscow in the summer of 1957 as part of the World Festival of Youth it was overwhelmed by Soviet Jewish visitors anxious to make contact. When an Israeli soccer team was scheduled to play in Moscow a year later it was estimated that more than 60 percent of the fans were Jews, some of whom had traveled long distances to see a Jewish team play. By the mid-sixties residual memory combined with growing evidence of exclusion and the awareness that there existed a thriving and concerned Jewish community abroad raised the level of consciousness of Soviet Jewry. Most were not yet ready to consider emigration as a solution but the preconditions were in place. Still, had the Soviet leadership pulled back from its policy of purging Jewish talent the Soviet Jewry movement might not have developed as it did. [22] To discover how Israel, a nation consistently condemned by Soviet media, nevertheless became a reason for Soviet Jews to put their lives at risk we turn next to the development of the informal networks on which the Soviet movement would be based.

▪ The newly established Jewish state played the crucial role of reconnecting the "lost" Jews of the Soviet Union to the Jewish world. Its actions to encourage Soviet emigration represented a goal Zionists had always aspired to. The exercise of sovereign Jewish power to protect or save a diaspora community was in effect supportive evidence of the validity of Zionist ideology. It also filled another aspiration, this one not accepted by all Jewish communities, that Israel could act as the legitimate agent for world Jewry. That rationale was used during the negotiations with Bonn over reparations for the victims of the Holocaust.

Both Israel and American Jewry harbored groups of former Russian Jewish immigrants who had settled there in the first decades of the twentieth century and who continued to maintain a strong interest in their former homeland. Occasionally small numbers of immigrants successfully joined these communities and kept idealized childhood memories alive, including knowledge of the spoken language. In the interwar years interest in the well-being of Soviet Jewry was also maintained by the American Jewish Committee (AJC), the Jewish Labor Committee, and the Congress for Jewish Culture.[23] The practice of requesting government diplomatic intercession or simply inquiries regarding the fate of individuals or groups was renewed after the Roosevelt administration extended diplomatic recognition to Moscow in 1933. For historical reasons the concern about Soviet Jewry was stronger in Israel, where old-timers were often highly placed in government and in the founding kibbutz movement and the Labor Party. In the twenties some members of the extreme left of the kibbutz movement had chosen to return to the Soviet Union to devote themselves to building the new Socialist society. Others were all too aware that Russia's pervasive anti-Semitism had not been changed despite the clauses forbidding it in the constitution of 1936. Israel's concern for Soviet Jewry went beyond kinship and Jewish law. It was reinforced by the sense that the resettlement of Soviet Jews in Israel was a natural solution to Israel's impending demographic crisis that also solved the problems of security and the ability to live a Jewish life for the Soviet Jews. The Jews of Eastern Europe who might have become Israel's natural population stock had been decimated in the Holocaust. The demographic shortfall was compounded by the failure of the world Zionist movement to attract sufficient numbers. In 1948 Israel faced the most fecund population in the Arab world with barely a million inhabitants. In theory Soviet Jewry's immigration to Israel seemed to be a natural fit. For Israel it represented not only the fulfillment of the Zionist imperative of "ingathering of the exiles" but also a solution to its dire need for population. Paradoxically, it was the Kremlin that held the critical demographic card. That Soviet Jewry would be called upon to play the role of lifesaver seemed natural. Much of the Zionist idea was incubated within Russian Jewry, and the *Yishuv*'s initial population stock was composed in good measure of Eastern European Jews. The kibbutz, which was Zionism's pride and joy, with its volunteer collectivism and its fixation with the soil and agriculture, was clearly the realization of a Tolstoyan Narodnik (populist) vision of how life is best lived. In short, Israel needed Soviet Jewry at least as much as it imagined Soviet Jewry needed it.

The quest for immigrants began before the state was established in 1948.

Vague assurances made at the outset of the war proved to be not much more than empty gestures. When the war ended Israel was compelled to scramble for population to arrive at the critical mass necessary for statehood and security in a hostile Arab world. *Bricha,* the Hebrew designation for an illegally organized immigration operation, brought thousands to Palestine, but it was probably more valuable as a Zionist public relations ploy to highlight the plight of Jewish refugees and the *Yishuv*'s heroic role in receiving them than it was in making a dent in the population deficit.[24] An effort was mounted by the Jewish Agency to Zionize the survivors in Europe's displaced person camps but again the results were disappointing. In those years, too, the pull of America was strong.[25] The immigration from North Africa presented other problems, and the growing immigration from Romania was expensive. Soviet Jewry seemed to be the best answer if a way of getting people out could be found.

The absorption of Jews from North Africa nearly broke the back of Israel's fragile economy. It raised the question of whether Israel could indeed absorb a mass emigration from Russia. Friendship treaties with Syria and Egypt in 1950 showed that the Kremlin was drawing ever closer to the Arab world. Israel too reappraised the possibility of establishing a friendlier footing with Moscow in order to open the door for emigration. In the years that followed Moscow in a sense virtually held Israel hostage to its need for Soviet emigration. Israel hesitated to enter military pacts with Western nations in the hope that Moscow would view it as a neutral in the Cold War. Thankfully, Washington did not invite Israel to join Middle East Treaty Organization in 1954. Tel Aviv had spoken out during the trial of the "killer doctors" and watched silently as Israeli citizens, some former members of *Bricha,* and negotiators of the arms deal with Czechoslovakia were accused of being Zionist spies.[26] Even after the Sinai war (1956) Israel had not given up hope that a deal might yet be made to tap Russia's Jewish population source. Israel now used all public forums available to speak out against Soviet depredations against Jews. By the time Moscow broke diplomatic relations in 1956, Israel had become the primary voice calling world attention to the plight of Soviet Jewry. A high point in using the United Nations as platform to call attention to Soviet antireligious depredations came in April 1965 when Israeli Justice Haim Cohen made an impassioned plea for the right of religious communities to publish religious texts. Such a right was denied as a matter of course in Russia. The UN Human Rights Commission accepted the proposed amendment to its charter. Two years later the concept of having a special high commissioner on human rights, which Israel and other states had been advocating, also became a reality.

But Israel's basic dilemma remained unresolved. The Soviet "friendship" treaties with Arab countries were preliminary to a massive flow of arms to Egypt and Syria that threatened to weaken Israel's security and push it ever closer to becoming an American client state in the Cold War. In the short run Israel was militarily secure but in the long run its viability depended on immigration, which to some degree was in Moscow's hands. That delicate situation compelled Israel to deal softly with Moscow's implacable hostility, far softer than militant activists thought was necessary. It often resulted in the sending of mixed signals to activists in America and the Soviet Union, with poor results.

For the almost 100,000 signers of a petition delivered to the Knesset in April 1965, Israel's voice for Soviet Jewry was not loud enough. The petitioners urged the government to consider the Soviet Jewry issue more openly and condemned Nahum Goldmann who, like Henry Kissinger, believed that the issue was best handled through "quiet" diplomacy. The diplomatic approach did not sit well with those who had already settled in Israel, represented by the Union of Former Prisoners of Zion and the Association of Immigrants from the Soviet Union. In the United States, too, the Union of Councils for Soviet Jewry (UCSJ) and many members of the Student Struggle for Soviet Jewry (SSSJ) often found them in opposition to Israel's policy on the Soviet Jewry issue because of what they believed was an opportunistic posture.

Israel's dilemma was compounded by the awareness that the possibility of endangering Soviet Jewry was a real one. By the 1960s there was a growing sense that Moscow's extreme reaction to a comparatively minor power was abnormal and may have been partly triggered by an awareness that diplomatic ties had permitted members of its consular delegation to make seemingly innocent trips in their diplomatic cars flying the Israel flag, which was sufficient to bring Jews out of the woodwork. Armed with addresses received from relatives and former Soviet immigrants who had in earlier years settled in Palestine, hundreds of contacts were made and material about Israel distributed. The people involved in this sometimes dangerous work reported that, given sufficient incentive, at least fifty percent of Soviet Jewry would immigrate to Israel. Resettling millions of Soviet Jews in Israel was not a dream; it could become a reality. The passion for Israel was especially strong in the newly incorporated Baltic states, the Caucasus, and republics such as Georgia. A communications network, probably little more than a list of names of likely activists, was developed and gave the Israelis a good source of information on what was actually happening. It was the beginning of reestablishing a link between Soviet Jewry and the outside Jewish world. Jerusalem's hopes that the groundwork for emigration was being developed would soon be dimmed. The KGB was fully aware of the forbidden connection now maintained by family visitors and "tourists" from abroad and transmitted its information to the Central Committee of the Communist Party of the Soviet Union (CPSU).[27]

But even with the controls available to Soviet security it proved difficult to halt the traffic entirely without damaging the profitable Soviet tourist trade and the reputation of a free society it was anxious to nurse. Soon there were hundreds of visits yearly from visitors bearing gifts that included everything from religious items to patent medicines. The visitors arrived not only from Israel but from the United States and Britain. The visits had an impact not only on the applicants, soon dubbed "refuseniks," for visas that had been rejected by the Office of Visas and Registration (OVIR) but also on the hundreds of visitors who crammed into small apartments to listen and learn of a strange movement without formal structure, composed of people so impassioned by their commitment as to risk the well-being of themselves and their families. Such heroic types were not often seen in the West.

The visits were of course not coincidental but well-planned by a little known bureau within Israel's foreign ministry. As early as 1952 Moshe Sharett had established what was euphemistically called a liaison bureau (Lishkat Hakesher, or Lishka) whose short-run task was to improve contact between Soviet Jews and outside Jewish communities. A second goal was to heighten the profile of the emigration issue through public relations and other techniques and to activate the free Jewish communities of the West for that purpose. Offices within the Israel embassy that reported directly to the prime minister soon became active in Paris, London, and New York. Already in existence were procedures and practices that could be used to permit a trickle of emigrants to leave. If the emigration of Soviet Jews was linked to the existing notion of family reunification, a rationale for immigration to Israel could be established. Some even held out hope that Moscow could ultimately be convinced to cooperate with such a limited emigration. However, if the enterprise was projected as rescuing Jews from a tyrannical regime or an immigration that would ensure Israel's security and perhaps even its claims to the West Bank, the effect would be entirely different. Israel preferred this gradual exodus, which would also solve the absorption problem. But the *Hasbara* (educational public relations effort), emanating from activists in America and the Soviet Union did not always follow suit.

That decision to move into high gear on the emigration issue was made at an informal meeting in August 1955 between Ben-Gurion, foreign minister Sharett, and Shaul Avigur, a ministry official with experience in managing Aliyah Bet, the illegal immigration that brought thousands of Holocaust survivors to Israel. From the outset, coordination problems were encountered. The subcommittee to activate western Jewries had Nahum Goldmann, who was there in his dual capacity as president of the World Jewish Congress and the World Zionist Organization, as one of its members. He opposed "emotional" protests and was a strong proponent of "quiet diplomacy" that he envisaged would be conducted privately by people like himself. Though similar to the strategy preferred by Israel, it made him anathema to the militant activists in the Soviet Union and the United States. For its own reasons Israel too, though now convinced that many Soviet Jews wanted to leave, often found itself opposed to the protest ritual mobilized by activists. In addition, Israel's hope for diplomatic ties with Moscow, on which the success of the moderate approach depended, proved to be chimerical. Moscow broke diplomatic relations with Israel for a short period in 1953 and again in 1967. After that year the administrative work, mostly concerning visas, was done by the embassy of the Netherlands.[28] Meanwhile, the Russian-speaking Nechemia Levanon, appointed as an agricultural attaché in Moscow but actually charged with creating the links to Soviet Jews, was expelled for his activities in 1952 and replaced by Binyamin Eliav, who later became consul general in New York. After relations were resumed in 1953 the Israeli consular teams traveled far and wide to make contact with surviving Jewish communities. Soviet security must have been puzzled since nothing that came under the classification of intelligence collecting was conducted on these trips, which were devoted to simply establishing contact between Russian Jews and Israelis who could speak Russian. Soviet diplomatic personnel had reciprocal rights to travel in Israel. But in fact these visits to the Soviet hinterland were not innocent fact-finding trips. The reports yielded crucial evidence about the leaders or people who could be contacted and the degree of readiness for emigration in the various far-flung regions in Russia's vast interior where Jews lived. Since it was exclusively an Israeli operation, the goal, especially away from large urban centers, was to awaken Jews to the possibility of resettlement in Israel.

In 1958 Levanon was placed in charge of the bureau's diaspora operation, and Aryeh Eliyahu broadened activities in the Soviet Union, adding such things as Hebrew classes and information libraries.[29] But until 1967 Israel, sensitive to the fact that Moscow was in a position to threaten Israel's existence by its extensive armament program of her Arab neighbors, rarely spoke about emigration directly. These were left for discussions at the UN Commission for Human Rights forums and other international forums. Nor did Israel confront Moscow on her treatment of Jews. The material distributed contained no anti-Soviet references. There was fear that such rhetoric would threaten the safety of the very Russian Jews Israel hoped to protect and perhaps attract as immigrants.

While walking a diplomatic tightrope, the bureau carried forward its mission of activating the American Jewish effort. When Meir Rosenne was appointed ambassador these activities went into high gear. The new ambassador was convinced that American Jewish leaders' preoccupation with Israel's security without considering the emigration issue ultimately militated against Israel's interest. He saw the Soviet Jewry issue as a means to handle at once Israel's security and its demographic instability. Using the informal Jewish network in Washington, during the Kennedy administration, he and Ambassador Avraham Harman familiarized Sen. Ribicoff, Sen. Humphrey, and Justice Arthur Goldberg, among others, with the problem of Soviet Jewry. It was these connections within the Kennedy administration that marked the birth of an American government interest in advocating emigration rights for Jews. According to one observer, it "was clear case in which American Jewish concern followed the government, rather than the other way around." It was an interest that all subsequent American administrations were aware of but did not push with equal vigor.[30]

The initial organization of the Soviet Jewry movement was largely a Zionist enterprise that reached out to non-Zionist agencies such as the AJC and UAHC. In these early years few questioned that the goal of emigration would be resettlement in Israel. For a moment Israel played the role of protector and leader of world Jewry that Zionist thinkers had envisaged. Not only did Israel create and maintain the basis of the world Soviet Jewry movement from the early fifties to the end of the 1967 war, but Israel also controlled the contacts and the detailed information to keep it going. But almost from the outset Israel's assumption of the leadership role was not automatically accepted by all, especially not by the new organizations that had made their debut in the Soviet Jewry arena and who were not affiliated with the National Conference on Soviet Jewry (NCSJ).

Israel's proprietary feelings stemmed partly from the fact that it had created the movement. That it would claim a major role in determining the movement's direction was predictable. Yoram Dinstein, the representative of the Lishka in New York, may have sounded self-congratulatory when he rated the program as the "only success story of Israeli foreign policy since the birth of the state." When Dinstein assumed his post in 1966 few believed that there was a Soviet Jewry problem, "not even sovietologists."[31] Men such as Richard Pipes thought it was an Israeli invention. By the time Dinstein returned home a few years later, the issue held a high place on the Cold War agenda. But the breaking of diplomatic relations at the end of the 1967 war tended to marginalize Israel's role as a player in the Soviet Jewish drama. Israel witnessed the bridge to Soviet Jewry it had laboriously developed through its diplomatic mission threatened by the KGB and an independent-minded American movement. Circumstances had placed America and its Jewry in a better position to win the prize for which Israel had worked so hard and invested so much.

■　　In contrast to its European brethren, American Jewry emerged from World War II in better condition than it had entered it. The war permitted Jews, many for the first time, to break out of the urban ghettoes of the large northeastern seaboard cities where they were concentrated. The thousands of young Jewish males that had either enlisted or were drafted after September 1940, when the first peacetime draft was instituted, saw the breadth and beauty of the country. After demobilization thousands of Jewish veterans resettled in these areas.[32] The absorption of over 100,000 displaced persons, supplemented by a steady trickle of Jewish emigrants from Hungary, Israel, Cuba, Iran, and later the Soviet Union barely affected the rapid full acculturation of American Jewry, now overwhelmingly native born.[33] The years spent in the armed forces were themselves an intense Americanizing experience. For American Jewry the effect of the war was twofold: The Americanizing process was accelerated and, related to that, the northeastern center of Jewish life, anchored in New York City, was sufficiently defused to allow other centers to develop. Whether the reverse side of that intense wartime acculturation was the beginning of a decline in Jewish identity or merely a change in the kind of identity is difficult to determine. Closer scrutiny reveals that many of the changes were already present in the interwar years. What is clear is that American Jewry emerged from the war more confident and secure.

The comparatively high education level of American Jewry had been partly responsible for its rapid emergence from the depression. In the postwar years the rate of professionalization was accelerated further by the GI Bill, which thousands of veterans used to complete their education. The rising socioeconomic indices also included a growth in per capita income and a tilt in the Jewish occupational profile toward managerial positions. Even such seemingly innocent things as the increase in life expectancy showed that Jews had joined the general march of postwar prosperity in America. They had in fact gotten out in front of it. *Fortune Magazine* identified a new group of newly wealthy Jews dubbed "egghead millionaires" in the forefront of that march. That appellative referred to a stratum of Jews who combined a newly learned professional skill with business acumen to accumulate

great wealth.[34] If the success of postwar United Jewish Appeal fund-raising campaigns is any indication, such increase in per capita income was the rule rather
than the exception in the postwar decade. Jews were involved in establishing themselves in the middle class. That may be one of the reasons for American Jewry's
sluggishness in responding to the Soviet Jewish crises. The privatism generated by
the postwar prosperity and the effort and energy expended to make one's fortune
made the giving of philanthropy an acceptable alternate to the giving of oneself.

Notwithstanding the materialism and vulgarity they were endlessly cautioned
about by the disproportionate number of social commentators who came from
their ranks, the relentless march to middle class status and prosperity was welcomed by most American Jews. But there were fears and shadows in Jewish life that
prosperity could not eliminate. For one thing, America's earliest reaction to the
Cold War took the form of McCarthyism. Its hysteria, while not directed at Jews
per se, carried some frightening implications for a constituency that was probably
the nation's least enthusiastic cold warriors. After their disproportionate vote for
Henry Wallace in the election of 1948 it took little to convince some that Jews were
not in the political mainstream of American life.[35] It was not the first time in the
American Jewish experience that Jewishness and Communism or political radical-
ism were uttered in the same breath, but in the 1950s a series of espionage episodes
seemed to substantiate the caricature. During a two-year period news of the arrest,
trial, conviction, and finally execution of the Rosenbergs wracked American Jewry.
For some Americans it was a substantiation of the linkage between Judaism and
Communism, but for many Jews the execution of the Rosenbergs was a clear case
of anti-Semitism, especially in the execution of Ethel Rosenberg.[36]

For some, that the trials of Rudolf Slansky in Prague, of the "killer" doctors in
Moscow, and of the Rosenbergs in New York were held within the same four-year
time frame on either side of the iron curtain served as evidence of an anti-Semitic
conspiracy. The trials were dissimilar in most respects but the taint of Jewish disloyalty was unmistakably similar. Unfathomed by most Americans was that while
American Jews positioned themselves slightly to the left of center on the political
spectrum, it was the democratic left that become known for its early awareness of
the true nature of Stalinism. A coterie of dissident Communists along with former
Jewish Bundists and Labor Zionists became the group most aware of the murderous nature of the Soviet regime. In the examination in chapter 4 of the anti-
détente group that became the staunchest advocates of the Jackson-Vanik
amendment, it is noted that they were neo-Conservatives who often trace their

roots to a loose group of former Communists and Socialist democrats once active on the Jewish left.

■ These socioeconomic and political factors played a role in determining the terms on which American Jewry would become fully involved in the Soviet Jewry movement. But for an explanation of their passion for "rescue" we must turn to how American Jewry played its witness role during the Holocaust. Although an occasional survivor's memoir was published in the early fifties and the generation that lived through the experience was certainly aware of it, one heard little about the Holocaust immediately after the war. The so-called boomer generation born in the immediate postwar decade that came to maturity during the seventies learned about the fate of European Jewry during their adolescence in the sixties. It may have started with the Eichmann trial in 1961–62 and the publication of a cool administrative history of how it was done by Raul Hilberg, *The Destruction of the European Jews*. But it was the publication of a journalistic account by a researcher for CBS, Arthur Morse, that figures most directly in the anger of American Jewish activists. There were few American Jewish activists who hadn't read *While Six Million Died,* which placed the blame for the indifferent response to the death camps first on the Roosevelt administration, which the parents worshiped, and by implication, on the lack of concern of American Jewry.[37]

By 1963 the Holocaust was on the road to becoming a paradigmatic episode in the American Jewish experience. For young Jewish activists the victimization of Jews was not a random historical datum but rather a warning signal that something has gone awry in the prevailing nation-state system and that an act of massive social cannibalism such as the Holocaust could happen again. In the Jewish community the slogan "Never Again" had a resonance far beyond the members of the Jewish Defense League (JDL) who introduced it. The parallel with the events in the Soviet Union between 1948 and 1953 were too close to be ignored. "There is a dreadful moral trauma that haunts many of us," said Abraham Joshua Heschel at an address delivered at the Jewish Theological Seminary on 4 September 1963, "the failure. . . . To do our utmost . . . to save the Jews under Hitler. [The] nightmare that terrifies me today [is] the unawareness of being involved in a new failure, in a tragic dereliction of duty [toward] Russian Jewry."[38] Jewish activists entered the arena not to solve Israel's demographic problems but to do for Soviet Jewry what they thought their parents had failed to do for the Jews of Europe. The rescuer role they assumed released enormous energy but it would also become the source of much conflict. A similar awareness of prior failure may have fueled the favorable reaction by State Department personnel at the consular level, especially the American embassy in Moscow. Their supportive activities stood in sharp contrast to the customary indifference or hostility toward refugees by consular officials in the thirties. Of course, as one researcher points out, this time around the problem, at least in its early stage, did not seem to call for America having to absorb the refugees.[39]

The Holocaust gave young Jewish activists a reason to concern themselves about Soviet Jewry but, as an idealistic age cohort, their concern also had a general humanitarian impulse. Some spoke of a need to make a difference. Several participants have spoken of a spillover effect from the civil rights struggle that affected the struggle to "overcome" for Russian Jewry as well. Some participants were undoubtedly first involved with the civil rights movement but the precise number is difficult to quantify.[40] Ostensibly this change of allegiance occurred when the Congress of Racial Equality, the leading civil rights organization in the fifties, purged the leadership of the civil rights movement of white activists, many of whom were Jewish. More likely is the possibility that there was transference of the confrontational tactics developed by the antiwar and civil rights movements. According to one observer, "Shoving it in people's faces worked."[41]

The agitation for Soviet Jewry began slowly by drawing in religious leaders and intellectuals during the early sixties. In its early incarnation it was a human rights rather than an emigration movement.[42] As early as September 1950, fifty scholars, writers, and academicians, including Martin Buber, Bertrand Russell, Reinhold Niebuhr, and Albert Schweitzer convened in Paris to draw attention to the depredations that preceded the Doctors' Plot during the so-called Black Years. The mobilization of the voices of well-known intellectuals was effective and elicited an early response from the Soviet leadership to Bertrand Russell's letter to Khrushchev.[43] In 1948 many nations, excluding the Soviet Union, had signed the UN Universal Declaration of Human Rights. "Freedom of movement," on which the right to emigrate was based, was from the outset part of the human rights agenda, but it was overshadowed by such better known and popular rights as freedom of religion and speech. In these early years some Soviet activists believed that focusing the nascent Soviet Jewry campaign exclusively on the right to emigrate positioned it on too narrow an ethnic basis. It could too easily be viewed as an abandonment of those who struggled to democratize the Soviet system. Despite that, fear of the worsening situation in the Soviet Union, especially the increasing number of arrests and imprisonment of Jews for "economic crimes," ultimately led to a decision to separate from Soviet dissidents to focus on a solution by emigration. We return later to this decision and the problems it entailed.

Strangely, it was a denial of a practice among religious Jews, the ban on the baking of matzohs by several Soviet cities beginning in 1957, that led to the 1964 appeal for matzohs from abroad that fueled the still-muted protest ritual.[44] Stranger still was that the individual letters of concern solicited from political leaders such as Eleanor Roosevelt, Bishop James Pike, Sen. Kenneth Keating, and Jacob Javits and congressional resolutions sponsored by Sen. Thomas Dodd, Rep. Charles Buckley, Rep. Leonard Farbstein, Sen. James E. Murray, and Sen. Jacob Javits preceded Jewish pressure generated by mass protest rallies. The State Department's earliest expression of concern to Moscow was made in response to reminders by Jewish congressional representatives and others involved with Jewish constituencies, such as Sen. Keating. Such notes of diplomatic concern were routine for the department, but in the sixties they were undoubtedly sent with greater alacrity in order to head off complaints, fueled by the knowledge of the department's poor showing during the Holocaust.[45] Jewish leaders were not alone in asking for intercession from the postwar administrations regarding Soviet depredations. Congressmen such as Charles Vanik, who represented constituencies with representations of immigrants from Soviet-occupied areas in Eastern Europe, proffered a drumbeat of requests for intercession and concern.[46] Within the prevailing Cold War context the Washington's response to Soviet depredations on the congressional and executive levels occurred well before a mass public relations campaign alerting the general public was organized. Jewish leaders were not alone in calling for government response to Soviet depredations. The temptation to compare government and communal response during the Holocaust years, when the Jewish plea remained a voice in the wilderness, with their response during the Soviet Jewry episode, when anti-Soviet voices joined their quest, does not yield any great historical truth.

The early protests for Soviet Jewry were random and unsponsored. Jewish defense agencies entered the fray only after organizational difficulties were overcome. But protest rallies, large and small, sometimes served as a calling card for the debut of a new organization or grouping in the growing movement. A conference on the status of Soviet Jewry that convened on 12 October 1963 led to the establishment of the American Jewish Conference on Soviet Jewry a year later (AJCSJ).[47] The birth of the militant SSSJ can be traced to a protest meeting of students at Columbia University on 27 April 1964, which was followed five days later by a silent march to the Soviet UN mission on Park Avenue.

In fact, the history of Jewish defense organizations did not hold out much hope that a cohesive response could ever be organized. Before World War II, the Jewish communal organizational network was the most extensive of any ethnic community in America. Jews generated the highest number of organizations per capita. Every interest and ideology, even a shadow of an ideology, produced an organization. There were the major national defense organizations, each with its own style and politics, each representing a different constituency. There were public relations organizations, fraternal organizations, labor and Zionist organi-zations, organization of presidents of major organizations, religious organizations in triplicate for each of the separate branches of Judaism, political organizations, veterans' organizations, and a growing number of professional organizations. Each developed a separate appetite for funds. Withal, American Jewry was not governed in the sense that Israel was governed. The proliferation of Jewish organizations and agencies reflected the openness of American society, a model of the American world envisaged by Tocqueville. But the abundance of organization created problems of governance and coherence. The rallying cry of the Zionist-oriented American Jewish Congress (AJCong) during the twenties was a call for democracy in Jewish life. But in practice, that call often meant that organizational anarchy prevailed so that one almost wished for a Louis Marshall to impose some order as he did during the abrogation struggle in the early decades of the century. Only the annual meeting of the general assembly of the local federations (Council of Jewish Federations and Welfare Funds [CJF]) gave some semblance of governance. It produced an overall agenda and budgetary priorities. In the sixties the Soviet Jewry issue had not yet made its debut as a national Jewish concern.[48]

The omnipresence of organizational rivalry and duplication of effort is crucial to an understanding of the American Jewish response to the Soviet Jewish crises.[49] There was little agreement on how to fund the effort and which organization or combination of organizations or totally new single issue organization should take responsibility for the effort. In the latter case the cry of the existing agencies protecting their turf was: "Who needed yet another Jewish organization?"[50] The issue was made more complex by Israel's role as activator. Its involvement with Soviet Jewry contained much that could draw the commitment of young activists, especially the human rights aspect. But Israel's motivation also involved a national interest, bringing immigrants to the national homeland and a Zionist ideological element, and "ingathering." Both were bound to come into conflict with the simple quest to "rescue" persecuted Jews that drove American activists.

Even before the Slansky trial in December 1952, American Jewish organizations responded to the news of Soviet depredations. Predictably, most sensitive to what was happening in the Soviet Union was the Jewish Labor Committee, whose Europe-born members had sometimes experienced Soviet excesses firsthand. It organized the first protest rally on 21 December 1952, and some members later picketed the offices of the Communist Yiddish daily *Morning Freiheit*. It was the similarly politically inclined Congress for Jewish Culture that started a petition movement by leading intellectuals to let Jews leave. Organizations such as the AJ-Cong and umbrella organizations such as NJCRAC periodically issued press releases and featured an occasional article on the situation in their house organs. The American Zionist Council convened a meeting of thirty-four Zionist-oriented organizations even before the Doctors' Plot made the headlines. But their ability to act was hampered by limited budgets. When Isaiah Minkoff, executive director of NJCRAC, urged that international public opinion be mobilized to counteract Soviet anti-Semitism, the instrument and budget to do so did not yet exist. In 1952 such calls were largely unheard. For the leadership group who had witnessed the Holocaust, little seemed to have changed since World War II. In those years the AJC, convinced that the Jewish penchant for protest rallies and emotional actions at the grassroots level was a waste of time, similarly refused to participate in a mass protest rally in to take place on 16 February 1953 in Manhattan Center. The rally featured the usual speeches and resolutions but little beyond that to build a permanent organization concerned exclusively with Soviet Jewry. When an opportunity developed for a delegation of Jewish leaders to speak with Khrushchev, who was scheduled to meet with Eisenhower on 15 September 1959, the organizational leaders could not resolve the predictable jurisdictional conflict that followed. The Jewish Labor Committee opposed any meeting. A proposed ad hoc committee composed of Jacob Blaustein, past president of the AJC, Phil Klutznick, chairman of the Conference of Presidents, and Nahum Goldmann, president of the World Jewish Congress, did briefly meet with Khrushchev, but no one agreed about the crucial question: for whom did they speak and what would they say?

The AJC's organizational style was originally introduced by Louis Marshall and in the postwar years fully developed by its executive director, John Slawson. It strategy was to speak to power holders directly and to build coalitions with non-Jewish groups to give the issue as broad a political base as possible. As news of arrests of Jews increased in the early sixties, the AJC recruited the voices of such world-renowned luminaries as Albert Schweitzer, Bertrand Russell, and Norman Thomas, who could sound a moral appeal. But despite the amplification of their statements in the media, the impact in Moscow was not discernable. Like Berlin during the Holocaust, Moscow seemed immune from moral suasion.

The AJC, which was the first of the major defense organizations in the field, was shaped by an organizational culture that had always been averse to emotional public displays and mass rallies. It preferred working through insiders such as Meyer Feldman, Kennedy's special counsel, and other leading members of the administration and through Congress. They conceived of themselves as an elite leadership group speaking to another. In that way personal negotiations could generate new solutions unencumbered by organizational problems. Unlike AJC's response during the Holocaust, when it opposed the Zionist enterprise, it now welcomed the counsel of Israel's liaison office.

The "reunification of families" idea that had been used by Moscow several times in the fifties and sixties allowed the Soviets to permit some emigration without opening the floodgates. The idea of using family reunification may have come out of that kind of organizational synergy. It was rooted in the sense that the emigration could be managed through back channel diplomacy. But after the tension created by the Cuban missile crisis, the Jewish problem was overshadowed but did not vanish from the diplomatic correspondence. Kennedy asked Ambassador Harriman to raise the issue of the arrest of Jews with Khrushchev in 1962. But the State Department viewed such presidential requests as politically motivated and remained reluctant to intercede diplomatically on what it viewed as an "internal matter." Llewellyn Thompson, Harriman's successor, informed Label Katz, president of B'nai B'rith, that he believed that such diplomatic intercession would be counterproductive.[51] It would be a comparatively new presence on the political scene that would play a key role in bringing the Soviet Jewry case to the fore. The increase in Jewish senators and representatives from both parties and non-Jewish political leaders who unhesitatingly spoke out on Jewish causes formed one wing of this group. Another was formed by congressional assistants who acted behind the scenes to play a pivotal role in writing legislation and in political strategizing.

At the grassroots level yet another development was occurring outside the Jewish establishment. Beginning in cities such as Cleveland and San Francisco, groups of Jewish activists, unhappy with the slow response of the mainline organizations, were planning their own programs to bring the plight of Soviet Jewry to public attention. It would lead to the establishment of the UCSJ, a federated organization in which these local groups and federations came together. For the next three decades it acted as a gadfly for the movement.[52]

At the same time, Nahum Goldmann, anxious to have the World Jewish Congress, of which he was president, represent world Jewry in negotiations with Moscow also approached Soviet authorities for direct talks. He apparently assumed that Moscow was aware of his preference for "quiet diplomacy." He had after all stated several times publicly that it was a mistake to agitate too "noisily" for Soviet Jewry because it would not be effective and would increase the danger the Soviet Jews faced. But few cared to follow a self-appointed leader, and for the more militant activists he had become anathema. There was a sense that Israel preferred private negotiations and was generally opposed to confrontational protest, unless orchestrated by the Lishka, and shared Goldmann's "quiet" approach.

The organizations, the AJCSJ, the UCSJ, the SSSJ, still in nascent form, were in place and so too was the conflict about tactics and strategy, which was the signature of the Soviet Jewry movement, as it had been for every previous organized rescue effort of American Jewry. What had not yet developed was a coherent organizational response to the worsening situation in Russia. The Jewish organizational world continued to be characterized by jurisdictional disputes regarding turf that were only partly resolved by the establishment of the AJCSJ in 1964. It was born as an organizational hybrid and was dysfunctional from the outset. The line between having a separate agency or a federated response of existing agencies could not easily be fudged. The establishment of the successor agency in 1970, the NCSJ, was an improvement, but the problem of who makes policy and who pays was never fully solved. At the same time little common ground could be found for day-to-day operations. There was a line between activists, who believed that confrontational tactics such as those employed in the civil rights movement were necessary, and the representatives of the Lishka, who still held out the possibility of behind-the-scenes negotiations. The idea of a repetition of the mass protest ritual of the Holocaust years also was opposed by the AJC, which considered them more cathartic than effective. Paradoxically, the AJC, which would play a major role in creating the NCSJ, considered itself an agency apart in the Jewish organizational world. It belonged neither to the NJCRAC nor to the Conference of Presidents.

The difference in approach went beyond generational and cultural background. Isaiah Minkoff, the Yiddish-speaking president of NJCRAC, and Lewis H. Weinstein, its chairman, called for a worldwide campaign for Soviet Jewry as early as February 1953. A decade later Rabbi Abraham Heschel, affiliated with the Jewish Theological Seminary and whose reputation among younger activists was considerably enhanced by his strong support of the civil rights movement, warned the leadership of NJCRAC that unless a campaign with a separate agency to address the Soviet Jewry issue was formed he would campaign to create one. A separate agency with an independent appetite for funds and autonomous action was the last thing that main line agencies wanted. Finally, Lewis Weinstein called a meeting of the Conference of Presidents and invited Heschel to speak. The AJC was invited to attend as an observer. The meeting was a stormy one. There was general agreement that action had to be taken but little consensus on what to do and who should be responsible for actually doing it. It was decided to convene a high profile national assembly in Washington, a kind of American Jewish conference on Soviet Jewry, reminiscent of the disastrous conference convened in 1943 when news of the Final Solution had been fully confirmed. Meeting at the Willard Hotel on 5 and 6 April 1964, there was surprisingly unanimity to proceed with establishing a new agency. Only Agudath Israel opposed the final resolution in which the twenty-four organizations promised "not to exacerbate cold war tensions" and vowed to find the resources and energies to call the world's attention to the oppression of Soviet Jewry. The emigration solution was not yet in the picture.

That may be one of the reasons why Israel, which had played the central role in building a bridge to Soviet Jewry, had no official representative at the meeting. American organizations were now primed to act for protecting Soviet Jewry in place. They did not yet think in terms of extrication and resettlement in Israel. Yet by the 1960s Israel's unofficial presence in American Jewish affairs was well established. As a sovereign state it also maintained a separate government to government diplomatic contact. Nechemia Levanon and Meir Rosenne maintained contacts with the State Department and Yoram Dinstein used his post on Israel's UN mission to guide the Jewish organizations that were headquartered in New York. It may have been an exaggeration to claim to have laid the groundwork for the American movement, as Dinstein did. But the Israeli team was first on the scene and became active with Jewish communal and American political leaders.[53] Practically, the Israeli mission had better access to the administration than the nongovernmental organizations representing the Jewish community. Their exasperation must have grown as they listened to non-Zionist AJC and B'nai B'rith speak of the Soviet Jewish problem as basically one of restoring Jewish cultural life and ensuring human rights. Israel had from the outset an additional motive, aliyah, that they hoped might ultimately be arranged on a government-to-government basis, as it was with Romania.

But how could a flow of emigrants to Israel be best assured? Before the 1967 war the Israelis were anxious not to antagonize Moscow and therefore counseled a less confrontational approach. They played a major role in setting up the complex governance of the first national organization, the AJCSJ, in 1964. Yoram Dinstein, who succeeded Meir Rosenne as head of the Israeli operation in the United States, speaks of the AJCSJ as "essentially our creation."[54] When the financing and the rotational leadership of the agency proved inadequate, Dinstein again became involved because the AJCSJ was "in terrible shape and I had constantly to deal with its survival" and to "nip the opposition stemming from Cleveland in the bud."[55]

The delicate relationship between the growingly active Jewish organizations and the Lishka delegation in Washington began to show signs of strain after the 1967 war when Israel became more forthright and confident in its confrontation with Moscow that, Israel was convinced, had encouraged Egypt's bellicosity. Moscow had in any case broken diplomatic relations with Israel. A year later Ilya Rippes, an activist from Riga, protested the invasion of Czechoslovakia by attempting self-immolation before the Soviet embassy in Prague. Fearing loss of the information network derived from sources within the Soviet Union, Dinstein rejected a strategy, advocated by the JDL and other militants, to showcase the immolation incident as a protest against the denial of the right to emigrate.[56] Several months later the conflict assumed a bitter tone when Dinstein opposed an American tour for a particularly militant activist Yasha Kazakov[57]

More likely to account for the diminishment of Israel's authority was the maturation of the American movement. In addition, the break in diplomatic relations hampered Israel's ability to operate from within the Soviet Union. Israel's monopoly of information was first broken by Michael Sherbourne, a London schoolteacher who, using a direct phone line, was able to provide the required information that the British Board of Deputies published in a weekly bulletin titled *Jews in the USSR*. More important, the more confrontational position Israel assumed after the 1967 war was insufficient to satisfy militants such as Jacob Birnbaum and Glenn Richter, founders of the SSSJ, who were successfully drawing young Orthodox Jews into the movement. They had become convinced that if the secular leadership of the mainline organizations was not precisely incompetent, then they were lacking in moral spiritual fiber to do the work that had to be done. The seeds of the disunity that would plague the movement in the seventies were planted in the sixties.[58]

That division was also rooted in the duality of Israel's motives, which viewed Soviet Jewry in terms of emigration to Israel. The muted approach to Moscow that was transmitted to the mainline organizations allied with Israel was based on the assumption that Moscow would ultimately negotiate on the emigration question and the conviction that the possibility of changing Soviet policy by public protest alone were slim. On the other side were the militants affiliated with the UCSJ and the SSSJ, closely linked to the militant activists in the Soviet Union who were similarly convinced that constant steady pressure on Moscow could bring a breakthrough on the emigration issue.

Once focused on the problem the American agencies did what they do best, they programmed and processed. Because of its "inside the loop" tradition, especially its contacts with the State Department, the AJC played a particularly noteworthy role that complemented that of the Israeli team and later came in conflict with it. In August 1962 it alerted the newly appointed ambassador, Foy D. Kohler, to the Soviet Jewry problem, and later it played the same role when former Ambassador Llewellyn Thompson became Kennedy's advisor on Soviet affairs. It was in the area of research that the AJC traditionally reigned supreme, and for a time its research was used by the American UN mission. The head of the American delegation to the UN Human Rights Commission was Morris Abram, who had been president of the AJC. But under the presidency of Philip Klutznick, B'nai B'rith also brought its research department to focus on the Russian Jewish issue. William Korey, a former professor of Russian history, was transferred to the Washington office where his knowledgeable research reports combined with a lucid narrative style soon made their weight felt. It was Korey who produced the earliest papers placing the emigration issue in the context of human rights. That would give the movement outside Russia the broad base of support it needed among the churches and civil rights groups. A report Korey wrote in December 1960 that showed the impact of the war on Jewish families established a rationale for limited emigration on the basis of family reunification. The *vyzov*, actually an affidavit from concerned relatives abroad, became a crucial document during the seventies.

▪   In one sense the 1967 war in the Middle East was a predictable event. There was the lesson of the Sinai war in 1956 in which Soviet intercession and threats virtually removed the danger of defeat. There was an expensive Soviet-supplied arsenal waiting to be used and there was the need to show one's mettle in the perennial quest for leadership in the Arab world. For Cairo the time seemed ripe to redeem its reputation after the humiliation of 1956. But that was not to be. Instead, Cairo emerged from the war with a deeper sense of shame that was as keenly felt in Moscow as in Cairo and Damascus. What was unforeseen was that Cold War power calculus would be altered by the totality of the Arab defeat. Client states for the contending superpowers had fought as proxies, and those of the Soviet Union were decisively routed. Although Israel's humiliating victory acted like adrenalin for the Soviet Jewry movement, it made more remote the possibility of the realization of the Soviet emigration goal by means of a Soviet concession.

The victory was followed by an acceleration of movement activities and an optimistic spirit. Partly that was attributable to the general euphoria that greeted

Kosygin's "free to go" statement of 3 December 1966. There was an increase in exit visas issued after that statement.[59] At home a breakthrough that strengthened the movement's link to the civil rights movement occurred when Bayard Rustin, the strategist behind the movement, tangled openly with the first secretary of the Soviet embassy and accused him of "evasion of the stubborn facts" regarding anti-Jewish discrimination.[60] The Soviet Jewry issue gained additional prominence when it was included on the agenda of the UN's Human Rights Commission that met in Geneva in March 1967.[61] There Morris Abram, the American delegate to the commission, clashed with the Soviet representative, Jacob Ostrovski, concerning the creation of an office of high commissioner of human rights. Abram, incensed at the publication of the Kitchko book, accused the Soviet government of the crudest type of anti-Semitism. By April, evidence that a congressional link had been forged came when 282 congressional representatives, approximately two-thirds of the House, joined in a Passover eve appeal to the Soviet government to ease religious and cultural restrictions on Jews.[62]

The Soviets too intensified their agitational propaganda with its now standard anti-Zionist invective. They responded to the Geneva Human Rights initiative by charging that a nation guilty of aggression in Vietnam could hardly act as an acceptable advocate of human rights. Just a month after the statement, which was followed by an increase in applications for visas, ten members of Israel's consular staff were expelled for "espionage and Zionist propaganda," and articles appeared in the Soviet press discouraging Jews from applying for visas or having contact with Israelis. Soviet security was busily rolling up the communications net Israel had built. It almost seemed as if the raising of the decibels of the debate between spokespersons for the Soviet Jewry movement and the Kremlin was a harbinger of what was about to happen in June. It was the war that changed everything in post-Holocaust Jewish history. It revealed that the Soviet animus against the Jewish state reached far beyond the normal requirements of the international class struggle, the governing doctrine of the Marxist state.

To understand the next round of the struggle to leave the Soviet Union it is necessary to fathom the full impact of the victory on the mentality of activists within and outside the Soviet Union. The victory marked a shift in the tectonic plates of the Cold War, which in turn determined the power arrangements that served as the context of the emigration movement. But on the eve of battle few of the decision makers fathomed what was at stake. Washington's initial reaction to the developing crises was to try to get Israel to hold off its attack so that diplomacy could do its work.[63] Washington greeted the decisive victory without touting, lest

Moscow's humiliation itself become a problem in maintaining international stability. But the American press and especially the Anglo Jewish press could not be so contained. There were pictures of Israeli soldiers praying and weeping at the Wailing Wall and everywhere stories of a remarkable feat of arms. One historian called it a "defining moment" in Jewish history.[64] Others were more reserved, viewing Israel's victory as so decisive that it would never again be able to claim the appealing image of David slaying Goliath.[65] For American Jewry, which was historically conditioned to prefer winners in history rather than its victims, the victory was especially welcome. Its faith in Israel was confirmed, and they demonstrated it in an increase in philanthropic dollars and a spike in the number choosing to resettle there. In the twenty years between 1948 and 1968 Israel received about 10,000 immigrants from the United States, compared to the two years between 1969 and 1970 when it received 12,000.[66] In the Soviet Union the momentum for activism and applications for emigration grew.

The Soviet Union was unprepared for the defeat. Radio Moscow was jubilant at initial reports of Egypt's success on the field of battle but soon became aware of the resounding defeat suffered by the client states. Then the rhetoric emanating from Moscow went from vituperative to choleric. By the use of misinformation and disinformation regarding the imminence of an attack, Soviet leadership clearly had helped bring on the war. Now the Soviet Union had become a victim of the very misinformation fed to Nasser. Despite Furtseva's earlier denials of an aspiration to liquidate Israel, many activists within and without Russia became convinced as a result of the circumstance of the outbreak of war that that was precisely the aim of Soviet leadership.[67] Ilya Ehrenburg, the journalist and writer who mysteriously maintained an entrée to Soviet leadership, observed that had there actually been an Arab massacre of Israelis it might have led to pogroms in the Soviet Union.[68] The vituperative anti-Zionist campaign that followed the war was based on a decision probably taken at the highest party levels at the end of July.[69] Paradoxically, the Soviet propaganda machine reverted to a Tsarist myth, a modern version of *The Protocols of the Elders of Zion,* which had been forged by the secret police. But rather than Judaism it was Zionism that was now viewed as a vast conspiracy that threatened the entire world. Soviet Jewry would be the first on the list to feel the sting of an outraged, frustrated Soviet leadership. Together with Arab states, a campaign was begun in the United Nations to force Israel to withdraw from the occupied territories. Whatever the intent of Soviet agitprop might have been, the message heard by Soviet Jews was clear: they were no longer considered loyal citizens of the Soviet homeland. It is in that sense that Soviet information strategy itself helped create the sense of separation that was behind the wrenching decision to emigrate.

Like Jews the world over, Soviet Jewry underwent a change in consciousness as a result of the 1967 war. The victory buoyed their spirit and for some undoubtedly it built confidence that Israel would be there should it become possible to emigrate. In some cases it may have strengthened the resolve to do so. Emigrants speak of a growth in ethnic pride. Jews could be warriors as well as violinists and chess players, an image more appreciated by their Russian neighbors. The image of a fighting Jew, rather than the martyrdom associated with the traditional religious culture, was associated with Israel, offspring of the Zionist movement. There were more Yiddish and Hebrew songs, poetry, and the omnipresent Jewish jokes. The Soviet movement was now circulating what may have been the most widely read samizdat in the Soviet Union. Included was *Tamizdat,* books authored in the Soviet Union and published in the West that then came back for circulation in the Soviet Union.[70] Withal, one needs to add that with the exception of the Jews of Georgia, the deepening of national consciousness was probably more nationalistic or Zionistic than religious or cultural, if these aspects can be so neatly separated. The increase in Hebrew study on a group and individual basis was usually a secular Zionist enterprise, not a religious one. Some question whether the "reawakening" of Jewish identity was triggered by the intensification of anti-Semitism. They point out that the hunger for cultural education and a growth in the informal means of obtaining it was cumulative and began well before the war.[71]

Whatever the source of the awakening, the conversion to Zionism was limited to an urbanized numerically small group who often brought to it the passion of the convert. Their influence among Soviet Jews went far beyond their numbers. It was abetted by Voice of America programs and Kol Israel beamed in Yiddish. The momentum for cultural renewal and the desire to emigrate that often accompanied it came from within, and one can only speculate about its mysterious sources. The awakening of national consciousness was not confined to Soviet Jews. It spread to the Baltic and Volga Germans and the Crimean Tatars and Armenians. The release of about three thousand Jews in 1968 on the basis of family reunion was probably based on the hope that the nationalist spirit could be stilled by allowing a handful of catalysts to emigrate, a practice well known in the Tsarist period. It was a miscalculation. The release of some merely whetted the appetite of others for emigration.

Nevertheless, the larger assimilated group of Soviet Jews was not yet ready to cut itself off from mother Russia to live in social and economic limbo. In an informal survey of the post-Gorbachev emigration one researcher found that only 1 percent identified the Six Days' War as "the most important event in twentieth century Jewish history," whereas 43 percent considered the establishment of Israel itself as such an event.[72] But the preconditions for emigration had been planted in this group too, not by conversion to Zionism but by the realization that there was no future for Jews in Russia. In a word, it was the Russian role in bringing on the war and the worsening Jewish condition that followed that fueled the emigration movement up to 1975.

Withal, there is danger in overstating the Kremlin's monolithic approach to its Jews. Aware of the price the Soviet Union was paying in the war of images, not all Soviet leaders went along with the anti-Semitic vitriol in the months that followed the war. Andrei Gromyko, the foreign minister and Yuri Andropov, formerly head of the KGB, had broader views of what was happening abroad worried about the cumulative effect of the charge of "discrimination" and anti-Semitism being trumpeted in every public forum. They suggested that "in order to contain the slanderous assertions of western propaganda," 1,500 visas be issued per year "to be granted to individuals of advanced age without higher or specialized education." The central committee of the CPSU passed such a resolution calling for a kind of annual quota. It also stated that in 1969 the KGB and the foreign ministry would introduce a proposal for such a limited exodus of the unwanted and until that time Soviet Jewish citizens would be "permitted in exceptional cases" to visit Israel.[73] Clearly those Soviet activists who insisted that the Soviet Union's sensitivity to criticism from the outside could be used to gain leverage were on to something. Andropov and Gromyko were aware that the defeat on the field of battle could easily be followed by an even more decisive defeat in the propaganda war. Already sizeable portions of the Soviet, Polish, and Czech intelligentsia had made their opposition to the war clear by open demonstrations and petitions.[74] Opposition to the 1967 war culminated in Sakharov's balanced statement finding the United States to blame for the continued war in Vietnam and the Soviet Union for "irresponsible encouragement" of retrogressive Arab powers. At the same time, opposition of the international Communist movement was fully expressed at a World Conference of Communist Parties held in Moscow in June 1969 when the Australian delegation refused to sign the customary concluding statement. Democratic centralism, the euphemism used by Communist parties the world over, to rationalize the "rallying 'round the flag phenomenon" once the leadership had made its decision, seemed to be breaking down. That became more apparent when the Warsaw Pact was ordered to attack Czechoslovakia.

The victory also exacted a diplomatic price from Israel. Except for Romania,

Israel was now isolated in Eastern Europe, where the best hope for the mass immigration existed. More important, the breaking of diplomatic relations acted to
reduce Israel's leverage within the Soviet Jewry movement.[75] Israel could no
longer develop and cultivate the net that had been built by its diplomatic staff in
the prior decade. As the idea of a Jewish emigration from the Soviet Union became
more possible to envisage, its potential of threatening American Jewry's crucial
ties to Israel became a reality. Israel's interest in Soviet Jewry clearly went beyond
the humanitarian. In April 1969 a delegation of American Jewish leaders met with
the new ambassador Charles Yost to explain that both Israel's security and the
well-being of Soviet Jewry were important to American Jewry: "The issues must
be separated," explained a delegation to the State Department, "and . . . one
should not be [considered] at the expense of the other."[76] From the State Department's view, whether it concerned preparations for peace negotiations in the Middle East or the Soviet emigration issue, it was difficult to see light at the end of the
tunnel on these Jewish issues.

Directly related to the emigration issue was the nettlesome issue of the disposition of the West Bank, which had been taken from Jordan. Aware that the territories could become a burden rather than an asset, the president of Israel, Levi
Eshkol offered to return the territories with only minor modifications of borders.
Should the territories be annexed, as proponents of the "greater Israel" movement
advocated, the demographic crises that threatened to undermine the Jewish character of the state would be exacerbated by an addition of the million and a quarter
Palestinian inhabitants of the territory. That would inevitably increase the urgency of resettling Soviet Jewry in Israel, perhaps even in settlements on the West
Bank.[77] The territories issue had the potential of undermining the moral high
ground on which emigration was based should Israel's demographic motives overshadow the humanitarian aspect of mass emigration.[78] The West Bank territories'
link to Soviet emigration would require an even greater political balancing act by
Israel vis-à-vis the Soviet Union. Small wonder that President Levi Eshkol characterized Israel's postwar posture (in Yiddish), "Shimshon der Nebhishder" (Samson
the weakling).[79] Despite the victory Israel was more than ever required somehow
to avoid further ruffling of Moscow's feathers. Both mass emigration, which related to the long-term security of Israel, and immediate physical security, which
could be affected by the armaments sent to Arab neighbors, remained in
Moscow's hands despite victory in the 1967 war.

■   In the years after the June war the desire of some Soviet Jews to emigrate was
a minor note of malaise in the Soviet empire. The fateful decision that some are

convinced marks the historic juncture after which the Soviet control system failed was the Warsaw Pact invasion of Czechoslovakia in August 1968.[80] Like the 1967 war the invasion of Czechoslovakia triggered worldwide protests, including a demonstration on Moscow's Red Square where a group of protesters led by Pavel Litvinov, the grandson of the Jewish foreign minister during the United Front period in the thirties. When the protesters were arrested Andrei Sakharov called Yuri Andropov, the head of the KGB, warning that those arrested must be released, adding "Communist Parties in the West are following developments."[81]

The invasion signaled how insecure the Soviet leadership had become. No Brezhnev doctrine, granting the Soviet leadership the right to defend Socialist regimes when threatened, seemed able to restore confidence. In its historical context the intensification of agitation for emigration should be seen as one of several symptoms of restlessness in the Soviet bloc. Though it developed in Soviet society rather than in the empire, compared to the Prague Spring it was a minor one. But the Jewish issue was always there. One of the first things Alexander Dubcek did was to appoint a commission to investigate the Slansky trial.

If the tempo of protest is any indication, the Soviet Jewry movement had also come of age. In August 1969 eighteen Jewish families from Georgia addressed a letter to the UN Human Rights Commission demanding the right to immigrate to Israel. Three months later seven Jewish student activists led by Hillel Levine staged a sit-in protest demanding staff and funds at the annual general assembly of the CJF meeting in Boston. The sit-in tactic was borrowed from the civil rights movement but the cause advocated, among others, was that organized American Jewry show a more active concern for Soviet Jewry. And just before the year ended on 29 December 1969 the JDL graduated to a more radical tactic by striking at Soviet facilities in New York, Tass, Intourist, and Aerflot. In March 1970 a new more militant organization, the UCSJ, was formally established. And perhaps more fearlessly than before, in October 1970 more than 15,000 Moscow Jews gathered in front of Moscow's great synagogue on Simchat Torah to dance Israeli dances and sing Israeli songs. That month too more than two hundred petitions from Soviet Jews had been received in the West. Most asked for the right of emigration. The movement had arrived.

THREE The Curtain Rises

The years between 1967 and 1973 were not auspicious for arousing an American interest in the "rescue" of Soviet Jewry. The divisive war in Vietnam tended naturally to overshadow a problem that would hardly have drawn attention even in the best of times. Israel had won a remarkable victory in the June 1967 war and for a moment the implacable hostility of her Arab neighbors expressed itself through verbal vitriol and UN resolutions. America, without whose intercession there could be little impact in Moscow, had as its primary foreign policy objective to extricate itself from the Vietnam quagmire with as much of its self-esteem intact as possible. Paradoxically, it would need Moscow's good offices to do so.

Richard Nixon, whose political career was thought to have ended with his defeat in the 1962 California gubernatorial race, seemed to rise like a phoenix out of the ashes to capture the Republican nomination in 1968. He ran on a peace platform but there would be no peace in sight for the next seven years, the period when the Soviet Jewry issue would ripen. The challenge faced by Jewish activists, to make themselves heard over the noise of other events and to transform a minor distraction to a Cold War issue, seemed like a "mission impossible." How that was achieved is a fascinating story.

■ At the beginning of the seventies the emigration issue was barely a blip on the monitor of international happenings. Moscow was aware that its 2.7 million Jews gave it leverage in the Middle East arena of the Cold War, but that was no substitute for victories on the battlefield. The Arab states that it had befriended were proving to be capricious allies; in their humiliation they were blaming their defeat in the 1967 war on the inferiority of Soviet weapons. But after Soyuz 5 achieved the first space linkup in January 1969 and Soviet engineers successfully completed the gigantic Aswan High Dam project in July 1970, Russia's image as a world power in possession of superior engineering and technology was partly restored. Moscow, after all, shared their belief that Israel was a major regional nemesis. Yet when it became clear that Moscow was reluctant to supply the arms needed for a return match with Israel in 1972, Egypt broke its recently signed friendship treaty with the Kremlin. In reality, despite its overwhelming victory in 1967, Israel was more than ever surrounded by an irreconcilable Arab world and dependent on American goodwill and arms.[1] Egypt, Syria, Algeria, and Iraq broke diplomatic relations with the United States as a result of the war, making Moscow's link to the Arab world seem stronger than ever. By 1969 a left-wing regime had become entrenched in Sudan, and Libya's pro-Western King Idris was toppled in September by the highly unstable and viscerally anti-American Muammar Qaddafi. From an outside perspective Israel's remarkable victory in 1967 seemed to have had little impact on basic power arrangements in the Middle East.

Though Israel entered the seventies more than ever dependent on American goodwill its position in the Nixon administration was not fully secure. In the election of 1968 Jews had overwhelmingly supported the Democratic candidate, Hubert Humphrey, with 81 percent of their vote.[2] Nixon signed legislation on 16 July authorizing up to $85 million to help the resettlement of Jews and other refugees. A disproportionate sum of the money, which would be distributed by the State Department, was earmarked to resettle Jews in the United States and Israel. But a request during the 1968 campaign by Rabbi Israel Miller and Lewis Weinstein, the leaders of the American Jewish Conference on Soviet Jewry (AJCSJ), to bring the mistreatment of Soviet Jews before the UN General Assembly received short shrift.[3] In the election of 1972 Nixon did succeed in almost doubling his Jewish voter support from 17 percent to an unprecedented 35 percent, despite the fact that George McGovern projected himself as the peace candidate and accused Nixon of silence on the Soviet Jewry issue.[4] At the Republican convention a strong "right to emigrate" plank was included in the party platform to accompany the customary pro-Israel plank. Jewish voters were aware that Nixon's strong support of Israel was based more on strategic than on domestic political considerations. He understood that Israel with its well-trained reserve army and American-equipped air force was an indispensable Cold War asset. The thirty Syrian tanks that crossed into Jordan on 21 September 1970 quickly scrambled back across the border when, at the president's behest, Israel's air force threatened. Yet Nixon would not publicly acknowledge Israel's part in rolling back the Syrian threat. Instead, he insisted that Jordan "under Hussein's courageous leadership saved itself."[5] Notwithstanding the efforts of Max Fisher, a rare Jewish leader who was a loyal Republican and raised millions for the party, Nixon's bridge to the Jewish community could not bear heavy traffic. Jews were prominent in campaigning and helping to finance the McGovern campaign.[6] In the crucial election campaign of 1972 Jewish leaders such as Sen. Abraham Ribicoff, former governor of Connecticut, aided by Marvin Mandel, the Jewish governor of Maryland, played important roles in winning the nomination for McGovern. Interestingly, Sen. Henry "Scoop" Jackson, whose presidential ambitions were thwarted in the primaries, received little support from prominent Jews involved in politics despite his strong stand on Soviet Jewry. Jackson was considered a "cold warrior" but the primary interest of the Jewish voter was focused on stopping the war in Vietnam. Though McGovern continued to attack Nixon on his silence on the Soviet Jewry issue and for making "false claims" about having spoken out on the issue at the Moscow summit conference in May, for the Jewish voter the Soviet Jewry issue was not yet sufficiently important to balance the war in Vietnam that Nixon had promised to bring to an end.

The Jewish relationship to the Nixon administration on which access depended remained problematic during his second administration.[7] The administration was slow to respond to Egypt's violations of the armistice by placing surface-to-air missiles in the forbidden Suez Canal zone. The rearming of Israel with the F-14 jets it had lost over the canal was slower than the Soviet resupply of Egypt and Syria. After the Nixon-Brezhnev Moscow summit in May there was much uncertainty among activists about whether Nixon had actually brought up the Jewish question and in what depth. A purported statement by Nelson Rockefeller, governor of New York, that an agreement to allow 35,000 Jews to emigrate annually had been reached was vehemently denied by the governor.[8]

Nixon was acutely sensitive to the Jewish political presence in American politics, probably more than was warranted by the reality. He sensed that Jews were not taken with his persona and frequently resorted to popular anti-Semitic epithets when referring to Jews.[9] Henry Kissinger, his national security advisor and secretary of state, who later made light of them, was not spared hearing them.[10] There were a disproportionate number of Jewish names on Nixon's famous hit list. The feeling of distrust was mutual but on the Jewish side it was balanced by awareness that a connection to the administration in power was essential. During his first administration the Middle East question and other matters concerning Jews were assigned "exclusively" to William Rogers, his secretary of state, and Joseph Sisco, his assistant secretary. "I did this," he explained, "partly because I felt that Kissinger's Jewish background would put him at a disadvantage during the delicate initial negotiations for the reopening of diplomatic relations with the Arab states."[11] But the principles of realpolitik that governed the administration's

Middle East policy were not easily extended to human rights issues concerning Soviet Jewry. Nixon and his principal foreign policy advisor were simply not interested in human rights and could not fathom that image and world opinion
generally had some weight in human events.

Nixon's renown in the foreign policy arena would not come in the Middle East
but in the opportunity to play the so-called China card. The secret visit by Henry
Kissinger to China in July 1971 followed by secret negotiations and Nixon's formal
visit to China seven months later altered the balance of forces in favor of the West.
The new threat from China now buttressed by American support became the
major concern of Soviet policy makers. Adding insult to injury, in 1978 Congress
granted most-favored-nation (MFN) status to China, something Moscow had un-
successfully hoped for but never realized. Moscow's insecurity was compounded
by growing evidence that the ramshackle Soviet economy could not provide both
guns and butter. It would be that weakness that some believed would make the Soviets amenable to negotiations on lowering tensions in the hope of somehow winning favorable trade arrangements and credit from the West. That became the
Cold War context for the idea of allowing emigration for some Jews. A contemporary version of such a quid pro quo, embodied in Henry Kissinger's linkage, called
for the United States to provide favorable trade, including some technology and
credit, in turn for the Soviets halting the flow of arms to Vietnam and pushing
Hanoi to the negotiating table. The possibilities for Kissinger's linkage were enhanced in 1972 when the Soviet economy experienced its worst harvest since 1963
and successfully negotiated a major grain purchase from the United States.

■   The single most important foreign policy issue against which the emigration
of Soviet Jewry is viewed is the policy of détente, which had roots in both the Eastern and Western camps. Aware that either side could destroy civilization by the
push of a button, détente was primarily aimed at scaling down the level of armaments and finding alternate means for the two rival systems to compete. There
was little doubt in the West that in a fair contest it would prevail. The earliest transaction associated with détente concerned an exchange of trade for disarmament.
In its 1950s incarnation the ideas of trade-offs such as trade and credit for release of
Soviet Jewry were not yet present. In the later context of the Cold War, Soviet Jewish emigration continued to be a comparatively minor issue for the Kremlin. For
Henry Kissinger, détente's principal proponent, it meant that the prevention of
nuclear war had the highest priority. He did not so much oppose Soviet Jewish emigration or general humanitarian concerns as he ranked them below the need for a

stable world order. Detentists argued that immigration policy was in any case everywhere considered an internal affair, nowhere more so than in the Soviet Union, which guarded its sovereignty more jealously than most nations. But that did not mean that some informal arrangement to release a certain agreed upon number each year could not be reached through informal arrangements.[12] The highest policy priority belonged to SALT I, which got underway in 1971. The détente policy of the era of Nixon and Kissinger was not based on mutual trust to find a new way to manage the Soviets, now a global power that could inflict enormous damage on the nation. From a domestic perspective, given a losing unresolved war in Vietnam, domestic turmoil in the nation's cities, and the growing military strength of the Soviet Union as felt in the Middle East and in the horn of Africa, the years between 1969 and 1972 were not propitious to call upon the United States to help extricate Soviet Jewry. The basic problem of détente was that although Washington and Moscow were both strong advocates of peace, the motivations for supporting détente were different. During Khrushchev's tenure the Soviets had begun to speak of "peaceful coexistence," which outwardly resembled the accommodations position developing in the West, especially in West Germany. But growing internal instability in the Soviet bloc forced the Kremlin's hand. The "Socialist camp" shared the fear of a thermonuclear holocaust but that did not mean that one could freeze "the march of history" to delay the inevitable Socialist end of days. Moscow had signed the first nonproliferation treaty with the United States even while it was inciting war in the Middle East and crushing the Prague Spring. It saw no inconsistency because they were done in defense of "progressive" societies. At a conference of Communist and workers parties in 1979 Brezhnev called for an "intensification of the struggle against capitalism and imperialism on a global scale" while simultaneously "conducting a struggle for peace."[13] There was, moreover, a strategic advantage for the Soviet regime in freezing the status quo. It allowed it to stabilize its western front in order to better confront the threat from China on its Asian border. When the emigration issue was later placed on the scale of things Washington might be willing to bargain for, Soviet reluctance to deal with the issue directly was more problematic than activists imagined. It posed domestic as well as foreign relations problems. "Every new Jew who arrives in Israel," declared the premier of Lebanon to Sarrav Asimov, the Soviet Ambassador, in March 1971, "is more dangerous than a tank, cannon or fighter plane." As much as Soviet spokespersons minimized the numbers released, the emigration issue contained a potential of weakening the ties to its Arab clients.[14] Predictably, there would be little inclination in Nixon's troubled second administration to complicate relations with Moscow by adding the nettlesome Jewish issue to the negotiating brew. There was fear that détente policy could be held hostage by the Jewish emigration issue. It was pointed out that under the cover of humanitarianism the Soviet authorities had already allowed thousands to leave the Soviet Union on the basis of family reunification. To press the Soviets on the emigration issue would inevitably lead the parties involved to having to make an agonizing choice between mitigating the possibility of a thermonuclear disaster by negotiated disarmament with inspection and emigration of handful of "discontents," whose aspirations for emigration, according to Soviet authorities, were not shared by the majority of Soviet Jews. Few had forgotten the chilling Cuban missile crisis in 1962. The Kremlin leaders, they reminded Sen. Henry Jackson's congressional team, possessed the power to destroy civilization, and there is ample evidence that they would do so, under stressful conditions. In such a case the former choice of negotiation and accommodation was the only responsible one. The Soviet Jewry movement came to fruition at the historical juncture when a "softening" of the Cold War policy was in the offing. In American politics how one stood on the emigration issue was highly correlated with that movement, which was embodied in the détente policy.

The opponents of détente viewed such a transaction as a form of surrender and continued their opposition even after the rapprochement with China gave Washington superior leverage in negotiating with Moscow. Opposition to détente continued to build especially after Andrei Sakharov spoke out against it in 1973. It was with the Jackson-Vanik Amendment in 1973 that the emigration of Soviet Jewry also became part of the anti-détente approach. Its legitimacy derived from the support of Sen. "Scoop" Jackson.

The anti-détente forces that enlisted the Soviet Jewry movement to its banner offered several counterarguments to Kissinger's "peace or death" alternative. The siren song of prosperity through peace, they pointed out, meant in effect locking millions of people into their captive state. Détente without accompanying democratization was futile and would generate an even a greater threat to peace because the struggle to liberate oneself from tyranny was intrinsic to the human condition. One should not rely on the goodwill of the Kremlin whose tyranny the detentists would legitimize. Soviet disarmament promises could not therefore be trusted. For activists, the intensification of persecution of dissidents and Jews in the post-1969 Nixon years was evidence enough of the misuse the Soviets were putting détente. That remained true even when the Soviet turned the emigration spigot on and off when SALT or other treaties were about to be signed. The emigration figures for the first three years of the decade (1971–73) were the highest yet achieved. Still, there was something disingenuous when the opponents of détente suggested that Nixon was "soft on Communism" because during the Nixon years the defense budget actually reached new highs. Nixon insisted that relaxation of international tensions served the national interest and did not mean that the nation was letting its guard down.

The Soviet Jewry issue, which in its final incarnation presented emigration as the most practical solution, witnessed prominent American Jews taking positions on both sides of the détente debate. Important among those who opposed the concessions demanded by détente were associated with Sen. Jackson's "Bunker," a group of congressional assistants mostly of Jewish origin led by Richard Perle, Jackson's congressional assistant. Those supporting détente were loosely associated with Henry Kissinger.[15] Morris Amitay, an Israeli born former student of Kissinger at Harvard and now congressional assistant to Sen. Ribicoff, saw a broader Jewish influence. "There are now a lot of guys at the working level up here who happen to be Jewish," he observed, "who are willing to make a little bit of extra effort and to look at certain issues in terms of their Jewishness, and that is what has made this thing go very effectively in the last couple of years."[16] Yet the Jewish aspect which emerged during the debate over the Jackson-Vanik Amendment was not couched exclusively in terms of the Jewish interest. We shall note later that in the first stages of the debate the Jewish interest had not yet firmly crystallized and that neither Kissinger, Jackson nor Perle thought only, or even primarily, in terms of the Jewish interest. They were simply trying to assure that the "good guys," at least their version of them, would prevail. To be sure, Jackson possessed a genuine interest in universal human rights and harbored a deep emotional feeling for the refuseniks. But his press releases and speeches inevitably spoke of the crucible experienced by all who lived under the totalitarian yoke, not only Jews who desired to leave the Soviet Union. Some of Kissinger's staunchest supporters of détente were to be found in the American Jewish community whose organizations had assumed a prominent role in the peace movement. There was in addition a group cohort of Zionist leaders led by Nahum Goldmann and Rose Halperin who came to their position on détente not from a strategic point of view but from a practical one. They were convinced that the activists were exaggerating the threat to Soviet Jewry and that popular protest was ineffective and endangered the very people they sought to help. Members of the Lishka delegation naturally were primarily concerned with the more important issue of Israel's security. Like Kissinger, Nechemia Levanon, who headed the bureau's delegation (Lishka), wanted to negotiate the release of Soviet Jews privately. It should "in no way" [be allowed to become] "another theme in the Cold War agenda." Instead, sympathy should be built up slowly and quietly "so that it could get maximum support and sympathy in the widest circles of public opinion in the West." Needless antagonism of the Soviet Union by the activists should be avoided.[17] Only later, when no response from Moscow was forthcoming, did Levanon change his mind. A Sovietologist in his own right, Levanon did not need Goldmann to apprise him of the inherent dangers of the operation. It was his knowledge of Russian history and culture that served as the basis of his friendship with Malcolm Toon, who was to become ambassador to Israel and Moscow, and Henry Kissinger, Helmut Sonnenfeld, Max Frankel, Peter Gross, and many Jewish congressmen on the Hill.[18] The Soviet Jewish emigration issue played no direct role in the Vietnam debacle, but its involvement in the détente debate, though minor, gave it a voice. Neither did American Jewry as a community figure in the Watergate scandal that ultimately brought the Nixon administration down. The ascendancy of the emigration issue to prominence in American Soviet foreign relations is attributable primarily to its alignment with anti-détente forces who opposed greater trade concessions to the Soviet Union. In the context of the Cold War, calling attention to Soviet depredations served American interest. "It's never been very hard to persuade the United States and its political leadership that the Soviet Union is made up of bad guys," observed Phil Baum, executive director of the American Jewish Congress.[19] It was in that context that the Cold War became the midwife for the development of the Soviet Jewry movement. Withal, there was no official Jewish caucus in Congress in the early seventies, and Yoram Dinstein, the Lishka agent in New York, commented ruefully that in the sixties all there was to be mobilized for the Soviet Jewish causes were two senators, Javits and Ribicoff, and one former Supreme Court judge, Arthur Goldberg.[20]

▪   Had the Kremlin acceded to the requests by a comparative handful of Jews to be allowed to emigrate, the Soviet Jewry movement might never have gotten off the ground. Before 1970 a phased yearly emigration might have acted as a safety valve. Instead it abetted the campaign for emigration by fueling it with cases of inequity. The campaign against Zionism became increasingly vitriolic. Yet Soviet leaders were not of one mind on how to handle the issue of applicants for emigration.[21] Yuri Andropov and Andrei Gromyko counseled that a certain number of aged Jews should be allowed to leave periodically. But there were conditions in Soviet domestic and foreign affairs that militated against the simple solution of allowing the still proportionately small number of Jews who wanted to immigrate to Israel to do so. There were continuous complaints from Arab leaders concerned that emigration would strengthen Israel. In these early years the Soviet authorities had a ready answer. The number leaving was minuscule compared to the primary source of emigrants to Israel, which was the Arab states themselves.[22] But as the issue drew more attention the Kremlin could no longer deflect the problem. Soviet authorities began to view talk of mass emigration from the Soviet Union as a form of anti-Soviet propaganda and were particularly disturbed that the Chinese press had also joined in.[23]

Preference for granting visas to older retired applicants from the non-European parts of Russia and the later imposition of an education tax on those applicants with higher degrees may indicate that the Soviet authorities were also concerned about a "brain drain."[24] Later involvement with security matters became a stumbling block for receiving an exit visa. These applications were rejected no matter how old and remote such contact was. We shall be able to note later that when the agitation over the head tax became so intense the Soviet response was not to collect the tax but not to revoke the enabling regulation either.[25] Clearly the party leadership was in a quandary.

Finally, there was concern that the release of Jewish emigrants, even if only bound to rejoin families in Israel, would be contagious. The term "refusenik" applied to less than one of six applicants, but that was a sufficient number to awaken hopes among the Volga Germans and the Armenians.[26] There is little direct evidence that there was collusion between the three groups seeking to emigrate. The German and Jewish emigrants had in common that a "home" country beckoned them to return. Otherwise, the situations and strategies of the three groups wanting to emigrate diverged. The Soviet Jews rattled the closed gates whereas the Germans let West German authorities bargain quietly for their release. They profited from the Jewish lead and from Jewish agitation for emigration. The claim of family reunification was limited to Jews and to a lesser extent Armenians. Like the Jews, the ethnic Germans remained culturally distinct and also endured discrimination based on fears about their loyalty. Stalin's suspicion was strengthened by the fact that during the war 350,000 *Volks* Germans were resettled by Himmler's SS, as part of the notorious *Lebensborn* program to reshape the map of Eastern Europe according to Nazi racial principles.[27] Though the Jews wishing to leave were a comparatively small group, the emigration issue had potentially high resonance in the media. In nations where the citizens are comparatively content the emigration rate is low. The movement advertised the low quality of Soviet life. For Soviet policy makers the loss of scientists and technocrats, disproportionately present in Soviet Jewry, ultimately came down to a matter of prestige as well as economic well-being.

■ How did the emigration of a foreign minority assume such importance in Russian-American relations? Part of the answer lies with a remarkable group of Soviet activists who at the outset only dimly realized that what they were proposing entailed not only a basic change in Soviet governance but also in gaining support from the American government. To understand the refusenik mentality we need to abandon the notion that theirs was a revolution of the Soviet Jewish masses from the bottom up. Viewed against the background of Soviet class structure the refuseniks were in fact a relatively privileged elitist group. Perhaps the best way to think of the refuseniks is as the Soviet equivalent of a metropolitan Jewish community such as one could find in New York or any major American city. Some were drawn from the top rung of the Soviet technocracy, science, and culture.[28] A good portion consisted of well educated middle echelon types, a kind of secular urban/urbane group, and the best the Soviet Union had. They were not an officially organized group, which was in any case prohibited in the Soviet Union, but rather a loosely bound band held together by a common background and experience of adversity. Once having applied for a visa the applicant lost all status in Russian society. The process of being refused a visa created a leadership cadre. Benjamin Levich, Alexander Lerner, Mark Azbel, Alexander Voronel, Viktor Polsky, Vladimir Slepak, Alexander Lunts, Victor Brailovsky, and Vitaly Rubin, all former well-established members of the Soviet intelligentsia, who upon rejection were no longer able to function in Soviet society, became the informal leaders of the movement. Often kept in social limbo for years, they formed their own community. If they were observant it was usually a relatively recent addition in their return to Jewishness, which had caused them to place themselves outside of society in the first place. They celebrated the Jewish festival days of the religious calendar but in a cultural way. Many could be classified as converts or *baal t'shuvahs* (returnees) who clung passionately to their newly discovered Judaism and Zionism, so much so that the Israeli consular employees who had contact with them were sometimes astounded at their passion and motivation about a Judaism and a Zionism they hardly knew. They learned Hebrew in secret; they sang lilting Yiddish and Hebrew songs rarely heard abroad any longer. The last step, applying for the exit visa, usually meant losing your position and living in economic limbo for an indefinite period of time.

Undoubtedly, the role played by the refuseniks occupies the center of any historic explanation of the remarkable development of the Soviet Jewry movement. But it was also the overreaction of Soviet authorities to their provocation that forms part of the story. We turn next to examine three such events, the reaction by Soviet authorities to the Leningrad kidnapping and trial, the Brussels conference, and the imposition of the education tax, which catapulted the Soviet Jewish problem to world attention.

▪   From the outset there was something about the Leningrad hijacking that seemed odd. It ran against the character of the Soviet Jewry movement, which relied on verbal protest rather than violence.[29] In the midst of the post-1967 Soviet anti-Jewish campaign a group of young men, led by Vladimir Bukovsky, a non-Jewish dissident, and Edward Kuznetsov, planned to hijack an Aeroflot airliner with the goal of fleeing to nearby Finland. About twenty plotters mostly from Riga and Leningrad were involved. Before the plan to seize an Aeroflot plane at Smolny airport could be implemented the group was apprehended. Arrests and house searches followed in Moscow, Riga, Leningrad, and Kharkov. So rapid was the KGB response that the sense that it had foreknowledge of the event and was planning to exploit it to discredit the activist movement is possible.[30] By the end of June 1970 over two hundred Jews thought to be involved with the scheme were placed under arrest. In fact the "plot" was poorly conceived and faced opposition from within the group and the Israel foreign office who counseled against it in December 1969. Most of the conspirators were from Riga and had first to find their way to the Leningrad area. Only Mark Dymshits, who was subsequently sentenced to death, was an experienced pilot.

The first sign that a public relations disaster for the Soviet Union was in the offing was inherent in the strategy of staging such a trial itself. From its early days the Kremlin had displayed a penchant for elaborate showcase trials designed to illustrate the workings of its legal system. But the purge trials of the thirties, the Slansky trial, and the disastrous Synyasvsky trial in 1966 as well as smaller trials in the satellites inevitably backfired. Speculation that torture was involved in producing the spectacular confessions abounded in the Western press, which began with the assumption that the trials were staged for propaganda purposes. The trial of the alleged hijackers was no exception, especially when it was learned that it would be closed to outside observers, except relatives. By 1970 the Western world had had its fill of staged Soviet trials.

Yet hijacking was a crime that had become particularly onerous in the public mind. If the act could be linked directly to the Jewish emigration movement it was hoped that the onus of criminality would spill over and deflate its reputation at least for the Soviet public. But the strategy had two flaws that caused it to boomerang. Hijacking for some nationalist cause and taking lives such as practiced by the Palestine Liberation Organization was indeed universally condemned. But hijacking a plane in order to gain one's freedom was a different story, especially when it was clear that no harm was intended either to passengers or to property. That was the argument Sakharov made in his telegram to Brezhnev.[31] Instead, the trial highlighted the heroic lengths the desperate refuseniks were willing to go to gain their freedom. The Soviets had miscalculated regarding the impact on world public opinion because they had no idea of how favorably such an "escape to freedom" would play in the West. In the massive protest that followed the trial the public clearly rooted for the hijackers, who had been given savage sentences.[32]

There was an intense public reaction to the severity of the sentences. Faced with people who simply wanted to leave the country, a right taken for granted in the West, the Western press took a special interest in the case. Communist parties in the West inquired how they might respond to the hundreds of inquiries that they were receiving. The French Communist organ Lunette found the severe sentence incomprehensible. No hijacking had actually occurred, they pointed out, so why the ferocious sentencing? Of the sixteen originally arrested only eleven had been chosen for trial and of these, two non-Jews seemed to have been included in order to deflect charges of anti—Semitism. Nevertheless, the protests across Europe mounted in intensity. Included was an appeal from U Thant, secretary general of the United Nations. Only the Soviet campaign to "save" the Rosenbergs had seen anything like it. Twenty-four separate diplomatic requests asking for clemency were received in Moscow. In some respects the international outrage was greater than that over the invasion of Czechoslovakia in August 1968. The protest seemed to have taken on a momentum of its own. There was a promise of diplomatic intervention by Pope Paul VI, including cables from Catholic cardinals and bishops. Moscow was inundated with appeals from dozens of national and international Christian bodies, including the World Council of Churches, National Council of Churches, the Primate of the Greek Orthodox Church, and dozens of Protestant denominations.[33] Sometimes coverage of the protest was coupled with the Angela Davis case in the United States, as if to show that no special animus against the Soviet Union was intended. The protest ritual would not have been complete without a congressional resolution which was introduced by Rep. Edward Koch of New York.[34] Absent from the diplomatic protest was any note of concern from the State Department. The belief was that the Soviet Union had grown so sensitive to intervention in what it considered an internal affair that diplomatic intercession could endanger the defendants.[35] Finally, less than two weeks after sentencing on 29 December 1970, the Judicial Committee for Criminal Cases of the Russian Soviet Federated Socialist Republic Supreme Court in Moscow commuted the death sentences to fifteen years and lowered some of the heavier sentences. The public relations campaign had succeeded in reinforcing the contention by Soviet activists that pressure from abroad was the most effective way of contending with the Soviets.

▪   The idea of enlarging the impact of the Soviet Jewry issue by convening an international conference was on the drawing boards well before the Leningrad hijacking. The idea has several sources but its most persistent advocate was the Lishka, which overcame the opposition of the three international agencies already in the field, the World Zionist Organization, the World Jewish Congress, and the International Order of B'nai B'rith, who jealously safeguarded their turf as international agencies working in the Jewish interest.[36] Invitations for a large meeting of 800 delegates from 38 countries and dozens of international agencies and nongovernmental organizations had been extended to convene in Brussels on 23 to 25 February 1971.[37] Coincidentally, the Brussels meeting was scheduled when the momentum from the Leningrad trial was still strong so that it seemed as if matters conspired to raise the visibility of the emigration movement. At least the Soviets thought that was the case as they planned to counteract the effects of the "Zionist anti-Soviet conference."[38] There were press releases and press conferences, including one featuring Jews insisting that, unlike a handful of "Zionist traitors," Soviet Jews were content and patriotic. Attending was a delegation of Soviet Jews who were barred from the conference, as was the Jewish Defense League (JDL), which had switched from exploiting the domestic racial tensions triggered by the Ocean Hill–Brownsville conflict to the Soviet Jewry issue in 1969 and then gained new attention after its assault on the Aeroflot offices in New York.

If the aim of JDL was the disruption of the conference, that might have been achieved more easily by waiting until the Jewish organizations tore each other apart. One of the basic splits was generational. The young American activists gathered around the new journal *Genesis* and condemned the conference as "the most telling evidence of the moral bankruptcy of world Jewish leadership since the Holocaust."[39] Though the conference itself was an Israeli operation there was opposition in Israel concerning the strong focus on human rights rather than emigration. The postconference evaluation was often negative. The playwright Paddy Chayefsky did not think the conference would have any effect, and one reporter concluded that the conference was like a "Hadassah ladies meeting."[40]

But the organizers viewed the conference as a success. Recalling that at the first international conference convened in 1955 American Jewry was barely represented, Levanon thought that the massive American representation in Brussels indicated that the Soviet Jewry movement had become worldwide.[41] The 85-year-old Ben-Gurion, ignoring the advice of Nahum Goldmann, was in attendance as was Elie Wiesel and the discoverer of the polio vaccine, Albert Sabin. As the three international organizations had feared, Brussels did give birth to a new agency to deal with the campaign on a worldwide basis, the World Conference of Jewish Communities on Soviet Jewry. The "Declaration of Solidarity" that ended the conference was significant for its open Zionist appeal. It called the "civilized world's" attention to the Soviet Union's flagrant violation of human rights in cutting its Jewish population from its Jewish roots. The declaration closed with the well-known words of the spiritual "Let My People Go," which became the most frequently used slogan of the Soviet Jewry movement. A five-member delegation was appointed to present the declaration to the UN's Commission on Human Rights meeting in Geneva where Rita Hauser, the American delegate and a member of the board of trustees for the American Jewish Committee (AJC), delivered a strong fifteen-minute address on Soviet mistreatment of Jews. At Brussels, Israel supposedly "came out of the closet." But we shall note that the penchant of Israel's foreign office for keeping a low profile continued through the seventies.

As in the case of the Leningrad trial, the conference's real contribution stemmed from the international attention from the media, thanks to Soviet overreaction. That response placed it in a Cold War context and gave the nearly five hundred media representatives in attendance something to write about. It was one of several miscalculations by Soviet propaganda experts that helped put the movement on the map.[42]

In its desire to discredit the emigration movement, the Kremlin clearly inflicted a grievous wound upon itself. It converted what might have remained an insignificant meeting in Brussels into a media event. With one blow it demonstrated that its emigration policy was indeed shaped by anti-Semitism. Instead of discrediting the emigration movement it strengthened it, as thousands of new visa applications were received. One observer speculates that the negative international reaction so dismayed "higher party circles" that it led to an easing of visa restrictions in 1972, when 12,000 were issued. With the Leningrad trial and the Brussels

conference, which marked the culmination of intense activity by the Soviet government to suppress what they believed to be a Zionist conspiracy, the Soviet
Jewry movement, which had become hyperactive in the final months of 1970, entered a new phase of militant activity. In historical perspective the period between
the Leningrad trial and the Brussels conference marks a high point in the development of the Soviet Jewry movement.

■   The imposition of a head tax on emigrants was yet another public relations
debacle for the Soviet authorities. Unlike the Leningrad trial, which likely was incubated in the Soviet security service, the idea of a head tax probably emanated
from the lower levels of the Soviet officialdom, especially the extensive OVIR bureaucracy. It was then approved by the Central Committee of the Communist
Party of the Soviet Union. The difference in origin is important. The labyrinthine
process of clearing the Soviet Union before emigration administered by OVIR
could be life-threatening in its own way, but there was little physical threat and risk
of ending up in the Gulag, as was sometimes the case when tangling with the
KGB.[43] The decision to emigrate was in practice an act of daring based on desperation. It could lead to social ostracism and almost always meant a loss of the applicant's economic security. Few Russians thought of the right to leave a country as a
natural human right.

While Soviet reasoning behind the education tax might have been defensible,
the selective way it was implemented raises some question regarding its real purpose. In applying the tax the Soviet authorities argued that society was losing an
asset that they had developed and, like Romania and other states that imposed
such a tax, the state was entitled to some compensation. The citizen's right to education and the prior services to society such a trained emigrant may already have
performed did not figure in the decision. In practice people with special skills
deemed to be necessary for the national welfare were denied visas. For these applicants formal education, like exposure to classified information, became merely an
instrument to prevent the applicant's emigration, though these applicants were
customarily no longer allowed to practice their profession. The group so taxed included not only technocrats and scientists but also artists, dancers, curators, and
certain categories of the professorate. Despite a concerted effort to lower the proportion of Jewish students and faculty in the universities and in certain professions, because Soviet Jewry still boasted the highest level of education, the tax
strategy allowed the soviet government to restrict the outflow without having to
simply prohibit it.

The tax made its debut during the Brezhnev/Nixon summit in Moscow in May 1972, at the peak of the détente period. Despite the Leningrad hijacking trial the right of emigration had not yet become a Cold War issue. On the agenda was the signing of two accords, the SALT I agreement and a less-publicized agreement concerning the principles of international conduct. But the preliminary informal government-to-government discussions linking trade with Soviet behavior had begun, and there were rumors of a certain number of emigrants, perhaps 35,000, being allowed to leave yearly. Emigration was not an exclusive part of the diplomatic mix. The Nixon trade proposal also spoke of credit and MFN status for the Soviet Union. That was where matters stood when news of the head tax on emigrants with a higher education reached Washington on 3 August 1972. It was Nechemia Levanon who had the first intelligence and a copy of the Soviet administrative ukase to put it into effect. Because the decree applied to all emigrants, Jewish and non-Jewish, the Soviet Union could not be accused of discrimination. But in effect it did signal out Jews because they were the ones who disproportionately possessed higher education degrees and were overwhelmingly the candidates for emigration. It did not impact on all Jewish emigrants because the Jews of Georgia or Uzbek rarely held such higher degrees.[44] In a word, the education tax hit precisely those urbanized, educated newly Zionized Jews who composed the refusenik cohort, precisely the group one would target if one wanted to discourage visa applications. Again, Soviet authorities did not foresee that they had opened a can of worms. Henry Kissinger, who was handling the trade negotiations that were a crucial part of his détente policy, was taken by surprise by the tax levy. When Ambassador Dobrynin was called in to explain he could find no explanation except to say that it was a clumsy "bureaucratic bungle." But evidence was accumulating that it was hardly that. According to information available to the Dutch embassy, the Soviets had been discussing such a tax at the highest levels for some months.[45] It was implemented by Michael Suslov, a hard liner, while Gromyko and Brezhnev were vacationing. The Soviet motives, as usual, were unclear. The most obvious purpose of the tax was to stem the "brain drain." But there is something of an ethnic conceit in that explanation. Jews played an important role in the Soviet intelligentsia and technocracy, but they composed less than 1 percent of the population. Soviet cultural and scientific life could easily have proceeded without them.

What the Soviet authorities again failed to foresee was the reaction abroad. The charge of ransoming was first sounded in Israel, where the Knesset passed a resolution appealing to "enlightened opinion" to fight the tax. Again the now-

familiar cast of characters, church groups, well-known scholars and Nobel laure-
ates, ambassadors, and human rights groups protested the tax. Again the Soviet
authorities were taken by surprise. Why the fuss? Israel had been paying a head tax
for Jews released from Romania's Communist regime under Nicolae Ceausescu,
and West Germany would do something similar in the form of loans to the Soviet
Union. Again the emigration issue was pushed to center stage and again the State
Department counseled that the matter could best be settled through quiet behind-
the-scenes diplomacy. Strangely, Israel may not have discounted some kind of fiscal arrangements to get the emigrants moving to the homeland. Ambassador
Yitzhak Rabin was silent on the matter and as late as March 1973 insisted that
American interference in the tax matter would prove to be counterproductive.[46]
For a moment Israel and the Jewish organizations toyed with the idea of defraying
the projected extra cost involved through the Migration and Refugee Assistance
Act of 1962. But such a subsidization of a Cold War opponent would have received
little support from the American taxpayer. Moreover, there was nothing to prevent
the Soviet Union from increasing the tax and finding other ways to milk the American money cow.

Again the Soviet leadership found itself in a dilemma, this time triggered not
only by the massive outcry against the "ransom" demand that in the Jewish community was compared to Goering's "Flight tax" imposed after *Kristallnacht* in 1938
and the ransom proposal of Hjalmar Schacht for the release of German Jewry.[47]
But primarily it was the delicate negotiations that were in play between Congress
and the administration over the Jackson amendment that impacted on Soviet decision makers. In March 1973 Victor Louis, a journalist close to Soviet leaders, revealed that the "diploma tax" would not be revoked but would be allowed to fall
into disuse in the near future. Nonetheless, the administration of the education tax
was repeatedly raised throughout the series of congressional hearings on the Jackson amendment in 1973.[48] The politburo was disturbed by the negative reaction. At
its meeting in March 1973 a perplexed Brezhnev observed that "Zionism is making
us stupid, we take money from an old lady who has received an education." Better
to let such Jews go on a controlled and quiet basis.[49] It seemed like Brezhnev's complaint was well grounded but the humanization of Soviet policy on emigration was
still far from becoming a reality. But something new had entered the arena. Spearheaded by an organized Soviet Jewry movement, Jewish leaders were becoming a
force able to influence the emigration issue through the American government.

■   Once awakened to the possibility that Soviet Jewry could be extricated, an organizational structure had to be developed to mobilize American Jewry for the en-

terprise. Two alternate strategies were possible, either to use the extensive existing organizational structure or to create a new organization designed specifically for "rescuing" Soviet Jewry.[50] Part of the organizational conflict that developed stemmed from the fact that in the absence of a conscious choice both alternatives came into play. That was partly the source of the conflict between the National Conference on Soviet Jewry (NCSJ) and the Union of Councils for Soviet Jewry (UCSJ). From the outset the task was hindered by the perennial problem of organizational turf, which organization should do what task and, more important, who would pay for it. Not surprisingly American Jewish communal politics turned out in the end to be budgetary politics.

Motivated partly by Ben-Gurion's quest for immigrants, Israel was far ahead of American Jewry in recognizing the extricating some Soviet Jews. We have seen that one of the objectives behind the establishment of a secret "office without a name" or liaison bureau within the foreign office was to organize Jewish communities in the diaspora, particularly American Jewry, for the rescue task. A good part of the early groundwork for the American soviet Jewry movement is attributable to this early initiative. The bureau's role in the United States became one source of the several conflicts that wracked the American movement. When agents of the Lishka came upon the American scene, with the exception of some organizations of the old social democratic left, the Verband, the Jewish Labor Committee, and the Workmen's Circle, they found little concern about Soviet Jewry in the early sixties. "In those days my main role," states one of the bureau's agents, "was to persuade people that there was such a problem as Soviet Jewry."[51] As late as 1972 American Jewry was little aware of Soviet Jewry.

Much of the credit for changing that situation belongs to one man, Moshe Decter. Decter understood that it was not that American Jewry was indifferent to the fate of Soviet Jewry but that its primary attention, the issue of Israel's security, was uppermost in their concern. Unlike Ben-Gurion and the leaders of the Labor Party in Israel, few American Jewish leaders paired the problem of Israel's security with the possibility of extricating Soviet Jewry for resettlement in Israel. Undaunted, Decter wrote and researched and generally played the role of a one-man public relations office for Soviet Jewry. He established his small research bureau in a little cubicle of an office that the American Jewish Congress allowed him to use. From there flowed an endless series of reports and fliers and also plans for rallies and marches. One was held at Hunter College, a short distance from the Park Avenue headquarters of the Soviet UN delegation. The first march on the Soviet "embassy" was organized from there together with Phil Baum, then the assistant executive director of the American Jewish Congress (AJCong). The march and protest before that building and others that housed Soviet diplomatic personnel became a ritual. Decter had the financial and moral support of the Lishka but except for some volunteers, he had no staff. His instinct for public relations combined with the passion of the activist kept his operation alive. Speaking of the tactics of the civil rights marchers, he informed an interviewer that he operated on the general principle that "if it's okay for the goyim, it's okay for us."[52] In October 1963, sensing the need to attract non-Jewish voices to the Soviet Jewry struggle, he organized a conference of American intellectuals to discuss their status of Soviet Jewry. Speakers included Martin Luther King, Justice William Douglas, Walter Reuther, Bishop James Pike, and Norman Thomas. An "Appeal of Conscience for the Jews of the Soviet Union," the report of the conference, was widely circulated. But emigration as a solution was not mentioned. Within the year the Soviet Jewry issue began to appear on the liberal agenda of matters that deserved attention. Infused with a lifelong commitment to Zionism, Decter's ideological proclivities corresponded roughly with the growing number of Russian refuseniks who saw their future as citizens of the Jewish state. It was the stories of their confrontational activism that inspired Decter and gave him material for his publication. He republished in several languages the eloquent petition from Georgian Jews (6 August 1969) in which they pleaded to be allowed to go to Israel and was gratified when he witnessed his activities finally bearing fruit during the Leningrad trial. Yet for years his was a voice in the wilderness. Some leaders of the American Zionist movement considered him a "loose canon" and even as his message began finally to be heard he remained a marginalized figure appreciated mostly by the Israeli representatives of the Lishka and some insiders of the growing movement.

At the heart of the American Jewish organizational effort was the National Conference on Soviet Jewry, which was reborn out of the wreckage of the AJCSJ in June 1971. The birth of the new organization was not an easy one, and its control of the Russian Jewry movement was always contested. It occurred only after a six-year period of trial and error in which the five organizations most directly involved tried to find a way of reconciling the innumerable conflicts entailed in establishing a new single-purpose organization that would nevertheless be answerable to the mainline organizations who would determine its policy and its budget.

The need for such an organization was felt as early as September 1963 when a delegation composed of Supreme Court Justice Arthur Goldberg, Sen. Javits, and Sen. Ribicoff spoke to Kennedy about their concern about the treatment of Jews in the Soviet Union. They discovered that there was little knowledge or interest in the matter in the Kennedy administration. Secretary of State Dean Rusk suggested that the problem was best handled through private discussions between Soviet officials and Jewish leaders. But contact with the omnipresent Soviet Ambassador Dobrynin on 29 October 1963 produced only total denial that there was a Jewish problem in the Soviet Union. After the meeting Goldberg expressed a need for some continued public pressure to get the issue known. But little came of the efforts to organize before Kennedy's assassination in November. A month earlier a meeting of Rabbi Uri Miller, then president of Synagogue Council of America, and Rabbi Abraham Heschel, of the faculty of the Jewish Theological Seminary, agreed to join efforts to educate the Jewish public on the Soviet Jewish issue. They were aware that in their proposed move from "quiet diplomacy" to "responsible protest" they were embarking on a long and arduous journey.

The next step was a two-day founding conference that convened in Washington in April 1964. Chaired by a noted civil rights lawyer and president of the AJC, Morris Abram, and keynoted by Arthur Goldberg, who for a time occupied the "Jewish seat" on the Supreme Court, the conference was off to a good start. In attendance were the representatives of twenty-seven Jewish organizations. The delegates constituted themselves into a permanent body, but there remained the challenge of finding a way to resolve the question of organizational turf. A subcommittee to do that and report back to the conference was created. It was composed of the presidents of the organizations most involved; NJCRAC (National Jewish Community Relations Advisory Council), the umbrella organization for all community relations organizations; the Conference of Presidents, originally established by Nahum Goldmann to speak to the administration on matters concerning Israel and related foreign policy issues. Also included was the Synagogue Council of America, which was the organizational base of Rabbi Israel Miller, who was one of the earliest leaders active on the Soviet Jewish problem.

From the outset the AJC, a defense and community relations organization whose organizational mission and experience in foreign affairs gave it a special interest in the Soviet Jewry area, assumed an inside track in the development of an organizational structure. The AJC's experience in forming interdenominational and interracial coalitions that are essential to bring specific interests, such as emigration of Soviet Jewry into the political process, would become crucial for the new organization. Many of the AJC's leaders also traditionally served on the board of the Joint Distribution Committee, which would become a principle funding agency for emigrants. But like other affiliated organizations, the AJC was not fully comfortable in the proposed new organization despite the fact that its organizational core, represented by Richard Maass, Jerry Goodman, and David Geller, who replaced Goodman at AJC and became coordinator of the GNYCSJ, and later Morris Abram, stemmed from its ranks. It had not joined the Conference of Presidents because it opposed the idea of a single Jewish voice speaking for American Jewry. Though it later soft-pedaled the question of its organizational autonomy, its conflict with the NJCRAC, which purported to speak for all community relations organizations, persisted.

The Jewish organizational arena was already crowded, and creating yet another agency that had not yet found support among American Jews meant in effect that funding would have to come from the agencies already in the field. The affiliated organizations were being asked to surrender mission as well as funding. The alternative was for each organization to form its own Soviet Jewry department but by 1963, twelve years after the MacIver report spoke of wasteful duplication, it was understood that a single purpose organization in which all the relevant agencies would have a say was the most practical way to operate. The Conference of Presidents would under ordinary circumstances coordinate the effort that concerned government involvement. But its mission was primarily concerned with Israel, and although representatives of the Lishka had played an important role in finally getting the American Jewish effort off the ground, to permit the Conference of Presidents to play the major coordinating role would raise question of Israel's role in American Jewish governance. Rabbi Schindler, leader of the American Reform movement, who opposed direct Israeli involvement, did not cherish entering negotiations with State Department officials who jokingly referred to the Jewish delegation as "Dinitz's little boys."[53]

Because Israel's control of the movement rested partly on its control of the flow of information from Soviet activists, that issue became the nub of a conflict. When the UCSJ requested that the list of 800 refuseniks be made available to them, Dinstein refused the request, fearing a security compromise. It was eventually honored by his successor, Yehoshua Pratt, who succeeded Dinstein in April 1972. But the problem of information control was not resolved until Israel's monopoly was broken. That happened when Michael Sherbourne, an English school teacher activist, was able by use of the telephone to virtually construct his own network of information, which he freely shared.

We have seen that even before the 1967 war generated a new confidence among activists, a conflict over strategy had developed between confrontationists and accommodationists. The former group was convinced that the only way to wring better treatment for Soviet Jewry was through direct pressure. Militant factions in Cleveland, Philadelphia, San Francisco, and Long Island, who banded together to form the UCSJ in 1972, followed the lead of the increasingly militant activists in the Soviet Union.[54] They had with them the younger generation of activists who were often familiar with the tactics employed in the civil rights and antiwar movements. Opposed to them were leaders such as Nahum Goldmann of the World Jewish Congress who, like Henry Kissinger, maintained that much more could be achieved by avoiding the humiliation of a world power concerning a matter what was considered to be an internal affair. Though eventually referred to as the "establishment," an appellative frequently heard in the antiwar movement, the fact that nonestablishment groups such as Agudath Israel and Chabad (Lubavitch) that had long-term connections in the Soviet Union and also opposed confrontation tactics indicated that something broader was involved.

Finally, a decision to establish a new single-purpose organization was made. But all kinds of special adjustments would be necessary. The AJC, which had traditionally assumed the role of interlocutor between the Jewish community and the administration, would now join the Conference of Presidents, which reserved that role for itself. The militant Committee on Soviet Anti-Semitism (CCSA) in Cleveland, which favored a nationwide mass membership multiethnic organization, could not be accommodated in the new scheme and went on to become the nucleus of the UCSJ formed in March 1972. The conflict was thereby virtually built into the basic organizational structure and grew naturally out of deeply felt differences in how Soviet Jewry might best be served. The presidents of the organizations involved in the single-purpose effort met on 5 May 1964 to officially proclaim the new agency, but it was clear from the outset that the elaborate mechanism designed to resolve organizational rivalry about "turf" and budget would not produce an effective operation. There was an executive board led by a rotating chairmanship between five organizations, the Conference of Presidents, the American Zionist Youth Foundation, the AJC, and NJCRAC. The first director was Albert Chernin of NJCRAC, who served until June 1968 when he became executive director of Philadelphia's Jewish Community Relations Council. It was Chernin who created New York's Coalition for Soviet Jewry, a forerunner of the Greater New York Conference on Soviet Jewry (GNYCSJ), which went on to organize the first formal rally on Hammarskjold Plaza in 1966. The Soviet Jewry issue was then still couched in human rights terms and became a kind of American Jewish version of the Afro-American struggle for civil rights. Included in the executive committee of the AJCSJ group was Yehuda Hellman of the Conference of Presidents, Jerry Goodman of the AJC, and Jack Baker of the Anti-Defamation League.

Almost before it got started the new organization threatened to collapse under its own weight. Hellman, who conceived of the Conference of Presidents as a kind of foreign policy arm of the American Jewish community, believed that the Soviet Jewry organizations should be under its umbrella.[55] That would ensure the "coordination" with the interest of Israel's foreign office, but the Conference of Presidents itself would not contribute to the budget of the new organization. The AJC, the agency that would contribute both money and key personnel, was not a member of the Conference on principle. The budget and staff to be provided by the constituent organizations did not materialize in sufficient quantities to ensure operations. The Conference of Presidents soon was at loggerheads with Isaiah Minkoff, president of the NJCRAC, who advocated a looser arrangement and a limitation of the newly proposed organization's contacts with grassroots organizations with which NJCRAC dealt on a daily basis in eighty-seven cities and through its eighteen member organizations. In the end, NJCRAC took the new hybrid organization under its wing by providing contact with the grassroots organization and providing minimal staff, including a highly competent and knowledgeable organizer, Albert Chernin of its Philadelphia office.

In those early days, plagued by conflicts and budget problems, the new organization was barely able to remain afloat, much less to popularize an issue not yet well known to American Jewry. The organization could offer to lead, but there was no assurance that there would be followers. Moreover, the question of who was to do the leading remained unclear. Relations between Lewis Weinstein, chairman of NJCRAC, and Morris Abram, president of the AJC, were civil but the gap between the two could not be bridged even over a proposal of dispatching a delegation to Moscow to meet with high-level Soviet officials. The conflicting interests and operational styles within the new organization seemed irreconcilable. Yoram Dinstein, the aggressive agent of the Lishka who took much credit for helping the organization get underway, claims that "prior to [his] arrival the Conference existed on paper and did nothing." That may not have been quite accurate but it was, in the words of Rabbi Herschel Schacter, its chairman from 1970 to 1972, a "paper tiger."[56]

Part of the problem stemmed from the unresolved relationship between the American movement and Israel. That was in turn shaped by the difference between a well-situated, secure diaspora community and a Jewish community developing in a beleaguered national container. Involved American Jews, reflecting the American political culture in which they were nurtured, tended to assume the moral high ground. They wanted to "save" Jews qua Jews. The Israeli effort on the other hand was motivated by an ideology of ingathering and *raison d'état*.

But Dinstein's observation about the ineffectiveness of the AJCSJ in these early years contained some truth. Much of the activity related to street action, picketing the Soviet embassy and consulates, made headlines but the activists that conducted them looked upon the AJCSJ as part of the establishment. The AJC's distaste for emotional protest rallies, organized by the rival AJCong during the years of the Holocaust, had not totally disappeared. But with the civil rights movement the confrontational tactics of the Student Struggle for Soviet Jewry (SSSJ) and even the JDL had become part of the political language of America. At least the militants in Moscow and New York were doing something and in the process making the Soviet Jewish issue known. They argued that the AJCSJ acted more like a think tank that was reluctant to get its hands dirty. Clearly the aspirations of the two rival organizational groupings to help Soviet Jewry were identical, but their tactics and organizational cultures were antonymic. The militant tactics of SSSJ and CCSA in Cleveland seemed more in keeping with the time. Yet the grassroots activities of the NCSJ and the UCSJ actually complemented each other, especially in the crucial area of public relations. "It was the grass roots membership of all Jewish organizations which gave the National Conference its clout," observed Nechemia Levanon.[57] But that confluence of goals could not forestall conflict concerning among other matters the question of the Jackson-Vanik Amendment and the role of Israel in the emigration question.

It did not take long before it was discovered that the confrontationist tactics used in the civil rights struggle worked equally well against the Jewish "establishment." The annual meeting of the general assembly of the Council of Jewish Federations and Welfare Funds (CJF) by dint of control of the federation budget appropriations acted as the highest governing body of American Jewry. In 1969 several hundred students led by Hillel Levine conducted a sit-in at the general assembly of the CJF in Boston. Despite the unseemliness of the tactics they seemed to produce results. In 1970 the general assembly meeting in Kansas City approved $100,000 for the Soviet Jewry campaign, which is what the militants had demanded. The Leningrad trial in December generated new levels of militancy that could not be contained in a ramshackle organization such as the AJCSJ. It was time to restructure.

Aware that the organization they had created was not capable of carrying out its mission, a Joint Committee on Restructure was created in the fall of 1970, and its report was made public in March 1971. Given the political realities of Jewish organizational world it would have been difficult to mount the kind of program favored by the militants. As in the case of its predecessor the AJCSJ, the NCSJ remained an umbrella organization for some twenty-seven agencies. Not all were equally weighty nor did they share a common passion for Soviet Jewry. The Zionist organizations naturally viewed the Soviet Jews in terms of immigration to Israel. Defense organizations such as the AJCong also viewed it as a human rights issue, whereas religious organizations such as the Synagogue Council of America hoped for the ending of persecution and the restoration of Jewish culture and religious life in place. Rabbi Israel Miller, who was asked by Secretary of State Dean Rusk to state precisely what he wanted, replied simply "let them live or leave." The most difficult groups under the umbrella were the coordinating organizations, the CJF, which was the closest thing American Jewry had that acted as controller of the purse, and the NJCRAC, which acted as a coordinator of the hundreds of local Jewish community relations councils. It was a crucial agency for the functioning of the NCSJ because it could serve as a conduit to the hundreds of local communities where American Jews actually lived their lives. Aware of its strategic importance, the NJCRAC did not lightly surrender access to what might become a competing organization seeking grassroots contact.

The most problematic of the coordinating organizations was the Conference of Presidents of Major American Jewish Organizations (the Conference of Presidents), an umbrella organization that reserved for itself the right to speak for American Jewry on foreign policy issues. The Conference of Presidents usually placed the security of Israel first and jealously guarded its monopoly on access to the administration and to foreign governments. Though the newly restructured NCSJ reflected American Jewry's concern for Israel, it became apparent that Israel's specific aspirations for aliyah were not easily accommodated, especially when they did not correspond to the aspirations of the Soviet emigrants. Few had bothered to question what the Soviet Jews themselves wanted beyond the refuseniks' desire for emigration. The answer came after 1975 when it became increasingly apparent that the new visa applicants entering the emigration stream desired resettlement elsewhere.

The Israeli Foreign Service had come to believe that Soviet opposition to emigration could be defused if it was confined to a specific group immigrating to a specific destination. But the charter of the new organization did not confine emigration of Soviet Jewry solely to Israel but instead broadened the destination of the emigrants to "Israel and other places." According to Yehoshua Pratt "this was the price we had to pay to Isaiah Minkoff."[58] Minkoff, the chairman of NJCRAC, had a non-Zionist Bundist orientation and was convinced that a viable Jewish culture could be rebuilt in the Soviet Union. Paradoxically, one of Israel's strongest supporters for an independent militant organization was Bertram Gold, executive director of the AJC, which had historically been anti- and then non-Zionist.

The founding charter of the renamed organization, the NCSJ, called for a budget of $235,000 and an additional $8,300, a one-time donation by NJCRAC. Additional resources were to be made available in service, such as clerical help, and members were to pay dues. Together with the GNYCSJ, which was established at the same time of the restructuring, an undetermined amount of federation funds would be made available. The new structure and name change did not alter the fact that the NCSJ would remain chronically underfunded and hampered by its inability to strike out on its own.[59] After one year of operation there was a budgetary shortfall of $100,000, due partly to unforeseen expenses incurred in financing Solidarity Day. By June 1972 it had only $2,000 in the bank and had debts of $13,000. It could not meet its payroll.[60]

The restructured organization's prognosis for realizing the goals outlined in the joint conference report were poor. It had no means of getting to the Jewish grass roots and no way to speak truth to power without the interference of NJCRAC and the Conference of Presidents. A link to the local communities was crucial for the effectiveness of the NCSJ. There was one ray of hope. Because he seemed to be able to muster a certain detachment from the hot political temper of Jewish communal politics, Richard Maass, who had served as head of the AJCSJ while also serving as chairman of the AJC's foreign affairs committee, was appointed to head the new NCSJ. He brought with him Jerry Goodman, who directed the committee's foreign affairs department, to serve as executive director of the new organization. In the meantime, events within the Soviet Jewry movement seemed to have taken on a momentum of their own. Goodman, a graduate of Habonim, the Labor Zionist Youth Organization, was a particular source of satisfaction for Dinstein because it ensured Israel's continued influence in the organization. "Jerry was on our side from day one," Dinstein observed. After Pratt discussed the appointment with Charlotte Jacobson they too agreed that "Jerry was in Habonim and he is the right man."[61]

The UCSJ, which came into formal existence in March 1972, nine months after the NCSJ, was not bound by the strictures of powerful coordinating organizations such as the Conference of Presidents or NJCRAC. By 1970 there had developed many local nonaffiliated groups in cities such as Cleveland, Philadelphia, and San Francisco that acted like gadflies, alerting local federations and branches of the mainline organizations to the situation in Russia. Organized around the militant CCSA in Cleveland, six such grassroots organizations organized themselves into a loose federation. They were the most viable of the dozens of voluntary au-tonomous councils for Soviet Jews that had sprung up before and during the Leningrad hijacking trial in 1970. Some were new but others formed around local chapters of NJCRAC and national organization such as Hadassah or the AJCong. In some cases it might have been a religious congregation that served as the or-ganizing seed.

Not all were able to sustain themselves. The San Francisco area produced such a group as early as 1965 but when the Soviet Jewry issue momentarily vanished from the screen it discontinued operations. When it was reformed three years later it became one of the most militant of UCSJ's affiliates. By 1989, the year this study ends, the UCSJ claimed a worldwide dues-paying membership of 100,000. It had local councils in almost every state and in more than fifty cities. Its strength came directly from the growing passion the issue aroused at the grassroots level, which related to the travail of the refuseniks. Its response was often immediate rather than long range and strategic, which was the penchant of the NCSJ. In 1970 Louis Rosenblum of Cleveland's CCSA, Harold Light of the Bay Area Council, Si Frumkin of the Southern California Council, and several other local activists formed the UCSJ as an umbrella organization for the network of grassroots or-ganizations that had come into existence. Rosenblum's memorandum to the local action councils spoke of "the failure of the AJCSJ to generate or support sustained community action in support of Soviet Jewry."[62]

Five major local councils formed the UCSJ's organizational core.[63] The promi-nence of California's local Jewish communities in its early organizational effort is another clue to its contrast with the NCSJ. It reinforces the sense that the UCSJ was more reflective of American political culture than the NCSJ. Louis Rosenblum, a particularly energetic organizer, became its first president. Significantly, its na-tional office was located in Cleveland, housed and nurtured by the militant CCSA, away from the influences of New York. To the chagrin of the officers of the NCSJ it opened a small office in the capital well before the NCSJ and proved itself a skilled lobbying agent during the Jackson-Vanik negotiations. Its imaginative pub-lic relations programs, the "Adopt a Refusenik Family Program" and the Commu-nity and Bar Mitzvah twinning program, were incubated in its local councils and then transmitted through its informative journal *Alert* or its newsletter the *Quar-terly Report*. The council became a communications hub, maintaining extensive telephone contacts to keep track of developing events in the Soviet Union. Fre-quently it was the first to distribute news of the latest developments. Two of its most fruitful liaisons were with the Medical Mobilization for Soviet Jewry and the Legal Advocacy Center for Soviet Jewry.

Because it was the most activist and youngest section of American Jewry, the UCSJ's most significant though informal affiliate was the independent SSSJ. Much of the effort to hold this group together is owed to Jacob Birnbaum, a far-seeing charismatic leader working out of New York's Yeshiva University. He was the first to demonstrate the possibility of mobilizing Jewish youth coming out of the Modern Orthodox movement and also the civil rights movement. These would eventually coalesce in a loose federation known as the SSSJ. Much of the activism was conducted by the SSSJ or similar groups in areas of Jewish population concentration, especially the greater New York metropolitan area. Their style was an amalgam of the direct action of the civil rights and peace movement played out in a Jewish context. "The voice may be Jacob's, but the hands are Uncle Sam's," noted one observer.[64] There were sit-ins and lie-ins, chaining oneself to fences at the Soviet mission, chanting of slogans, and dozens of specialized techniques to win public attention. But, like the mainstream movements, the activities of the SSSJ though confrontational were nonviolent.[65]

One can only speculate about the reason for such engaged activist types appearing in disproportionate numbers among young religious Jews. Though the circumstances are different, the similarity in typology between Jewish activists in the Soviet Union and their American counterparts in the SSSJ may indicate that it is more a Jewish than an indigenous phenomenon. Paradoxically, militant groups were often compelled to seek financial support from the very "establishment" they held in contempt. In February 1972 an officer of the SSSJ asked the NCSJ for $5,300 to create a political awareness committee "to try to educate primarily the student public . . . in terms of political activities on behalf of Soviet Jewry." The cause was a good one but the applicant seemed unaware that the NCSJ was sorely strapped to meet its own budgetary needs and was in any case not a funding agency. The request was turned down because the "proposed committee would be . . . sponsored by parts of the Jewish community not now linked to the work of the NCSJ."[66]

The tensions between the NCSJ and the UCSJ went beyond differences in organizational structure. The NCSJ was a reflection of the existing organizational establishment, which meant in effect that the security of Israel played a major role in its strategic planning. The Lishka's representatives in the United States claimed a major role in bringing the NCSJ into existence. The UCSJ, which became a competing agency, was closer to the grass roots of Jewish America; its Zionism was not exclusive. It was also concerned about human rights as reflected in the domestic struggle for civil rights. Once established it quickly developed a sense of its organizational autonomy and a sensitivity about taking orders from the agents of the liaison bureau active in the United States. The matter came to a head first in March

1968 when Dinstein accused Louis Rosenblum, chairman of Cleveland's CSAS, of having encouraged the disruption of the AJCSJ's biennial conference. Again in 1970 an overzealous Dinstein arranged for the discharge of the chairman of the California SSSJ from the Jewish Federation Council of Greater Los Angeles. When Zev Yaroslavsky refused to back down, Dinstein supposedly threatened: "I shall see to it that my government destroys you."[67] There followed a letter to Yitzhak Rabin by Louis Rosenblum requesting that the foreign office put a halt to Dinstein's "tiresome, bullying tactics."[68] At the same time, Levanon claims to have been instrumental raising funds for organizing the UCSJ and the SSSJ. It was only after 1970 that what he believed was the UCSJ's anti-Israel posture disappointed him. Though most of its members considered themselves staunch Zionists, the UCSJ would not allow itself to become simply an instrument of Israel's foreign policy. It insisted on maintaining an independent electronic communications net with activists in the Soviet Union, and it maintained close ties with the international human rights movement and the Helsinki monitoring committees that came into existence after 1975.

After 1975 a UCSJ delegate attended every Helsinki follow-up conference. In 1980 it formed its own human rights center and appointed the noted Roman Catholic priest, Robert Drinan, as its chairman. It also maintained close personal relations with Soviet activists, and ten years later the noted refusenik Dr. Leonid Stonov established a UCSJ human rights bureau in Moscow. For that action it was condemned by CJF and the NCSJ, who believed that the newly established Israeli consulate was better able to defend the rights of Soviet Jews.[69] We shall see presently that its staunch support of the Jackson-Vanik Amendment after 1985, when a growing number of Jewish leaders were willing to deal with Moscow on the emigration question, became one of its most controversial decisions. It followed the general consensus among the activists in Moscow, but a growing number of American Jewish leaders, such as Phil Baum of the AJCong, called for negotiations lest the American Soviet Jewry movement remain virtually dead in the water. Baum's fear was born out by the lean period between 1980 and 1987 when few visas were issued. Yet by 1989 the UCSJ, whose voice was central to the development of the Soviet Jewry movement, had become a cry in the wilderness. Somehow a turn in the road after Gorbachev's perestroika had been missed by its leadership. How and why that happened is an interesting aspect of the story that will come up again in a later discussion.

■   The reader may wonder how it was possible for a few underfunded organizations that could find little common ground to confront a problem almost unknown to the public and shunned by the administration in power to emerge two and a half decades later with their goal realized. Part of the answer can be found in its public relations campaign, which capitalized on the plight of the refuseniks. By public relations we refer to the use of the print and film media as well as physical protest to get the story known. That skill had to be developed virtually from scratch.

Some activists naively assumed that there was a caring world ready to listen to the moans and groans of a "persecuted" people, but that turned out not to be the case. The effort to get the story known was supported by an informal worldwide Jewish information network that was aided at critical moments by a hapless Soviet government that furnished heartrending incidents as if to demonstrate its inhumanity. News stories about the Leningrad hijacking trial, the education head tax, the trial and imprisonment of an activist such as Sharansky, and dozens of other incidents appeared almost daily in the media. Cumulatively they awakened the interest of a world concerned about the human dimension behind Soviet depredations. It was that concern rather than yet another tale of victimization of the collective Jewish people that drew attention to the emigration story.

The files of the NCSJ and the news coverage of the movement by the Jewish Telegraph Agency in its daily bulletin are primarily devoted to the hundreds of mundane day-to-day happenings that make the news and are then picked up by the press. The stories might concern an arrest in Kharkov or a trial in the Ukraine based on a trumped-up charge of embezzlement or the Soviet delegate in a subcommittee of the UN's Economic and Social Council charging "world Jewry" with trying to subvert Soviet authority. There is a photo in the local newspapers of a group of activists who have chained themselves to the gates of the Soviet UN mission. A good proportion of the activity of the activists was devoted to making "noise" or calling attention to those who were. Stories of victimization of the innocent served as basic ammunition to awaken concern. Most activists realized that getting the Soviet Jewry story into the headlines was a good part of the battle, and much energy was devoted to finding ways to do that by both the NCSJ and the UCSJ. The American Soviet Jewry movement was in a sense primarily a public relations agency. Almost everything that was done was related to it. Much of the newsworthy stories emanated from the activities of the activists at the grassroots level. Among the most imaginative of these regional groups were the GNYCSJ, an umbrella group for eighty local organizations, and the San Francisco Bay area group. Both organizations issued extensive press releases and bulletins and maintained close contact with news services. All groups publicized their activities and made personalities available for interviews on the media. They did the myriad things necessary to gain exposure. Associated groups of lawyers, scientists, doctors, and dentists came into existence. When it became apparent that refusenik scientists who remained too long out of the loop would lose their skills, the American Committee for Concerned Scientists assumed the task of sponsoring seminars in Russia to keep them up to date. The program, which ran into difficulties, was publicized in the press. There was even a group of congressional wives for Soviet Jewry. Great care was taken to ensure that all religious denominations were involved and that interracialism was stressed. Typical was the program for human rights for Soviet citizens create by the Soviet Jewish Task Force of Bridgeport. The strategy called for getting as broad an American public opinion base as possible. The idea was to get away from the notion that human rights were only a Jewish issue.[70]

There were occasions when the high priority given to public relations posed problems concerning exaggeration, which is inherent in the public relations process. People who sacrificed their well-being for the cause of emigration were not merely fuel for propaganda but sometimes the stories seemed exploitative and undermined the fact that the Soviet Jewry movement had authentic heroes. The mundane act of applying for an exit visa meant positioning oneself outside the social order and endangering one's livelihood, even one's habitation. These steps were not taken to get the attention of the media so that the emigration problem could be showcased. But their stories did inspire and create sympathy. For the historian an important question is whether public relations inevitably design reality so that it is difficult to distinguish fact from fiction and the significant from the mundane. But how does one fit the heroism often witnessed among the Soviet activists in the historical narrative without stretching credibility? That kind of total commitment and self-sacrifice we witness among the refuseniks was not new for those familiar with Russian Jewry. At the turn of the century the term "mad Russians" was applied to Russian immigrants who threw themselves wholeheartedly and passionately into the task of organizing the Jewish labor movement or establishing a Kibbutz. The *brenendiger,* the burning ones in Yiddish, was a recognizable Eastern European Jewish type. The things that seem ordinary to citizens living in a politically free world, from greeting visitors to signing a petition, were mortally dangerous to life and limb in the Soviet Union, which was an ordered but basically lawless society. Viewed from the perspective of public relations, the hundreds who tangled openly with the KGB were worth their weight in gold. Their crucible fueled the public relations process with tales of injustice and cruelty by the Soviet authorities and heroism and self-sacrifice by the "victims."

It took years before Soviet leaders became aware that they had entered upon a losing battle.[71] Paradoxically, public relations in the West gave some measure of protection to the refuseniks, even while it exploited their victimization. It helped bring the relatively minor emigration issue to the fore as a just cause and it made the word "refusenik" into a badge of honor. It was discovered that a caring group could be created by making the crucible of the refuseniks known. Avital, the wife of the imprisoned Anatoly Sharansky, surely believed that the more political leaders she visited to explain her crucible, the sooner her husband would be released. But those who arranged the well-publicized visits to heads of state were aware that she was a public relations treasure. Dressed in the modest style of Orthodox women, she helped create an image of faith and its link to human resiliency. The Scharansky story contained an aspect of love thwarted by a demonic government an irresistible theme in the Western world. The concern about Sharansky's health in prison became the subject of innumerable diplomatic dispatches and was continually raised by emissaries in Moscow. It puzzled Soviet authorities, who were slow in realizing that they were confronted with a public relations disaster.

The public relations campaign would have been ineffective had the Soviet regime been immune from its impact. But the reverse was known to be the case. Soviet authorities were extremely sensitive to the opinion of the outside world.[72] They too understood that the realization of their goals would not be signaled by the signing of a peace treaty but was somehow related had to their effectiveness in the public relations area. The impact of Soviet activists went beyond furnishing stories to the media. "Soviet Jews showed us how to speak up," observes Malcolm Hoenlein, the first director of GNYCSJ. "It was their putting themselves on the line that made the essential difference."[73] Even the names used, "prisoners of Zion," "conscience," "refuseniks," and slogans such as "Let my people go" or "Solidarity Sunday" conjured up a sense of urgency. Behind the public relations strategy was the assumption that there existed a universe of obligation, a caring world whose conscience could be aroused to intervene for Soviet Jewry. That a post-Holocaust Jewry could still generate such belief is at once a tribute to human hope and perhaps, innocence.

The public relations effort was not only widespread and continuing; it could also be highly imaginative. On the occasion of a Brezhnev visit to the United Nations, activists took over a little island in the East River facing the UN building and placed a six-foot-high sign that read "Soviet Jewry Freedom Island." They then hired a boat and invited 150 reporters on board to meet such notables as Percy Sutton, the president of the borough of Manhattan, Bob Abrams, borough president of the Bronx, and others. The complaint by Kurt Waldheim, UN General Assembly president, to Mayor Lindsay produced no results, and unexpectedly the press of the Chinese People's Republic took great delight in reporting the story. So did other newspapers.[74] Sometimes the tactics employed had comical twists, as when on the occasion of their sixteenth anniversary the Bay Areas Council for Soviet Jewry had someone dressed as a woman deliver a birthday cake to the oft-picketed Soviet consulate, prepared by "Rent-a-Yenta."[75] On another occasion a helicopter was flown over the Sugar Bowl football game with a "Free Soviet Jewry" banner. Notes were slipped into programs prepared for a performance of the Bolshoi ballet company reminding the recipient of the plight of Soviet Jewry. Not all events were equally successful nor was the flow of events uniform.[76] The pace of events tended to accelerate when something important such as a summit meeting was scheduled.

Virtually every public relations technique developed in the civil rights and anti–Vietnam War movement as well as some original ones was employed. The most effective was the annual Solidarity Sunday, whose origin is claimed by Yoram Dinstein, among others. The massive crowds it attracted was soon noted by presidential and senatorial hopefuls who requested to speak at these rallies, thereby ensuring press coverage. The wearing of bracelets or the carrying of signs with the name of a refusenik personalized the activity and became popular among young people. The idea was probably borrowed from the Vietnam war aftermath in which bracelets with the names of soldiers missing in action were sold. There were also "prisoner of Zion" T-shirts and posters, bumper stickers, buttons and seals, people-to-people greeting cards. Speaking tours of refuseniks became popular after 1971. A separate campaign was mounted to have the Voice of America broadcast Yiddish programs to the Soviet Union in the belief that there continued to exist a large Yiddish-speaking audience in the Soviet Union. A congressional resolution to finance such broadcasts cosponsored by Rep. Vanik was introduced in 1971 but didn't get very far. The convening of an international scholar's seminar in 1978 proved particularly vexing to the Soviet authorities, who refused to issue visas for many of the participants. One of the most effective techniques was a "tourist" program to the Soviet Union in which the visitor brought gifts such as medicines and prayer books and shawls. The impact of such visits may have been greater on the visitor than on the Soviet Jewish families that hosted them for an evening. There were all kinds of family pairing programs for bar mitzvahs or Jewish holidays. In August 1972 the NCSJ sent out a directive to national agencies to encourage adopt-a-prisoner and adopt-a-city programs. A commission on trade and commerce was established to cope with the data spun off as the Soviet trade issue heated up. There were mass letter-writing programs to congressional representatives and to Soviet political leaders. There were literally hundreds of ads and paid advertisements about the plight of Soviet Jewry in major and local newspapers. There is some evidence that by 1970 the planners had developed the ability to organize and coordinate rallies on a nationwide basis.

Most of the attention-getting practices of the American Soviet Jewry movement was designed for education of the public for the long run. But a portion, in all likelihood copied from the civil rights struggle, was based on civil disobedience. Tactics included going limp in public places, sit-ins and lie-ins to disrupt some activity, and raucous behavior at mass meetings of the "noninformed." In one or two cases stink bombs were deployed in auditoriums to bring the message of Soviet Jewry. Such tactics were used by younger activists who argued that such happenings were far more likely to get media coverage than staid rallies or meetings to preach to the converted.

It is probably awareness that such tactics could also call attention to an otherwise marginal organization that brought the JDL into the arena. The JDL carried these tactics to new heights that sometimes bordered on violence, beginning with the harassment of Soviet consular and diplomatic officials, disrupting touring Soviet ballet and theater companies, and random shooting on a Soviet facility.[77] But the hunger for attention was insatiable and required ever more outrageous acts. It peaked in November 1971 when four shots were fired into the Soviet UN mission in New York and a bomb damaged the offices of Sol Hurok, the leading impresario for Soviet performances in the United States. In April and May the leaders of JDL, including Rabbi Meir Kahane, were arrested on the charge of smuggling dangerous explosives. But its first attempt to gain international attention failed. In February 1972 the JDL attempt to crash the Brussels conference had been a halted in its tracks by the Belgian police acting at the behest of Golda Meir, chairperson of the presidium of the conference.

The JDL's activities triggered controversy in the Jewish community. The general feeling was that calling attention to the brutal behavior of the KGB was not well served by demonstrating violence in turn. Dobrynin, the Soviet ambassador, pointed out the irony that the embassy staff and Soviet officials posted to the United States were, as a rule, much in favor of lifting emigration restrictions and like himself were recommending liberalization to the policy makers in Moscow. He warned that he would no longer send such advice to his superiors.[78] In defense, members of the JDL were quick to point out that American Jewry was again being indifferent to the fate of their brethren. Indeed, the "never again" slogan seemed to have a cathartic effect on all young militants. Moreover, they pointed out that their tactics were quite effective in drawing attention to the cause of Soviet Jewry, which, after all, was everyone's goal. If getting media coverage was the litmus test for success then the activities of the JDL should be rated highly, they argued. Instead, they were almost universally condemned by the movement's mainstream.

At the opposite end of the public relations spectrum was the attention gained from political quiet and cumulative action, such as statements read into the *Congressional Record,* congressional resolutions, and congressional hearings. Few citizens kept track of these hearings, and press coverage was usually confined to the back pages. But as the subject of Soviet Jewry repeatedly came up in Congress it became part of the nation's political dialogue. News of the plight of Soviet Jewry distilled downward from the nation's opinion-making elites, its journalists, pundits, and congressional representatives. Before the hearings on the Jackson-Vanik and Stevenson amendments, the hearing of a subcommittee of the House Foreign Affairs Committee chaired by Rep. Benjamin Rosenthal drew together the nascent community that was forming around the Soviet Jewry issue. Held on 9 and 10 November 1971, the hearings were based on the Anderson-O'Neill resolution that had been signed by more than one hundred congresspersons. It urged the State Department to raise the issue of Soviet violations of the UN Declaration of Human Rights before the General Assembly. Congressman Rosenthal added a specific request that the Soviet government also be urged to "permit Jews and all other citizens to emigrate freely."[79]

The hearings turned unexpectedly to an assessment of the real danger faced by Soviet Jewry. The testimony of Richard T. Davies, deputy assistant secretary for European affairs, raised a storm among the emigration advocates. Davies's testimony acknowledged the special hardship of Jewish life in Russia. But he did not believe that most Jews were experiencing an "unusual ordeal" or that they were living in a "state of terror." Instead, he pointed out that Soviet Jews remained Russia's most-educated, well-situated national minority. Davies's observation was substantiated by Sol Polansky, formerly secretary of the American embassy in Moscow, who testified that Rep. Edward Koch's testimony that Soviet Jewry lives "in a state of terror" was "exaggerated."[80] For Jewish advocates Davies's testimony was disappointing because it stole their thunder, which was based on the target centering the exclusion and persecution of Soviet Jewry. They feared that it would weaken their priming of Nixon for the summit talks scheduled to be held in Moscow in May 1972. The attack on Davies began almost as soon as his testimony ended. Rita

Gluzman, a former refusenik, insisted as did several others that "our spirit is in terror" and spoke on the need to maintain continuous pressure on the Kremlin. Hans Morgenthau, who chaired the special committee of academics, spoke of spiritual terror even while agreeing that the conditions of Jews in Russia were not analogous to those in Nazi Germany between 1939 and 1940.[81] William Korey pointed out that conditions have worsened since 1967 when the Soviets began their anti-Zionist campaign. Judd Teller, the noted Yiddish journalist, felt that the Davies testimony was in poor taste.[82] Most eloquent and passionate was the response of Mikhail Zand, the noted Soviet orientalist who had finally been allowed to immigrate to Israel in 1970 after worldwide publicity. Zand maintained that "hundreds of thousands would be ready to go" if exit permits were quickly made available.[83] Though the State Department supported a congressional resolution calling on the Soviet government to allow Russian Jews to emigrate, Davies complained of "being deluged with cables and letters in connection with my statement." Strangely, Moshe Decter, who was considered to have almost single-handedly nurtured the movement into existence, felt "duty bound" to take exception to the attack on Davies, which he thought was caused by poor reporting that took the Davies testimony out of context. There were certain nuances that Davies might have mentioned to avoid misunderstanding, but "I want you to know," Decter wrote to Davies, "that I regard your statement . . . to be the best statement ever made by a high official of the government."[84]

The contretemps is interesting because it highlights the problem of exaggeration, which is inherent in many hard-sell public relations efforts. Davies was observing that the victimization stories had been exaggerated. On the other side, Soviet officials such as Dobrynin and Brezhnev repeatedly denied that such a problem existed at all. Others simply did not care for the promotion of a Jewish problem generally. Nahum Goldmann decried the shrillness of the protest. "If only we would shut up and leave matters to him instead of carrying on in this vacuous fashion," said one observer describing Goldmann's utter contempt for the "hysterical" activity of the activists.[85] "It is time to acquire a sense of responsibility and to put a stop to the hysterical agitation practiced by Israel and still more by American Jewry," wrote Goldmann in 1978.[86] In 1974 Rabbi Arthur Hertzberg, president of AJCong, had reached a similar conclusion. He blamed Gromyko's rejection of an informal agreement between Kissinger and the Soviet leadership concerning an annual Jewish emigration quota on Sen. Jackson's untimely boast at a press conference that he had brought the Soviet Union to its knees on the emigration question.

Goldmann and Hertzberg were not alone in condemning the shrillness the public relations campaign had assumed. Nechemia Levanon, who claimed a prominent role in developing the American movement, opposed the public relations campaign on emigration for getting too caught up in the rhetoric of the Cold War. It would be counterproductive since Moscow was bound to resist humiliation.[87] Glenn Richter, the codirector and founder of SSSJ, also concluded that occasionally the "noise" generated by his troops backfired.[88] Professor Dan Miron of Tel Aviv University, who was heading a delegation visiting the Soviet Union in 1971, admitted that for some emigration was a "burning problem" but noted that his sense was that "the problem of emigration is overemphasized . . . the majority of Jews in the Soviet Union are integrated and they will remain Soviet Jews." The desire for contact with outside Jews is there, but they do not necessarily want to leave the Soviet Union.[89] The dropout problem that developed in earnest after 1976 was for many who had grown disenchanted with the Soviet emigrants evidence that those in the Zionist-oriented refusenik cohort were not representative of Soviet Jewry.

For the Zionist-oriented refuseniks, no confirmation that emigration was paramount was required. Their lives were based on the assumption that an authentic Jewish life could only be lived in Israel and that therefore any actions that were done, including raucous public demonstrations, were legitimate. They could point to examples when the light of publicity, as in the case of the Georgian Jews whose eloquent petition to settle in Israel in November 1969 led to their being allowed to emigrate almost immediately. Some well-known refuseniks, such as Mikhail Zand, were similarly ushered out of the country after their names made the headlines in the Western press. Publicity might play lightly with the facts but it could also save lives. We shall note later that the question of whether the public relations effort had an impact on Soviet policy remains an open one. Some Sovietologists believe that although there may have existed a sensitivity to world opinion, Soviet public and foreign policy was driven by internal developments. It was intrinsically driven rather than extrinsic.

But lest the Soviet Jewry movement be dismissed as merely a public relations phenomenon, it should be remembered that there are many real problems in the world that never become known because, unlike the Soviet Jewry situation, the resources to mobilize an effective public relations effort are not available. National groups such as the Kurds and the Roma have suffered almost in silence for generations. To observe that the direness of the Soviet Jewry condition was overstated does not mean that it did not exist. Those who became targets of the KGB, those who were denied admission to schools despite the fact that they were well qualified, and those who suffered the slings and arrows of anti-Semitism provoked by the government propaganda apparatus were victimized by a cruel system. To argue, as some do, that Soviet Jewry suffered like other captive people in the Soviet empire misses the point. For many Jews, especially those whose identity after the 1967 war was based on Zionism, the need to leave the Soviet Union and resettle in Israel was imperative. What the activists did was to submit a new datum, that Soviet Jewry needed "rescue," and used it to pierce the iron curtain. That is less dramatic than trying to jump the Berlin Wall but far more effective in the long run.

What of the price paid by activists who experienced the enormous daily stresses of living outside the system? Some like Sharansky spent the best years of their lives in prison and gave up promising careers. Were they merely fodder for the public relations mill or is there some kind of reward for daring to become actors or resistors in history? The question, which is reminiscent of the role of the hero or individual actor in history, deserves our special attention. There are few such instances of heroism in the experience of modern mass society. Our concern relates to the authenticity of the hero whose role is publicized by public relations. Are heros or actors diminished when we for our own interest call attention to their courage? Would their role have been more elevated had they endured in silence? There is no easy answer to such questions, but it is certain that the Sharanskies and the Nudels would have remained unnoticed if it were not for the ability to get their names known in the West through the public relations network. Their sacrifice made an impact because they were not allowed to become anonymous. They became the fuel through which the Soviet Jewry movement was energized. It allowed them to become actors in history, and it allowed the movement to become a fact of history. The struggle for emigration of Soviet Jewry was not won by divisions and battalions but by a brilliant deployment of public relations activities that gained the attention of the world. It got the world, especially the Jewish world, to care. In order to "let my people go" there had to be a way of "let[ting] my people know."

■ At the outset of this discussion we wondered how the tribulations and the desire to emigrate of a comparatively minor Soviet national minority became an issue in the Cold War. Public relations was a weighty factor but the prominence of the emigration issue was could not have been achieved by public relations alone. The actual instrument for catapulting Soviet emigration onto the world stage related to the Cold War instrument developed in the context of American politics, specifically the Jackson-Vanik Amendment to the Trade Act of 1974. Some maintain that the contribution of the amendment was more in the area of public relations rather than a deleterious impact on Soviet economic development. The genesis of the amendment, especially the interplay of political ambition with a desire for adding a humanitarian dimension to foreign policy, is the subject of the next chapter.

FOUR Jackson-Vanik

*The Elusive Search
for an Economic Lever*

How the welfare of a beleaguered Soviet Jewry became a concern of American foreign policy is a story full of happenstance. The Nixon administration's attention can be attributed to the Jackson-Vanik Amendment, which proposed a transaction whereby the Soviet Union would receive trade and credit access in return for the release of Jewish applicants for emigration. The prognosis for such an arrangement was poor. Moscow's emigration policy was conceived not in relation to what was viewed as Washington's "ethnicized" politics, but on the basis of its own national needs and interests. Yet, based on Cold War needs, the momentum for this unlikely transaction of trade and credit in turn for concessions from Moscow developed.[1] For activists of the Soviet Jewry movement the Watergate imbroglio turned out to be a blessing in disguise. The Jackson-Vanik Amendment, which was also a congressional challenge to the president's control of foreign policy, weakened the Nixon administration sufficiently to permit an opening for the Soviet emigration issue. The congressional battle for it achieved in a short period what the public relations effort alone would have taken years to realize. For a moment it seemed like Jewish concerns were becoming Americanized or, better, there seemed to be a convergence of American and Jewish interests.[2]

■ The two years from 4 October 1972, when Sen. Jackson introduced his amendment on the Senate floor, to the day President Ford finally signed the new trade agreement on 3 January 1975 were ones of unusual turmoil in the international arena. The Cold War seemed more threatening than ever, especially in Middle East and Africa, which had been the latest scene of Soviet expansion. The war in Vietnam had lost public support yet the promised peace seemed impossible to achieve without compromising the nation's superpower status. In October 1973 a surprise attack by Egypt across the canal in tandem with Syria in the north looked momentarily like it might succeed in bringing Israel to its knees. In the final round Israel prevailed and with it American prestige. But the war proved what Anwar Sadat had wanted to prove, that Israel was vulnerable. An unforeseen dividend of the war was an Egypt with restored self-respect ready for a peace that would be based on the new power realities.

For the time being the Middle East situation seemed stable. but the war in Vietnam still festered. Washington policy makers thought that one avenue to a respectable peace could be achieved by removing Moscow's support from the North Vietnamese. That was the genesis for the idea of exchanging access to American trade and credit in turn for Moscow's help in bringing the Vietnam war to an end. The Jackson-Vanik strategy was a variation of that strategy. Both were based on the assumption that the ailing Soviet economy desperately needed such help. But there was little evidence of such desperation in its aggressive foreign policy between 1972 and 1974 when the Jackson-Vanik Amendment was being considered.

Hanging over the lingering war in Vietnam was an unexpected domestic happening that was bound to weaken the ability of the administration to project its power in the international arena. The Watergate scandal had little bearing on the nation's military strength but it represented a crisis in leadership. Henry Kissinger, who virtually alone managed the nation's foreign policy during the crisis, insisted that the nation's foreign relations were unaffected. But the fact that the welfare of a foreign minority could trigger an effort to influence Russo-American relations was in some measure evidence that the Watergate scandal had already tilted the delicate balance between the executive and legislative branches in the foreign policy process in favor of the latter. Without Watergate, Jackson-Vanik might never have become part of American trade policy and the Soviet emigration issue might not have come to the fore.

The strategy of linking trade and credit benefits to Soviet Jewish extrication was not part of Kissinger's well-known concept of linkage. The idea of such a transaction developed in the early years of the Cold War and had nothing to do with Soviet Jewry. Moscow's failure to respond to American policy goals in the immediate postwar years was in fact one of the reasons why the Soviet Union was not granted most-favored-nation (MFN) status while more than one hundred other trading partners were as a matter of course.[3] The use of trade policy to wring concessions from Moscow had the support of religious groups but at the same time had to contend with pressure from the business community to expand East-West trade. Concurrent congressional resolutions calling for religious toleration were passed in May 1965 and again in April 1972 but made no specific mention

of the persecution of Soviet Jews or the possibility of linkage of trade and emigration. In an early direct congressional approach to the emigration of Soviet Jewry,
the newly elected Rep. Edward Koch, sent to Congress by a heavily Jewish district
in Manhattan, proposed a resolution to admit 30,000 Soviet Jews in 1970 but little
came of it.[4]

Only gradually did the idea of "freedom of movement" and withholding trade
and credit until Soviet emigrants were released become part of a trade package. "If
they want trade and technology from us," said the Israel-born Morris Amitay, who
served as Sen. Ribicoff's staff assistant and was the principle strategist behind the
amendment, "let them pay for it in what we want to get from them—persecuted
Jews."[5] The trade-for-emigrants transaction never won the approval of the Nixon
administration, which by 1971 viewed the liberalization of East-West trade as a
building block in its détente policy. The basic aim of that policy was to "manage"
the Soviets by offering enticements that it was assumed the Kremlin desperately
needed to stabilize its overextended economy. The administration's trade legislation, which included provisions for granting direct credit as well as credit guarantees, was submitted on 10 April. It promised to create a new economic order by
"building a fair and open trading world." Over a year later on 27 September 1972,
Jackson put an end to months of rumors by announcing that he would be offering
an amendment (section 10) to the Russo-American Trade Relations Act of 1971
with the Soviet Union. The announcement set the stage for a three-year conflict
fought on three interrelated levels, a personal one between Henry Kissinger and
Scoop Jackson and his assistant Richard Perle, an ideological one between those
who supported détente and those who opposed it, and a political one between the
executive and legislative branches of government.

▪ The use of trade and credit as a lever to exact better behavior from the Kremlin, as later proposed in the Jackson-Vanik Amendment, was from the outset a
highly controversial matter. To what extent Soviet policy makers would consider
the release of Jewish emigrants in exchange for favorable trade and credit arrangements with the United States was unknown. Much depended on the condition of
the Soviet economy, which was difficult to read from the outside. Moreover, its
poor performance needed not directly affect its continued ability to devastate any
enemy in wartime.

On one hand, Soviet planners had demonstrated an ability to focus resources
in a designated area, which resulted in some important technological breakthroughs, especially in space technology. Its military technology was usually able

to match that of the United States and in some cases Soviet military equipment, known for its sturdiness and simplicity, proved to be superior in the field. With the help of Western know-how and training, Soviet technology had surprisingly been able to keep up with U.S technological advances in many areas. On the other hand, such breakthroughs were achieved at great cost to the Soviet living standard. There are some who maintain that without the purchase and theft of Western technology, the Soviets would have fallen even further behind.[6] Soviet leaders were under pressure to close the growing gap between the Soviet standard of living and that of the West, especially housing and automobile ownership. Raising the standard of living required a lowering of the disproportionate share of its budget earmarked for military spending and required trade and credit from the West as well. Favorable credit terms were particularly important because the Soviet economy produced little capital on which it might finance its growth internally. Particularly troublesome was the Soviet agricultural sector, which had been collectivized by Stalin. The problem came to a head in the 1960s when after a series of bad harvests the Soviets were compelled to turn to the West for the purchase of grain. In 1965, to the dismay of American wheat farmers, the Soviets turned to Canada to avoid the Commerce Department regulation that 50 percent of exports of farm products must be shipped in American bottoms, which meant an increase in delivery price of $6 per ton. Though the price the Soviets were willing to pay was low, the sale of thousands of tons of wheat to Russia could have meant prosperity for the American wheat farmer and the lowering of expensive government farm subsidies. But until 1972—the year a three-year $750 million grain deal, later dubbed "the great Russian grain robbery," was completed, enabled by the Commodity Credit Corporation—the profits from grain sales to Russia went mostly to Canada and France. The loss of trade aroused concern among American policy makers over the question of whether national security was in fact enhanced when credit or technology was withheld in a market where buyers could make their purchases elsewhere. Those who favored the sale argued that the loss to the American economy also had to be factored into trade policy. The withholding of certain strategically useful products was not a new policy. The concern about providing the Soviet Union with technologically advanced items in radar and later in computer technology occurred almost simultaneously with the deteriorating relations between the two super powers. The Allies watched helplessly as the Soviets dismantled Germany's surviving industrial plant under the reparations clause of the Yalta agreement. As early as 1949 the nations of the West had formed an informal consortium to restrict the export of strategic goods to the Eastern bloc but thereafter the huge Soviet market was a constant temptation to which European and American business periodically succumbed. As in previous administrations, President Johnson operated on the premise that trade could be a "powerful tool of national policy" that would allow the United States to "influence the internal development and the external policies of European Communist societies along paths favorable to our purpose and to world peace."[7] Trade was also a factor in Kissinger's détente policy. He was convinced that trade and credit would "leaven the autarchic tendencies of the Soviet system."[8] To the dismay of the anti-detentists, the trade agreement with Moscow signed on 18 October 1972, which replaced the more stringent Export Administration Act of 1969, provided for long-term loans through the Export Import Bank to finance Soviet purchases. It also contained a request to Congress to approve normal MFN status for Soviet imports, which was granted to most trading nations as a matter of course but had been withheld from the Soviet Union.

Under the Nixon administration the United States switched from a trade denial policy to recognizing its economic and diplomatic benefits. Trade became not only a worthwhile goal in its own right but would bring other benefits such as reducing the record balance-of-payments deficit. It might also be used as an inducement for Soviet leaders to follow a more cooperative policy toward the West or at least stimulate the liberalizing tendencies within the Soviet Union. The export controls for militarily useful technology to the Soviet Union were kept in place but nonstrategic trade was encouraged. In practice, however, the new computer technology often had dual usage, just as tractor plants built in the Soviet Union by Western firms in the thirties were quickly converted to tank production during the war. It was that liberalization of trade policy that first aroused political leaders such as Sen. Henry Jackson.

During the early years of the Nixon administration top American firms were encouraged to sign "technological exchange" agreements with Moscow. Like traditional free traders, detentists believed that trade would draw the Soviet Union into the family of trading nations and soften the harsh class struggle imperatives of Communist ideology. An understanding of that detentist mind-set is requisite for understanding what happened in 1973 when linkage between trade and the release of Jewish emigrants came to the fore. Kissinger's primary aim was to seduce the Kremlin to withhold new military supplies from North Vietnam and encourage Hanoi to negotiate. The exodus of Soviet Jewry was not involved in the envisaged transaction. What was new in the Jackson-Vanik Amendment was the extension of the economic weapon beyond security considerations to a humanitarian purpose.

At the same time, it marked an effort by a group of Democratic legislators to gain control of Cold War policy. For Jackson the withholding of MFN status came to more than simply wringing better treatment for Soviet Jewry. Behind it was the conviction that liberal trade policy would strengthen Soviet military power. The neoconservatives, whose influence on policy was growing, believed that an old Leninist policy of getting from the West the very rope with which to hang them still prevailed in the Kremlin.[9] The notion that Soviet military power was formidable was reinforced after the Soviet-trained Chinese People's Liberation Army displayed its mettle in Korea. The Soviet economy grew rapidly under Stalin despite the fact that it was cut off from Western trade. The sense that the Soviet's retardation in the new information technology meant that it was falling behind the West did not become a certainty until the Reagan administration.[10] The importance of trade and credit did not impress the military strategists as much as it did the policy makers in America's think tanks. In the short run the Soviet technology deficit made little difference in strategic considerations. Whether or not they had the latest computers, the Soviet arsenal contained ICBMs that could deliver thermonuclear bombs.

■   In Washington the sides on trade policy, which was at the heart of détente, were sharply drawn. The administration would be able to count on an important section of the business community involved with grain, oil, gas, and metallurgy. There was hope for additional sale of pipes for petroleum drilling and other technology. Three months after the Great Grain Robbery came the administration's plan for a comprehensive trade agreement. It called for the expansion of trade and a settlement of the lend-lease debt that for decades had placed a legal hold on any new trade agreement. After long negotiations, Secretary of Commerce Peter G. Peterson announced in September that the negotiations over lend-lease debts would soon be resolved.[11]

The prospects for the proposed trade agreement looked good and although the talk of emigration for Soviet Jewry had grown in intensity since Kosygin's permissive statement regarding family reunification in 1966, the Soviet Jewry emigration issue and the mistreatment of the refuseniks had not yet become a talking point in the Cold War dialogue. In the final months of 1970 stretching to the fall of 1972 there were few clues to the troubles that were ahead for the administration. Despite differences over SALT I, Kissinger, head of the National Security Agency, was not yet convinced that he and Sen. Jackson were at loggerheads on how to deal with Moscow. Until October 1972, when Jackson actually introduced his amendment, the Nixon administration's plans for a new trade agreement had bipartisan support and seemed eminently realizable. But under the political leadership of Jackson and the addition of a Jewish human rights element that hopeful prognosis changed. It was not a normal extension of the détente formula for world stability.

Strangely, the congressional move to link trade directly with the right of Soviet Jews to emigrate did not originate with Jewish organizations or with the so-called Jewish lobby. Israel could be counted upon to support any policy that improved the hope of aliyah from the Soviet Union. But an ever-cautious Yitzhak Rabin, Israel's ambassador in Washington, believed that open support for pressure on Moscow would be "counterproductive" and considered the amendment an entirely American issue. As Israel went so did the Conference of Presidents.[12] On the eve of the negotiations for the Jackson-Vanik Amendment the idea of linking the benefits of trade with and credit from America with some Soviet concession such as suspending the head tax and facilitating the emigration of Soviet Jews was in the air.

■   Some attribute its crystallization to a small band of loosely organized Soviet Jewish activists who goaded their American and Israeli counterparts. In turn they brought the idea to "the Washington group," the name sometimes given to a band of congressional assistants led by Richard Perle, Morris Amitay, and Mark Talisman.[13] At the same time a similar idea linking trade to emigration by including it as an amendment to the Export Administration Act of 1969 scheduled for renewal in 1972 surfaced at the National Center for Jewish Policy Studies established by American University professor Harvey Lieber and Washington attorney Nathan Lewin. But the road to such a direct linkage was not a smooth one. Early proponents had to overcome the hesitation of American Jewish organizations and Israel's reluctance to become directly involved in an American legislative process. Jackson assured the Israelis that his amendment was the "best hope" to enhance emigration but rarely spoke of Soviet Jewry exclusively.[14] In 1972 Israel's voice in the American Soviet Jewry movement counted for much, which may account for the initial hesitation of the restructured National Conference on Soviet Jewry (NCSJ) to support such a bold and conspicuous Jewish input to proposed legislation.

As the 1972 presidential campaign reached its zenith, the Soviet Jewry question was at last receiving some attention. We have already noted McGovern's charge in August that Nixon had given too little attention to the question during his Moscow summit meeting in May.[15] That together with the efforts of the Union of Councils for Soviet Jewry (UCSJ) and other Jewish agencies to get a plank on the

Soviet Jewry issue into the party platforms brought the emigration question into the campaign. In turn for allowing Republicans to cosponsor his amendment, Jackson agreed to soft-peddle the issue until after the campaign. Though the Jewish note sounded was minor it dismayed Nixon's campaign managers.[16] At the Democratic convention Jewish support predictably went to McGovern. He was nominated to head the ticket by Gov. Abraham Ribicoff, who was rumored to be a candidate for the vice president's slot on the McGovern ticket, along with Gov. Marvin Mandel.[17] Three weeks later Republican Party stalwarts came to Miami to hammer out their platform. Richard Maass, chairman of the NCSJ, departed from his prepared text in a speech before the platform committee to denounce the new Soviet education tax. As promised by Sen. John Tower, chairman of the Republican Resolutions Committee, the platform included a strong plank on Soviet Jewry. But for most the possible linkage between trade policy and the head tax was had not yet entered political consciousness. The Soviet Jewry emigration issue had arrived on the American political scene but had not yet become a Cold War issue.

The forging of a link between trade and Jewish emigration awaited a speech by Sen. Javits delivered in New York's garment district in August and again on the floor of the Senate. His rationale was clear. Significant progress had been made on the pending trade agreement, especially on the nettlesome lend-lease payback issue, but there would be "trouble" if the Soviets did not abandon their education head tax. "The minute Javits spoke," observed Malcolm Hoenlein, director of the Greater New York Conference on Soviet Jewry, "everyone knew something was going on."[18] But as a Republican and a Jew representing a pivotal state, Javits was careful not to overextend himself and threaten his access to the Oval Office. Having introduced the issue he reverted to the human rights aspect of the Soviet Jewry problem and rarely publicly mentioned the possible quid pro quo of trade and credit for emigration. Perhaps resenting Jackson's preemption of his position as advocate for Jewish interests since the 1960s, Javits interposed several objections when the campaign to mobilize popular backing for the amendment was organized.[19]

The showcasing of the emigration issue in Congress was focused on congressional resolutions proposed in February by senators Jackson and William Brock III concerning religious freedom and financial aid to help absorb the Soviet emigrants in Israel. When the Kremlin's education tax came into effect in August it changed the terms of the debate. The tax led to Javits's declaration on 17 September warning that the pending trade agreements would face "trouble" over the new Soviet exit visa policy.[20] The education tax thus provided the first opportunity to raise in the Senate the issue of the mistreatment and the right of Soviet Jewry to emigrate. A giant step forward had been given to the Soviet Jewry movement by the Soviet bureaucracy.

The education head tax that drew congressional attention to the Soviet Jewry issue and the solution proposed by the Jackson amendment was promulgated in the Soviet Ministry of Education and imposed by OVIR in August 1972. Issued as a "Decree of the Presidium of the USSR Concerning Reimbursement of State Expenditures on Education by Citizens of the USSR Departing for Permanent Residence Abroad," the regulation featured a sharp gradation of taxes, with the most prohibitive attached to higher degrees from highly rated universities. The reaction of the press viewed the head tax as a particularly cruel form of ransom.

The 1972 presidential campaign presented an opportunity to raise the emigration issue by focusing on the education tax. Despite the warnings of his chief of staff, H. R. Haldeman, regarding the futility of trying to win the Jewish vote and pocketbook for the campaign, Nixon remained determined to make inroads on the Jewish electorate. He looked to two Jewish Republican stalwarts, Max Fisher and Jacob Stein, to help him do so. On 28 September Nixon met with thirty-two Jewish supporters brought together by Fisher to explain his strategy regarding the proposed amendment. He stressed the importance of using diplomatic channels rather than "demagoguery," which would be "counterproductive." That was the reason why he intended to keep the problem of the education tax out of the public debate. Usually an able political tactician as well as a ferocious political in-fighter, Nixon unaccountably surrendered the issue on which the early struggle for the trade agreement would revolve to his opponents. But true to his word, he spoke to Gromyko and Dobrynin about the problems the head tax was creating for the prospects of the administration's proposed trade agreement. On 4 October Secretary of State William Rogers met with a more select group of Jewish leaders to give assurance that the department was concerned about the tax and the persistence of harassment, especially of visa applicants, and was doing all that it could to mitigate the cruel situation of the Jewish refuseniks. As the conference drew to a close Rogers was informed by Richard Maass of the prevailing mood in the American Soviet Jewry movement. The congressional initiative to offer Moscow a linkage between the benefits of détente and the removal of the education head tax was being considered from several angles by the Jewish leadership, but the tax itself was unacceptable and could not stand.

When the Soviet authorities realized that they had blundered, they stopped administering the order, although the statute itself remained on the books. Few heeded the subtle change that had taken place in the growth of Jewish support for Jackson. Joined by Jewish communal leaders, the senator was now submitting specific conditions that the Soviets would have to meet to get the benefits of American trade and credit. In the year-long negotiations that followed, Moscow would be requested to permit a yet to be agreed upon number to leave annually, and they would have to offer assurances that the harassment of the refuseniks and geographical and occupational restrictions on emigration would cease. In short, Moscow's blunder opened the gate for its emigration policy to be strongly influenced by a foreign power acting as an agent for Soviet Jewry, an unprecedented intrusion into its sovereignty.

■ The actual provisions of the amendment were hammered out over several meetings of the Washington group in the offices of Sen. Ribicoff. But at the first meeting in September 1972 there was little agreement on strategy. The confrontational approach favored by Richard Perle and Morris Amitay, which would link trade and emigration, was rejected. Instead, alternative measures, such as a nonbinding congressional joint resolution favored by Sen. Humphrey and Sen. Javits, an open letter to the Kremlin, or a visit with Dobrynin to press the case against the education tax, were considered.

The earliest proposal proffered by the Perle group did not directly place a yearly emigration quota on the table. It only viewed trade and credit concessions encompassed in granting MFN in exchange for lifting the education tax. The final product embodied in section 10, the legal designation of the amendment, contained three main points: No "non market economy country" could be granted MFN or receive credit in any form, direct or indirect, which denies their citizens "the right or opportunity to emigrate to the country of their choice." The longest section of the amendment proposed denying trade and credit privileges if the requesting government imposed "more than a nominal tax on emigration or on the visas or other documents required for emigration for any purpose or cause whatsoever." The waiver provision that permitted the president to unilaterally end these restrictions once the president determines that the county is no longer in violation of these regulations was already present in the original proposal, but its terms were not yet spelled out and would become a source of continuous controversy.

The overwhelming reaction to the education tax overshadowed the opening provision of the amendment, which called for a prohibition of credit for a general denial of the right to emigrate, even when taxes and fines were not involved. The clause was potentially broad ranging in its effects, and together with the later Stevenson Amendment, which limited the extension of credit to the paltry sum of $300 million over four years, it could have brought Soviet-American trade to a virtual standstill. It remained for the congressional assistants who fashioned the daring direct link between trade, credit, and emigration to sell it to their patrons and then to Congress itself. They would face the implacable opposition of the Nixon administration, which saw the amendment as an attempt to undermine its policy of détente.

Finally, on 4 October, after warning at a preceding press conference that the head tax must go lest the pending trade agreement would have Congress to deal with, Jackson introduced his amendment on the Senate floor. It was aimed primarily at abolishing the tax. The notion of the right of movement would come to the fore later. The introduction of the amendment became one of several lines drawn between those who supported détente and those who were convinced that any concession to Moscow such as those contained in SALT endangered American security. The Soviet Jewry problem was on the way to becoming part of the Cold War debate. There was a feeling of optimism among the activists after the amendment was introduced. It would quickly bring the Soviet Jewry issue to the fore. At the same time there was uncertainty about making the refugee issue the center of the Jewish agenda. One of the things that endeared Jackson to the activists was his introduction of a bill, "A Two Year Program of Aid to Resettle Soviet Jews in Israel." A total of $250 million for 1972 and 1973 was requested. Some doubted the wisdom of placing two Jewish issues on the American political agenda. There was a difference between government appropriations for Israel's defense and a proposal to help fund resettlement of the emigrants in Israel. The former could be viewed as serving the national interest but how could resettlement aid for Soviet Jews in a foreign country be defended?

A supportive plank for Israel in the platform of both parties had become almost standard, but the addition of yet another "Jewish" plank was not a simple affair. For most Jews the Soviet Jewry issue seemed less urgent than ending the war in Vietnam or maintaining the integrity of the civil service merit system that had been challenged in the Ocean Hill–Brownsville section of Brooklyn.[21] The Democratic platform committee had little trouble in including something on Soviet Jewry. But by the time the Republicans came to Miami for their convention Anwar Sadat had expelled his Soviet advisors. Courting Egypt too ardently might affect the Jewish vote, whose sensitivity had intensified as a result of the Soviet-imposed education tax in August. On 5 September came the unexpected attack on Israel's Olympic team in Munich by a group of Palestinian terrorists. The reaction of the Jewish community was visceral. These were after all athletes, a symbol for many Jews of normality, of the new modern Jewish man.

As election day approached the idea of a quid pro quo was in the wind that would give the Soviets MFN status in turn for a liberalized emigration procedure that would allow Jews and all others who so desired to emigrate and also halt the harassment of visa applicants. On 12 September Sen. Ribicoff openly mentioned such a linkage on the Senate floor, and six days later at the behest of Max Fisher and Jacob Stein Jewish leaders again met with Secretary of State Rogers, who officially handled Middle East and Jewish matters, to explain what had to be done. It was becoming clear that Jackson's link between Soviet trade and emigration was gaining momentum. Sen. Jackson and Sen. Javits openly spelled out the emerging quid quo pro on the Senate floor. On 26 September Jackson again urged the NCSJ, whose position had not yet crystallized, to support the resolution that he would introduce in October. Rep. Vanik had already offered an amendment, identical in most details to Jackson's Senate resolution on 22 September. The stage for a protracted debate was set.

■   At the 28 September meeting with thirty-two Jewish Nixon supporters corralled by Fisher in the Oval Office, Nixon promised to use his influence to pressure Moscow on the head tax Nixon followed through and Dobrynin dutifully brought the message to the Politburo. The effect was dramatic. An angry discussion between Brezhnev, Andropov, and Kosygin occurred on 20 March 1973. The exasperated Brezhnev blamed Andropov for mishandling the tax matter and providing fodder for the Soviet Union's enemies. He spoke of Nixon's pressure on him to undo the tax: "Nixon is in favor . . . but many senators are against, merely because we are collecting a fee from Jews." Brezhnev suggested five hundred "individuals of secondary importance" be released immediately and noted with chagrin that "Zionism is making us stupid." [22] For a moment there seemed to be more pressure in Moscow than in Washington, where Jewish emigration was considered a campaign sleeper issue for the Jewish section of the electorate whose leadership was under pressure from the more militant activists here and in Moscow to get behind the Jackson initiative. But to do so was not without political risk since Nixon was projected to win a second term. It was one thing when Jewish voters continued to pull down the lever for the Democratic party and quite another when they became a thorn in the side of an already beleaguered presidency by undermining the strategy of détente.

By October the Soviet Jewry issue had gained traction. Nixon invited Gromyko and Dobrynin to Camp David to warn about the damage the education tax was doing to the prospects of granting MFN for the Soviet Union. Pleased that Kissinger was using his office as a favorite diplomatic "back channel," the Soviet diplomat confided that the tax was a "blunder" committed by a lower echelon bureaucrat while Brezhnev and Gromyko were vacationing on the Black Sea. But secretly apprised that hardliners in the Kremlin were actually behind the tax, Kissinger did not believe the ambassador. The problem was how to disarm the tax without publicly humiliating the Soviet government. The delicate negotiations regarding the outstanding lend-lease debt being conducted by Secretary of Commerce Peterson were coming to a conclusion. That would clear the decks for the two national leaders to sign the new trade agreement in October and to seek congressional authorization for the promised MFN and the credit lines that came with it. It was important to show the Jewish leadership that the administration could deliver the end of the ransom-like head tax. Additional assurances that the onerous tax would be phased out was given by Rogers at a meeting with the triumvirate that had become most closely associated with the amendment issue, Max Fisher, Jacob Stein, and Richard Maass. From his position as president of the NCSJ, which was becoming the major Jewish agency to deal with the Soviet Jewry issue, Richard Maass again informed Rogers that the initiative to link the "benefits of détente," as Maass delicately put it, with the trade treaty were well under way and that there should be no doubt that the Jewish leadership would stand behind it. Indeed, as Maass was speaking Jackson introduced his amendment to the Conference of Presidents, warning that if the head tax were not rescinded the amendment would become part of the pending trade act. The recruitment of a majority of the Senate as cosigners before the adjournment of Congress was a sign that Jackson's threat was not an idle one.[23] A week later, as part of an appropriations bill, the House passed a $50 million financial package to help the settlement and absorption of Soviet Jewish emigrants in Israel. It was a far cry from the $250 million Jackson had requested in February, but the mood of Congress was clear. On 18 October, just two weeks before the new election, the U.S.-USSR trade agreement was signed, but the crucial MFN provision and the question of credit extension awaited congressional action.

▪ It was a seemingly innocent burglary in the Watergate apartment complex where the Democratic Party campaign headquarters was housed that would bring the conflict over détente, to which the issue of free emigration from the Soviet Union was linked, to a new level. From the Republican perspective Nixon's landslide victory over McGovern in the election of 1972 contained a Jewish dividend. Nixon had received 39 percent of the Jewish vote, a higher than normal percentage. Some imagined that the Republicans were finally on the road to loosening the Democratic hold on the Jews that began with their love affair with the New Deal and Franklin Roosevelt.[24] More important, the Soviet Jewry issue would be resolved through the "quiet diplomacy" the administration favored. A rumored prior agreement with Jackson to keep the emigration issue out of the campaign in turn for permitting Republicans to become cosponsors of his amendment muted talk of the issue.[25] But despite an increase in Jewish popular support for Nixon the Jewish distaste for Nixon had not appreciably abated. According to Kissinger, the administration's Jewish supporters were "outgunned" in their efforts to detach the Jewish voter from supporting the Jackson amendment. Most Jewish organizations supported Jackson "or didn't know how to dissociate from him."[26] But that did not take into account that a highly political president, aware of the priority Jewish voters gave to Israel's security, might subtly use that heartfelt need to disarm the resistance to his trade bill. "Personally I can get better results for you," Nixon assured Golda Meir without mentioning the price. Ambassador Yitzhak Rabin spoke of Kissinger "asking the impossible of us."[27] In fact, it would be the role of Israel that repeatedly became central in the American Jewish consideration of the Soviet Jewry issue.

Kissinger acknowledged that a heavily accented German Jewish refugee and an anti-Semitic fallen Quaker made an "unlikely pair."[28] But they agreed that the emigration issue posed a threat to the détente policy. For the moment there was complete consonance with Israel, which did not yet view the amendment as an asset. Anxious above all to retain the administration's support, Israel insisted that what happened in Congress and with American relations with Moscow was an American affair. In determining Israel's policy at any given moment one had to differentiate between its public pronouncements and the voice emanating from private "insider's dialogue," which was often at variance with it. As we shall learn later Israel's desire to reestablish relations with the Soviet Union made it a possible candidate, in the eyes of the Nixon administration, for projecting its influence on American Jewish leaders against the amendment. Yet the American Israel Political Action Committee (AIPAC), the principle lobby for Israel, began by helping to line up support for the amendment and only fell into line weeks later. Its role was important because as a tax exempt institution the NCSJ was prohibited from openly lobbying. The Nixon administration's hope of thwarting the passage of the amendment were also raised when communal leaders such as Rabbi Arthur Hertzberg and Charlotte Jacobson, president of the World Zionist Organization's American section, did not support the amendment. It allowed the White House to choose and thereby empower the particular Jewish leaders it wanted to talk to. By exploiting the unclear lines of communal authority that permitted the co-optation of leaders favorable to the administration, much confusion was sewn.

But when it became clear that the Jewish leadership was moving to support the amendment, White House aide Leonard Garment and Peter Flanigan, who led the administration's campaign to prevent the amendment from reaching the floor of the Senate, tried to keep the Jewish leadership fragmented.[29] It soon became clear that the Jackson-Vanik Amendment imbroglio would prove no exception to budget considerations, which characterizes much of Jewish communal politics. As early as 1971 hackles were raised when the UCSJ started a food parcel program for "prisoners of conscience." Zionist organizations felt that "Jewish money" should be spent in Israel to help the hard-pressed Jewish Agency resettle Soviet emigrants. Lest funds be diverted, it was proposed that all fund-raising be done through the United Jewish Appeal and the Council of Jewish Federations and Welfare Funds, which served as the collecting and budgeting agency in most Jewish communities and where support of Israel continued to be strong. Behind the budget fracas was the crucial issue of determining who controlled the Soviet Jewry movement.

In the end Jackson faced the reality that the Jewish organizations would require time to mobilize and unify behind the amendment. Hearing Cairo's threats of war, Israel needed to take special care not to cross the Nixon administration, on which it was dependent for arms. At the outset of 1973 just as a cease fire in Vietnam had been put in place it looked as though the amendment had gained considerable momentum. Rep. Vanik's proposal introduced as part of a foreign assistance bill (HR16705) on 22 September and containing almost identical provisions to Jackson's bill had attracted 238 cosigners by February 1973. The drumbeat of public relations continued to focus on the education tax from which Soviet authorities were in the process of withdrawing. The idea of a "trade for visas" deal was still new and smacked of overreach to some. Speaking to Jewish student leaders at the University of Maryland, Jerry Goodman, the director of the NCSJ, cautioned militant activists about any move to cut all trade with the Soviet Union. Trade, he argued, was still needed as a lever to win compliance from the Kremlin. The Jackson amendment allowed for a policy of "balanced tension," which is the most practical strategy for emigration and gaining an end to harassment. That tension would become unbalanced if the promise of trade and credit was withheld. There were others who argued that freeing a handful of Jews was an insufficient reward for what was being offered to the Kremlin.

The administration too sensed that it faced a struggle in Congress to get a new U.S.-USSR trade act on the books. It tried in vain to prevent the legislation from being introduced on the floor of the House and Senate. Peter Flanigan, chairman of the Council of Foreign Economic Policy, recruited Georgy Arbatov, the well-known director of the Soviet Institute of America Affairs, to lobby before the Soviet American Trade Conference. But when he suggested subtly to a convention of the National Association of Manufacturers that Jackson-Vanik would provoke anti-Semitism in the Soviet Union because it gave Soviet Jews a special status and treatment, Sen. Ribicoff , sensing that a threat had been made, requested that Arbatov be asked to leave the country.[30] That did not end the efforts of Soviet trade officials to generate support for the trade act. Several Soviet trade delegations touting the profitability of trade with the Soviets followed Arbatov's mission.[31] Ten days after Arbatov's declaration, George Shultz, secretary of commerce, headed an American delegation of businessmen and economists to visit their Soviet counterparts. Shultz, who later became a passionate advocate of the Soviet Jewry cause, explained the emigration problem to his hosts and extended a token $10 million credit, as if to say that there would be more to come should there be movement on the emigration question.

Meanwhile on 15 March Jackson introduced his amendment. It was followed a month later by the submission of the administration's trade bill to Congress. The lines of the conflict that would last two years were drawn. The formal arena would be the hearings of various committees in the House and Senate, but a good part of the battle was also fought behind the scenes through leaks to the media, meetings with leading American Jews in the Oval Office and at the State Department, and all sorts of personal pressure on the historical actors. Behind the scenes those in the administration mounted a fierce no-holds-barred battle to turn back what they perceived as a challenge to its control of foreign policy. The White House had subtly conditioned rejection of the amendment with continued administration support of Israel. As a last resort Max Fisher, the administration's point man, called Stein, Maass, and Jacobson to Washington for a meeting on 2 November. There they were told that the administration needed an unequivocal statement of support for the Trade Reform Act, which meant telling Jackson to withdraw the amendment. These tactics had considerable impact especially on those leaders who placed the security of Israel uppermost. But the Jewish organization continued to support the amendment perhaps with less fervor. Wilbur Mills, who had been lured away from full support, rejoined the Jackson forces that now rallied his supporters. He invited the Jewish leadership to his office to buttress their sagging spirits.[32] In a heated meeting the group was chastised not by Jackson but by Sen. Ribicoff, who resented the administration's strong-arm tactics. A week later Jewish organizations reaffirmed their support of Jackson-Vanik in its original form. The administration efforts to defeat the Vanik amendment now continued to the floor vote on 11 December, where Title IV, which the administration had successfully removed, was restored by a three to one majority.

The administration did not capitulate. On 19 April fifteen Jewish leaders were called to the White House where a memorandum of assurances from Soviet leaders was read. It informed the group that the Soviet authorities were open to negotiation on the basis of private and quiet diplomacy such as the president had outlined. They assured the leaders that such an approach would yield the best results. In response, four days later an open letter from one hundred Soviet activists urging the need for sustained pressure on the Kremlin by supporting the amendment, precisely the reverse course suggested by Kissinger, was received by Jewish leaders and quickly transmitted to the press. The letter, which reminded them of the consequences of their silence during the Holocaust, was a turning point.[33] It was followed two days later by news that the NCSJ, the major Jewish interest organization for Soviet Jewry, favored the Jackson-Vanik Amendment without reservations. In May Jewish leaders were finally able to inform Kissinger of something he already knew, that support for the amendment in the Jewish community had grown and the chances of turning it around were slim. In the House the Vanik amendment had already gotten 279 cosigners, a sufficient number to win a floor vote. Kissinger may have found it bitterly ironic that he, of all people, should be requested to inquire about the fate of forty-two "prisoners of conscience." Release from their prison sentences, explained the activists, would serve as evidence of the good intentions of the Soviet authorities.

■   As Kissinger prepared for his trip to Moscow, scheduled for the first week in May, he must have already been aware of the seriousness of Jackson's challenge to the conceptual basis of his foreign policy. The day before he was scheduled to depart he again met with the now-familiar group of Jewish leaders, Max Fisher, Jacob Stein, and Richard Maass, to review the situation. But disharmony had developed in the triumvirate because Maass, as president of the NCSJ, was now openly supporting the amendment. Fisher and Stein remained loyal to the president. An administration move to eliminate Maass from future meetings was forestalled when the two Republicans insisted that Maass be present at Oval Office meetings. That first week in May also witnessed a massive Solidarity Sunday rally in which an estimated 100,000 people marched down Fifth Avenue to call attention to the Soviet Jewry problem. For the 10,000 protesters at a rally on the West Plaza listening to Jackson explain in lucid terms why trade and tyranny cannot be mixed, the attendance by Fisher and Stein at a dinner for Brezhnev in mid-June seemed like an act of betrayal.

The division between those for and against emigration was also deepening abroad. For the Palestinians the small trickle of emigrants was a portent of things to come. The Palestinians noted with bitterness that a Soviet emigrant who had no connection with Israel and might not even be Jewish had the right to settle in Israel, whereas they spent their lives in refugee camps, unable to return. The first of two attempts to disrupt the flow of emigrants out of the Soviet Union to the debarkation point at the Schoenau Castle in Vienna was staged by a group of Palestinians on 19 June. But the bomb planted on a nearby autobahn exploded prematurely, killing the terrorist. A second attempt occurred a week prior to Egypt's surprise attack on the Jewish holy day of Yom Kippur, this time on the train leading to Schoenau. Two startled emigrants were kidnapped. The incident called attention to an aspect of the emigration issue given little attention by the media, the role a massive exodus of Soviet Jews could play in fueling the intractable Arab-Israel conflict.[34] The October Organization of Petroleum Exporting Countries (OPEC) oil embargo, which raised the price of oil by 70 percent and promised to cut production by 5 percent each month until Israel withdrew from all occupied territory, was only peripherally related to the emigration issue. But evidence of a collective Arab reaction to the October war by using its oil weapon added a new ingredient to the Middle East problem that could complicate the emigration process. In 1973 most Soviet emigrants were resettling in Israel.[35]

In the interim, both measures were making their way through the legislative process. On 19 June the House Ways and Means Committee began consideration of the administration's new Trade Reform Bill. Wilbur Mills, the powerful chairman of the committee, allowed himself to be convinced to support the combined Jackson-Vanik Amendment by adding his name to it so that it was officially known as the Jackson-Mills-Vanik amendment. The administration also possessed an arsenal of rewards that could bring the honors hungry chairman to the administration's side. After Brezhnev spoke to Congress, Mills received a special invitation for a luncheon with the Soviet leader at Blair House. That proved sufficient for the moment to detach Mills from the Jackson camp. His Ways and Means Committee was temporarily removed from considering the amendment by a parliamentary maneuver calling for the elimination of a clause barring credit and credit guarantees that the Republicans on the twenty-five member committee argued belonged in the province of the House Committee on Banking and Currency.

For Jewish communal leaders the October war that highlighted Israel's dependence on resupply from the American arsenal also made them prone to the administration's suasions. Brezhnev's threat to intervene militarily to enforce the delicate cease fire that protected the surrounded Egyptian army also had its effect. But ultimately pressure on Jewish leaders came too late. By the time the October war broke out the amendment already had 285 cosponsors in the House and 77 in the Senate, and there were signs that Moscow had softened its position regarding dealing with Congress on its emigration policy.

A more serious conflict occurred in the Senate Foreign Affairs Committee, where Sen. Fulbright had warned against the influence of the "Jewish lobby" on American Middle East policy. His opposition was now extended to the movement to pry open the gates of the Soviet Union by using trade and credit as a lever. Jackson was not a member of the committee but that did not prevent him from confronting Fulbright's pronouncements. He spoke of the amendment as an American effort to bring "a tiny bit of freedom for Jew and Gentile in the USSR," which Fulbright saw as "idealistic meddling."[36] Contrary to Fulbright's assumption, the notion of an American role as facilitator and helper for Jewish refugees was not a new departure. It first came into play in early August when Attorney General Elliot Richardson was asked to use his parole authority under the refugee law to admit eight hundred Soviet Jewish emigrants who had rejected settling in Israel. The administration's generosity did not come without a price. It was used by Max Fisher, who had interceded on the emigrant's behalf directly with the president, as evidence of the administration's good intentions.

In the meantime, Nixon planned to use the confirmation hearings for Kissinger's assumption of the secretary of state post before the Foreign Relations Committee to press again for the practicality of "quiet" diplomacy and the need to avoid the distortion of the policy-making process that would result from the congressional initiative. But the committee meeting was canceled, and on 18 September Kissinger was approved without the customary cross-examination. Congressional confirmation of the amendment was not yet assured. Many weapons remained in the administration's arsenal, including the possibility of modifying the amendment to return the key decision regarding credit and MFN to the president's office by means of the amendment's waiver mechanism. Mills's illness, which required a leave of absence, opened an unexpected opportunity to reshape the Vanik amendment. On 13 September Rep. Al Ullman, who became acting chairman in Mill's absence, and Rep. Herman T. Schneebeli, the ranking minority member, were invited to the White House for a special luncheon. The full-court press to halt the momentum did bring some defectors from the list of cosigners. The administration now focused on a measure proposed by two California congressmen, Rep. Pettis, a Republican, and Rep. James Corman, a Democrat. Rather than a direct denial of MFN and all that went with it, the status of Soviet compliance would be granted on the basis of an annual report to Congress on whether there was "reasonable progress" on "freedom of emigration" and "free expression of ideas." After the report was received Congress would retain for ninety days its power to deny MFN status and should it choose to veto, the president would require new congressional authority to grant it.

The president would have preferred to have sole power to extend credit grants but was willing to settle for the Corman-Pettis proposal, which still left much of the decision in executive hands. Much depended on who would generate the report and what "reasonable progress" meant. The question of harassment of visa applicants was becoming ever more important for the activists. Clearly there would have to be some monitoring system in place to make certain that the Soviets were in compliance. This first attempt at finding a middle course was rejected but in 1975, under the Ford administration, a slightly altered version of the so-called waiver provision became part of a proposed new settlement.

The high point reached by the administration with the Corman-Pettis proposal quickly became a low point after Congress received two letters from Andrei Sakharov, the Soviet physicist and Nobel Prize winner whose reputation as a courageous dissident was at an all-time high. The letter urged Congress to support the Jackson-Vanik Amendment and warned those who would deal with the Soviet authorities that they could simply not be trusted. Sakharov took precisely the reverse position of Kissinger who argued that détente, the best hope for survival, would be subverted by the amendment. Sakharov argued that the passage of the amendment was essential for genuine détente, which required a degree of internal freedom in order to not lock in the millions who lived under Communist tyranny. Such a mass incarceration, he argued, could not possibly serve as a basis of a stable world order. Rejection of the amendment would be a betrayal of the thousands who were victims of Soviet suppression. Sakharov's arguments, which hit the emotional hot points of the Cold War, were echoed in the congressional debate over the amendment. A week after the letter became public Sen. George McGovern, whom Nixon had roundly defeated in 1972, addressed the opponents' favorite argument against the amendment, that immigration policy is everywhere an internal matter and that the United States could not base its foreign policy on restructuring the policies and institutions of societies it may find abhorrent. "If we don't interfere in internal affairs," queried McGovern, "what the hell were we doing in Vietnam?"[37] It was a telling point especially since the Export Administrative Act of 1969 the Vanik Amendment sought to improve considered trade as an instrument of foreign policy.

We have noted that such was always the case in postwar trade policy with the

Soviet Union. It was in fact the policy of détente that marked a departure from standard practice. But at a news conference before Kissinger left for Moscow on 26 June 1974, an embarrassing question was posed by a Soviet journalist to Ron Ziegler, Nixon's press secretary: "Would you agree to making U.S. trade with the USSR dependent on the solution of the racial problem in the U.S.?"[38] The point was well taken, and a press conference was not the place to explain that the United States had embarked on a course to solve its racial problem whereas the Soviet Union seemed to be moving in the opposite direction with its Jews.

■   As the first phase of the congressional debate ended and the trade bill was reported out of the Ways and Means Committee on 26 September, an event that would change everything occurred in the Middle East. Egypt and Syria mounted a surprise attack on Israel on 6 October, the holiest day on the Jewish religious calendar.

The Yom Kippur War had both a short- and long-range impact on the Jackson-Vanik negotiations. The former concerned the crucial question of resupply. Did the administration attempt to use Israel's critical supply situation to wring concessions on the compromise idea of a presidential waiver? The answer would involve the role of Kissinger directly since by October Nixon was so deeply mired in the Watergate inquiry and the question of the tapes that the administration's foreign policy was, in effect, being run by Kissinger. As a foreign-born American he keenly felt the strangeness of the historic moment. He was managing American foreign policy and in heavily accented English reassuring the American public that Watergate had no effect on the American presence in the world.[39] But privately he was telling Jewish leaders that the story of allowing Israel to "twist in the wind" over resupply was false and that there ought to be some gratitude toward the administration for the generosity of its support.

Russia's belligerent threats during the war and suspicion of the administration's aims strengthened communal support of the amendment. The war resolved the ambivalence many peace-oriented Jewish liberals had toward the anti-détente Jackson amendment. Were Sadat's goals limited or was the war a joint attempt with Moscow to finally eliminate Israel? In either case the authenticity of Moscow's peace goals and beyond that its reliability as a partner in détente was open to question. It is on the question of Soviet intentions in the war on which a judgment about détente, especially among Jewish voters, ultimately rested. For Kissinger the most important result of the war was the effect it had on solidifying the opposition to his détente policy.

What remains a mystery about the relation of the emigration problem to the Yom Kippur War is the Kremlin's extreme reaction. It is true that Israel's victory threatened a Soviet Cold War asset in which Russia had invested heavily. But how Soviet Jews could be related to that is not easily discernable. Yet Moscow's treatment of the refuseniks, the general harassment of Jews, the conjuring up of a world Zionist conspiracy, the expenditure of millions of rubles on crassly anti-Semitic books, the setting the stage for war against Israel in 1967, and Moscow's refusal to recognize Israel after the humiliation of 1967 were evidence of an overreactive pattern of behavior. Clearly this was no ordinary hostility. Moscow's reaction to the Jewish presence in the family of nations, according to Golda Meir, went beyond the limits of an unfriendly policy to a murderous one. That rage came to the surface again in the Yom Kippur War and in the end we will have to come to historical terms with Soviet rage against Jews and their state and learn how it fits into our story. The Soviet Jewry movement is not only developed by activists but fueled by the series of overreactions and missteps by the Kremlin.

Meanwhile, negotiations on the amendment remained virtually suspended until March 1974 because Nixon, preoccupied with the daily televised Watergate hearings, felt too weakened to take on Jackson and his allies. On 10 October, four days into the war, two presidential assistants, John Ehrlichman and Donald Segretti, resigned. That was followed ten days later by the famous "Saturday night massacre," the firing of Special Prosecutor Archibald Cox and the resignation of Attorney General Elliot Richardson. The negotiations with Jackson had become "a dialogue of the deaf" because, according to Kissinger, Jackson no longer had an incentive to "strike a deal on the numbers."[40]

On 28 October in the Senate and in the House on 9 November, as a troubled peace returned to the Suez Canal area, now secured by a 10,000 man UN peacekeeping force, the legislative war over the trade bill entered its final round. The OPEC oil embargo, which began as the negotiations for a cease fire were underway, caused a 70 percent rise in fuel prices. The long lines at the gas pumps reminded Americans that their love affair with the automobile could be disrupted by events abroad. The bargaining over the trade act was ready to resume once the disengagement agreement was implemented in January. A new factor in the negotiations was that the war more than ever convinced supporters of Israel that a massive infusion of Soviet emigrants was necessary to give Israel the security, demographic and otherwise, to withstand the sustained threat the state faced from its neighbors.

The new round of negotiations on Jackson-Vanik took on a special urgency. To restore some semblance of a working détente policy after the war, Kissinger needed a proposal to bring to Moscow for a scheduled meeting in March. Unlike the aftermath of the June war, when Moscow emerged with its presence in the oil-rich Middle East intact and in some cases improved, the war in 1973 offered no such compensations. Despite threats and bluster Moscow could not shield Egypt and Syria from the defeat on the battlefield. The Soviet Union had been kept out of the postwar peace negotiations and the result of its expensive armament of Egypt was that in April Sadat, dissatisfied with the quantity and quality of Moscow's support, virtually ended Egypt's eighteen-year alliance with the Soviet Union. Egypt, a key anchor for Soviet influence in the Middle East, was in the process of switching its loyalties to Washington. Kissinger was wont to attribute his success in neutralizing the Soviet threat in the Middle East to his nuanced diplomacy. But others recognized that the American position in the Middle East was earned as much by Israel's victories on the field of battle as by brilliant moves on the Cold War map.

The negotiations between Jackson and his coterie, Sen. Javits and Sen. Ribicoff and sometimes including leaders from the Jewish community, and Henry Kissinger and his advisors that occurred during the two-month period of February and March 1974 concerned two issues: The first was to reach an agreement on a legislative mechanism that would allow the executive branch to retain control of the actual implementation of trade and credit policy while granting Congress some check on Soviet compliance. The second issue was to determine an annual quota of exit visas to be granted by the Soviet authorities. Given the deterioration within the Nixon administration following the Watergate revelations and the determination of Jackson to impose a liberal emigration policy on the Soviet government, the odds on achieving a breakthrough were slim.

In February Kissinger met once again with Jewish leaders for yet another effort to convince them that outside pressure would not appreciably change Soviet behavior toward its Jews and that the best opportunity for emigration lay in an unofficial agreement to include quotas to be granted exit permits. Two days after the meeting the administration's extension of liberal credit terms under the Soviet Union's existing arrangements was questioned by Sen. Clifford Case of the Foreign Relations Committee. Suspicious that the administration had been bypassing Congress by using little-known executive agreements to extend preferred credit rates to the USSR, Case asked for a "full airing" of existing trade arrangements.[41] It was a sign of the growing suspicion that would surface in the March hearings before the Senate Finance Committee.[42]

Kissinger was aware that the hearings were the beginning of a process that would help determine the fate of the détente policy. But sensing that the momentum favoring the amendment could not be stopped, he now sought to reformulate it so that it would still work for the administration. Sen. Russell Long, the chairman of the Finance Committee, was presented with a list of those who would testify for the next round of hearings representing the administration's "Big Guns." [43] George Shultz, secretary of commerce, put forward new language for the waiver component in the amendment that would allow the president to implement the credit provisions and Congress to exercise a check on Soviet compliance. [44] The question of numbers of emigrants to be granted exit visas proved even more difficult to resolve because Jackson's position, ostensibly based on humanitarian principles embodied in the Declaration of Human Rights, demanded nothing short of total freedom to leave and return to one's country. Kissinger complained of Jackson's tactics. He suggested that Jackson's objective was not to reach an agreement but to gain Jewish support for his forthcoming second bid for the presidency. Why else would Jackson raise the ante every time a proposal was on the table? The number to be granted visas annually changed from 40,000 to 65,000. When Jackson left for Moscow the actual number to be granted visas was still unclear. But in the tough bargaining that followed the Yom Kippur War Jackson reluctantly agreed to the waiver proposal, which partially restored the executive initiative.

As in 1973 the administration made good use of a timely dispatched Soviet delegation of twenty-six "experts" on Soviet American trade headed by Foreign Trade Minister Nikolay S. Patolichev to build up support in the business community. The visit was hardly coincidental, and the impact of OPEC's oil embargo would possibly create a favorable public opinion linking trade and prosperity. But the administration's strenuous efforts to disarm the amendment were futile. A Jewish delegation informed Kissinger before he departed for Moscow that Jewish communal support behind the amendment had solidified. By the time the hearings concluded on 11 April the House had already passed the Vanik amendment.

Kissinger's return from Moscow was the signal for the administration's final attempt to find a workable compromise. A meeting with Jackson and Javits and another with Gromyko allowed Kissinger to reveal that there had been some movement on the question of visa quotas though the precise numbers could not be discussed. After hearing a report on what had transpired at the meeting, the executive committee of the NCSJ on 26 April also expressed its strong support for Jackson-Vanik. On 5 June, a day before the anniversary of D-Day, the beleaguered Nixon spoke at the Naval Academy in Annapolis. It was an occasion to again enunciate his views on attaining world peace to the graduating midshipmen. Perhaps he was already aware that his tenure as president was about to be curtailed and that historians would find the saving grace of his administration to be the strong hand it played in the foreign policy area. That brought him naturally to the Jackson amendment, which he denounced indirectly as interfering with the administration's efforts to make the world a safer place. Détente did not mean letting the American guard down, he argued. It was détente that raised the hope and prospect for peace in the Middle East. It could play a similar role in the Cold War.

Unsaid was that much depended on regaining some flexibility in the Jewish community. Soon after Nixon's Naval Academy address a new meeting was scheduled with key Jewish leaders to seek a formula that would satisfy all parties. That included the Israeli government and its need for the emigrants and American Jewry and its need to "rescue" Soviet Jewry. The militant American and Russian activists were not party to the negotiations because neither would have been satisfied with anything less than total release of all who wanted to emigrate. But the 6 June meeting convened by Max Fisher and Jacob Stein did in fact have some new Jewish faces: Arthur Hertzberg, a well-known rabbi and president of the American Jewish Congress, and Charlotte Jacobson, a powerful voice in the American Zionist movement. Neither was fully convinced that the amendment served the Jewish interest as they understood it. Like Sen. Javits they were not averse to finding a formula that could bridge the differences between the two sides.

The American Jewish position was in fact "soft" on several strategic aspects of the emigration issue. Professor Hans Morgenthau, a leading academician and spokesman for the realpolitik school in foreign policy who had been recruited for the movement by Moshe Decter, presented an accommodationist position at a congressional hearing in 1971. He believed that the Soviet Jewry movement should focus on "attainable" goals and abandon the idea of mass immigration in favor of "selected cases of personal hardship." At the same time he advocated a much stronger support in place to save Soviet Jewry from "spiritual cultural extinction."[45] There was disagreement about which tactic would bring out the highest number of Soviet Jews, a confrontation on human rights grounds such as favored by Jackson and the militants or a quiet "informal" agreement with the Soviet authorities that would permit a certain agreed upon number to leave monthly. The latter was the path proposed by Kissinger. If this was the likely alternative, how many should be allowed to leave annually? The Soviets spoke of 30,000, approximately the number released in 1972. But Jackson, who believed that all should be released on principle, proffered the 100,000 figure and immediately publicized that number in the press. That was three times the number the Soviets ever permitted to leave per year. It was a figure that Kissinger did not feel was achievable and with which Sen. Ribicoff, Jackson's partner, was also uncomfortable. The bargaining area was predictably somewhere in the middle, between 45,000 and 65,000 to be granted exit permits annually. For Jerry Goodman and Malcolm Hoenlein, it mattered less whether the quota agreed to by Soviet authorities was 45,000 or 60,000. They considered that the fact that quotas were offered at all was a sign that the Kremlin was reachable on the emigration issue. More important, it meant that Brezhnev's story before Congress declaring that he would be happy to give the Jews who wanted to leave exit permits but he could no longer find Jews to give them to was untrue. Goodman and Hoenlein took the Soviet offer of annual quotas as evidence that there continued to be pressure to leave the Soviet Union.[46]

That is where matters stood when Nixon and Kissinger traveled to the Moscow summit on 5 July. For Nixon it was a vain attempt to recoup from the damage that Watergate had done to his administration. He would demonstrate that at least in the foreign relations realm he still reigned supreme. But that was not to be. The amendment was not a major issue of the meeting. Brezhnev again informed the president that visa applications had declined. Moscow had made its move on emigration and now it was up to Washington. Jackson had chosen to visit China at the moment that Nixon was in Moscow, as if to remind the negotiators that the Cold War was now tripolar. The next move was up to Moscow, declared Jackson, acting like he was already making foreign policy. It must end the harassment of visa applicants. If that happened and Moscow showed a human face, he was ready to work out "a sensible arrangement." That may have been a response to Sen. Fulbright's declaration on a popular television program, *Meet the Press,* that he as chairman of the Foreign Relations Committee saw no need for the amendment, which ought to be revoked in light of developments.

The return from the summit was followed by the customary debriefing. Echoing the Soviet line, the State Department informed congressional leaders that Jewish applications for visas had declined.[47] Nixon's resignation was only months away, and stories that he was personally responsible for the delay in resupply during the Yom Kippur War now resurfaced in the Jewish press.[48] Nixon had reminded Jewish leaders that without a trade agreement there was nothing to oblige the Soviet authorities to issue any exit permits at all. There was an element of truth in that assertion, which was similar to the point made by Jewish leaders such as Max Fisher, who favored a compromise. That reality might also have become clear to the Jewish leadership group that again met with Kissinger on 24 July. Some changes had taken place that made an agreement appear to be more possible.

Rabbi Israel Miller, the most experienced of the Jewish leaders on the Soviet Jewry issue, was able because of the multiple posts he held to overcome a problem faced by the NCSJ, which was obligated by its founding charter to check every move it made with the Conference of Presidents. The leadership of the NCSJ had also changed when Richard Maass was succeeded by a well-known lawyer, Stanley Lowell. Before Kissinger met with the seventeen leaders, Maass, Lowell, and Max Fisher were invited for a preliminary meeting in which the now-familiar territory was again explored. Leonard Garment, who acted as the administration's liaison with the Jewish community, was also present.

The discussion focused on the same area Kissinger had covered in a prior meeting with Jackson, Ribicoff, and Javits. He presented a detailed description of what had transpired in Moscow. Détente, on which peace depended, was a "two way street." There had to be something in the hopper to get the Soviets to cooperate. Trade and credit would not only benefit our economy, it would help bring the Vietnam peace negotiations to a successful conclusion and solve the emigration problem in a satisfactory way. That is where the matter of the amendment stood when the Watergate scandal finally forced the resignation of the president on 8 August. On the following day, Vice President Gerald Ford, who was not a cosigner of the Vanik amendment and was a staunch supporter of the benefits of Soviet-American trade, took the oath of office. It was Watergate, not the endless negotiations over a trade agreement, that held the public's attention in 1974 and well into 1975. The cast of historical actors that would finally produce a trade agreement with the Soviet Union remained in place, including its two most important actors, Henry Kissinger, who represented continuity from the Nixon administration, and Henry Jackson, who was already planning his primary campaign for the Democratic nomination.

The negotiations continued on 15 August with Jackson, Ribicoff, and Javits trying to come to some arrangement while the trade bill was held up in the Senate Finance Committee. At the same time Rep. Edward Koch introduced an amendment to the Export-Import Bank Bill that would halt all bank credits to the Soviet Union until the Senate acted on the trade bill. Considered on the House floor on 21 August, the Koch move further increased the pressure on the administration. Kissinger insisted that "a reasonable solution can be achieved" but he had to have something in hand that he could defend and transmit. He could not outright demand a specific figure such as 60,000 exit permits without offering something in return.[49] In an effort to counteract Washington rumors that he was trying to mobilize American Jewish resources for his next presidential bid, Jackson again stressed the broad humanitarian principles on which his position on the trade act rested. "I assume there will be a substantial number of gentiles as well as Jews applying to emigrate," he told reporters.[50]

Meanwhile, the Russians seemed to have lost interest. In a tough speech delivered to the U.S. Soviet Trade and Economic Council that convened in Moscow on 15 October, Brezhnev mentioned that as it stood the trade act was not acceptable. William Simon, the new secretary of the Treasury, assured his Russian counterpart that the administration expected to have a treaty in place before the end of the year. The Ford-Brezhnev summit at Vladivostok to prepare the ground work for SALT made no official mention of things other than preparation for a second SALT conference to be held in a year. But at home, months of negotiations had finally produced a breakthrough on the power sharing through the waiver mechanism. All that remained was to reach agreement on the number to be released. The bargain was sealed by a "letter of agreement" between Kissinger and Jackson containing the outlines of the agreement. It seemed a minor point but it turned out to be an impossible hurdle for the opponents of the amendment.

The letter was an "ingenious formula" conjured by Kissinger who understood that the Soviet government could never agree to a public humiliation inherent in an American diktat determining its immigration policy.[51] Even less could they tolerate an American senator known for his anti-Soviet posture to dictate that policy. Hence there was an exchange of letters, jointly worked out by Kissinger's principle assistant, Helmut Sonnenfeldt, together with Jackson, in which the points ostensibly agreed to in informal discussions with Soviet authorities would be set. The written agreement was not between the Soviet Union and the United States, but between Kissinger and Jackson. All that was required was Jackson's signature to seal the bargain. It was an "extraordinary" arrangement that ensured a steady flow of emigrants while removing Jackson's hand from the administration's throat, if only for the moment.[52]

But to Kissinger's dismay Jackson "ratcheted matters up" by proposing that the preferential treatment given to visa applicants in the provinces, where the education and professional level was lower, be listed as one of the harassments the Soviet authorities would eliminate.[53] Then he insisted that the three senators (Jackson, Javits, and Ribicoff) prepare an interpretation of the letter to have available precise interpretations for every Soviet assurance.[54] As it turned out the procedure was full of loopholes that ultimately raised new hackles. The most obvious one was that there was no way of confirming whether what Kissinger's restatement of what the Soviet authorities agreed to was truthful. Lowell and Jackson agreed that in their letter of response to Kissinger the phrase "we have been assured that" should be substituted for "we are satisfied that," in order to pin Kissinger down. But Soviet assurances, if they were given at all, by Dobrynin and Brezhnev, were given orally. To request further assurances from the Soviets would have deprived Kissinger of the "wiggle room" he required to maneuver. Much therefore depended on Kissinger's truthfulness, which was precisely what Jackson found wanting. In the letter exchange it was truly a case of the devil being in the details, but precision and detail was what it could not contain. The letter was full of what Kissinger called "creative ambiguity."

After enumerating the prohibition of specific forms of harassment, such as the requirement that adult emigrants receive the permission of their parents to emigrate, Kissinger's initiating letter contained no specific annual quota to be granted visas. The rate of emigration, the letter stated, "would begin to rise promptly from the 1973 level and would continue to rise to correspond to the number of applicants." Jackson's demand was specific: "We would consider a benchmark—a minimum standard of initial compliance—to be the issuance of visas at the rate of 60,000 per annum."[55] Some of the ambiguity could be traced to the lack of clarity in the Soviet emigration policy and the way regulations were administered. Privately, they agreed to release 40,000 emigrants per year but publicly they would not acknowledge such an intrusion or that they had agreed to stop harassment. Kissinger was careful to deny that the letter of exchange represented a formal guarantee from the Soviets.

For the leaders of the Soviet Jewry movement there was a kind of magic in having a letter behind which the government would ostensibly stand. The agreement was hailed by Lowell and Rabbi Miller with the condition that there would be carefully supervised Soviet compliance. The refuseniks, however, harped on the untrustworthiness of the Soviets on the grassroots level. They insisted that an agreement that does not have some form of oversight of the Soviets was not worth the paper it was written on.[56] For Jackson, distrust extended to Kissinger himself. The battle was far from over. For unexplained reasons Kissinger called off a planned third letter in which he would approve Jackson's response to his first letter.[57] The Jewish leadership that had slowly come to fully support Jackson now screamed out in pain at the prospect of the administration's betrayal. It was Javits's talent for legal wordsmanship that produced an acceptable answer and saved the day. The operative paragraph of the third letter would be attached as the final paragraph of Kissinger's first letter. The administration's limit on only two letters would be upheld and the compromise would remain intact. After a few additional wrinkles were ironed out, the new version was submitted for approval. The waiver agreement that allowed the president to waive clauses a and b of section 402, containing the Jackson-Vanik Amendment at the heart of the compromise, allowed the Congress to have its say and at the same time play a watchdog role. But the initiative to make and oversee policy returned to the president where it had always resided. The challenge of Congress to the president's foreign policy-making power was not yet fully played out. It would take additional months for the Jackson-Vanik imbroglio to be resolved. After a one-month recess there would have to be additional consideration by the Senate Finance Committee followed by action of the full Senate and finally action by the Senate-House Conference Committee before the amendment was ready to be voted upon by both houses. All that would have to be completed before 20 December when the second session of the 93rd Congress was scheduled to adjourn. The NCSJ alerted its members to keep up the pressure.

▪   Its collapse came eight days after the letter of agreement was made public. In a secret letter to Kissinger, Gromyko denied ever having agreed to such an intrusion in the internal affairs of the Soviet Union. At the same time Jackson would dispute the lower than 60,000 quota figure. When, within sight of his goal, Jackson raised the ante further by insisting on an annual quota of 100,000, Kissinger finally understood that what was intended was not merely the release of the refuseniks, but the elimination of the policy of détente. Perhaps it had little prospect for success to begin with, going beyond the separation of powers system by means of an elaborate scheme of letters and engineered by a heavily accented and disliked secretary of state.

Behind the scenes there were signs that the letter of agreement was not working. It came from the Soviets who, perhaps reacting to Jackson's bravado at the concluding news conference in the White House briefing room, now formally denied that there was an agreement. President Ford stated that Jackson had "behaved like a swine" and then hastily announced to the press that no Soviet pledge on a specific number of Jews that would be permitted to emigrate had been given.[58] Kissinger's letter carefully avoided stating a specific number but Jackson understood that 60,000 would be "a minimum standard of initial compliance" and thereafter the rate of emigration would rise until it corresponded to the number of applicants.[59] It would be used like a benchmark by Congress to judge the good faith of the Soviets, who were in fact obliged to change from a restrictive to a liberal immigration policy. Now Gerald Ford, who in the interim had succeeded

Nixon, was saying no specific number or even standard had been agreed upon in the long negotiations over the agreement. For those who distrusted Kissinger it served as additional evidence that Moscow and Washington were acting in tandem to check the ill effects the Jackson-Vanik Amendment might have.

It availed little. The Soviets would not be babied along, at least not in public. "We responded, we gave you the sign," Dobrynin angrily observed when Jewish leaders would not back away from the amendment, "now what is your counter response." [60] Moscow found no one with whom to negotiate. On 26 November the Trade Act of 1974, its waiver clause rewritten, was finally reported out of the Finance Committee where it had been holed up for almost a year. On 11 December, a year after it had passed the House, the Trade Act of 1974 passed the Senate and was on its way to a conference committee to iron out the minor differences between the two measures. The bill emerged a week later, supposedly now ready for Ford's signature, when the delicate house of cards collapsed.

Unheralded, a measure was quietly incubated in a subcommittee of the Senate Banking Committee by Sen. Adlai Stevenson III limiting the Export-Import Bank's credit to the Soviet Union to a total of $300 million dollars over a four-year period without prior approval of Congress. Two days later the Senate overwhelmingly passed the Jackson and the Stevenson amendments together. Such a paltry extension of credit combined with the Kremlin's other reservations about the Jackson amendment made its rejection of the agreement a foregone conclusion. That would remain the case even with the president's power to waive restrictions for a maximum of eighteen months, which softened the amendment. On 18 December, two days before Congress was scheduled to vote on the entire package, the Soviet newspaper *Tass* published Gromyko's original letter "categorically reject[ing]" the agreement. It came as a surprise since at the November summit meeting at Vladivostok, Brezhnev had reconfirmed the agreement embodied in the letter exchange with Jackson. Moreover, Sen. Russell Long, who would act as floor manager of the trade bill, wrung an agreement from President Ford that he would not oppose congressional passage of a cargo preference bill to favor U.S. shipping. After Congress passed Section 402 of the Trade Act (the Jackson-Vanik Amendment) on 3 January, Ford signed the entire bill a week later.

On 14 January, having faced Gromyko's earlier denial that such an agreement was ever entered into, Kissinger made public the Soviet rejection of the treaty. As if to add salt to the wound, Moscow at the same time also rejected a plan for a $7 billion joint venture to develop the Yakutsk gas fields in Soviet Asia. Ford, an inveterate free trader anxious to toll some diplomatic victories before the 1978 election, keenly regretted the failure to come to an agreement on trade with the Soviets. He informed Sen. Long of his intention to introduce new legislation to correct the flaws of the newly passed trade law, and he issued Executive Order 11846, which in compliance with the trade act created a new East-West Foreign Trade Board.[61] True to his word, the efforts to purge the trade act of the amendment went forward and with it the arguments about what happened and who was to blame. Senators Jackson, Javits, Ribicoff, and Vanik also issued a joint statement stating that they believed in the efficacy of trade but also in the Universal Declaration of Human Rights. They hoped that the Soviet Union would find it possible to cooperate "at some future date."

In his news conference on the evening of 14 January, Kissinger, foregoing an opportunity to blame the sponsors of the amendment, expressed his continuing intent to "bring about improved relations between the United States and the Soviet Union" but clearly détente had been given a blow from which it would not soon recover.[62] Why a battle-hardened Kissinger risked dealing with a mercurial Senator Jackson whose real motive he suspected was to undermine the policy of détente is not as puzzling as it seems. It was in fact a desperate effort to salvage what remained of détente and the executive initiative on which it depended. "[He] had that kind of exaggerated self-confidence," according to one of Jackson's assistants.[63] But assurances that an acceptable trade agreement would come to pass in the next congress were no longer credible. Kissinger's public career would soon end.

In the meantime July 1975 witnessed a disastrous shortfall in Soviet grain production that triggered a five-day buying spree in the American grain market. The massive purchase of 345 million bushels of wheat, corn, and barley without special long-range credit arrangements created the impression that the Jackson-Vanik imbroglio may have been much ado about nothing. The members of the U.S.-USSR Trade and Economic Council which, after its founding in 1973, lobbied endlessly against the amendment, were happy. But the unforeseen giant sale, though it was below the minimum of six million metric tons set by the Ford administration, seriously upset the American market by raising the domestic price of grain products.

After the debacle Kissinger encountered problems with Jewish communal leaders who denied that the blow to détente was somehow a Jewish responsibility. He was informed that his "effort to rewrite history" did not play well in the Jewish community. It was not the Jackson amendment that "inflamed the Russians" but the accompanying limitation on credit.[64] When Gromyko's letter of repudiation was made public, Stanley Lowell and Charlotte Jacobson, acting as members of the executive board of the NCSJ, agreed to withhold public comment until there was some clarification. All the organizations accepted the stricture on issuing press statements except the American Jewish Congress (AJCong), which had had serious reservations about the amendment all along and now planned a statement explaining its position. It argued that if Gromyko's statement were true, then the trade act containing the objectionable amendment did not warrant Jewish support. Only the intercession of Stanley Lowell, who was also chairman of the AJCong Governing Council, prevented an open split in Jewish opinion from becoming newsworthy. In the end neither Kissinger, who was less than truthful, nor Jackson, who some felt was using the Jewish communal support for his own purposes, could be trusted. Eugene Gold, a former president of the NCSJ, took the position that the Jewish community had been "screwed" and that they should now call for a veto of the Trade Act.[65] A few days later, after Ford had pledged to use the waiver, a letter stating the NCSJ position on the events that had transpired was finally sent to the White House. It seemed as if the final disposition of the Jackson amendment, which had not originated in the Jewish community, would also not be determined by it.

■   Many questions concerning the Jackson-Vanik Amendment imbroglio remain unanswered. Was there an unspoken commitment made to Kissinger by the Soviets that was then repudiated by Gromyko in his 26 October letter? In the vain hope that he could still make some adjustments on the numbers with Jackson, Kissinger informed neither Congress nor the Jewish leadership of Gromyko's earlier letter repudiating the agreement. Were Jackson's motives political, as Kissinger maintains, or were they propelled by humanitarian concerns? Was the contretemps caused by a last desperate effort by Kissinger to protect his détente policy by finessing the Kremlin. But within days a new congressional development, the Stevenson amendment to a routine bill extending the life of the Export-Import Bank, delivered the death blow by severely limiting the crucial credit outlay required by the Soviets to carry on.[66] In the words of Peter Lakeland, a former aide to Senator Javits, "it just got sprung out of nowhere," and caught both the White House staff and the Jewish leadership by surprise.[67] Was there simply bad staff work that did not pick up the threat the Stevenson Amendment posed? Kissinger believed that the amendment was actually Jackson's doing in order to get a "double lock" on East-West trade policy.[68] Jackson, who may have viewed it as a kind of backup for his amendment, announced his support together with eighteen other senators whose position was probably related to their opposition to the pending

SALT agreement and to their chagrin regarding the Great Grain Robbery of 1972. Like the Jackson amendment before it, the Stevenson Amendment did not emanate from Jewish sources. The momentum for cutting credit to the Soviet Union had anti-détente roots that exploited the emigration issue brought to the fore by the Jackson amendment.

Finally, there is the question of determining to what extent Moscow's failure to approve the trade agreement affected Soviet economic well-being and the condition of Soviet Jewry. Some researchers believe that the withholding of suitable credit arrangements under the Jackson amendment played only a minor role in determining Soviet behavior. But when the Stevenson Amendment further limited credit the Kremlin may have decided to cut its losses. The Soviet leadership, after all, had witnessed how an issue concerning the fate of Soviet Jewry was brought to the very center of the American foreign policy-making process. For them it indicated the prevalence of a strong Jewish influence in the American corridors of power. For some it may have buttressed an image of a Jewish conspiracy prevalent in pre-Revolutionary Russia. It may be that "Scoop" Jackson also thought in terms of Jewish political influence. But if his motivation was to garner Jewish political assets for his next campaign to win the Democratic 1976 presidential campaign, then like the Soviets he may have overestimated Jewish political clout. The Democratic nomination went to a relative unknown, Jimmy Carter, the Democratic governor of Georgia.[69] The Jewish voter in that election reverted to its traditional loyalty to the Democrat party to help Carter gain his narrow victory.

But Max Fisher and Henry Jackson deserve some attention because the role they played inadvertently confirms what some Soviet leaders believed about Jewish influence in the corridors of American power. Fisher's position does not lend itself to normal categorization as a Jewish leader. Despite the absence of an official position as a leader of a Jewish communal organization and his atypical conservative political views, his voice was heeded in the Jewish organizational world and in Israel. Raised in a small Midwestern town and a star college football player and a lifelong Republican, Fisher was accepted as one of their own. He was an enormously successful party fund-raiser and very generous with his own fortune.[70]

He began to play that bridging role between the Republican party and the world of Jewish politics as a supporter of George Romney, the former governor of Michigan and a Republican presidential hopeful in 1968. At one point in his career, Fisher held every major leadership post in the Jewish philanthropic and Zionist world. Yet he was not a shtadlan in the ordinary sense.[71] He provided American Jewish leaders with an access to the Nixon administration they otherwise would not have had. But it came at the price of adherence to the administration's policy of "quiet" diplomacy. He projected an unusual influence in the Republican Party, which in 1970 boasted few moneyed Jews who also held important leadership positions in the Jewish Agency for Israel, a unique quasi-official agency of the world Zionist movement. He first approached the Nixon administration in 1970 seeking intercession to gain clemency for the convicted Leningrad hijackers. True to his word, he convinced a number of United Jewish Appeal's "big-givers" to contribute to the Republican Party. For a time his was the only Jewish voice that was heard in the Nixon Oval Office. It was Fisher who suggested to John Mitchell, who became head of the Nixon campaign team in 1972, that the Soviet Jewry issue was one of the keys to increasing the Jewish vote for Republican candidates. As distasteful as Nixon may have seemed to the Jewish voter, Fisher endlessly pointed out that it was from the president's office that the awesome power of the American government was exercised. The Soviet Jewry movement could not hope to be effective without Nixon's support. The same advice was given to Israeli political leaders. He aim was to make the Conference of Presidents the official voice of American Jewry and himself the official channel. But in the case of the Jackson-Vanik Amendment the Cold War entanglement that was linked to the question of détente became too much, even for Fisher. He could weaken Jewish support at critical junctures by calling in dozens of political debts owed to him by Jewish leaders, but in the end he could not deliver the Jewish community to the administration.

If Fisher garnered only mixed support from American Jews the affirmative feeling for Scoop Jackson is virtually unanimous. Only George Shultz is rated close to him in appreciation. In years to come historians may conclude that Jackson's amendment had little to do with the Jewish interest and everything to do with Jackson's hatred of the Soviet system and his presidential ambitions. American Jewry's hesitant support of the amendment, which eventually catapulted the Soviet Jewish emigration issue unto the Cold War agenda, signaling it out from the many similar human rights questions, served as a political lever for Jackson's ambitions. Kissinger initially considered Jackson an ally with minor tactical differences. But he soon changed his mind and viewed him as an implacable foe of détente with an all-consuming ambition to occupy the Oval Office. There is much in Jackson's background to affirm the notion that his interest in the Jewish aspect of Soviet repression was fortuitous and became merely one of several human rights issues to which he committed himself. A Norwegian Lutheran from Washington with little prior contact with Jews, there is little in his political career to indicate a special feeling about Jewish victimization. Washington had few Jewish voters. He spoke of his visit to the notorious Buchenwald concentration camp as "the most profound experience of his life," but there are some who question the veracity of the story.[72] First elected to the Senate in 1941, Jackson took advantage of Roosevelt's exemption of members of Congress from the draft.

Whatever the case, Jackson's seeming political opportunism was balanced by sympathy for history's victims, which was sustained throughout his political career. He was one of the Senate's earliest supporters of the civil rights movement. Most of his press releases on the Jackson-Vanik Amendment also focus on other suppressed groups in the Soviet monolith. Jews were not his exclusive concern. His opponents considered Jackson a political opportunist but his friends and assistants viewed him as a rare combination of political acumen and idealistic motivation. Kissinger considered him the toughest political opponent he faced because he was not so much a "Cold Warrior" as "a master psychological warrior."[73] His animus was focused specifically against the Soviets. He felt deeply for those victimized by the Soviet system but he applauded the Nixon administration's opening to an equally tyrannical China, which he felt would lessen the Soviet threat. Like Melvin Laird, secretary of defense, he opposed the détente that produced the SALT agreement. Both believed that the Soviet Union posed a special threat to the nation and was the crueler despot. Unlike Kissinger, who sought to manage the crises, Jackson's goal was to eliminate the Soviet system, preferably by peaceful means. He saw himself as the political leader with the vision to fulfill that goal. The practical politician in him must have made him aware that American Jewry had become a formidable influence on the American political landscape. His assistant, Richard Perle, with whom he had a close relationship, kept him apprised of the neoconservative wave developing in American Jewish political culture. But Jackson remained an old-fashioned conservative in foreign policy. He might even have sensed that without the financial and political support of the Jewish community that supplied a considerable proportion of his campaign funds it would be difficult to win the presidential nomination in 1972 and 1976. But clearly his strong support of Israel and the Soviet Jewry movement went beyond mere political opportunism. All who worked with him attest to his genuine feeling for the plight of Soviet Jewry. His political alliance was strongest with organized labor, with whom he shared a firm long-standing wariness of the Soviet Union. He was a strong proponent of defense spending, but again there was a strange duality. As in the case of the amendment the "Senator from Boeing" was doing good while doing well. But in the end the matter of Jackson's political opportunism was not relevant once the Soviet Jewry problem became a Cold War issue. Once that happened it no longer belonged to the Jewish community alone. It became part of the larger Cold War arena and would be buffeted by its thrusts and parries. Unanswered is the question of whether the Jackson-Vanik Amendment foiled a better opportunity to "rescue" Soviet Jews through the administration's strategy of a staggered emigration on a yearly basis. The answer to that depends on the question of trust. Could the Soviet government have been trusted to carry out the informal agreement Kissinger had reached with Gromyko? History gave neither side an opportunity to test that proposition.

▪   For those who believed that the ups and downs of Soviet emigration policy and treatment of Jews are best correlated with events outside the Soviet sphere, the months following the failure of the Ford administration to find a compromise on Jackson-Vanik were full of foreboding. No longer involved in a negotiation, the Soviet authorities could give full vent to their wrath. The years after the passage of the Jackson and Stevenson amendments were especially bitter ones for the refuseniks, so much so that some wondered whether those legislators advocating the amendment had not overreached.[74] Lowell cabled to Kissinger that new arrests and low immigration figures for the month of February indicated that the Soviet authorities were exacting their pound of flesh. As president of the NCSJ, Lowell demanded an immediate American response by raising the issue at the meeting of the UN Human Rights Commission in Geneva.[75] As predicted, Soviet repudiation of the trade agreement translated into loss of leverage in Moscow, where it counted. Release of "refuseniks" now occurred most often on a case-by-case basis, sometimes through intercession of businessmen such as Donald Kendall of Pepsico and Armand Hammer of Occidental petroleum.[76] With the exception of 1979, emigration entered a lean phase that lasted almost seven years. The hope for help from Moscow to bring the Vietnam debacle to an acceptable close unwound. In April 1975, four months after Congress passed the Trade Act, the North Vietnamese disregarded the Geneva peace agreement and captured Saigon. Yet in August the Soviets signed on to the Helsinki Accords, which would go far in resolving the emigration crisis on an internationally agreed upon human rights basis. At the time few suspected that the accords would be one of the keys to gaining the release of the Jews who wanted to leave.

The two-year struggle over the Jackson-Vanik Amendment marked the first round in the struggle against the policy of détente. In the 1976 campaign right-wing Republicans joined Jackson and his neoconservative supporters in condemning the détente policy until Ford ruled out the use of the term in his speeches.

Kissinger himself was purported to have said, "Détente is a word I would like to forget."[77] Small wonder, in 1973 he had witnessed the Soviets directly threatening Israel, and in 1974 Moscow committed Cuban troops to Angola. Speaking of the Yom Kippur War, Richard Maass responded to Deputy Secretary of State Kenneth Rush, who argued against the amendment, that "[he] cannot help feeling that had the détente been real there would not have been a war."[78] The domestic impact of the Jackson-Vanik Amendment was devastating for the Nixon administration. It was one of the few issues that conservatives could sponsor that also attracted liberals, an unbeatable combination.

Another way to view the amendment is to see it as part of a congressional reassertion of its prerogative in the foreign policy area after having ignominiously given it up with the Gulf of Tonkin resolution.[79] One reaction was the War Powers Act of 1973 which established stringent rules for consulting congress before troops could ever again be committed to hostilities. Together with Jackson-Vanik, they mark the end of the so-called imperial presidency to which Nixon aspired. Even while Kissinger insisted that Watergate had no effect on the management of America's foreign affairs he must have understood when negotiating with Jackson and finally offering him a Letter of Agreement that his control of and ability to make policy had been compromised.[80]

◼ There is something almost comical in the reversal of roles that occurred in the conflict over the Jackson-Vanik Amendment. What one sees is a Christian senator leading a reluctant Jewish cavalry in an attack to open the gates of a closed society so that their brethren may come to the Promised Land whose gates are guarded by a heavily accented Jewish refugee. But if the Jackson-Vanik imbroglio and the Jewish emigration issue that was at one end of it are framed as a political issue at home and a Cold War issue abroad, then they emerge as a paradox. From one perspective the Jackson-Vanik Amendment marked a great Jewish victory, a turning point in the long history of American Jewish advocacy before the American seat of power. For some Jewish activists it may have compensated for the failure to energetically play that role during the years of the Holocaust. It was the first piece of human rights legislation passed by Congress aimed at ameliorating the condition of an oppressed foreign minority. That it addressed a Jewish concern and boosted the moral of the activists here and in the Soviet Union should be seen as an added dividend. It was the militant activists here and in the Soviet Union who became the most passionate supporters of the amendment. American Jewry ultimately supported the amendment but many continued to be far from certain about its benefits and the political motivation of its backers. Despite that doubt the incorpora-tion of the amendment into the trade act over the staunch opposition of the White House enhanced the perception of American Jewish power at home and in the Kremlin. It is not unreasonable to imagine that Soviet leaders then, as Muslim leaders today, came to believe that Jewish influence in the corridors of American power was supreme.

Finally, and perhaps most important for American Jewry, the Jackson-Vanik Amendment helped remove the stigma of Holocaust abandonment that for so many American Jews had become part of their cultural baggage. In universal terms too it can be argued, as Sharansky did, that the Jackson-Vanik Amendment was a great victory for the forces of justice and humanity because it represented the first example in American-Soviet relations of a policy based squarely on a human rights position.[81] Above all, it strengthened the hands and hearts of those forces within the Soviet Union, Jewish refuseniks as well as non-Jewish democra-tizers that had come to believe that they stood alone in their struggle against So-viet tyranny.

Sometimes the perception of victory is only in the eyes of the beholder. Noth-ing that the Jackson-Vanik Amendment promised came to pass. Once the lure of trade and credit were taken off the table the Soviet leaders stopped transacting business and the position of Soviet Jewry actually worsened. Except for a tempo-rary increase in emigration flow in 1973, 1974, and 1979, there was no discernable alteration of Soviet emigration policy until Gorbachev came to power in 1985. After 1979 it became almost impossible to leave the Soviet Union. The American economy gave up the trade that might have come its way had the Soviets accepted the trade agreement. Organized labor lost the possibility of an expanded job mar-ket. The U.S. Treasury lost almost $1 billion dollars that might have come to it as part of a payback for lend-lease.[82] Most important, the Jackson-Vanik Amendment simply did not work in its basic motivation of changing Soviet behavior. Soviet policy was hostile during the October War period in the early stages of Jackson-Vanik. The Soviets invaded Afghanistan in 1979 and used Cuban proxies in Angola in 1982. All of the above are what led Professor Marshall Goldman to conclude that Jackson-Vanik was economically "counterproductive" and diplomatically only of limited effectiveness.[83]

The arguments for the amendment emanating from the anti-détente position were no less unforgiving. Scoop Jackson and his followers were convinced that "softness" toward Moscow was itself a cause of instability and threat. In signing SALT I on 30 September 1972, the opponents of détente argued that Kissinger was, in Lenin's words, being a "useful idiot." At the final hearings of the Senate Finance Committee in December 1974, Sen. Harry Byrd, disturbed that the Soviet Union received $587 million in the three years prior to the amendment, posed a question to Kissinger in the same vein: "Whatever its intended purpose, does not the extending of long-term credit to the Soviets get them out of an economic bind while permitting them to continue their high rate of defense spending?" [84] It was a crucial question whose answer only remotely related to Jewish emigration. What the critics of détente found wanting was a trade transaction that put fungible money into the hands of a would-be aggressor. The amendment to the Trade Act of 1974 was their answer to that.

We have noted that in the American Jewish polity the question of retaining the amendment became a cause of much rancor between the more militant UCSJ and the NCSJ. The AJCong especially had to be cajoled by Stanley Lowell, president of the NCSJ, not to break the common front in support of the amendment. Feeling that an opportunity to extricate all of Soviet Jewry in a staggered way had been lost, Phil Baum, its assistant executive director, rued the rigidity of the Jewish leadership.[85] Rabbi Hertzberg, president of AJCong, openly accused a group of extreme militants led by Benjamin Levich, whose "heads are on the bloc," and whom Moscow will never release, of pushing for extremes rather than negotiating Soviet Jewry out of Russia.[86] Conflict over the amendment also placed an additional strain on the delicate relations between American Jewry and Israel. There was fear that the militant activists would fail to understand that the security of Israel rested on the goodwill of the Nixon administration to resupply the Israel arsenal after the October war.[87] Sometimes the arguments on either side balanced each other so completely that they could not be resolved. The Soviet activists, now "intoxicated" with their victory, argued that as long as the weapons of coercion remain in their hands no assurances given by the Kremlin should be trusted. Those who insisted on flexibility argued that the best results were achieved by the process of negotiating itself. That is the way the silent concessions on the education tax, the increased emigration after 1973, and the promise to reduce harassment were achieved.

Few foresaw the demise of the Soviet empire and fewer still were able to foresee the strange turn the emigration issue would take when it was reframed as a human rights rather than solely as a Jewish issue. In the discussion that follows we learn how the Soviet Jewry issue was transformed when a new breed of Soviet Jewish emigrants chose not to settle in Israel.

FIVE Dropping Out

The conflict over the Jackson-Vanik Amendment did not come to an end when the Soviets rejected the informal agreement on its implementation. It would reemerge periodically as the trade law came up for reconsideration. The determination of the Ford administration to push for removal of the amendment was now matched by Moscow's seeming indifference.[1] But in the American Jewish polity, where there were endless arguments concerning the drop of emigration rates and their possible relationship to Moscow's repudiation of the trade agreement, the support behind the amendment began to fragment by 1977 and especially after 1980 when it became apparent that without the allurement of credit the Soviets would not play the game.[2]

At the same time the motivation of the Soviet Jews seeking to emigrate was also undergoing a change. The applicants for visas were less likely to possess a burning desire to settle in the Jewish homeland and more likely to seek haven where economic opportunity for themselves and their children could be found. When these emigrants arrived at the processing center in Vienna they were increasingly likely to disregard the Israeli visa that enabled them to leave the Soviet Union and choose to resettle elsewhere.[3] (Henceforth we refer to them as "dropouts.")

After all else is peeled away the dropout phenomenon is partly attributable to a legal quirk in the peculiar improvised administrative structure of the Soviet Union. We have seen that the Soviet Union did not recognize that there could be a desire to leave and therefore had no immigration law as such. Rather, there was a series of ad hoc regulations involving special cases such as the repatriation of Poles between 1956 and 1958. Another factor was the absence of diplomatic relations between Israel and the Soviet Union even though an Israeli visa was the only legal way to leave Russia. Occasionally there were individual cases of reunification of families that were sanctioned by the Soviet authorities as a humanitarian gesture. It was this precedent that allowed the Soviet authorities to conceal what might otherwise be construed as a vote of no confidence in the Soviet system. The Jewish emigration was based on this fragile reed. Emigration required a *vyzov*, a written notarized statement from a "first degree" family member to serve as evidence of the existence of such a relative with whom to be reunified and an affidavit of support. Much to Israel's chagrin the Soviet authorities did not seem concerned when the Israeli visa, for which the *vyzov* was intended, was used to go elsewhere. In several cases the KGB used the Israeli visa as an escape valve to rid themselves of particular troublesome non-Jewish dissidents.[4] Undoubtedly, the exodus of Soviet Jews would have been considerably reduced had the emigrants not been aware that once having left the confines of the Soviet Union access to the United States was possible.

But that access was not possible before World War II, the period when the restrictive Immigration Act of 1924 that featured a quota system based on the national origins was in effect. As noted previously, the law and its amendment in 1929 were rooted in the fear that the nation was about to be flooded with millions of penniless Jews from war-devastated Eastern Europe. The effects of the restrictive immigration laws were devastating during the years of the Holocaust. But generally unknown was the fact that the Roosevelt administration did circumvent the immigration law in two cases. In 1938 Roosevelt allowed the extension of visitor visas for six months, and in 1940 the State Department also ordered the admission for internment, outside of the immigration quotas, of German natives living in various Latin American countries thought to be involved in espionage or otherwise threatening to American security under the Declaration of Panama and the Act of Havana. Again in July 1944, the Roosevelt administration permitted a thousand survivors, most Jewish, to temporarily enter the United States on the same basis.[5] Gradually, a process of circumventing the immigration law by a series of emergency measures implemented by executive order or administrative decree was put in place. But in the years following the war this token generosity, which resulted in sheltering almost a thousand survivors in Oswego, New York, under the Army Relocation Authority, was reversed. Under the Truman administration Congress was reluctant to admit displaced persons. The Displaced Persons Act of 1948 was an emergency bill almost as intent at excluding Jews as the original Immigration Act of 1924. News of the Holocaust did not yet arouse congressional sympathy. The American Jewish Congress (AJCong) and other Jewish agencies advocated that the act be vetoed. Nevertheless, the first Jewish displaced persons began to enter the country under its refugee provision. By 1948 Congress began to think seriously that, rather then depending on ad hoc emergency bills tailored for each case, the basic immigration law should be more liberal and flexible to fit the new

Cold War situation. The law to admit displaced persons in 1948 and 1950 and the admission of thousands of Hungarian refugees after the 1956 uprising are examples of such ad hoc laws. In 1953 the Refugee Relief Act admitted 200,000 additional displaced persons and put the basic tenets of American refugee policy in place.

These additional refinements and those added in the sixties would not have been necessary had the controversial McCarran-Walters Immigration Bill (1952) become the omnibus measure refugee advocates hoped for. Instead, it revealed that the old Nordic supremacy idea on which the quota system was based was still alive and well. The measure was passed over Truman's veto but in his veto message a new rationale for admission of refugees was given. It was not only necessary to offer a haven to those in need for humanitarian reasons but a properly structured immigration law would also enable us to enrich our economy with skills possessed by these potential new immigrants.

Ironically, the McCarran law finally recognized the special needs of refugees in the context of the Cold War by distinguishing between immigrants and refugees. The years that followed witnessed a series of refugee laws culminating in the Migration and Refugee Assistance Act of 1962, which set aside a number of places for refugees and also ensured financial support for transportation, housing, and retraining, if necessary. In addition the law strengthened the parole provision of the U.S. Immigration and Nationality Act (1952) that gave the attorney general the authority to grant entrance to the country on a case-by-case basis.[6] In 1965 the preference formula based on national origins was finally swept entirely away and replaced by one including, among other criteria, reunification of families. A finishing touch was added in 1976 when the limit of annual refugee admissions was raised from 20,000 per country to a ceiling of 120,000 total refugee admissions. Needed skills received preference but, while gaining access to America remained difficult, the legal basis for emigration from behind the iron curtain was now in place and was supplemented by generous refugee assistance laws in 1962 and 1980.[7]

In a word, by 1972 American immigration policy had developed from a restrictionist basis to a comparatively liberal one for Cold War refugees. That change proved a very seductive one for those desiring to leave the Soviet Union, but it also contained serious flaws that became a factor in the conflict that would later develop regarding the dropout problem. Congress followed the definition of "refugee" established by the Geneva Convention, which speaks of candidates having to have a "well founded fear" of what their fate might be should they return to their country. The definition of refugee also required candidates to be outside of the country of their nationality. The irony was that in order for Soviet Jewish emigrants to become refugees under American law they had first to obtain visas from Israel because that was the only way to leave the Soviet Union.

For the potential emigrant the process of leaving the Soviet Union was full of uncertainty. We have already noted that once the emigrants' intentions became known as a result of their applications for exit visas, it usually meant placing themselves in social and economic limbo. Employment position and income could be lost, housing could be threatened, and often the hostility of neighbors could make life uncomfortable. Choosing to emigrate meant choosing to enter a pariah state that could last several years before the precious visa was finally in hand. For some applicants who had run afoul of the authorities or who could be accused of having been exposed to classified security matters, the necessary exit permit never came. Before it was granted emigrants had still to undergo an approval process from their "connectors," supervisors at work, their concierges, the police, and sometimes permission from relatives. Not surprisingly, the process resembled the experience of checking out of a penal institution. Undoubtedly the discrepancy between the number of *vyzovs* issued and the number actually used is related to the defection of those who found the process so onerous that they could not go through with it. For those who prevailed and succeeded in getting out the mechanics of dropping out could be equally daunting.

The emigrants would arrive by overnight train to Vienna, which served as a central processing center for the Jewish helping agencies. Because they traveled on an Israeli visa a representative of the Jewish Agency for Israel (JAFI) would conduct the initial interview. Here dropouts had to know beforehand that, despite the cajoling of the interviewer, they could not be compelled to settle in Israel. They also had to overcome the uncertainties of their position as dependent emigrants to insist on becoming a dropout. At Schoenau Castle, where the processing took place, the knowledge that the American Jewish Joint Distribution Committee (JDC) and the Hebrew Immigrant Aid Society (HIAS), backed by the Austrian government that hosted the operation and standing ready to support the right of emigrants to choose, helped them withstand the interviewer's psychological pressure to continue to Israel. If they prevailed they would then be handed over to representatives of HIAS and JDC for further processing. After 1978 the two agencies, the JDC assuming responsibility for housing and support and the HIAS for all activities related to furnishing them with the required papers, transportation arrangements, and "close relative" documentation, were able to offer a comparatively attractive package to the emigrants as a result of an appropriation by the Carter administration that almost matched the financial outlays of the two agencies.[8] In 1979, $140 million was awarded by the federal government to fourteen refugee absorption projects, far outpacing anything that Israel could offer to lighten the cost of resettlement. That largess later became a bone of contention when Israel claimed that the emigrants were being seduced to dropout by the government-supported Jewish social welfare agencies. The Israeli complaint was a portent that the efforts of Jewish legislators and leaders to open the American gates to Soviet emigrants were setting the stage for conflict between the American Jewish and Israeli Soviet Jewry movements.

The dropout phenomenon was present from the year that the emigration trickle started.[9] Between 1972 and 1976, 14,927 settled in the United States with HIAS assistance and an additional 720 per year emigrated directly without the Israeli visas based on family reunification.[10] The total dropout rate of about 10 percent might have been higher between 1966 and 1971 had there been a viable American alternative. It was partly due to the growing American support for refugees and partly the removal of a fifty-year ban on emigration by the Politburo in the spring of 1971 that set the stage for *Neshira,* the Hebrew term for dropping out.

By 1973 the original Zionized emigration began to thin and was gradually replaced by emigrants who were the end product of three generations of forced assimilation and knew little about the Judaism to which they were heir. Having seized upon an opportunity to leave, sometimes evidenced by as little as the word *Yevrei* stamped in their internal passport, they too became subject to the limbo state of visa applicants. Some of the most militant refuseniks possessed little sense of their Jewish identity at the outset of the emigration process. Some revealed that it was the abusive emigration process itself that converted marginal Jews to politicized refuseniks with a strong Zionist bent. In the early years most continued to identify with Russian culture.[11] Between 1967 and 1975 those who chose to emigrate formed a small percentage of the 2.1 million Jews, estimated by the Soviet census of 1970. Of these, the dropouts composed a still smaller group. By 1980 those proportions had changed. The Soviet Jewish emigration stream remained proportionately small but the number rejecting resettlement in Israel now formed the majority. They stemmed from the urban centers of European Russia, primarily major cities such as Moscow, Leningrad, Odessa, and Kiev but also middle-sized cities such as Kharkov, Minsk, and Volgograd.[12] Compared to the average Soviet Jew, the dropouts possessed a higher level of formal education and professionalization.[13] The fact that the dropout cohort especially possessed some characteristics of an educated elite may partly explain Moscow's reluctance to part with them.

That comparatively high education level may also have served as the fuel for risking emigration because positions commensurate with their educational level had become limited for their children as a matter of public policy. Positions in the military, diplomatic corps, and certain branches of academia were virtually off limits for Jews. Children could no longer aspire to the social status level achieved by their parents. Education remained a particularly strong value in Soviet Jewish family life. The general limitation of opportunities for higher education had a drastic effect because in Soviet society, where a professional posting was assigned by government, the link between higher education and professional certification was very direct. Surveys done of dropouts in Rome by HIAS cite the sharp curtailment of educational opportunities for Jewish children as the most frequent reason given for the decision to emigrate.[14] The dropouts were an urbanized elite group conditioned to achieve with nowhere to go in Soviet society and penalized for a Jewishness they hardly knew.[15] There was in this condition a formula for a social explosion that instead took the form of an emigration movement. Despite decades of social engineering to refashion Soviet Jewry to better fit into Soviet society and economy, in 1970 it continued to bear a strong resemblance to the urban and often urbane Jewish population aggregations in the West and, like these communities, the rate of intermarriage was high. That too was reflected in the dropout pool and frequently played a role in rejecting resettlement in a Jewish state. Affected by the rise in national consciousness that came with the victory in the June 1967 war, the earliest group of emigrants composed of Zionists, many possessing the passion of the newly converted, was almost exhausted by 1975.

It was from this stratum that the militant activists who energized the world movement were drawn. The picture composed from the rudimentary anecdotal impressions of social workers shows that by 1978 two-thirds of the emigrants gave non-Zionist reasons for emigration and rarely mentioned their need for cultural fulfillment, a favorite rational presented by Zionist activists. Eduard Kuznetsov, involved in the Leningrad hijacking in 1971, noted simply that the emigrants "are not Zionists, or any other ists."[16] By 1987, Kuznetsov's observation might have been extended. Not only were the dropouts not Zionists, more than 25 percent of emigrants were not Jews, according to Jewish law.[17] Some Soviet authorities may have been close to the truth when they counseled that given better treatment and access, Zionist sentiment among the emigrants would not be strong enough to cause Jewish families to uproot themselves. But they failed to consider the impact of native anti-Semitism, especially in the 1980s, and a government policy of exclusion that increasingly denied Jews access to the channels of mobility in Soviet society. Jews were upwardly mobile in the twenties but that was less true in the seventies. Unlike the free societies of the West, Soviet society offered no alternate path such as small business to find an outlet for talent and energy. That loss of hope fueled the ranks of the refuseniks, some of whom had achieved prominence, especially in medicine and the sciences, but then found themselves with no place to go but abroad to continue their development. Above and beyond the possibilities opened by U.S. refugee policy and the support role of the JDC and HIAS, a crucial factor in the emigration of potential dropouts was the feeling that Soviet government and society did not mean Jews well. There was no hope for a future.

Some residual sense of Jewishness remained despite the systematic destruction of the cultural institutions, the schools, and religious institutions through which ethnic identity is transmitted. One fourth of those questioned expressed affinity for Yiddish and Jewish folk songs, even in their Stalinized versions. Many were still able to recall a Passover Seder or a Yiddish-speaking grandparent. There was in the pool of those who chose to emigrate an unknown number for whom even a nostalgic sentimentalized version of Jewishness carried great weight. But with the exception of a small minority that memory of a memory rarely translated into a desire to shape one's life according to the religious tenets of Judaism. Whether they were zionistically oriented or potential dropouts, the emigrants were overwhelmingly secular and russified. At the same time there was also a sense of pride in being Jewish. According to the anecdotal record it was based on a mundane conventional wisdom that Jews do not drink or beat their wives. Jews from the isolated communities behind the Urals or in the Caucasus, where stronger Jewish identities were still generated, were less likely than heartland Jews to dropout.[18] When such Jews emigrated they were still able to imagine that they were returning to Zion.

At the same time that urban life accelerated assimilation it also placed potential emigrants in a better position to consider applying for a visa. Often they had access to "outside" information through the network of prior emigrants who kept them posted on two matters crucial to their decision: the economic and security situation in Israel that related to finding a position commensurate or nearly so with their training, and what the "on the ground" situation was in Schoenau Castle where the initial processing occurred. After about ten days dropouts would be transported to Rome for further processing by HIAS. The period of uncertainty until access to the United States or other countries could be arranged was trouble-some not only for emigrants but for the personnel of the JDC, who assumed fiscal and social responsibility for the emigrants and their families while HIAS took care of the paperwork. This outside source of information emanating from earlier em-igrants who wrote back to family and friends would play an important role in the immigration process and is similar to earlier waves of immigration. It was a Jewish version of the "America letter" cited by Marcus Hansen, a Pulitzer prize-winning American historian of immigration, who viewed the "how to" information and general appraisal of the situation those letters contained as an important source of the immigration ebb and flow.[19] In the case of Israel where absorption facilities were sometimes poor and economic conditions were wanting and war threatened, the letters were often negative. Predictably, the controlled Soviet press gave wide promotion to such negative descriptions of the situation in Israel and often embel-lished such reports with erroneous information to discourage visa applicants. That too affected the dropout rate as did the difficulty of learning Hebrew from a Slavic base language. What is difficult to measure is the effect of the attitude of the Israelis who understood the need for immigration but at the same time resented the sacrifice it entailed. The reception in Israel, a key part of the difficult absorp-tion process, became the source of much difficulty and complaints to write home about.

After 1975 conditions grew more favorable to begin the long emigration process. In contrast to earlier years, 75 percent of the applicants received permis-sion to leave within six months. To the dismay of Israel the dropout rate rose and continued to do so even after care was taken to make the emigrant as comfortable and welcome as possible. Israel's special efforts had little effect because in most cases the decision to drop out had been made early in the emigration process.

After the rejection of the Trade Act of 1974 Soviet authorities seemed unen-cumbered by considerations concerning the welfare of their economic system. In an effort to break the organized activists who now existed in virtually every major city, the Soviets turned to extreme forms of suppression; at the same time, the number of granted exit permits increased. It was hoped that this strategy would siphon off the leadership while helping to soften the American stand on disarma-ment and the granting of trade credits at the same time. With the exception of 1978 and 1979, when the Soviets wanted to get SALT II on the books and a new op-portunity to rework the trade relations existed, the years after 1975 were among the darkest for the Soviet Jewry movement. After the Soviet invasion of Afghanistan in 1979 ended the hope that SALT II might still be ratified or that a revised trade act containing generous credit provisions would be approved by Congress, Soviet authorities began reducing the number of exit permits. The *vyzov* procedure was more stringently enforced so that only "first degree" relatives, spouses, siblings, and children could be validated as "close relatives." Control of the mails sometimes enabled the KGB to block delivery of these crucial papers.[20] In Minsk young people, some beyond the age of forty, were now required to have permission from their parents to emigrate. Hoping to cut off the sources of funds that enabled visa applicants to support themselves while in economic limbo, Soviet authorities proposed imposing a 65 percent tax on all currency transfers from abroad to take effect in January 1976. The goal of the stricter regulations was to crack down on the emigration flow and cut it off entirely if possible. The rationale presented by the Anti-Zionist Committee of the Communist Party of the Soviet Union (CPSU), composed of prominent Soviet Jews and established in 1973, was that the family reunification program that began after World War II has been completed. There were no more applicants. The message was clear but it was more a Soviet aspiration than a reality.

Though some researchers challenge the barometer theory that sees the emigration flow related to events outside the Soviet Union, there is little doubt that as the hopes of détente diminished, so too did the flow of emigrants. The signing of the Helsinki Accords in August 1974 hardly diminished Cold War tensions. The final curtain on the war in Vietnam came down in April 1975 when the Communists cast aside the Geneva peace treaty and occupied Saigon. Photos of American helicopters evacuating desperate Vietnamese were featured in the media. But with the ending of this chapter in the Cold War, Kissinger's quest for Soviet mediation to bring the war to a satisfactory close was no longer operative. A burden had been lifted from American shoulders and with it the emigration of Soviet Jews, never a major concern, lost some of its Cold War urgency within the Ford administration. It barely warranted mention when the Democratic and Republican party platforms were drawn up in July and August of 1976.

The denouement came with Carter's boycotting of the Moscow Olympics scheduled for the spring of 1980. A massive sale of grain for which special low credit rates had been arranged was embargoed. In 1978 renewed possibilities for revising the trade law broke down after Sen. Jackson rejected the idea of abandoning the 60,000 annual benchmark of exit visas to be granted. To rub salt into the Kremlin's wounds in 1979 the Romanian government, which had been making a handsome profit by releasing its Jews, was granted MFN, as was the arch enemy of the Soviet Union, the People's Republic of China. In their turn the insecure Soviet authorities gave security organs a free hand to suppress dissidence. Included in their net were the Sakharovs, who were sent into an internal exile in Gorky after having spoken out against the invasion of Afghanistan.

■　In the face of the worsening situation within the Soviet Union the leaders of the Soviet Jewry movement mobilized all efforts in the area of public relations, which was in effect the only weapon remaining in their arsenal. Few were yet convinced that the Helsinki Accords would furnish a new instrument to pressure the Kremlin. That campaign to "soften" the Soviets continued unabated. At its high point it included the convening of a second international conference in Brussels to be held in February 1976. But beyond the noise, the attention-getting tactics, and mass rallies honed sharp from years of practice it was evident that without the availability of the carrot and the stick, the Soviet authorities no longer saw a need to make concessions. It was a bitter lesson for members of the Conference of Presidents and the executive committee of the National Conference on Soviet Jewry (NCSJ), who as late as July 1975 sent a cautioning statement to seventeen senators who had recently returned from being feted in the Soviet Union, which sounded suspiciously like they believed that they had retained a controlling voice in the making of foreign policy in the Soviet trade and emigration area: "The ball is now in the Soviet court and before any thought can be given to modifying the law of the land we must see action by the Soviets."[21] But little "action" from Moscow was forthcoming and lean years for the movement lay ahead.

That seemingly insoluble difficulty with the Soviet authorities was compounded by the early negative communal reactions to the absorption of the thousands of dropouts in the United States. As in the case of the Industrial Removal Office during the years of the massive Eastern European immigration at the turn of the twentieth century, it was decided that the key to successful absorption was dispersion into the interior. That required a matching of the immigrant's occupational profile with the needs and capacity of the local receiving community. The model seemed the soul of rationality on paper except that few communities believed they "needed" Soviet emigrants, and few Soviet emigrants desired dispersion to smaller Jewish communities located in the Midwest and South. Like their historic predecessors they hungered for the life in and the opportunities of the big city. By 1979, 42 percent of the emigrants had settled in New York, and seven years later the percentage had risen to 51 percent. Everywhere the cost was born by the local federations already burdened with the increase in expenses entailed in providing communal support for the aging Jewish population.

The dropout refugee stream was unusually rich in skills and talent, but these were not always relevant to the American labor market. How many shoemakers does a small community need? The per capita cost of resettlement often proved to be beyond the capacity of the local federations.[22] It was Mark Talisman, former aid to Sen. Vanik and founding member of the Washington group and who, by using Rep. Jonathan Bingham's precedent of getting an allocation of $25 million in the federal budget of 1973 to help underwrite the resettlement of Soviet immigrants in Israel, was able to convince Congress to extend that government largess for resettlement of the dropouts in America.[23] We have already noted the successful effort by the HIAS to get the emigrants reclassified as refugees, which gave them a special status outside the quota system by placing them under the State Department's Bureau of Refugee Affairs. When it developed that the State Department required evidence that there was "flight from persecution" and that the allotment of numbers of refugees to be admitted annually had to be shared with refugees from southeast Asia, Central America, and the Caribbean, the representatives of HIAS transferred many of the refugees to the attorney general's parole authority, where support was less generous but acceptance into the country more certain. The enlistment of American government aid to resettle dropouts became a crucial factor in Israel's opposition to the role of the JDC and HIAS in the emigration process. The activities of these agencies not only made an American haven more accessible, they also competed for U.S. government funds that might be allocated for resettlement in Israel. In 1973 the UN High Commission on Refugees declared a definition of "refugee" favorable to Israel. Soviet emigrants were not classified as "refugees" but would be considered "Israeli-protected persons" from the moment of their arrival in Vienna. That was the legal definition preferred by Israel because it recognized the status of the Israeli visa and indirectly of Israel's proprietary rights to resettle the emigrants. The UN definition challenged the American one that, by viewing the dropout as a refugee under American law, opened a way for the Jewish welfare agencies to apply for government matching funds.

Aside from the high cost for local federations, the absorption of the dropout ran into other problems. American Jewish patrons who thought they were rescuing a beleaguered Jewry were often disappointed in their clients who were not as Jewish as they would have liked and whose disaffection from Soviet-style state socialism translated into political conservatism to the right of the American Jewish political norm. The Soviet Jews who settled in America soon earned an undeserved reputation for criminality and misusing the welfare system. "They lie, they cheat, anything to get what they want, . . . [many] lack the basic concepts of humanity, let alone Judaism," observed one Queens Rabbi, blaming the Soviet system for having "done its work only too well."[24] By 1980 the passion for "saving" Soviet Jews had become confined to those whose impressions of Soviet Jewry were based on their original contact with the idealistic Zionized refuseniks of the early seventies.

Withal, the change of fortune of the Soviet Jewry movement that occurred after the Soviet rejection of the informal arrangement undertaken by Kissinger seemed to spur even greater effort on the part of the NCSJ and the dozens of local groups operating under the umbrella of the Union of Councils for Soviet Jewry (UCSJ). The knowledge that America's gates were open to refugees increased the request for *vyzovs* and exit permits dramatically between 1976 and 1979. The Soviet crackdown ensured a steady stream of victims whose plight could be publicized in the ongoing public relations campaign. Sharansky's arrest on the charge of treason on 15 March 1979 and his subsequent imprisonment was made into a cause célèbre with the help of his devoted wife, Avital. The six-hour interrogation in the notorious Lefortovo Prison and the numerous depredations thereafter would be publicized by a special committee headed by Rep. Robert Drinan. A proposal by the well-known attorney Alan Dershowitz to run a daily ad in the New York Times until such time as Sharansky was released was discourage by the NCSJ.[25] Aware of previous disasters in staging show trials, the Soviet authorities hesitated to commit themselves to yet another trial. No ordinary prisoner, Sharansky refused to be defended.[26] Something had changed in the ability of the KGB to conceal their activities behind closed doors. Almost every trespass in the Sharansky case was soon known to the outside activists and was duly broadcast to the world. In a perverse way the Sharansky trial, by raising the hope that the heavy-handed Soviet authorities would again blunder as they had in the Leningrad kidnapping trial (1970) and the case of the education head tax, might improve the ebbing fortunes of the Soviet Jewry movement.

Structural weaknesses within the NCSJ, intended as the organizational expression of the collective American Jewish communal effort, continued to plague the movement. A series of compromises implemented when the organization was restructured in 1972 left the NCSJ financially dependent and prohibited from developing its own grass roots. That important connection that entailed communication with local agencies such as federations and Community Relations Councils (CRCs) was supposed to be the provenance of the National Jewish Community Relations Advisory Council (NJCRAC), but in practice it hampered the activities of the NCSJ. The continuous tensions with NJCRAC concerning contact with the local communities broke out into open hostilities in 1978. The strength of the UCSJ, which had become the NCSJ's competitor, lay in its federated grassroots structure. Unlike the NCSJ it possessed control of its own grass roots. In contrast, precisely what the role of the local CRCs should be in relation to the NCSJ had constantly to be clarified.[27] Its financing was insecure. By mid-1976 the NCSJ's function was jeopardized when the Large City Budgeting Conference of the Council of Jewish Federations and Welfare Funds (CJF), which oversaw funding of NCSJ, questioned the need for an associate directorship position and the continuance of its Washington Office.[28]

In the midst of this test of the NCSJ's organizational and financial viability, the Jackson-Vanik conflict, which had consumed much of the organization's energy, was entering a second round. The push to undo the amendment came from the state, commerce, and treasury departments, supported by sections of the business community anxious to tap the Russian market. All were willing to make necessary trade concessions in turn for Soviet assurances of good faith on the emigration question that they believed held American foreign policy hostage. In addition, the united front presented by Jewish organizations in support the amendment had again weakened. The American Israel Public Affairs Committee now joined AJ-Cong and informed the NCSJ that in any forthcoming negotiations between the United States and the USSR "sacrifices in other areas" might be necessary to ensure the continued security of Israel. That translated into trade concessions to first ensure commitment to the security of Israel. So apprehensive was Jerry Goodman, the director of the NCSJ, concerning the possibility of a repeal of Jackson-Vanik that he recommended that there be a contingency to fall back on in case that became necessary.[29]

■ Lack of organizational cohesion, the historical bane of American Jewish organizational life, which increased between the elections of Carter in 1976 and Reagan in 1980, fed the sense of crisis that beset the Soviet Jewry movement. We have noted that jointly with the reorganization of the NCSJ in 1972 the UCSJ was experiencing a spurt of growth. By 1973 it had about twenty affiliate local organizations around the country. Some of these local organizations, such as those in Cleveland and the Bay area, were fully established, internally funded groups. Others were more ephemeral and were organized on an ad hoc basis that functioned from activity to activity.

The major difference between the two organizations was in the way they came into being. The UCSJ developed from the bottom up and the NCSJ from the top down. By its founding charter the NCSJ was a creature of what came to be known as the "establishment." It could not reach out to form its own grassroots membership nor could it speak directly to political leaders and agencies as an autonomous agency with its own voice. Financially it had become dependent for yearly allotment of funds on the Large City Budgeting Conference of CJF. If the NCSJ was hampered by the control of the mainline organizations and a chronic shortage of funds, the UCSJ suffered from the opposite malady. It had a central council and claimed a mass membership of 50,000 by the mid-eighties, but it was organized as a loose federation, which meant it sometimes experienced difficulties in getting grassroots consensus so that its leadership could be players on the level of national politics. Its activism was based on a conviction that pressure from below was crucial for the "rescue" of Soviet Jewry. Without it there would be no political negotiations at the government level. Picketing a local Soviet consulate was requisite for negotiating with top decision makers. The NCSJ was rigidly held by the existing world of Jewish organizations, and the more impassioned UCSJ sometimes encountered difficulty at the government level where compromise and bargaining were required. By the time of the struggle for the passage of Jackson-Vanik Amendment one could note the development of a kind of division of labor between the two organizations. The NCSJ, with the connections and experience of its American Jewish Committee (AJC) connection, was able to speak directly to congressional and political leaders on a leader-to-leader basis. Richard Maass became part of the triumvirate that met periodically with Kissinger. The UCSJ also spoke to its congressional leaders and generated all kinds of pressure at the grassroots level. It became known for its militancy and activism and its close ties to the activists in the Soviet Union. Like Sen. Jackson, UCSJ leaders viewed emigration as a human right not restricted by family reunification or principles of national repatriation. The UCSJ became a staunch supporter of the Jackson and Stevenson amendments, which it did not abandon lightly. Nor did its commitment to the freedom of movement cease once the emigrants left the Soviet Union.

The NCSJ also ultimately came down on the side of favoring the amendment, but representing twenty-seven affiliate organizations both secular and religious as well as the full political spectrum of Zionist organizations, it had to walk a delicate line. It had also to be more cognizant of other Jewish interests, such as the general security of Israel, which continued to have the highest priority in the Jewish world. We have seen that by 1976, fearing that the trade act would be revised, the NCSJ was already thinking of a fall-back position. The interest of Israel, which was a third party to the struggle, became the focal point around which the organizational lines of conflict ultimately formed. For a time a kind of division of labor between the two organizations developed. There was much overlap and duplication especially in the lobbying activity undertaken by both agencies in Washington.

Until the 1980s the movement had enough momentum and energy to conceal the deep-seated rift that divided the two agencies and American Jewry itself. Not until the dropout problem became massive after 1987 did the divisions come to the fore in all their intensity. On the broad Jewish historical stage it revealed the demographic conflict that was concealed at the roots of the relationship between American Jewry and Israel. From the Zionist perspective, the very existence of a free and prosperous America had since the beginning of the century somehow subverted the real Zion by luring away its intended population stock.

A second effort to strengthen the international presence of the movement and to spur it forward led to a second two-day international conference convened in Brussels on 17 February 1976. Beneath these normal movement aspirations there were other reasons that reflected the malaise of the movement after Jackson-Vanik. As in the case of the first Brussels conference, the organizational initiative came from the World Zionist Organization, supported by a bevy of American "establishment" organizations associated with the NCSJ. The second Brussels conference marked a last-ditch effort by Israel to retain full control of the movement. At stake was the disposition of the dropouts, who composed 78 percent of the emigrant stream by 1980. That growing phenomenon was bringing the tensions between American and Israeli Jewry to a boiling point. Of all the conflicts roused by the emigration of Soviet Jewry, the dropout problem exposed the conflicted heart of the Jewish enterprise as never before.

Much had changed since the first Brussels Conference. In August the signing of the Helsinki Accords signaled a movement away from the Cold War sparring of the single-nation American initiative embodied in the Jackson-Vanik Amendment to placing the emigration problem on a universal human rights basis. Included among the 1,200 delegates from thirty-two states attending the conference were non-Jewish representatives of humanitarian groups as well as representatives of the National Interreligious Task Force on Soviet Jewry, an umbrella organization that focused on the right of emigration and freedom of religion. It was hoped that by inviting other human rights groups to Brussels the conference would rise above merely another conference where Jews talked about the persecution of other Jews. But although a greater emphasis on human rights could be noted the broader approach envisaged by the conveners did not materialize.

As in the earlier Brussels conference, the JDL, now operating under the more heroic name of the Jewish Armed Resistance, tried again to garner some of the attention the conference drew from the media to itself. Meir Kahane, its leader, used a press pass to gain access to the floor but was quickly expelled by the authorities. By 1976 the formally organized Soviet Jewry movement was almost a decade old and could produce living evidence of its effectiveness. It was represented by a new constituency, a delegation of no longer silent Soviet Jews who had been successfully resettled in Israel. Many were surprised at the voice they heard, and undoubtedly there were some on the left side of the political spectrum who rued the day these Soviet emigrants had found their political voice. What remained unchanged from Brussels I, and perhaps even intensified, was the extreme reaction of the Kremlin to a Zionist-sponsored conference. The Soviet pronunciamientos denouncing the conference outdid themselves in choleric anger. There were news conferences showcasing emigrants who had returned to the Soviet "homeland" after an unhappy stay in Israel and Jewish Generals, with chests full of medals, willing to testify about the goodness of Jewish life in Russia. There were ill-disguised threats to the Belgian government for hosting a "provocative" conference. In some paradoxical way all the conveners had to show for their effort was Moscow's paranoiac reaction to what it imagined was a "world Zionist conspiracy."

The conference could not conceal the deep rifts that had developed among the activists. Some concerned matters of organizational turf, this time played out on an international level. Rabbi Schindler, the leader of the American Reform movement, reacting against the Israeli instrumentalist view of emigration, advocated a greater investment for educating Soviet Jews in place, "to teach a Judaism which is actively relevant to the present generation of Jews." [30] Beyond the question of how best to establish an international organization to promote the interests of Soviet Jewry was the gulf between Israel and others on the aims and the future of the movement. Beneath that was the more perplexing question of the dropouts, which from a Zionist perspective constituted a challenge to its ideological principles.

It may have been the change in atmosphere after the Soviet rejection of the Kissinger agreement and the subsequent crackdown that prevented Brussels II from repeating the grand success of the first conference, which was convened in a flush of enthusiasm for a movement coming into its own. Getting the movement known and coordinating its far-flung activities is usually the primary purpose of such conferences. But the final Brussels declaration was more significant for what it did not say after its pro forma profession of support for the Helsinki process. Part of the problem was that the increasing number of dropouts compelled the activists to undergo a reality test that few could pass. The dropouts of the post-1975 years were nothing like the Zionized, heroic "mad Russians" of the early period. The movement now was compelled to deal with the real Jews of Russia, warts and all. That they had arrived at that stage was a sign of its success. But few realized that at the time.

■   One of the many prisms through which modern Jewish history can be viewed is through its perennial immigrations. The flow of Jews from areas that have become untenable to areas of safety is a constant in Jewish history. A study of immigration movements such as that of Russian Jewry in the nineteenth and twentieth centuries can yield an insight to the forces at work beneath the surface of the Jewish experience. For example, the rapid increase of the Jewish population in Eastern Europe played an important role in the massive East-West migration at the turn of the twentieth century. It was this emigration that furnished the stock of contemporary American Jewry while also producing a small counterflow for the *Yishuv*, the Jewish settlement in Palestine. In the early years of that East-West population movement there developed a demographic competition between the *Yishuv* and America. Small wonder that some Zionist leaders considered America as a hindrance to the realization of the Zionist dream of establishing a Jewish homeland. The uneven rivalry between the two Zions characterizes much of the history of twentieth-century Jewry. The constant lure of America haunted the first three waves of immigration that established the foundation of modern Israel. But with the rise of National Socialism the demographic question took a different turn. The 1930s produced a *Zwungsaliyah* for the *Yishuv*.[31] Because America had adopted a restrictive immigration policy in 1924 and much of the rest of the world was closed to Jews, Palestine was the one place where the Jews of Germany might have been welcomed. The possibility of resettlement shortly before the Holocaust momentarily raised hopes that the Zionist movement might yet be the instrument of Jewish salvation. But with the implementation of the British White Paper in May 1939, which limited immigration and land sales, that too was denied. Paradoxically, if German Jewry had been given a choice between settling in America or Palestine only 10 percent would have chosen the latter, a decision much like that made by the dropouts. But resettlement remains an intriguing alternative in Jewish history. Had there been no Final Solution, the settlement of the threatened Jews of Europe would still have been the limited by the absorptive capacity of the *Yishuv*. Other resettlement havens would have been required. The resettlement strategy was in fact seriously considered by Roosevelt but not in Palestine, despite the fact that before 1941 its vast experience in resettlement would have made

Palestine a good prospect for resettling a small portion of European Jewry. The Roosevelt administration considered more than 600 resettlement prospects in such areas as Brazil, Mindanao, and Baja California for the targeted Jews of Europe. But with the exception of a minor resettlement venture in the Dominican Republic, eagerly seized upon by the State Department, Roosevelt's search found few places outside a tropical rainforest or an arid desert that might be considered for the heavy capital investment required.[32] The Nazi regime also considered resettlement in Madagascar. In fact, resettlement became a code word used by Berlin to conceal the operation of the Final Solution.

The prospect for resettlement outside Europe placed the Zionist leadership in a quandary. Eastern European Jewry, which might have been the prime population stock of a newborn Jewish state, was being systematically destroyed, and the Zionist movement itself was being asked to lend its expertise to resettle surviving Jews anywhere else but the area that wanted and needed them. Should the limited resources of the world Zionist movement be made available for resettlement elsewhere to save Jewish lives? The Jewish leadership tried ultimately to do both: to settle those Jews who could enter with Palestine certificates while waging a political battle against the British Foreign Office's inhumanly restrictionist policy. During the final months of the war and in the months immediately after a desperate rescue operation, *Bricha* and *Ha'apala* were initiated to bring the survivors to Palestine.[33] Paradoxically, the novel *Exodus,* a fictionalized account of the smuggling of survivors into the homeland, sometimes inspired Soviet emigrants to make a similar decision to emigrate to Israel.[34]

After 1945 Jewish leadership in Palestine was forced to confront the bitter fact that the Jewish population that might have settled in a Jewish state was in ashes. A desperate search to solve its demographic problem would have to be found if the state was to be secure in the face of a fecund Arab population. "Mass immigration, it was for this that the state was established," declared Ben-Gurion, "and it is by virtue of this alone that it will stand."[35] Coincidentally, the Soviet emigrants whom Israel was anxious to attract were the descendants of the East European Jewish population aggregation originally earmarked in the Zionist vision for resettlement in the Jewish state. That too may account for the troubling proprietary interest that Israel expressed in the control of the Soviet Jewry movement and the emigration that was its primary goal.

Yet despite its desperate need and the feeling that Soviet Jewry belonged to Israel there was a duality in approach to the Soviet emigration question. In its early postrevolution years some Zionist leaders mustered considerable sympathy for what was happening in the Soviet Union. We have noted that the Kibbutz movement in its agrarian fundamentalism and the notion of renewal through labor had a distinctly Russian socialist flavor. When Ben-Gurion left Russia in 1923 he pledged himself and the Zionist labor movement never to antagonize or slander the Soviet Union or to betray his faith in the revolution. Mass immigration to the Jewish homeland carried forward under the Zionist ideological mandate of ingathering of the exiles could for practical reasons not be fully implemented before the advent of Hitler. What was preferred were pioneers to build the land rather than ordinary immigrants. The accusation of favoritism toward younger members of Zionist youth movements for the granting of Palestine certificates during the Holocaust was an oft-heard accusation. Suffice it to say that there existed within the Zionist movement an internal incompatibility between Israel's sense of itself as a Jewish state and refuge for all Jews who needed a haven and the practical needs of nation building that required selectivity in immigration policy. After the founding of the state when finding population stock was imperative, the resettlement of the Jews of the Maghreb proved to be such a traumatic experience that it forms the axis of Israel's politics to this day. It was as if Israel's short-term goals to survive and secure the Jewish state were at odds with its long-term goals to build a national home for all the Jewish people. In some measure the confusing zigzag Israeli policy on emigration was related to the historic tensions that Israel had experienced in having to bring almost its entire population stock from elsewhere.

There was a side to Israel's demographic problem generally unknown to the public. Its need to attract immigrants was compounded by the larger contextual problem of needing to stabilize its existing population. The problem was *yerida,* a Hebrew term meaning descending or emigration from Israel. Between 1969 and 1979, 510,528 citizens had left Israel, according to figures published by the Ministry of Labor and Social Welfare, whereas the Soviet aliyah brought only 384,000 to the country. The Soviet immigration, added to others who settled from other countries, barely compensates for Israel's population loss because of emigration. Israel needed immigration merely to maintain, much less enhance, its critical population mass. For Israel, Soviet Jewry, which was of culturally similar stock and possessing high skills, was viewed as a demographic lifesaver.

The activities of the Zionist movement in the postwar displaced persons camps was another episode in Israel's search for settlers. The survivors in these camps were referred to in Hebrew as *Sherit Hapleta,* the surviving remnants. The *Yishuv*'s effort to settle the displaced persons in Israel was packaged as a human salvaging project. It surely was that but it was also the Jewish state that was to be saved. The Zionist leadership did not mourn when the Truman administration proved as reluctant as the Roosevelt administration to admit the displaced persons.[36] The American Jewish welcome to displaced persons was not consciously motivated by demographic considerations. It was also a humanitarian endeavor. Yet some might argue that at another level there was awareness that American Jewry too needed a biological infusion. Like Israel its basic population stock was also Eastern European, and in the postwar decades it was no longer reproducing itself. The dirty little secret of American Jewish history was its prewar dependence, culturally and biologically, on the surfeit of Eastern European Jewry. American Jewish leaders preferred to speak in humanitarian terms of welcoming Jewish emigrants but clearly for those willing to see there were demographic factors involved as well. Later, Isaiah Minkoff, who possessed a vaguely non-Zionist Bundist mentality, related the Soviet emigrants to reviving the declined Yiddish culture in America. "Maybe a new exodus from the Soviet Union will bring . . . Russian Jews with Yiddish culture to the U.S.," he mused, "there would be a revival of Jewish life. . ."[37] That rationale was similar to that given by Israeli leaders, who were convinced that by compelling dropouts to settle in Israel, they were doing the right thing for them while at the same time serving the needs of Israel.

The context of the dropout phenomenon is to be found in the politics of demography. Since the mid–nineteenth century Jewish immigrants have had two alternative Zions, one in America and the other in the location of the ancient Jewish homeland in the Middle East. In the competition for Jewish immigration it has been the American Zion that has proven to be more attractive, at least from the vantage of holding out a higher standard of living. While Zionism has been the most important source of a sense of Jewish peoplehood in the twentieth century, in practice the decision that Jewish immigrants make about where to live is based on practical matters, not ideological ones. The decision of Soviet Jewish emigrants to drop out in the hope of settling in America was not unique in historical terms. It was in effect the same decision that had been made throughout the twentieth century by immigrant Jews. Some dismiss anti-Semitism and a search for Jewish identity altogether as motivating the decision to emigrate. "Psychologically, they were escaping from the Soviet Union and not going back to Judaism," explained Nechemia Levanon.[38] Another observer noted: "They may have been running away from anti-Semitism, but they weren't necessarily running to anything Jewish, and many of them were running away from Socialism."[39] Others, we shall later note, chose an internal emigration by eliminating the term *Yevrei* from their internal passport.

■　The conflict that developed over the dropout problem exposed a deep chasm between Zionist-oriented Jews and those who, at least in the primary motivations that shaped their lives, tended to personal development above the imperatives of ideology. It remained a latent problem until 1979 when more than 66 percent of the exceptionally large exodus (51,333) chose to drop out. At that point Israel's hidden fear that the entire emigration would be lost became an open one. Convinced that the uncommonly large emigration of 1979 would become the pattern for future years, Israel became more overt in its advocacy. Once before in the fall of 1974 Israel thought a working agreement concerning emigration had been reached with Moscow. But then Israel could still believe that the large majority of the emigrants would settle in Israel. Word was sent to President Ford and Sen. Jackson congratulating them on the "very gladdening" news. Assuming that the emigrants were destined for Israel, the transmission counseled that there should now be a great absorption effort.[40] Most shared that sense. In February 1972, also believing that the emigrants would settle in Israel, Sen. Jackson introduced a resolution for a two-year program to aid emigrant resettlement there. Now, four years later, almost unheralded, a full-blown threat to her national interest had developed.

In fact, it should not have come as a surprise since as early as 1973 there was evidence that Soviet emigrants might have other ideas about where to settle. By 1980 the emigration stream had again grown so small that there was little to argue about. It was not until Gorbachev's liberalized reform regime loosened the strictures on emigration that the dropout problem came fully into its own, accompanied by a bitter intracommunal conflict. Strictly speaking, that conflict was not between Israel and American Jewry. There were American Jews who advocated settlement in Israel and activists in Israel who acknowledged the impossibility of coercing settlement of unwilling emigrants. A group of Soviet emigrants in Israel warned that there would be a "drastic decrease" in the number seeking to emigrate to Israel if the gates to the United States were closed.[41] But other Soviet emigrants, such as Mark Dymshits and Iosif Mendelevich, both convicted in the Leningrad hijacking trial, vehemently opposed giving dropouts any help. The dropout phenomenon split all constituencies, including the emigrants themselves.

Ultimately, it was not only the question of coercion but of financial aid for the refugees that resolved the issue. Should the money raised in the American Jewish community be expended for resettlement of emigrants in America when Israel, the national home of the Jewish people, was willing to accept them with open arms? When Israel began to insist on measures such as cutting philanthropic assistance to the dropouts and doing all in its power to direct the emigration flow to Israel, polarization between the two sides began in earnest. Some cautioned that Israel's Zionist "monomania" was self-defeating and would compromise the Soviet Jewry movement. So convinced was Yoram Dinstein that the tensions would lead to a loss of idealistic young activists that he suspected that the Soviet authorities were deliberately encouraging the dropouts in order to undermine the Soviet Jewry movement.[42] For some American Jewish leaders, Israel's resistance to the emigrant's right to choose meant denying Jews the possibility of escape from a society and government that tyrannized them. The dropouts too complained that during the initial interview conducted by Jewish Agency personnel in Vienna, they were being made to feel that they were unworthy Jews because they wanted to go to America.[43]

Part of the problem was that Israel believed that having built the foundation of the movement in the Soviet Union, its primary goal was to encourage emigration to Israel. That goal had been affirmed at the Brussels conference. At first Israel did not acknowledge the growing proportion of non-Zionists in the emigration stream after 1975. It was assumed that the bad stories about the condition of prior emigrants in the government-controlled Soviet media had created a negative image of Israel among the potential new settlers. Zionist ideologues believed that the diaspora was in any case doomed by assimilation and that the future of Judaism was with the settlement in Israel. Why place the emigrants on a sinking ship? That "negation of the diaspora" attitude had developed early as part of an ideological baggage required to build a national homeland under difficult circumstances. It clearly was not the perspective shared be a growing number of emigrants. Nechemia Levanon called the dropout phenomenon a "Jewish tragedy" because the emigrants do not chose to settle in America to be Jews. "On the contrary I think they suffered as Jews . . . (and) many would be quite prepared to forget it to become as quickly Americans as they can."[44] The idea that the Jews choosing to come to America were doomed to be lost was not limited to Zionists living in Israel. Rabbi Irving (Yitz) Greenberg of the National Jewish Conference Center argued: "There is a real possibility that Russian Jews which will go to America or elsewhere, because they are uncommitted Jewishly, will assimilate and be lost entirely to the Jewish people."[45]

Others argued for the sacredness of the Israeli visa. "No one has the right to prostitute the Israeli visa," argued Morris Brafman.[46] Predictably, the most telling argument against the dropouts was the one that sought the moral high ground by arguing that emigration based on self-fulfillment and the quest for a higher living standard undercut the moral basis of an emigration based on a search for national identity and human rights. The intensely idealistic redemption or return issue had attracted many marginal Jews to the movement by strengthening their sense of Jewish identity. That would be undermined if the movement now became merely one to help Soviet Jews to attain a middle class life in America. If the dropout phenomenon was sustained, the Soviet Jewry movement would lose its universal appeal, which was based on a humanitarian response to suffering. But most common among "old time" Zionists such as Leon Dulzin, chairman of the World Zionist Organization, was a proprietary sense of ownership of a movement founded by Zionists: "Soviet Jews who arrive in Vienna on Israeli visas are enabled to do so all the thanks to the devotion, dedication, martyrdom of the Zionist activists in the U.S.S.R. and the direct involvement of the Israeli authorities. Once they arrived in Vienna, as free men, the Jewish people, as a whole has only one commitment toward them—the commitment to get them safely to their homeland, Israel."[47]

But for most American Jews, Israel remained primarily a worthy goal for their philanthropy. They did not consider themselves as living out their lives as Jews "on a sinking ship." Neither were they ever likely to become passengers on a one-way flight to Israel. One historian observed that Israel's policy on the dropouts "would suggest that the Zionist movement, as its opponents have long contended—does not treat the individual Jews as an end but as a means."[48] If Israel continued her hard-nosed tactics toward the dropouts the result would be that far fewer Russian Jews would choose to enter upon the risky emigration process.[49] For many American activists whose sensibilities were secular and liberal it was Israel's hard approach that treated the emigrants as biological material needed to fill a demographic gap that was problematic. It also had a negative impact on recruitment. The Committee of Concerned Scientists (CCS) affiliated with the NCSJ urged that without freedom of choice for the emigrants, the CCS would have difficulty enlisting internationally known scientists.[50] There was something in the mentality of the urban/urbane Jews that resisted coercion even if in their heart of hearts they sensed the historical rightness of Israel's claim to the emigrants.

Most American Jews continued to give the security and welfare of Israel their highest priority. Those who considered the immigration of Soviet Jewry as a movement to save Jews qua Jews wanted to encourage emigration to Israel. "I want them to remain Jews," said David Geller, an early activist associated with the AJC, "and I want Israel to be a strong state, . . .I think it should be helped."[51] For those who were religious Jews, bringing Jews to Israel, even if they wanted to settle in the American Zion, was not an infringement of their human rights, it was an act of repatriation. But to more liberal-minded secular Jews who had argued all along that the right of Soviet Jewish emigration was a human right, a forced immigration to Israel was an unacceptable alternative. In Israel too there were many who shared the feeling that an emigration based on compulsion was wrong. A few, such as Moshe Decter, a venerable founder of the American movement, hovered between the two positions. "I adopted the conventional American liberal civil liberties line which most American Jews and Jewish organizations did," said Decter. "You cannot force people to go anywhere they don't want to." But a year later, Decter changed his mind. The purpose of the movement was to save lives, but not just any lives. "It was the right to leave the country in order, hopefully, that they would go to Israel. . . . That was the whole purpose. . . . we need that rich human resource, which only the Russian Jews can give us."[52]

If the element of coercion troubled American Jews concerned with human rights, then the idea of rescue that prevailed among American activists troubled Israelis. The emigration of Soviet Jewry, they believed, was not a reenactment of the refugee crisis that preceded the Holocaust. "What troubled me," observed Levanon, "was that some very militant fighters for the freedom of Soviet Jews spoke about physical danger of Jews in the Soviet Union. I knew that there was no physical danger. But I knew that there was a danger to Jewish identity in the Soviet Union."[53] The Holocaust fixation of many activists in America led logically to the idea of rescue. They would do for Russian Jewry what they believed their parents failed to do for European Jewry during the Holocaust. That dramatic heroic motivation was a far cry from the Israeli activists, most of whom simply wanted more settlers in Israel to secure the Jewish state.

Religious Jews found the choice of Israel or America especially difficult to negotiate. According to Jewish law *pidyon shivuim* (redemption of prisoners), because it concerns the saving of life itself, must be given absolute priority over all else. The destination of the emigrants can therefore not be considered as part of the religious law governing the ransoming of prisoners. Accordingly, the Synagogue Council of America, one of the largest religious bodies, decided in favor of freedom of choice on the basis that destination is not relevant and that Jewish law mandates that all Jews must be helped. But there were exceptions among the observant who also held strong Zionist sentiments. Malcolm Hoenlein, executive director of the New York Conference and an Orthodox Jew, suggested that if there must be freedom of choice, let the choice be made in Moscow. Moreover, he pointed out, emigrants cannot legally be classified as refugees nor prisoners if there is a haven available to them. In 1987 the State Department came to the same conclusion regarding the refugee status of the emigrants. Mostly those who favored settlement exclusively in Israel feared that government and private funds raised to help the dropouts would inevitably cut into funds for Israel. On the other hand David Harris, who was on the scene in Rome and would become the executive director of the AJC, attributed the disconnect not to a question of money but to deep-seated cultural and generational factors. "We had entirely different understandings and expectations of each other as Jews," he observed. Jewish social workers expected to encounter people like their grandparents, grateful refugees "dripping with appreciation." Instead they encountered emigrants who knew exactly what they were entitled to and rarely had a word of appreciation.[54]

▨   Emigration to Israel from the Soviet Union had profound implications for the Cold War. As long as Israel had a demographic deficit the possibility that the Jewish state would unravel existed. But beyond that a growth in population might also strengthen Israel's claim to the West Bank. The State Department, whose goal was stabilization of the Middle East, was aware of the Soviet government's equivocal stand on dropouts as reflected in its lack of concern about the authenticity of the *vyzov*. But despite the high costs, it was reluctant to disrupt the existing arrangement that granted financial support to the refugees on the freedom of choice basis, lest it come under more congressional pressure. But after 1986 American political leaders would be under fiscal pressure to change its generous refugee policy. Behind that change is an interesting story of government-to-government pressure involving the relationship of the dropouts to Israel's security combined with Washington's growing concern about the cost of the absorption of thousands of prospective Jewish refugees from the Soviet Union.

The dropout phenomenon forced the Soviet Jewry movement to face a moment of truth about itself. For Zionists the demographic needs of the Jewish state added an unforeseen dimension. Israel had national interests that could come in conflict with the idealism and aspirations that energized the activists. For those of a Zionist sensibility the need for Soviet Jews to flee and the need for the Jewish state for settlers was a perfect fit. The rescue of Soviet Jewry ennobled the more political goal, the demographic rescue of the Jewish state. But the full truth lay elsewhere. It concerned the inability of the Zionist movement to attract and hold Jews on a voluntary basis, a crucial test of its viability, which was nowhere better illustrated than in the dropout phenomenon. Like the German Jewish refugees of the thirties, Soviet Jews would not have a Zion imposed on them. It was a distressing moment of truth, if not revelation, for those committed to the Jewish national homeland.

The agents of the Jewish Agency working in the processing centers in Vienna were unprepared to treat the emigrants the way a social worker treats a client. They believed that if the support structure put in place, which included a weekly allowance, board in available hotels, and some language and orientation lectures were removed the "natural" flow to Israel would resume. They accused HIAS and JDC, in whose charge the emigrants fell after the JAFI team had interviewed them, of "hijacking" the Soviet emigrants by offering all kinds of inducements. The emigrants were a way to keep the helping agencies alive because there had been no mass Jewish immigration to the United States since 1956, when Hungarian Jews came in numbers. Their generous private philanthropy and government aid to the emigrants was in reality a clever strategy to keep these obsolete agencies in business. It was a cruel charge indicating how deeply emotional the dropout issue had become. Despite clear evidence that the Soviet authorities were unconcerned they warned that the misuse of the Israeli visa would lead to Moscow's curtailment of emigration altogether. Moreover, the dropouts were using up the precious allotment of visas that would normally go to emigrants who wanted to go to Israel.

These charges and others and a series of proposals by Israel were made to head off the possible loss of the Soviet emigrants. Through the connection of Phil Bernstein, the executive vice president of CJF, the General Assembly of the CJF was asked to cut off all aid to the Soviet emigrants in Vienna and to limit HIAS's responsibilities to finding close relatives in the United States for those who could not be convinced to continue to Israel. The proposed new procedure would not eliminate freedom of choice because the emigrants could still apply directly to countries other than Israel for visas. But the ploy fooled no one, least of all the dropouts, who were aware that the only way to get out of the Soviet Union was with an Israeli visa. Convinced that the proposal was meant to curtail freedom of choice, which he insisted contravenes Jewish law, Lewis Weinstein, the former chairman of NJCRAC, let out a lusty cry of opposition. The proposals, which also included the idea of direct flights out of Bucharest to by-pass Vienna and Rome, came to nothing.

Without the cooperation of Moscow, which rejected direct flights, little could be done to bypass the American agencies. The Dutch embassy in Moscow that handled the administrative details of the emigration process for Israel rejected Israel's request that the question "What is your final destination?" be included in the application.[55] Similarly, Bruno Kreisky, the Jewish prime minister of Austria, rejected Israel's proposal that a refugee camp under Israel's control be established. After Austria assumed responsibility for the security of the emigrant processing operation, Kreisky also rejected Israel's proposal that his government guarantee that emigrants who enter the country with an Israeli visa be compelled to continue to Israel. For Israel it was a question of honoring its visa, but like the Netherlands, Austria was strongly in favor of freedom of choice. Israel's proposals designed to channel the emigrants to Tel Aviv, and the charges against HIAS and JDC were symptomatic of its fear that the desperately needed emigrants would be sidetracked and resettled elsewhere. Israel's leaders considered the struggle to "gather in" the emigrants as important as any military campaign, perhaps even more so in the long run.

In responses to Israel's onslaught, representatives of HIAS and JDC warned that if they were forced to leave the field, organizations such as the Tolstoy Foundation, the International Rescue Committee, Rav Tov, the World Council of Churches, and other unacceptable groups that viewed the Soviet Jewish migration as a fertile field to proselytize, would fill the vacuum.[56] With the high stakes involved what the emigrants wanted mattered little. The Jewish Agency filled the air with unrealizable threats, including withholding the list of names of emigrants to be processed. But that hardly convinced the federation leaders who would ultimately have to make the decision.

By mid-1976, the conflict had become serious enough for both sides to agree to convene in an effort to find a solution. After heated discussion it was decided to form a committee composed of eight representatives, four from each side.[57] In an effort to achieve a better balance and operational knowledge the Committee of Eight was increased to ten.[58] After weeks of discussion the committee made several minor concessions to those who advocated freedom of choice but otherwise came down solidly on the Israeli side. The emigrant's destination would be determined before he leaves Russia. Those choosing Israel would continue to be processed by the Jewish Agency and receive Israeli visas for direct transport to Israel. Those choosing to dropout and settle in the United States, Canada, or Australia would be free to apply for visas from those countries and be administered by HIAS and JDC. The "unintentional rewards" of U.S. refugee policy would be discontinued as of 1 February 1977. Every effort would be made to improve the absorption process in Israel. Under enormous pressure, the HIAS board of directors met on 26 October and tentatively voted in favor of the committee's proposal with a reminder that the original condition that bound the Committee of Eight, that nothing would be done that threatened the outflow of Jews from the Soviet

Union, remained in effect. The JDC executive committee followed suit. Its new president, Donald Robinson, supported the curtailing of its assistance program in Vienna to dropouts. The decision would now have to be ratified at the meeting of the General Assembly of the CJF, which acted as a governing body in matters concerning money, to be convened in Philadelphia in November.

By mid-1977 feelings ran so high on both sides that rather than settling the conflict, the plan provoked it. There was little prospect that a consensus report would be ready for a meeting of the Jewish Agency scheduled for Geneva in August. HIAS, JDC, and the AJC rejected the February deadline. A moving speech by Leonard Fine, a well-known writer on Jewish internal politics and editor of *Moment* magazine, helped convince the assembly to withhold approval of the committee's recommendation. A final vote was postponed and the issue was taken directly to the Jewish public. Carl Glick, the president of HIAS, and others spoke to the local federations in favor of choice while members of the liaison bureau and some members of the NCSJ executive board tried to convince federation leaders that Israel was more suitable for settlement. In the weeks that followed more local federations reported that they favored freedom of choice. Soon additional problems developed. The Israeli assurance that American visas would become available for the dropouts was seen as a fiction, despite Max Fisher's assurance that he would use his influence to get more. The Philadelphia meeting of the General Assembly of the CJF was a historic turning point. Israel learned that American Jewry would not always do her bidding. But time was on Israel's side. The politics of the refugee question in Washington and budgetary considerations that grew out of the unexpected large number who chose to emigrate after 1989 made it necessary to view the question in a new light.

The embarkation problem in Moscow was not so easily solved. The idea of giving the emigrant choice to be made in the Soviet Union about where to resettle was not only alien to the totalitarian state but also to the American definition of refugee, which applied only to someone outside of his or her native state. All were aware that within the framework of the totalitarian state there could never be free immigration, and therefore there could be no systematic Soviet immigration law. The prospect of getting an American visa and an exit permit and then to be granted refugee status were virtually nonexistent. When Rep. Edward Koch pressed to make 30,000 additional American visas available, he encountered stiff opposition from Herman Weissman, president of the Zionist Organization of America. For obvious reasons Zionists did not want easy access to America and were grateful when Max Fisher's endeavor to increase the number of visas was, for the moment, unsuccessful. More important, there was a risk of diminishing the emigration flow if the prospect of settling in America was withdrawn as Israel wished, because many applicants would then avoid the risky emigration process altogether.

Still, JAFI was aware that persuasion would be more effective than coercion of the dropouts. Delegations of former Soviet emigrants were sent to Rome to inform their compatriots of the "real" story of life in Israel. A course was organized to train sixty-five former Soviet emigrants to work with the dropouts in Italy.[59] In individual cases such efforts were sometimes successful, but the dropout trend continued on its upward trajectory. JAFI, which assumed the responsibility of absorption, also had concerns regarding its budget. A sizeable portion of the cost of resettlement was paid for by public and private American funds. There was apprehension lest American government funds earmarked for defense would be redirected to help settle the dropouts in the United States and Israel. In 1975 of the $40 million appropriated for transportation and maintenance of emigrants, only $5 million went to cover the cost of the dropouts. Whether government largess could keep up with the expected increase in Soviet emigration was doubtful. The American assumption of the cost of refugee resettlement was well established before the dropout problem, first with Hungarian refugees and then with Cubans. But that practice could be challenged if the cost became too high. In 1977, Congress appropriated an additional $25 million to support Soviet Jewish settlement and the State Department allocated a supplemental sum of $2 million to assist refugees settling in the United States. Carter endorsed the appropriation in 1978. Thereafter, the U.S. government matched HIAS and the JDC expenditures on a dollar-for-dollar basis while government funding was also extended to Caritas and other non-Jewish agencies. A claim by American Jewish agencies for matching funds for resettlement of emigrants in the United States could jeopardize JAFI's absorption and resettlement program, which was in some measure dependent on funding from America.

Fifty Jewish organizations eventually took part in the deliberations. Even before the Committee of Eight announced its recommendations there were signs that a strategy to mute the predictable protest by limiting media coverage would be of little avail. The agreement, which was in some sense a JAFI diktat, was coming apart. In the Jewish press the story line spoke of HIAS and JDC succumbing to Israeli pressure. In fact, believing that it was "acting in accordance with the highest precepts of the Jewish tradition" and "fulfilling . . . the wishes of the American Jewish communities," HIAS rejected the proposal. The deepening of passions on either side of the dropout question after the committee's report was predictable. Phil Baum viewed continued financial support of the dropouts as an unjustifiable expenditure of the Jewish philanthropic dollar. Just as vehement on the other side was a furious letter to the offices of the NCSJ that supported the committee report: "THIS IS OUTRAGEOUS! There is no way we will support *any organization* which is in favor of this despicable step—we must do everything possible to get out the Soviet Jews!"[60] The rift between the organizations also deepened. The AJC, which had assumed a prominent role in organizing the American wing of the movement, pointed out the subterfuge entailed in basing a solution on the prospect of the Kremlin honoring an American visa.[61]

The most serious conflict occurred between the two organizations directly involved with the emigration question, the NCSJ and the UCSJ. The line the NCSJ had to walk was not an easy one because the two major organizations to which it was bound, the Zionist-dominated Conference of Presidents and the NJCRAC, stood on opposite sides on the dropout issue. Legally the NCSJ was supposed to be nonpartisan but time and again it was called on to intercede on behalf of the dropouts. What should it do when HIAS requested help in finding families to vouch for the dropouts or when they were asked to help promote legislation for refugee relief or visas. How could such efforts be ignored? Ultimately the NCSJ came down in favor of freedom of choice but the opposition within its board by the Zionist-oriented organizations continued unabated. By the fall of 1978 the atmosphere had become so bad that Goodman suggested that a pamphlet be published celebrating the fifteenth birthday of the agency by setting the record straight.[62] The UCSJ had no such problems. Its position on the dropout problem was unequivocal. The saving of Jewish lives overrode all other considerations. The Soviet Jewry movement was organized for rescue of an endangered Jewry, not for emigration to Israel exclusively. The organization was for free choice and spoke out against what it considered Israel's manipulation.

In the face of American Jewish opposition the efforts to force the refugee stream to Israel grew more strident. In 1979 Israel again approached the Netherlands Ministry of Foreign Affairs to discuss the possibility of establishing a direct air link between Moscow and Tel Aviv to be flown by KLM. Israel undoubtedly offered to subsidize the venture but as in the prior case Amsterdam rejected the proposal. But Israel's pursuit of diplomatic contact with Moscow remained elusive and without it the dream of direct flight that would have bypassed the opportunity to dropout could not be realized.[63] A contretemps occurred when Levanon attempted to withhold 800 names of Israeli visa holders without which the American agencies could not process the dropouts. The problem of withholding names simmered for months and finally led to a protest by UCSJ at its convention in Israel in 1978. Disregarding a prior warning by federation leaders who subsidized JAFI in 1981, Leon Dulzin, the chairman of its executive, again threatened to withhold the names of arriving Israel visa holders. At one point Israel, undoubtedly fully aware that once an emigrant sets foot in Israel he or she automatically becomes a citizen and therefore can no longer qualify as a refugee under the U.S. refugee law, suggested to Carl Glick, president of HIAS, that it move its operation to Israel. The "Israel First" strategy had the additional liability of compelling emigrants to give up their refugee status under American law.

In October 1981 a second meeting of representatives of the agencies involved, JAFI, HIAS, JDC, and CJF, convened in Naples. After years of simply hoping to get HIAS and JDC removed from the processing of emigrants, Israel now proposed that the American agencies be limited to processing only those emigrants who had bona fide close relatives in the United States. All others would come under the control of the Jewish agency, which would also be granted an additional two-week orientation period devoted to a last-ditch effort to convince the dropouts to settle in Israel. Ostensibly that would bring most of the emigrants to Israel. Under some pressure HIAS agreed. But as HIAS officials had warned the percentage of dropouts did not decrease. Instead there was a steady increase in the number of emigrants without means of support in Vienna and Rome. It was apparent that no matter what the agencies decided, emigrants could not be compelled to settle where they did not want to live. As the number of emigrants increased, HIAS officials realized that they could not simply abandon the emigrants to their fate. That would break a pledge to the Italian government and to the emigrants who were trapped in a legal no-man's-land. By 1978, aside from the small community in Ladispoli and Ostia, a seaside resort near Rome where dropouts were housed awaiting American visas, they were causing a problem in several cities where they had settled. By 1978 there were 4,000 in Rome and almost as many in West Berlin and Brussels. The problem intensified in 1979, a banner year for emigration, due to a backup of emigrants who had to wait four to six months for processing. A planned airlift for 25,000 dropouts to the United States admitted under the attorney general's parole authority began in the April with the transport of 615 families in three jetliners. The problem was complicated by the "departees," emigrants settled in Israel who remained determined to get to the United States. A number of departees left Israel only to discover that they had become stranded in a legal no-man's-land since Israel would not renew their passports, except for a return to

Israel.[64] Phil Baum, the associate executive director of AJCong, who had previously advocated greater flexibility concerning the Jackson-Vanik Amendment, argued that "to say that they're trapped in Italy is silly . . . they can go to Israel. . . . If you want freedom then you come on the terms you can."[65] The problem was that those in the post-1975 emigration stream were motivated by a more personalized notion of freedom; they sought the freedom to fulfill themselves and to provide opportunities for their children.

After three months of trying to reconcile the two opposing positions, HIAS withdrew from the Naples agreement. Another solution would have to be found. "Freedom of choice" became the rallying cry for American Jews sensitive to human rights. That was, after all, what the American civil rights struggle in which some of the younger activists were involved was all about. In September the CJF met in New York to try again to come to grips with the conflicting interests of meeting Israel's demographic needs while heeding the voice of those who viewed Israel's policy as coercive. The public relations of the emigration movement had after all focused on the right of movement. It was ironic that Israel would now deny that right to the emigrants. The CJF had to contend with world opinion and the clear opposition of the State Department, which spent $25 million in 1980 to resettle refugees in Israel and only $15 million on the dropouts. The CJF members were aware that there were other agencies in the field anxious for their own reasons to help Jews.[66]

By 1978 it was clear that the attempts to find common ground between the Israeli view for the disposition of the emigrants and those who favored freedom of choice were not successful. A committee of the CJF met in Chicago in October 1979 in an effort to hammer out a resolution that would satisfy all in preparation for the forty-eight meeting of the General Assembly of the CJF scheduled to meet in Montreal in November. But the resolution passed by the assembly again fell between two chairs. On one hand it stressed the responsibility of American Jewish communities to provide help for all Jews who left the Soviet Union and to integrate them fully into American Jewish life. On the other hand it committed itself to encouraging as many Soviet Jews as possible to go to Israel. An amendment introduced demanding that dropouts depend on financial support on family funds and personal friends, rather than on welfare extended by the community, was defeated after a heated debate. The freedom of choice principle had become the consensus of American Jewry but only barely so since 40 percent of the delegates to the General Assembly voted for the amendment.

The split was along generational and ideological lines. The older delegates, most of whom had been brought up to consider Israel's security and welfare fore-most, inevitably favored the idea that Soviet emigrants should settle in Israel. For younger activists the demographic needs of Israel were important but secondary to individual rights. Apprehension regarding the high cost of resettlement preoc-cupied some delegates, especially when there were hints in the early months of 1981 that the Reagan administration was unhappy about the Carter administra-tion's generous aid to refugees. That aid covered about half of the cost of the op-eration. Meanwhile HIAS announced a new streamlined procedure shortening the amount of time the emigrants would stay in Vienna. To fulfill a commitment made by both HIAS and JDC in April 1977 a counseling program was introduced in Rome to familiarize the dropouts about life in Israel. It was hoped that the new procedure would lead more emigrants to settle there. It was in vain, and it would later be the rising cost of the refugee aid program that would become the decisive factor to resolve the impasse.

In June a meeting of the top level leadership from Israel and the diaspora com-munities again considered the options available but could come to no conclusions. The American leaders agreed that it would be best if the emigrants chose to settle in Israel, but they rarely went as far as Dulzin, who spoke of the dropout rate as a "calamity."[67] This time the prime minister of Israel himself resubmitted the pro-posal, which would limit HIAS and JDC to helping only those clients who had close relatives in the United States. But again there was opposition since that meant that those who did not would have no choice but to settle in Israel. Mean-while, the increasing number of emigrants in the stream in 1979 concealed the fact that Soviet emigration was about to experience a low that would last more than six years.

The presidium created by the Brussels conference expressed great concern about the increased rate of dropouts. If the increase continued Israel would receive less than 15 percent of the emigrants. Rejecting the fact that a new kind of emi-grant had entered the refugee pool, the Jewish agency continued to be convinced that the cause was related to the generous American aid package with which the agency could not compete. Still another committee was formed to confront the problem. Its composition barely concealed its strong Zionist orientation.[68]

In August, using the excuse that the Soviets would discontinue the emigration because of the growing dropout rate, the Jewish agency formally announced a unilateral plan for reducing the number of emigrants who receive American assis-tance. HIAS and JDC would limit their assistance to those emigrants who had close relatives in the United States. The remainder would come to Israel through

JAFI, and those who fell into neither category would be on their own. It was in fact, the same plan previously proposed by Israel that had been rejected by the CJF. The risk Israel ran in proceeding unilaterally was an indication of how determined it was not to lose this crucial population supplement. The policy would be enforced by withholding the list of emigrant names, which only JAFI possessed through Israel's visa bureau. Dulzin rushed to New York to explain the position to the leaders of HIAS and JDC and to the newly formed committee of the heads of the organizations involved in the Soviet Jewry issue. But his hopes that the majority American "freedom of choice" faction would give first priority to Israel's demographic needs were forlorn. For members of the UCSJ, who urged HIAS to continue its policy of aiding all Jews, human rights were uppermost. They were convinced that sullen, unwilling emigrants would not serve the demographic needs of Israel in any case. But like most American Jewish organizations that worried about Israel's future, the NCSJ's board, representing over twenty organizations, was unable to reach a clear consensus. Predictably, on 25 August HIAS hesitatingly reiterated its broad humanitarian policy: "The HIAS tradition is to serve every Jewish refugee in need, anywhere in the world, with compassion and understanding," read its carefully worded press release.[69] It also pledged to do its utmost to help bring emigrants to Israel. The lines of conflict were now sharply drawn. The following day, reminding everyone that the American government paid Israel $25 million a year for resettlement and in addition $1,000 for each emigrant going to countries other than Israel, the State Department again stressed its strong support for the concept of freedom of choice for the emigrants.

So the conflict went back and forth with little change in positions. As late as June 1985 one could still hear Dulzin arguing desperately that refugee status should be removed from the emigrants and that there should be direct flights from Moscow.[70] The dropout issue's full potential for ripping the community apart was avoided only by the fact that after 1980 there were precious few emigrants to argue about.[71] It was neither HIAS nor JDC nor JAFI that held the trump card. That remained with the leadership in the Kremlin for whom the emigration issue was pushed further into the background by the events on the domestic and foreign scene.

▪   The glimmer of what remained of the détente policy inherited by the Carter administration vanished with the Soviet invasion of Afghanistan in December 1979. The Iran hostage crisis simmered beneath the surface and eventually forced the secretary of state, who opposed Carter's daring rescue plan, to resign. The crisis of Soviet control in Poland, where Solidarity, a trade union coalition, sought independence and the right to strike, culminated in December 1981 with a declaration of martial law. It was yet another sign of the fragility of the Soviet hold of Eastern Europe. But few in Moscow read it that way. The bomb and the ICBMs to go with it assured them that the threat of mutual destruction would prevent precipitous moves. But Reagan's Star Wars proposal made in March 1983 threatened to undermine the certainty of mutual assured destruction on which peace was based. Aside from the rhetorical militancy the new president brought to the White House there was little to suggest that the Cold War was coming to an end.

In the election of 1980 the Republican defeat of Carter and Mondale was viewed by some as a portent for the sharpening of the Cold War. There were many involved in the Soviet Jewry movement who, seeing the doldrums the movement had entered into in the eighties, recalled the remarkable progress made when Scoop Jackson introduced his amendment in 1972. The struggle for Soviet Jewry seemed to thrive when cold warriors were at the helm. That and a strong stand on Israel's security may be part of the reason why Reagan received 37 percent of the Jewish vote to Carter's 45 percent, a comparatively high percentage for a Republican. The third-party candidate John Anderson received 15 percent of the Jewish vote, the same percentage given to Henry Wallace in 1948. What is most remarkable about the election of 1980 is that the combined vote for Reagan and Anderson was larger than the Jewish vote given to the Democratic candidate who, since the election of 1928, traditionally received a majority of that vote.

But while the dropout issue may have been unsettling in the Jewish organizational world it barely earned a blip on the monitor of crucial world issues. For the general public the elusive peace in the Middle East, which in 1982 entered a new more violent phase, overshadowed the Soviet Jewry question. The primary concern of American Jewry continued to be the security of Israel. To allay that fear the Reagan administration offered Israel a Memorandum of Strategic Understanding, which was in fact the next best thing to a formal alliance without undermining its posture as an "honest broker" in the Arab-Israel conflict. But the memorandum was aimed at the long-range threat posed by Moscow and did little to ensure Israel's security in the face of growing Palestinian Liberation Organization buildup in southern Lebanon. It was that buildup that served as the background for Israel's invasion of Lebanon in June 1982. The invasion, which was followed by the massacres at the Sabra and Shatila refugee camps, dominated the news and completely overshadowed the conflict over the disposition of the Soviet emigrants. The invasion of Lebanon did not improve Israel's security problem nor did it help convince Soviet emigrants living in limbo in Rome and Vienna that Israel offered a solution to their situation. After a bloody suicide bombing of the American Marines with heavy loss of life, America withdrew from Lebanon in the fall of 1983. A tally sheet of the invasion would show Israel's loss of goodwill in world public opinion and little else to show for it.[72] The disaffection of potential Soviet emigrants was also a concealed effect of the perpetual low level war that continued to beset Israel.

It was the death of Brezhnev in November 1982 and the succession of Yuri Andropov, former head of the KGB, which ushered in the last phase before the Soviet implosion. While there had been signs of instability in the Soviet orbit, few Sovietologists fathomed the depth of internal weakness in the Soviet system. One might argue that those involved in the Soviet Jewry movement, especially the Soviet activists, should have known that the end of the system was near. But although they had learned from bitter experience that the system was not as invulnerable as generally believed, few foresaw its total collapse on the very issue that they had agitated about for more than a decade, the freedom of movement.

But on the dropout front the struggle continued. There was yet another effort to find common ground between the Israeli and American effort at the Third International Conference on Soviet Jewry that convened in Jerusalem in March 1983. Aware that the dropout problem was tearing at the very foundation of the "One People" idea that bound Israel to the far-flung Jewish Diaspora, they sought to defuse the conflict by a preconvention decision to avoid discussions of the dropout problem. But Dulzin, the outspoken head of JAFI, could not be contained and again roiled the waters of the meeting with his outspoken insistence that the emigrants belonged not to themselves but to Israel.

A year later emigration reached its lowest point in 15 years.[73] It seemed like the problem was on the road to solving itself. But for Israel the need for demographic supplementation had become more urgent than ever. The unending low level war with the Palestinians, which now took the form of the Intifada, not only discouraged Soviet emigrants from settling in Israel but was a constant temptation for Israel's citizens to cast off the heavy burden of citizenship and settle elsewhere. Under Yitzhak Shamir, Menahem Begin's successor, there were again efforts to convince the Reagan administration to deny refugee status to the dropouts. But in Washington and within the world of American Jewish organization the freedom of movement issue, the rubric under which the Soviet rescue issue was now framed, was too politically hot to handle. Only an awareness of the cost of absorption would finally convince American political leaders that Israel was the best destination for the emigrants who, after 1989, could only claim to be refugees by a stretch of the imagination.

But that was still years away. The advent of the Gorbachev regime in March 1985 signaled the eventual liberalization of emigration and the end of government-sponsored restrictions on education and desirable positions. But the dropout problem persisted and Israel changed its tactics to intercede directly in Washington on a government-to-government basis. In the end, however, it was the concrete matter of economics and budgets that would determine what their destination would be.

The first phase of the dropout phenomenon brought the conflict between Israel and American Jewry to the surface. From many American Jews who considered themselves lifetime Zionists, Israel's wielding of state power to realize state goals came as a surprise. Three decades after the state had been founded devoted Zionists retained a highly idealized notion of the Jewish state as somehow exempt from the primary obligation of sovereignty. Like other states, *raison d'état* would be given the highest priority and in its name almost anything to ensure the state's security could be done. The image of Israel held by American Jews born in the twenties and thirties was of a nation composed of heroic pioneer founders, the daring social experimentation of the kibbutz, and the gallantry of its soldiers on the field of battle. The tenacity with which Israel pursued the dropouts served as a wake-up call. They were introduced to a Jewish state with a will to survive not only on the field of battle but in the intracommunal conflicts of interest. They observed Israel fight tooth and nail to "capture" the Soviet emigrants because, like Ben-Gurion, it viewed biological enhancement a matter of life and death. The survival of the Jewish state had priority over the right of the emigrants to choose or there would be no rights at all. In the end no holds were barred, even the threat of subverting the opportunity of Soviet Jews to escape, in order to bring this "biological material" to Israel. That accounts for the daring of the liaison bureau in setting up the net that enabled Soviet Jewry to plug into a worldwide Jewish network.

Until 1987 such rough tactics availed little. The choice to drop out, which was really a choice for settling in America, ended only when the prospect of settling in America was removed from the table. After 1989 many thousands settled in Israel who would have dropped out had the American alternative still been available. In a sense it was again a *Zwungsaliyah,* similar to the arrival of the German Jews in the 1930s. They too would have dropped out if there had been a place to dropout to.

There was not and that absence brought a highly skilled and productive population to the *Yishuv*. It was hoped that a similar condition would develop for Soviet Jewry.

A Reagan fully recovered from an assassination attempt in March 1981 easily won the election of 1984, again with an unusually high percentage of normally democratic Jewish votes. Seven months after his second inauguration there were rumors that Gorbachev would allow France to fly "several thousand" Jews from the Soviet Union to Israel, and Poland announced the opening of an "interest section" in Tel Aviv.[74] Suddenly the log-jam was breaking and things were changing for the better in the Soviet world. After six years of bleak prospects hopes could again be raised. Surprisingly, the changes in the Soviet empire's control system and the release of the Jewish emigrants like freed pigeons from their cages had little to do with actions taken in Washington or Tel Aviv. They had internal roots within the Soviet system. The release of the Jews followed from Gorbachev's general liberalization. Those who argued all along that Soviet emigration policy was intrinsically rather than extrinsically driven were proven to be right, at least in the short run. But surely the long-range causes of the liberalization, which had a desperate last-minute character, had much to do with Cold War policies and strategies that had been in place for years. The Soviet Jewry issue was a small part of that.

Finally, from a historical perspective there was really not much new in the dropout phenomenon. In the contest between the two Zions, America and Israel, it has always been the former that exercised the stronger pull. The dropouts were really in the historical mainstream. They were doing what their ancestors did at the turn of the century and for much the same reason. Involved in the emigration process were two different visions of the Jewish future. The first viewed Israel as the sole repository of the Jewish future, with American Jewry giving philanthropic support. The second, which was the one that most America Jews operated under, held a much broader view of where that future might lie. They were concerned about the Jewish state but not prepared to have their lives shaped by settling there. They were determined to shape their future for themselves.

Photo of Gov. Michael Dukakis signing Soviet Jewry Human Rights Proclamation, 26 May 1977. *Left to right:* Bailey Barron, Sudbury, SJ co-chairperson; Betty Dyer, Newton; Judy Patkin, SSJ co-chairperson, Lexington; Janice Weiss, Brookline; Ronya Schwaab, Watertown; Rabbi Michael Luckens, Canton; Gov. Dukakis; Rabbi Myer Strassfeld, Marblehead, ASJ Honorary Board of Directors; Rabbi Cary Yales, Lexington; Trudy Shecter, ASJ director; Jane November, Cambridge; Jan Forsythe, Maynard. The movement's message was amplified by the contact local activists maintained with their political leaders. © American Jewish Historical Society. All rights reserved. American Jewish Historical Society, Newton Centre, Mass., and New York, N.Y.

English course for refugees in Ladispoli provided by JDC while United HIAS Service processed their immigration papers, 1979–80. Courtesy of the American Jewish Joint Distribution Committee.

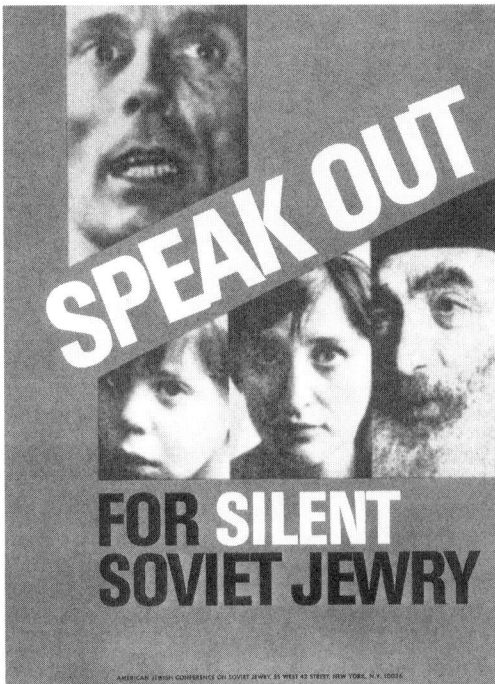

SPEAK OUT FOR SILENT SOVIET JEWRY

Poster of the American Jewish Conference on Soviet Jewry. Courtesy of NCSJ: Advocates on Behalf of Jews in Russia, Ukraine, the Baltic States, and Eurasia.

Poster of the Greater New York Conference on Soviet Jewry. Courtesy of the American Jewish Committee.

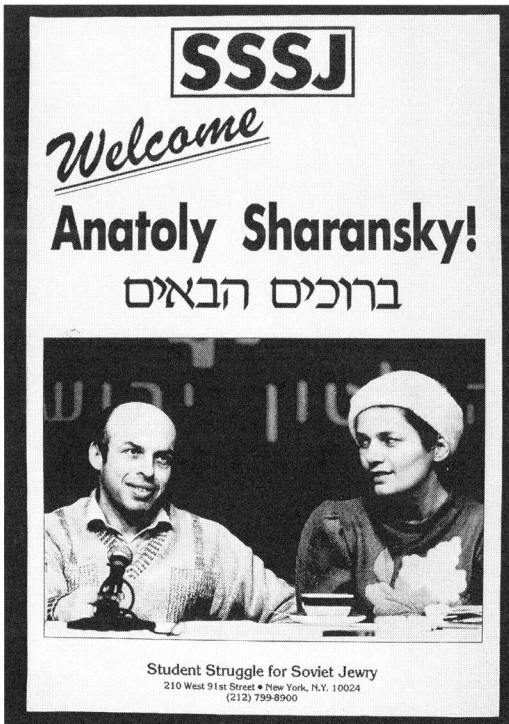

"SSSJ. Welcome Anatoly Sharansky! Bruchim habaim." Black-and-white poster by the Student Struggle for Soviet Jewry featuring a photo of Sharansky reunited with his wife after his release. It includes the address and telephone number of the SSSJ. 1986. Gift of Wendy Eisen. Collection of the Museum of Jewish Heritage—A Living Memorial to the Holocaust, New York.

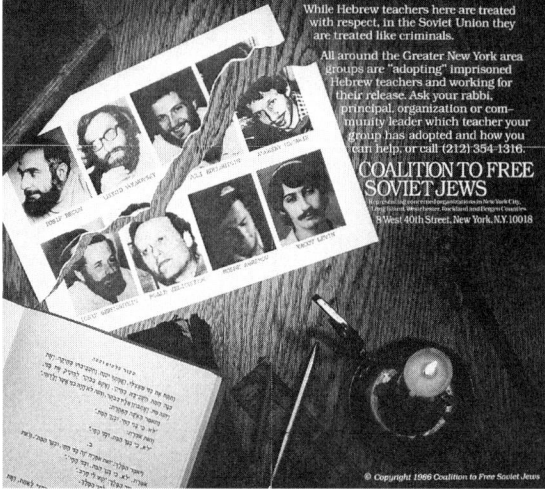

Poster protesting the arrest of Soviet Jews for teaching Hebrew and advising readers to become involved by "adopting" an imprisoned Soviet Jewish Hebrew teacher. Coalition to Free Soviet Jews. 1986. Gift of Hadassah, the Women's Zionist Organization of America. Collection of the Museum of Jewish Heritage—A Living Memorial to the Holocaust, New York.

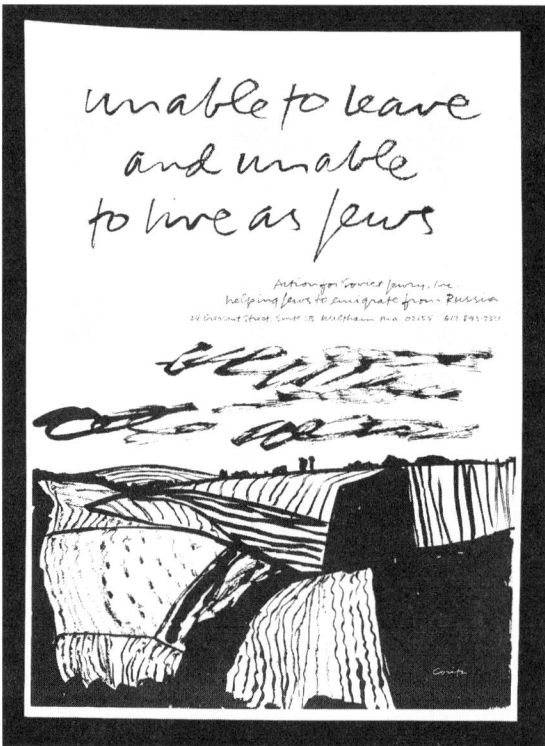

Black-and-white poster with illustration of landscape. Design donated to the organization by Sister Corita [Kent]. Donor cannot remember date, just that it was done at the height of the refusenik movement. Gift of Action for Post-Soviet Jewry. Collection of the Museum of Jewish Heritage—A Living Memorial to the Holocaust, New York.

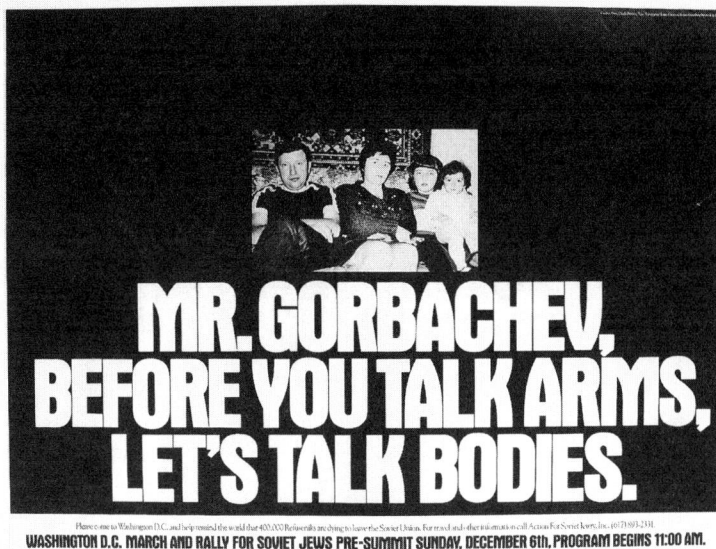

Black-and-white poster with photo of refusenik family, in English, 1987. Designed pro bono by Rossin Greenberg Seronick and Hill, a Boston advertising agency, for Action for Soviet Jewry. 1987. Gift of Action for Post-Soviet Jewry. Collection of the Museum of Jewish Heritage—A Living Memorial to the Holocaust, New York.

Black-and-white poster with impressionistic illustration of Moses with outstretched arm holding staff, the people of Israel crossing the Red Sea. Small text at bottom: "Moses did his part years ago to free the Jews. Now it's your turn. Write your elected officials or contact us today." 1980s. Gift of Action for Post-Soviet Jewry. Collection of the Museum of Jewish Heritage—A Living Memorial to the Holocaust, New York.

New arrivals in Vienna. Courtesy of the American Jewish Joint Distribution Committee.

SIX Of Human Rights

By all counts the relationship of human rights to the Soviet Jewry movement ought to be a direct one. The right to emigrate is after all listed in the Universal Declaration of Human Rights to which the Soviet Union ultimately became a signatory. Yet until the clamor for the right of Jews to leave Russia began it had a comparatively low resonance. People spoke of the freedom of religion or of speech but less frequently of the freedom of movement. That comparative neglect may be attributable to its singularity as a human right. What it seeks is not the right to enjoy all the freedoms guaranteed by law in a democratic society, but the right to leave, perhaps to enjoy those rights elsewhere. The freedom of emigration is the freedom to escape. So it was for Soviet Jewry.[1]

That emigration was a right to which all citizens were entitled was part and parcel of the public relations that we have seen was the way the movement got its message known. Sen. Jackson's image as a cold warrior, for example, overshadowed his abiding concern for human rights, which was part of virtually all his public statements on the Jackson amendment. "The fight for free emigration from the Soviet Union," he stated, "is part of the larger struggle for human rights in all lands and for all people."[2] But there was also a sense among the Soviet activists that the language of justice in a society that produced a gulag was an exercise in futility. In the Soviet world rights had to be bargained and paid for. The Jackson-Vanik Amendment was viewed as a bargaining chip to induce the Soviet Union to grant what citizens in democratic societies possessed by right. Most-favored-nation (MFN) status and credit were offered if Moscow would allow visa applicants with close relatives abroad to emigrate and in addition end the harassment of those who dared to apply for visas. Soviet activists were adamant in their view that pressure on the Kremlin had to be maintained. Many activists outside the Soviet Union, particularly those associated with the Union of Councils for Soviet Jewry (UCSJ), shared that view, and it was that insistence that set the stage for communal tension when some Jewish leaders were ready to negotiate the softening of the amendment in 1978 and 1979.

There is a fairly broad consensus that the Soviet leaders repudiated the trade agreement in January 1975 because the credit it wanted was virtually withdrawn by the Stevenson Amendment. When that happened the Kremlin lost interest in transacting business concerning the Jewish emigrants, and the numbers allowed to leave declined. Believers in the barometer theory, which postulates that Soviet emigration policy is driven by events outside Russia, were convinced that an error was made in offering the Kremlin a treaty. Clearly, when negotiating with the Soviets the best results were achieved not by making concessions but by withholding rewards and drawing out the negotiations so that the bargain could be sweetened by granting more exit visas. One researcher referred to that phenomenon as "linkage interruptus," by which he meant that the best results could be achieved when the bargaining was still going on.[3] Clearly some new negotiating strategy had to be found to replace the repudiated Jackson-Vanik Amendment. Jewish communal support for the amendment had in any case become a source of controversy, but the unexpected rise in emigration figures in 1978 and 1979 was interpreted by amendment supporters as belated evidence of its effectiveness, notwithstanding the fact that the suppression of activists had also intensified.

That human rights received a new emphasis at the historical juncture when the Jackson-Vanik Amendment seemed no longer effective is not a coincidence. The difference between the two approaches was that Jackson-Vanik was specifically designed to allow Jews to emigrate, whereas Helsinki's Basket III listed most human rights, including the general right of the freedom of movement, that applied to all captive peoples.

Moreover, the linkage of the Soviet Jewish emigration movement to general human rights was anomalous because activists within the Soviet Union had long since made it clear that they did not consider themselves "democratizers" or opponents of the regime. They were intent on leaving the Soviet Union rather than waiting for the day when Jews became acceptable in the Soviet political and social order.

For potential emigrants who were not imbued with Zionist ideology, the human rights movement offered some protection from their painful limbo state that followed the application process. An exit visa based on human rights also addressed a broader subject than the perennial persecuted Jews. Emigration would then become a natural human right rather than a betrayal of "mother Russia." More important, the idea of human rights itself had become a compelling sentiment in the Soviet bloc , whether it was called "Socialism with a human face" as in Czechoslovakia or simply "Solidarity" as in Poland. It was everywhere considered the desired direction of progress.[4] Its advocacy gave the U.S. a formidable weapon in the Cold War, though as the Carter administration would discover, it was one not easily wielded. It also proved to be surprisingly effective in improving the leverage for Soviet Jewry. The special crucible Jews faced in the Soviet Union was real, but in a world full of depredations the tribulation of a single group, as severe as it might be, was not considered exceptional. The campaign for emigration based on human rights placed the case for Soviet Jewry in the mainstream. When Soviet Jewry would finally be freed it would come together with all others who had been suppressed by the Soviet regime.

■ The displacement of the Jackson-Vanik Amendment by the human rights embodied in Basket III of the Helsinki Accords did not occur all at once. The conflict over the amendment's effectiveness raged on in 1978 and 1979, and its echoes continued to be heard until it was gradually bypassed by the exercise of the president's waiver authority. As long as the Soviet authorities continued to exercise their power to grant the exit visa the process of negotiating for the release of the emigrants was problematic. It permitted a tyrannical regime to extort a kind of ransom to be paid for people held captive.[5] Some thought that such payment, whether in trade and credit or money, was a dubious proposition. The very idea of bargaining for rights was repellent because it surrendered the moral high ground. But in Jewish law the actual redemption of prisoners, *pidyon shivuim,* the notion that such payments reward extortion and further encourage immoral behavior, was not considered relevant. The saving of lives is considered the higher morality. The *halachic* (religious law) assumption on which the case for paying ransom rests is also dubious because most Soviet Jews did not consider themselves prisoners, at least not more so than other Soviet citizens. The prisoner issue became convoluted when, for public relations reasons, the imprisoned refuseniks were dubbed "prisoners of Zion," which was soon changed to "prisoners of conscience."[6]

The American business leaders who pushed hard to break the grip that they believed the Jewish emigration issue held on the development of trade with the Soviet Union were not concerned about the moral issue. They considered the Jackson-Vanik Amendment a bad bargain from the perspective of business. For them and a number of key representatives, including Charles Vanik, an original promulgator of the amendment, the proposed reconsideration of the trade act by Congress scheduled for 1979 was an opportunity to recoup the losses the American economy sustained by the inflexibility of the act. Despite the fact that the president found alternate ways of extending good credit terms to Soviet buyers, the catalogue of missed opportunities and lost profit was growing.

Whether the amendment actually harmed the American economy is difficult to ascertain because the question is inextricably tied to coexisting strictures on Soviet-American trade related to national security. Far from being the sole or even the most important legislation restricting Soviet-American trade, the Jackson-Vanik Amendment was not concerned with exporting of high technology or strategic materials, which had a far greater impact on Soviet-American trade. The tensions that arose between free traders and cold warriors by the conflicting approaches to the use of access to the American market and credit for foreign policy objectives first came to the fore in the Carter administration. Secretary Cyrus Vance saw trade as a peace-generating, stabilizing factor, whereas Zbigniew Brzezinski, the National Security Advisor, was more inclined to use trade, especially the sale of technology, as a Cold War weapon. The Carter trade policy fluctuated between the two positions, leading one economist to label it "lightswitch" diplomacy because of its on and off character.[7] In 1978, despite considerable opposition to controlling the sale of oil drilling equipment and other high-tech products, the Carter administration prohibited the Sperry Rand Corporation from selling an advanced computer to Russia. But a year later, coming under pressure from the agricultural states, it permitted the sale of 25 million metric tons of grain under generous credit terms extended by the Commodity Credit Corporation. Introduced by Sen. Humphrey (S2385) and Rep. Paul Findley (HR10377) in December 1977, the bill soon gained the strong backing of the agricultural states. The sale served as an early wedge that circumvented the Jackson-Vanik Amendment.

In his testimony against the measure, Eugene Gold, chairman of the National Conference on Soviet Jewry (NCSJ), wondered why Congress would now "begin the steps which would dismantle this unique statement of concern for human dignity."[8] But there were portents that the common front of the Jewish organizations supporting the amendment was weakening. Without notifying its fellow members of NCSJ's executive committee, the American Jewish Congress (AJCong) announced its support of the extension of commodity export credits to the Soviet Union, breaking the common front presented in support of the amendment. Some considered the AJCong action as a first step in dismantling the Jackson-Vanik Amendment.[9] The use of trade as an instrument to wring better treatment was complicated by the thin line that had to be drawn between the sale of products that could affect national security and the refusal to extend favorable credit terms to serve a humanitarian purpose such as free emigration. In the heated atmosphere of the Cold War of the late seventies the distinction was often lost. Some general support for the Jackson amendment undoubtedly was rooted in its anti-Soviet character rather than the desire to right wrong. Rabbi Israel Miller, a founder of the Soviet Jewry movement, became convinced that government support of the Soviet Jewry movement was based on self-interest because it allowed them "to paint the Soviet Union into a corner on the human rights issues."[10]

The problem of evaluating the impact of trade restrictions was compounded by the refusal of the Soviet leadership to act as if they were headed for economic disaster. At a luncheon of the executive board of the U.S.-USSR Trade and Economic Council in response to Sen. Ribicoff linking the granting of MFN with the easing of emigration restriction, the Soviet minister of trade, Nikolai S. Patolichev, angrily declared to the gathered assembly, "We don't want your trade" and castigated American policy makers for being so exclusively concerned with Jews.[11] The Soviet minister's confidence may have been buoyed by the good news that an otherwise gloomy prognosis of the Soviet economy found forward movement in the crucial area of the development of its oil and gas industry. Based on its extensive petroleum resources the Soviet Union would become a seller rather than a consumer of petroleum products by 1985. When the Soviets repudiated the trade agreement in January 1975 the rapid increase in oil prices gave them a surplus of over a half billion dollars. The pressure for credit was, for the moment at least, not urgent.

Speaking of dynamics behind the move to soften the 1974 Trade Act, Marina Wallach, the NCSJ's agent in Washington, observed that "when the Russians desired, they seemed perfectly willing to pay cash as in the case of the grain purchase."[12] The awareness that other creditors and technologically advanced nations were picking up the trade that the United States had abandoned also became a factor in a movement to eschew using trade to moderate the behavior of the Soviet Union. Why should grain and general food products that had no direct strategic utility join the arsenal of economic weapons to control Moscow's behavior? argued the grain interests. In 1980 an export license was again denied to Sperry Univac Computer though it was purportedly only to be used for the forthcoming Olympic games. In the Carter administration, trade sanctions were turned on and off depending on the crisis raging at the time. They were imposed after the invasion of Afghanistan in December 1979 and all licensed exports were suspended and cereals embargoed in March 1980, pending review. Those who argued against the use of embargoes saw little evidence that these on and off again trade restrictions had any impact on Soviet policy.[13] The Soviet commissars could always turn to other developed nations, which were not as strictly bound by sanctions, to get reasonable credit terms and to purchase technology.[14] By 1980 American-Soviet trade was down by 3.7 percent.[15]

■   It was the concern about loss of markets that served as the background for the sharpening debate in Washington over the value of economic sanctions. Its outcome would be a factor in switching the emigration campaign from credit and trade sanctions to the morally elevated standard offered by human rights. The Jewish lobby, it was argued, held American trade policy hostage and compelled the American taxpayer to pay a dear price in markets and jobs.[16] "Remember Jackson-Vanik," argued one government official, "it was our one cannon ball. We loaded, we fired, and we missed. It didn't gain us a thing."[17]

Those concerned with human rights were hard pressed to convince the corporate leaders that there was more at stake than profits. If the West proved unable to put a brake on Soviet expansion abroad and suppression at home, they might end up losing more than business profits. Zbigniew Brzezinski, Carter's national security advisor, agreed with Soviet activists that the Kremlin must be kept under constant pressure and the nation's superior economic performance was the best place to begin. He was hardly alone in sensing Moscow's economic vulnerability but was more optimistic than most in sensing that it could be used to modify Soviet behavior.

That was the setting for the reconsideration of the Jackson-Vanik Amendment in 1978. It was part of a legislative process fueled by those in the business community and proponents of the détente policy who thought that the amendment was ineffective and counterproductive. But there was also a new element in the contretemps over the amendment. With the Helsinki Accords the human rights component of the amendment framed the conflict in a new way. In the post-Helsinki years the intensification of the Cold War widened the gulf between the two superpowers. The wielding of the trade weapon to wring human rights concessions did not concern national security directly. But its proponents now maintained that the amendment was a strategic as well as an ideological asset that came at a very low price because the disaffection within the Soviet Union was a self-starting affair requiring no nurture from Washington.[18] Besides, Jackson's supporters aspired to something more than another weapon to enhance national security. They imagined they were freeing the captive people of the Soviet empire.

The American Jewish posture regarding the amendment followed along somewhat similar lines. The idea of human rights had always generated a special passion in the Jewish community that went beyond group interest. The principle ideological buttress behind emigration was that it was a human right that belonged naturally to the citizen. What was missing was some means to make the Soviets comply with that right. Unexpectedly, the monitoring idea embodied in Basket IV of the Helsinki Accords coupled with the idea of follow-up conferences to review implementation gave it a binding character through what one researcher called a process of "shaming."[19] In a country that produced a gulag the idea of shaming into compliance may seem far fetched, but as noted the Soviet regime was extremely sensitive to outside opinion. Moreover, perhaps because it was denied to them, human rights had gained a special appeal among the people of the Warsaw Pact nations.

How to back up public support for human rights with an instrument to wring compliance proved to be problematic for the Carter administration. Rhetorically the administration was a strong proponent of human rights, but it was unable to come to a clear decision regarding the Jackson amendment, which addressed only one aspect of the human rights question. On one hand, as early as 1977 it favored a relaxation of the waiver and credit aspects that impacted on Soviet-American trade. On the other hand, by June 1979, when new congressional hearings on the Stevenson bill were scheduled, the Carter administration had not yet reached a decision on what course to follow. The continued Soviet refusal to negotiate on emigration, even to furnish the "formal assurances" of compliance that the Stevenson bill called for, would affect that decision. On Moscow's part there was the knowledge that without Sen. Jackson's support such a modification was in any case doomed to failure. Affecting both Washington and Moscow was the fear that if MFN were extended to China while it was denied to the Soviet Union, Cold War tensions that were already stretched to the breaking point by the discovery of an armed Soviet brigade in Cuba would intensify.

The impact of the amendment could be mitigated by lowering the requirement for the exercise of the waiver component that empowered the president to lower the restrictions on credit if there was sufficient evidence that the Soviet authorities were complying with the agreement to permit emigration and to halt suppressive activities. The arguments concerning enforcement related to defining what was meant by "sufficient." Instead of "waivering" the restriction year by year, Carter wanted to extend the waiver at one swoop to a three- or five-year period. The waiver became the battleground on which Congress and the president battled. Following in Nixon's footsteps, in November 1977 Carter requested that Congress soften the amendment's procedure by eliminating the requirement of assurances of compliance from the Soviet authorities and putting the question of credit extension back into the president's hands. The Ford administration too aspired to normalize trade relations with Moscow. But for Carter events conspired to move trade policy in the opposite direction. A major reason for that is attributable to Moscow's open expansionism in Angola, the horn of Africa, and the positioning of a brigade in Cuba. The threat from Moscow seemed more real than ever.

Carter's position was equally delicate on the domestic political scene. In order to realize his aspirations for a second term, he needed the support of the Jackson Democrats and the Jewish community. In the case of the latter it was not so much the size of the Jewish vote that had in fact lost proportional numbers compared to the black and Hispanic voting blocs, but its location in pivotal states. Jewish political influence was also amplified by its ability to extend financial support to the candidate of its choice. That was especially true of the Democratic Party, where more than 60 percent of its funds originated from Jewish sources. During the 1976 election campaign Carter's emphasis on human rights resonated strongly with Jewish voters, as did appropriate planks on Israel and the Soviet Jewry that matched those in the Republican Party platform. But for a group that traditionally voted democratic, Carter's support in the Jewish community was only lukewarm. Scoop Jackson or Morris Udall, who were strong on Israel but lost in the primary campaign, would probably have gotten more enthusiastic support than the "born again" Carter.[20] One Jewish pundit noted that "to them [Jewish voters] he is from a distinct region, a strange faith, [and] given to expressions of piety uncongenial to them."[21] For the moment Jewish support of the Jackson amendment was firm, but there was apprehension lest Carter, who spoke frequently of human rights, would group the emigration issue with other unsolved problems to be addressed when the situation was appropriate.

Matters took an unexpected turn when the congressional hearings before the subcommittee on international trade of the House Ways and Means Committee dealing with the renewal of the Stevenson Amendment were held in June 1979. The hearings concerned general trade policy, which entailed the extension of MFN to China, Hungary, and Romania as well as the Soviet Union. The latter two nations had previously agreed to the waiver policy requiring them to give yearly assurance of compliance with the liberalized emigration provision. The opportunity of Congress to play its version of the "China card" by extending MFN to the three Communist regimes while withholding it from the Soviet Union was too good to be missed. When Jackson was confronted with the inconsistency of his position he responded that the Soviet Union was the primary danger to world security. China was playing a significant strategic role in helping to deter Soviet expansion. Jackson insisted that the question of whether China would comply with section 402 of the amendment was less relevant in the case of China, where there were no Jews clamoring to leave.[22]

The subcommittee recommended granting MFN to China, Romania, and Hungary despite the fact that they did not meet the requirement that their economies be market driven. It was not Jewish political pressure that determined Congress's course but the renewed intensity of the Cold War. It was an attempt to humiliate Moscow by granting a long sought-for status to its opponent in the Socialist world. But that effort did not put the brakes on Carter's hope to repeal the amendment and restore the executive authority to determine credit policy.

Predictably, a somewhat tasseled and fragmented American Jewish leadership was in the forefront of the opposition to soften the waiver requirement. By 1976 the rank and file activists, particularly those associated with the UCSJ and the Student Struggle for Soviet Jewry, considered the amendment sacred ground. Some were convinced that if they had not quite bent the Kremlin to their will, the astounding emigration figures of 1979 proved that they must have done something right. Why abandon a policy that works? They took pride in what they thought they had achieved. "The organized Jewish community had created a law from beginning to end," noted one observer, "it identified a problem, placed it in the public eye, created legislation and moved it into law, overcoming the objections of the administration and Congress and the business community."[23] In the face of such strong convictions it would have come close to heresy, after the intensification of the Kremlin's anti-Semitic campaign, to retreat from supporting the Jackson-Vanik Amendment. Neglected was the growing evidence that after 1979 it was becoming virtually impossible for Jews to leave the Soviet Union. The voice of opposition to tampering with the amendment was particularly strong from the firing line in the Soviet Union. Soviet activists insisted that although the Soviet Union had signed the Helsinki Accords, there was no assurance that they would be implemented. The only thing that brought results was constant pressure from abroad. Sixty-eight refuseniks from nine Soviet cities appealed to Congress to continue their support of the Jackson Amendment "which at least, acts as an obstacle to the unbridled tyranny of the Soviet authorities in their emigration policies."[24] The fact that Scoop Jackson, who had become a great favorite among Jews of all political stripes, remained adamantly opposed to tampering with his amendment, carried weight.[25] Most important, though officially Israel could take no position on an American domestic matter and its distress at the high percentage of the emigrants who chose to drop out was palpable, its support for keeping the amendment unchanged was well known. The primary need was to get Soviet Jewry out. There would be time enough later to change America's generous refugee laws so that the flow of emigrants could be channeled to Israel, which needed and wanted them.

The possibility of communal polarization over the amendment had increased. Bertram Gold, the executive director of the American Jewish Committee (AJC), counseled that the conflict remain within the communal arena. But Hyman Bookbinder, acting as the AJC's Washington agent, a position that gave him a good vantage to view the practical political realities, noted that the higher emigration figures in 1978 and 1979 indicated that the Soviets were in fact responding. The ball was in the American court. A number of Jewish leaders favored keeping the amendment on the books but making some changes in the waiver authority provision to give the president more flexibility. Theodore Mann, the incoming chairman of the Conference of Presidents favored such a modification and predicted that within sixty days the amendment would be waived for twelve months and the Soviet Union would be granted MFN.[26] Richard Maass, who had been president of the AJC and as the president of the NCSJ probably was the person most responsible for the establishment of that agency, came to a different conclusion. He noted that there was no serious effort to negotiate with Moscow after its repudiation of the agreement. Aware of the increase in the volume in the grain trade without special credit benefits, Maass felt the problem could be traced to the nonnegotiable credit restrictions of the Stevenson Amendment. He opposed repealing the amendment but remained convinced that it could be better tailored to allow negotiations on emigration to begin again.

It was clear that by 1979 the emigration scene had changed. The increasing dropout rate gave credence to the Soviet argument promoted by the Anti-Zionist Committee of the Public, which declared that all Jews who wished to go to Israel had already done so. Most troubling for the NCSJ was the fact that the years of struggle to change the amendment when added to the years it required to bring it into existence had muddied the waters. The complex waiver provision was beyond the comprehension of the average newspaper reader. Some had lost track of the amendment and were inquiring if it was still in effect.[27]

Not all were as optimistic as Richard Maass, who wanted to restart negotiations with Moscow. After the doldrums in the years after 1975 and again after 1980, some had come to agree with Kissinger's prediction that the amendment would have a boomerang effect.[28] Surprisingly, the two originators of the trade-for-emigrants transaction, Sen. Vanik and Sen. Adlai Stevenson III, were now in favor of making concessions. The position of the NCSJ was particularly delicate because its rival organization, the UCSJ, was strongly opposed to softening the amendment, whereas the AJCong, one of its major constituent organizations, had already supported Carter's granting of credit for agricultural exports in 1978 and was supporting the Findley bill that would grant agricultural commodity credits to the Soviets in exchange for increasing emigration. Howard Squadron, AJCong's president, and Phil Baum, its associate executive director, saw an opportunity to restart negotiations with the Soviets after their repudiation of the trade act.[29] Jerry Goodman, testifying before the Committee on Banking in November, saw the possibility to do "some bargaining on behalf of human beings" should the opportunity arise.[30] This was not the time to abandon the commitment, Goodman observed, but the door was left open should such a moment materialize at some future time. Based on the advice of Marina Wallach, to assume an "intermediate" position on matters relating to a change in the Jackson amendment, the NCSJ took a more flexible position than that adopted by the UCSJ.[31] The conflict carried into 1979 with Moscow proving surprisingly amenable to back-channel negotiations on credit. Communal conflict about the amendment continued well into the eighties. As late as July 1983 when Edgar Bronfman, president of the World Jewish Congress, called for repeal of the amendment, he was roundly condemned for it by Morris Abram, chairman of the NCSJ.[32]

But clearly after the movement to soften the amendment was rejected the possibility of exacting concessions on emigration from Moscow on the basis of the trade credit linkage diminished. Between 1980 and 1983 the rate of emigration declined to a pre-1971 level and continued to be very low until 1987. The historian is left with the agonizing question of whether thousands of Jewish visa applicants, compelled to live in limbo, might earlier and more easily have gained their freedom had the amendment not been enacted in 1974 or at least softened in 1979. How one answers this question depends on the assessment of the character of the Soviet regime at a given moment in history. For those who believe that the rate of emigration acted as a barometer showing how outside events influenced Soviet domestic policy, enormous power was attributed to the amendment. Yet, strangely, such strong amendment advocates do not take responsibility for the sharp decline in emigration after a softening of its waiver provision was rejected by Congress in 1979. At the same time, those who maintain that Soviet policy was only minimally affected by outside factors do not come to grips with the diverse pattern of the German emigration in which neither the Jackson amendment nor the human rights movement played a role. Despite cordial relations between Bonn and Moscow, the notion that the two emigrations occurred in tandem is difficult to maintain after 1976. Although Jewish migration soared to new heights in 1979, German emigration remained low. There were periods when the reverse was the case. The oscillations of Soviet emigration policy have yet to be explained.[33]

The argument regarding the amendment's effectiveness after 1980 continued to the end of the decade and today is taken up by historians. Many would agree with the assessment of Professor Marshall Goldman, who became a consultant for the CSCE: "One cheer for the Jackson Vanik Amendment. Two cheers or more for Mikhail Gorbachev, and no cheers for the latter-day efforts of the Jewish community."[34] The low assessment of the Jewish community was based in some measure on the inability of the Jewish organizations to come to a shared estimate of the impact of the amendment and the intent of the Kremlin after Gorbachev.

■ The discovery of human rights as the Jackson-Vanik Amendment lost steam was not a planned or sudden change. It had in fact always been there and the relationship between the two was clear. The right to emigrate was a human rights goal to which the Jackson amendment, using the leverage of the American economy, could pressure for compliance. But the rejection of any softening of the provisions of the amendment to the Trade Act of 1974 and the Stevenson Amendment meant that the possibility of negotiating the emigration issue on the basis of trade and credit concessions had lessened. Something new would have to be found to keep the movement going. The problem was considered as early as 4 May 1975 at a Leadership Assembly convened in Washington where various "additional" options to the Jackson Amendment were considered.[35] An answer was found in the nature of the human rights issue itself, which, whether it spoke of freedom of religion, speech, or movement proved enormously difficult for the Kremlin to handle after Khrushchev's confessional speech at the Twentieth Congress of the Communist Party of the Soviet Union that virtually confirmed the worst that had been said about the regime. Evidence that its relationship to the Soviet bloc nations was not one of socialist fraternity but of an occupier had accumulated. It culminated in the Warsaw Pact invasion of Czechoslovakia in 1968. On the crucial public relations front the Soviet Union was losing much of the goodwill that it had won, especially in the third world. The amendment remained in place but willy nilly human rights became the new weapon of choice.

How to bring about compliance from the Soviets by merely talking of international standards of moral behavior posed a problem. The Soviet government and its satellites did not sign the Universal Declaration on Human Rights on 10 December 1948. But it was a signatory to the key protocols that followed: the UN International Covenant on Civil and Political Rights in 1973 and the Helsinki Protocol in 1975. The three declarations included in different forms the right to leave and return to one's country. But none had the force of international law, and Moscow understood them to mean that implementation would occur within the context of the signatories existing laws. It was an "internal matter." The problem was how to exact Soviet compliance with at least minimal standards. The answer was found in Basket IV of the Helsinki Final Act, which called for monitoring commissions for the signatories and triennial conferences to evaluate implementation.[36]

The United States did not come to the human rights issue bereft of experience in the human rights arena. Before Kissinger's realpolitik muted its play, human rights had a major motivational role in American foreign policy. It was played out in Congress where the struggle over the Jackson-Vanik Amendment was one of several legislative proposals that sought to introduce a moral component into foreign policy. It also had a presence in the State Department, which maintained a Human Rights Division under the assistant secretary for international organizations, and also in the U.S. delegation to the UN Commission on Human Rights, which in the heady days after World War II was headed by Eleanor Roosevelt. Its Universal Declaration of Human Rights, which contained the freedom of movement in its most pristine form, became the Magna Carta of the human rights movement. Separate government agencies, such as the U.S. Commission on International Religious Freedom, and nongovernment organizations (NGOs), such as Freedom House and Amnesty International, also played a role in what was essentially a human rights community. Human rights initiatives usually originated in Congress rather than the executive branch. Sen. Jack Kemp, for example, called for cosponsors on 18 October 1971 for a resolution conceived jointly with George H. W. Bush, ambassador to the United Nations, linking the right of emigration to the developing human rights campaign.

Predictably, there was resistance to wielding the human rights cudgel during the Nixon administration that went beyond Kissinger's disdain for the moralistic. The UN's Human Rights Commission was confined to a limited role in the Soviet Jewish emigration question because its influence had been undermined from within by nondemocratic nations. By 1969, except for its title, the commission had little to do with human rights.[37] Rita Hauser, a prominent attorney affiliated with the AJC, was Nixon's appointment to the commission. She soon recognized, as would Morris Abram, appointed to the commission in March 1968, that the U.N. was not a good venue for the remediation of the depredations against Soviet Jewry and so advised the NCSJ in May 1970.[38] She predicted that the Arab delegates would counter by citing Israel's human rights violations in the occupied territories.[39] A study by William Korey uncovered similar difficulties three years later.[40] Hauser had delivered a stinging address before the commission on Soviet human rights violations urging a more tolerant policy toward all its minorities including Jews. The address culminated with her expression of certainty "that the Jews of that country will add as much to Russian life as the Jews have added to the life of my country." Unaffected, the Soviet delegate, Nikolai Tarassov, responded with the now traditional reminder of lynching in the South and the existence of "serious anti-Semitic feeling" in the United States.[41] Yosef Tekoah, Israel's ambassador, also turned to UN Secretary General Kurt Waldheim with a request that an international commission be established to investigate the Soviet Union's violation of the Universal Declaration of Human Rights that had been recently ratified.[42] There was no response.

It was small wonder then that the initial reception of the Helsinki process was not enthusiastic. It was naturally viewed in the context of the weak response to human rights issues in the State Department and the United Nations. These bodies could now be circumvented. The human rights initiative would be taken up by the Helsinki monitoring groups. The State Department's Human Rights Commission, a small bureau, had been established as a subcommittee of an existing committee, with no budget of its own. It would be called into play when Congress passed the resolution authorizing the creation of the Helsinki monitoring committee in January 1976. But few gave the new hybrid agency composed of a melding of congressional and State Department personnel much chance to succeed.

The treatment of Soviet Jewry gradually became a human rights problem but that was not precisely a change for the activists. It simply meant that their public relations would now be coached in broader terms. Every player concerned with Soviet Jewry developed its human rights line, which served as the ideological underpinning and grist for the movement's public relations effort. In the Soviet Union as in Israel, activists couched their protests in human rights terms. In the Soviet bloc Alexander Dubcek's "human" as in "Socialism with a human face," referred to human rights. The civil rights movement had earned America goodwill in every corner of the world. "We Shall Overcome," its signature ballad, was sung everywhere. Unlike the trade and credit offered by the Jackson amendment, its currency was a nonnegotiable insistence on a higher standard of moral behavior. Supporting human rights convinced its advocates that they were on the right side of history. In the face of all predictions it proved to be surprisingly effective in the long run. Granting Jews the right to emigrate was the right thing to do, just as granting full civil rights to all citizens was in America.

The legal basis of human rights rested in international law, which meant it had no sanction except for the pressure of world public opinion and such penalties as could be mustered in particularly egregious cases. American foreign policy is often viewed as oscillating between the poles of idealism and realpolitik.[43] That impulse was not shared by the Soviet Union, whose position on human rights was closer to the international norm, which held that the protection of human rights in a nation other than one's own is not a legitimate part of a nation's national interest. Its foreign policy should not therefore include the attempt to shape the way another government treats its citizens. That, Kissinger complained endlessly, was precisely what the Jackson-Vanik Amendment was trying to do.

In a sense the Helsinki spirit that sought the universal adoption of human rights principles was an externalization of the civil rights impulse that had strong domestic support. Soviet Jewry was one of several groups targeted for amelioration, ranging from Tibetans to the Bantu of South Africa. The strategy of economic trade-offs in turn for some concession on human rights upon which the Jackson amendment was based was also precedented. The introduction of the previously mentioned (chapter 4, note 19) legislation by Rep. Bertram Podell and Rep. Thomas Rees was an early attempt to induce nonmarket nations to adopt human rights measures by the threat or inducement of trade. A direct attempt to compel regimes to adhere to human rights standards was introduced by freshman Rep. Thomas Harkin in October 1975 as an amendment to the International Development and Food Assistance Act of 1975. Harkin's resolution, which repeated a 1961 effort, set the parameters of the human rights issue by restricting security assistance and economic aid to regimes that had exhibited a "consistent pattern of gross violations of internationally recognized human rights." It was more far-reaching then the Jackson amendment.[44] But although it came to national attention at the same time as the Jackson amendment, withholding food and medicine for needy populations to gain some control over tyrannical regimes threw out the baby with the bathwater. As Rep. Millicent Fenwick put it: "It was not a question of who lives in the Palace but where the people are."[45] The desire to modify the behavior of the Soviets was similar to the Jackson amendment, but the target was too diffuse and did not have a human rights focus. The Jackson-Vanik Amendment was the first major international human rights legislation passed by Congress that possessed such a focus. The debate that followed the introduction of the amendment broadened the public interest in human rights issue. The link between the Jackson-

Vanik Amendment and the Helsinki Accords was their common aspiration to raise the standard of government adherence to human rights to a universal standard. However, the amendment focused on a single human right infringement, the right to emigrate and an end to citizen harassment. Jews were not specifically mentioned in the amendment but that their mistreatment was its focus was understood by all involved. When linked to the Helsinki process it gave the Soviet Jewry case a greater resonance. What had changed is that the victimization of Soviet Jewry could now really be seen as part of a pattern of suppression in the Soviet sphere. Unlike the years of the Holocaust Jews were not alone in facing the onslaught of a nation state fueled by a crusading ideology.

Jews in diaspora communities were not strangers to the idea of human rights anchored in international law. American Jewish scholars had gained considerable prominence in the area where human rights and international law intersect. During the period after World War I, when the League of Nations attempted to ensure the security and cultural identities of ethnic minorities on the redrawn map of Europe, Jews were fully involved. Louis Marshall, then leader of the AJC, was instrumental in helping convince the Wilson and Harding administrations and the Jewish leadership to support the national minority rights treaties. Despite the antagonism they generated in newly reborn nations such as Poland, Jews generally placed much faith in these treaties. But at the time of Marshall's death in 1929 it had become clear that the Zionist prognosis that foresaw that the minority rights treaties were at best a stopgap measure was accurate. But the minority rights treaties did reinforce a sense among Jewish leaders in the democracies that the "civilized world" could be relied upon to intercede in egregious examples of human rights depredations. But that seemed limited to states that had some pretensions of being parliamentary democracies. The story was different in the two totalitarian states that emerged from the chaos of World War I. The suppression of Jewish cultural institutions and general depredations inside the Soviet Union were well known in the twenties but, like the onslaught of National Socialism in the thirties, these regimes seemed peculiarly resistant to the human rights rationale.

Faith that an elevated moral code could improve behavior was so deeply rooted in postemancipation Jewish political culture that not even the world's indifference to the systemic slaughter of the Holocaust could fully dissipate it. Despite the Nazi penchant for genocide the hope of establishing a universal standard of behavior based on a recognized code of human rights emerged stronger than ever after World War II. The right of free movement, at the heart of this study, was embodied in the several human rights conventions that together created the human rights protocol.[46] With the exception of a failed attempt to include a "reservation" clause in the Universal Declaration of Human Rights in 1948, stating that implementation of the enumerated rights would be "in accordance with the procedure laid down in the law of that country," and the insistence that an optional protocol be included that prevented the United Nations from hearing individual appeals, the Soviet Union finally became a signatory of the International Protocol on Civil and Political Rights in 1973. Coincidentally, that was the year when agitation for Jewish emigration reached a high point.

It was undoubtedly the desire by Soviet leaders to alter the prevailing belief of a morally indifferent Soviet regime that led to their agreement to allow human rights to be considered in the Helsinki process. But the agreement barely concealed the fact that the Soviets approached human rights from a different perspective. From a Marxist materialistic point of view the right to eat outranked the right to speak or move freely. But Moscow was aware that the Western approach to human rights had strong support in international public opinion. For a state seeking legitimacy it was tactically wiser to support the democratic concept of human rights in theory, if not in practice. Until the United Nations published a study in 1963 entitled "The Study of Discrimination in Respect of the Right of Everyone to Leave Any Country, Including His Own, and to Return to His Country," few realized the importance of freedom of movement as requisite for the other better known rights. The West was compelled to agree with the caveat that the agreed-upon rights be implemented according to the country's laws. The Soviet Union had no official immigration law but many regulations ordering the emigration process. It could therefore claim with impunity that it adhered to the right of immigration as propounded in the international agreements to which it was a signatory. There were, to be sure, certain exceptions. An exit visa could be denied if applicants were charged with an offense or had not discharged their military service. That exception as well as others was later used to prevent emigration of Jews. Under pressure, the Soviet authorities sometimes made a gesture to humanize the system. But the broad principle of freedom of movement remained limited to the reunification of families. It had a humanitarian resonance that allowed the Soviets to claim that they were in adherence with the human rights provisions, if only on their own terms.

Moscow's participation in the Helsinki process went beyond public relations. The Soviet Union could, after all, claim to be the initiator of the process. Its support was rooted in the Soviet need to legitimize its postwar redrawing of the map of Europe that was ostensibly threatened by a revanchist Federal Republic of Germany. The initial call for the process came from V. M. Molotov, the Soviet foreign minister, in February 1954. He spoke of the need for an all-European treaty of collective security and an annual meeting for which the United States and China could only be observers. The call was followed in 1957 by another for a European security conference for the purpose of removing foreign troops from Europe and the general reduction of armaments. The idea was going nowhere when in September 1964, Poland's foreign minister, Adam Rapacki, proposed convening an all European security meeting for the purpose of declaring Europe's existing boundaries inviolate. Gradually new goals were added to the agenda to improve East-West relations. This Soviet version of détente included improved economic relations, increased cultural contacts, and cooperation in science and technology. These goals would become the building blocks of Baskets II and III of the Helsinki Accords. By the time the Warsaw Pact met in Bucharest in July 1966 the outlines of Soviet diplomatic strategy had become clear. The goal was to preserve the status quo in Europe, which from the Soviet perspective required the removal of American troops and weapons from Europe, all to be achieved under the umbrella of détente, which the Soviet's called "peaceful coexistence." In March 1969 another appeal came from the Warsaw Pact followed by the Prague Declaration in October, a year after the Warsaw Pact's crushing of the Prague Spring.

Clearly, the failure of Moscow's control system first in Berlin in 1953, then in Hungary in 1956 and finally in Czechoslovakia in 1968 had generated increasing concern within the Soviet bloc about its internal security. The Warsaw Pact's invasion of Czechoslovakia in August 1968 became a turning point in the Cold War. The West remained adamant in resisting Soviet demands to dominate a neutralized Europe. But in Germany the Willy Brandt regime, sensitive to the danger posed by an insecure Soviet Union armed with weapons of mass destruction, was willing to normalize the Soviet sphere of influence in Europe. In September 1971 Brandt's *Ostpolitik* ensured the permanence of the borders drawn along the Oder and Neisse rivers. The Mutual Balanced Forces Reduction in Europe followed as a matter of course. The German dimension concluded with the signing of a protocol in Berlin in June 1972. There ten nations began the multilateral preparatory talks that led to the protracted negotiations that culminated in the establishment of the CSCE, the international agency in which the Helsinki process would be housed. That was the situation when the first preparatory meeting of the CSCE was convened in Helsinki in September 1972. Based on the recommendations of these consultations, a three-stage plan was prepared for approval by the foreign minister of the ten nations involved. The newly constituted council then met for two years to work out a detailed security accord to include such things as a free flow of trade and information, cultural and scientific exchange, and other matters such as human rights.

Human rights was merely one of the topics on the agenda of the CSCE, and most participants gave it little weight. It was a necessary ornament to appease certain interests in the West but it was not expected to come to much. The issue first came to the fore in May 1970 when NATO nations responded to the invitation by insisting that European security include the question of human rights, including the free movement of people, information, and ideas and cooperation in the cultural, economic, technical, and environmental fields that would become the substance of Basket III. In a word, the Helsinki Accords, which included provisions for human rights, were triggered by the European security problem and by the Soviet Union's need to legitimate its position in the heart of Europe. Its approach was not far removed from the transaction proposed by the Jackson-Vanik Amendment. It said in effect that the Soviet bloc could have security and legitimacy if it modified its behavior on the human rights front. In a sense, the two were different sides of the same coin. The Jackson amendment tried to do on a government-to-government level what the Helsinki agreement sought by less confrontational means on the international relations level. Emigration of Soviet Jewry was the exclusive aim of the former, liberation of all captive people, the latter.

The negotiations that produced the Helsinki Final Act were convened in Finlandia House on 3 July 1973 and remained in continuous session for two years. All thirty-three European nations, except Albania, were represented. In recognition that the initiative for meeting came from Moscow the opening address was delivered by its foreign minister, Andrei Gromyko. Having divided their task into three commissions dealing with security, economic cooperation, and humanitarian contacts, the often tedious negotiations came to a close in July 1975 with the 40,000-word Final Act. A signing ceremony, attended by Ford and Brezhnev, was held in Helsinki on 1 August 1975.[47] The conferees were hardly aware that they had unleashed what was in effect a permanent continuance of the negotiations in the form of follow-up meetings and monitoring commissions for compliance. The two-year negotiation had hammered out behavioral guidelines that finally set the stage for the much talked about détente between the superpowers. Ironically, it would be the spirit of détente that was about to exit from the American historical stage.

Moscow's early enthusiasm for the agreement outpaced that of Washington. *Izvestia* ran a glowing editorial on the signing, and Brezhnev declared that the main thing now was to implement all the principles agreed upon. Soviet support of an agreement that contained human rights principles incubated in the West antithetical to its own idea of class struggle is not as mysterious as it seems. The Soviets did not take the rule of law with the same seriousness as the West and often confused law with regulation. For Moscow there was a public relations dividend to be gained from being on the side of human rights. Soviet leaders believed that the implementation of the nettlesome human rights code would be done in the context of their own laws that took precedence. "Soviet emigration law is made in Moscow not in the UN General Assembly," insisted one Soviet delegate. It was not an aberrant point of view because Henry Kissinger had repeatedly made the same point during the Jackson-Vanik debate. But the possibility that the Soviets miscalculated the general impact of the human rights issue cannot be excluded. In a sense the Soviets were inveigled into the human rights web by the rewards it offered, only to discover that once the agreement was signed they would be beaten black and blue on the human rights issue. Rather than the bourgeois niceties that the Soviets imagined them to be, human rights became a formidable Cold War weapon.

In contrast to Moscow's enthusiasm there was little applause for the Final Act in the State Department. Max Kampelman, who later headed the American delegation to the Madrid and Vienna follow-up conferences, wondered if there was any substance behind "the elegant and fine words" of the Accords.[48] But other observers were more hopeful. Comparing the conference to the Congress of Vienna, *Newsweek* observed that, "the strength of the Conference lay in the fact that the East and West had moved sufficiently far along the road to détente to be able to convene such a meeting at all."[49] The most balanced evaluation is contained in Rep. Dante Fascell's first annual report to the newly created Congressional Monitoring Commission on Security and Cooperation in Europe, delivered on 8 September 1976. The report acknowledged that the skepticism of the activists in the Soviet Union was well founded. The situation on the ground had gotten worse. New suppressive techniques such "psychiatric repression" had increased and additional thousands had been imprisoned. But he also noted that the Soviets were forced to "maneuver more intentionally" and "react more energetically" to charges of violations. He found that the opening of an "information channel to world public opinion" had already influenced certain western Communist Parties.[50] There was a public relations dividend to be gained from being on the side of human rights.

■   At first glance it seemed as if the Soviet Union received everything it wanted in the Helsinki Final Act. It was assured of the viability of the frontiers established at the end of the war, leaving its armies straddling the center of Europe. That principle was reinforced by citing the historic principle of "territorial integrity," which in the Final Act became the "inviolability of borders" of existing states such as the German Democratic Republic and Poland. But the greatest coup, seemingly addressed directly at the American effort to liberalize Soviet emigration policy through the Jackson-Vanik Amendment, was a reiteration of the sovereignty of nations principle, which meant that there could be no intervention in the internal affairs of sovereign nations. It addressed the reservation Soviet delegates had first raised in 1948 during the final promulgation of the Universal Declaration on Human Rights and had insisted upon thereafter. The state was the final arbiter of its behavior. But in practice, when the delegates yielded on the idea of follow-up conferences and the enumeration of human rights, it provided the West with what would prove to be a powerful change lever.

Moscow soon discovered that the Final Act it ratified in August 1975 went far beyond its original intention to buttress security and legitimate its position in central Europe. Cultural and scientific exchange and commercial contacts with the West were welcomed, but few Soviet leaders suspected that the human rights aspect of the Helsinki Accords would become a kind of time bomb that threatened the very foundations of their system. Jewish activists were equally unaware of the possibilities the Helsinki Accords held out. Despite months of negotiations a clause regarding the right of emigration was not included. Emigration continued to be limited to family reunification.

Soviet hopes for preserving the political status quo were destined to be shattered. The assurances Moscow wanted from the West were in fact not in any state's power to give. As long as the principle of national self-determination still existed the assurances given about borders could not be ensured by freezing the situation in central Europe as called for by Soviet Cold War strategy. Germans continued to dream of reunification, albeit by peaceful means. The Soviets also miscalculated on principle VII of the explosive Basket III, which concerned the human right to leave and return to one's country. Soviet activists moved fairly quickly to take advantage of it. Soon Moscow discovered that rather than stilling the voices for reform by failure to implement the human rights provisions, the Helsinki agreement actually amplified them. The monitoring groups assiduously collected evidence of Moscow's failure to live up to the provisions of the Accord. Ways were found to transmit them to Washington, where Rep. Fascell's Commission on Security and Cooperation in Europe, which was created to monitor the implementation of the Accords, published and distributed the findings.[51] They were then, often to the dismay of the European delegates, considered at the follow-up conferences. The Helsinki process openly challenged the Soviet control system, which undoubtedly was the primary reason for the violent crackdown that began in earnest with the exiling of Sakharov and the arrest and trial of the Helsinki Watch group.

Still, that did not happen all at once. It took several years for the monitoring procedure, called for in Basket IV, to come into its own. It was the formation of numerous official and unofficial Helsinki monitoring committees behind the iron curtain and the triannual follow-up meetings that slowly transformed a seemingly harmless process with no power to implement its findings into a formidable agent for change.[52] Matters did not all flow in the direction of the West. The satellite states the Soviet Union had established on the western border were legitimated by the Accords. But the transaction to achieve that status required some concessions in the area of human rights. Clearly, Moscow had little intention of implementing matters such as a liberal emigration policy that it had made certain were acknowledged as "internal affairs" in the final document of principles. "The Socialist countries firmly oppose and will prevent by all means in their power," declared a Hungarian Party leader, "attempts at ideological undermining made under cover of a 'free flow of people, ideas and information' in an effort to disrupt the unity of the socialist order and collective."[53] The crackdown on the Helsinki Watch groups that had formed themselves in Moscow and other large cities that followed was harsh.

Opposition was not limited to "free immigration" as the freedom of movement was sometimes called. A related right in Basket III, the principle of free exchange of information, was equally unacceptable to the Soviet security agencies. It was the ability to attract the attention of the Western press, a talent particularly associated with Sharansky, which encouraged the dissidents and gave them a measure of protection. In May 1976 three major Western journalists who had given some coverage to the dissidents were accused of espionage.[54] It was followed by a wave of arrests, first of those associated with the Helsinki Watch, Sharansky, and Yuri Orlov, followed by the arrest of twenty-five of the original thirty founding members of the monitoring group.[55] After demonstrations against the harassment peaked in June 1978, Vladimir Slepak, the father of the aliyah movement, and Ida Nudel, its mother, were arrested and sentenced to internal exile for "hooliganism." That was followed by the arrest of Josef Begun in 1978 and Igor Guberman, editor of *Jews in the USSR,* in 1979 and Victor Brailovsky in November 1980. By mid-1978 much of the leadership tier of the Jewish activist movement was behind KGB bars. Below them regional activists in Leningrad and Kiev and other Soviet cities were also subject to arrest for ten to fifteen days. There were reports of instances of KGB agents planting narcotics on those arrested, which meant a harsher sentence of forced labor, to intimidate emigration applicants who had become activists.

The number of applicants refused visas because of a supposed exposure to "classified work" also increased. After the years of comparative generous availability of exit permits in 1978 and 1979, a growing number of visa applicants would be stranded as the number of exit visas declined to a trickle. After 1980 the number of visas issued was below the 1972 level, despite the increase in the number of applicants. If the intent was to roll up the movement in the Soviet Union, the suppression backfired. It was estimated that the number of refuseniks, who had banded together in tightly knit communities for protection, had reached 40,000 by 1981. But as the KGB grip tightened, activities were disrupted. By 1978 there were comparatively few public demonstrations. Detained en route by the KGB, which had complete knowledge of their movements, only forty-four people managed to get to the Babi Yar memorial meeting that had become an annual event. In January 1979 inquiring U.S. officials were informed that no exit visas would be issued because the OVIR was too busy with applications for the forthcoming Olympics. Stricter regulations against "parasitism" and "hooliganism," the two most common charges against Jewish activists, were enforced. In a word, while Soviet officials were busily negotiating the Helsinki Accords with their complement of human rights, they simultaneously mounted a full-scale effort to destroy the movement within its borders. The years after 1980 were the most dismal years of the Soviet Jewish emigration movement.

The arrest and trial of Sharansky, the concerted effort to eliminate Moscow's Helsinki Watch, and especially the internal exile of the Sakharovs occurred at the same historic moment that the Carter administration was articulating a high priority for human rights and may have been Moscow's response to it.[56] When Sharansky and others were accused of being agents of the CIA it earned a personal public denial by Carter. More important, the arrest of Sharansky and the crackdown on the Helsinki monitoring groups indirectly widened the gap that had developed between the two major organizations, the UCSJ and the NCSJ. It seemed as if disunity, the great bugaboo of Jewish organizational life, reared its head precisely at the juncture when Soviet activists were under attack. The UCSJ was dissatisfied with the reaction of the NCSJ to the arrest Sharansky. Its newly established Robert F. Drinan Center independently monitored the Sharansky case, which was becoming a cause célèbre. It had also dispatched its own delegation to the 1980 follow-up conference in Madrid to showcase the Jewish emigration issue for the delegates. The Drinan Center soon became a point of confrontation with the NCSJ. Jerry Goodman, the executive director of the NCSJ, claimed that UCSJ's charge of passivity was based on "half truths and distortions" and "has only confused scores of good activists."[57] But by the 1980s it looked as if the UCSJ, with its thousands of members at the grassroots level, was overtaking the NCSJ, whose founding charter made it an organization of organizations and limited its ability to recruit rank and file membership.

We have already noted that the Nixon administration's reception of the Helsinki negotiations that began in 1972 was hardly cordial. The idea of a separate human rights area in the nation's foreign policy did not sit well with Kissinger, who considered it an intrusion on the policy-making power of the executive branch. His preference was for realpolitik and balance of power politics that viewed the conduct of governments toward their own citizens as an internal matter. Human rights was considered a "soft" area and not given a high priority. He viewed the commission being created by Congress as having a potential of preempting a policy task that fell within the purview of the state department and that because of its peculiar congressional mandate could not be easily controlled. His preference was for bilateral negotiations with the actual holders of power. To put the nation's faith in international agencies such as the CSCE was a waste of time and tends to obfuscate the issue at hand. Relations with Fascell's congressional commission, which came into being in 1976, were therefore cool. The State Department maintained formal activities, such as membership in the UN's Human Rights Commission, but they were viewed primarily in terms of their public relations value. Predictably, the antidetentists who argued that Kissinger was making fateful concessions to the Soviets found even less use for the Helsinki process. Jackson opposed Ford's going to the Helsinki summit to sign the Accords as did Reagan, also a presidential hopeful in 1975. Many believed that the Helsinki Final Act, especially the principle of the inviolability of borders, amounted to a betrayal of the people of Eastern Europe.

The concern for human rights was viewed more favorable in Congress. We have noted that the flocking of cosponsors for the Jackson-Vanik and other resolutions went beyond earning political capital. There were many in Congress who rejected Kissinger's hardness on the human rights issue. Over the years there were several resolutions and proposals for legislation seeking to use trade or aid as a tool to wring better treatment for persecuted groups in the Soviet empire.[58] A good example occurred in November 1975, three months after the Helsinki Final Act was signed. Sen. Alan Cranston introduced a human rights amendment that would have limited security assistance to any government that engages in a persistent pattern of human rights violations. It was really a version of the Jackson amendment writ large and predictably Jackson, more than ever convinced that the Kremlin could not be trusted, spoke in its support. "[If] the Ford administration insists on continuing to send American taxpayers money to bolster antidemocratic regimes . . . then it's up to Congress to undertake action stronger than non-binding sense-of-Congress statements." [59] Two years later when Carter made human rights the key note of his administration he was tapping into a similar sentiment in Congress.

Like prior administrations, Carter viewed the fulfillment of these humanitarian sentiments not through the CSCE but through government-to-government negotiation. Zbigniew Brezinski, his national security advisor, favored a more assertive American presence in the CSCE but conceived of human rights as primarily another arena where the Soviet Union could be exposed. The distrust of Helsinki stemmed primarily from those who feared a "soft" posture toward a hostile expansionist regime. Every concession was read as another "Munich" in the making. The conference was after all a Soviet idea. It took some time to realize that the Soviet initiative in forming CSCE was developing into something other than intended by Moscow. Rather than aiding in separating the United States from Europe, the CSCE harbored a surprisingly strong American influence that increasingly overshadowed Moscow's.

■   The reshaping of the Helsinki process into a formidable instrument to improve Soviet behavior is owed primarily to two remarkable members of Congress, Dante Fascell and Millicent Fenwick. Rep. Fenwick requires some attention because the figure she cut as an eccentric pipe-smoking member of the patricianate popularized when Garry Trudeau used her as the model for Lacey Davenport, a lead character in his popular cartoon strip, *Doonesbury,* is particularly misleading. Fenwick was outspoken and fearless and perhaps for that reason was considered eccentric. Beneath that eccentric exterior she possessed a serious commitment to civil rights that became a bridge to the human rights movement when she won her seat in the House in 1974 at the age of sixty-four. The informal title "the conscience of Congress," by which she became known among her colleagues, was not based on her eccentric character but on her engagement in the human rights movement that began when she became a committed supporter of the Soviet Jewry movement. [60] The precise circumstances of her recruitment occurred as a result of an invitation to join a mission to visit Soviet activists in Moscow together with Speaker of the House Carl Albert and others in August 1975. It was her impression of the Orlov circle in Moscow that was decisive. The visit was an unforgettable experience for the high-born Fenwick. She only fully realized the possibility that the recently signed Helsinki Accords held out for ameliorating the situation of the refuseniks after speaking to Yuri Orlov, who organized the Moscow Helsinki monitoring group, and Valentin Turchin, who was active in Amnesty International. But it was Sharansky, who spoke clear English and whose passion for the cause was coupled with humor and urbanity that converted her and Sen. Patrick Leahy, Rep. Sidney Yates, and Speaker Albert to the cause. She became single-minded in her pursuit of justice for the refuseniks and amelioration of their condition. When she returned from Moscow she introduced a bill (HR9466) to establish a Commission on Security and Cooperation in Europe to monitor the implementation of the human rights provisions contained in Basket III of the Helsinki Accords. The act would also furnish the legislative groundwork to implement the cultural interchange of ideas and people contained in the Final Act.

The Fenwick resolution, which was introduced into the Senate by Sen. Clifford Case, faced the opposition of the administration and languished in the House Committee on International Affairs. But eventually the proposal won the support of 96 cosponsors in the House, many of whom represented districts with sizeable east European ethnic constituencies. The lobbying of the Soviet Jewry movement, especially the NCSJ, which represented twenty-three organizations on its board, played a key role in garnering support for Fenwick's bill. The three-year struggle to bring the Jackson amendment into being had given them operational know-how and good political antennae on who was who on the Hill. The passage of the measure in October 1976 establishing a congressional monitoring commission marked a crucial juncture in the development of the Soviet Jewry movement.[61] Preoccupied with the continuing debate over the reshaping of the Jackson amendment, American Jewish leaders were late in recognizing the potential of the Helsinki process. When they finally did realize that if properly managed the human rights issue, as embodied in the Helsinki process, could develop into an alternative or supplementary strategy, it was almost too late. Some leaders lost confidence in the process because they believed that the concession to limit freedom of movement to the "reunification of families" clause in Basket III did not go far enough. But from Israel's vantage the existing clause legitimized and gave international sanction to the existing practice for emigration from the Soviet Union to Israel. It threw a moral cloak over its activities while holding out the hope of more emigration.

With advent of the Carter administration in 1977, the potential conflict of two diverse voices on the human rights issue, one from Congress and the other from the executive branch, was lessened. Carter had emphasized human rights in his inaugural and his appointment of Dante Fascell to the new administration's foreign policy transition team boded well for human rights advocates. Fascell also had a direct line to Cyrus Vance, the newly appointed Secretary of State, and it did not hurt that he was also chairman of the House subcommittee that authorized the State Department's budget. It was a well-connected Fascell who became chairman of the new commission. His drive did not go unnoticed. Within days of passage of the legislation Dante Fascell achieved the all but impossible task of procuring a suite of offices and a staff of thirteen, including ten researcher-analysts with appropriate language skills. Within months of Carter's inauguration the American team also became more active in the CSCE.

It was the monitoring provision of Basket IV that held the secret to the unexpected effectiveness of the Helsinki process. Everywhere small groups, some government sponsored, others composed of volunteers, sprang up to monitor and report on compliance with the human rights principle contained in the Helsinki Final Act. The NCSJ established its own committee to collect data on violations of Helsinki. The data would be passed to a coordinating committee chaired by Stephen Roth of the World Jewish Congress. Most notable were the committees formed in Moscow and Charter 77 in Prague.[62] Because its favorable political location gave it a special authority, the congressional committee assumed a central role in coordinating and debriefing the monitoring groups operating in the Eastern bloc nations. It was composed of personnel from the executive branch and Congress as well as three members each from the State, Commerce, and Defense departments. The primary task of the commission, soon to be cochaired by the energetic, knowledgeable Dante Fascell, was to prepare periodic reports on compliance with provisions of the Final Act.

In Fascell's hands the commission soon went far beyond its role. It held public hearings attracting media attention. It sponsored research and proposed visiting the Soviet Union for an actual investigation of the scene. A delegation visited Israel to personally interrogate recent arrivals. Within a year the commission became the megaphone for Eastern European ethnics in the nation who had a grievance against Moscow. Most important, it became the communications hub of the network of monitoring groups that had sprung up behind the Iron Curtain.[63] In 1978 these hundreds of reports were published in a nine-volume work that was distributed to Congress and the NGOs involved with human rights. The NGOs included the numerous Jewish organizations involved with Soviet Jewry.[64] It gave a government imprimatur to the information while creating its own special constituency for the commission. The activities of the commission were expanded far beyond monitoring compliance with the human rights provisions of Basket III, whose emigration clause actually still limited that right to the reunification of families.[65]

Sometimes it is as much as the character of the people involved as the worthiness of the cause that moves history in a given direction. Such was the case with the commission. Had it not been for the two founders it would probably have amounted to little. If Millicent Fenwick came to her role through her early involvement in the civil rights movement, Dante Fascell stemmed from an entirely different background. A child of Italian immigrants, he was one of those rare politicians who combined commitment and moral rectitude with a high level of political skill. What Fenwick and Fascell shared in common was a commitment to human rights and a feistiness of spirit that would not allow them to rest. From different areas of the political spectrum, they were bound by their common distaste for the "striped pants boys" of the State Department who rarely shared their enthusiasm for human rights. Kissinger would have preferred Ford to veto the Fenwick bill calling for a permanent commission. Yet as professional politicians both appreciated consistency. Despite his frequent talk of human rights, both mustered little confidence in him when it became clear that he was unable to apply the established standards consistently.

The commission would undergo its litmus test in October 1977 when the first follow-up conference was scheduled to meet in Belgrade. The United States would send a mixed delegation composed partly of professionals from the State Department drawn from its Human Rights Office and partly staff members of the Commission. Rep. Fascell and Sen. Claiborne Pell, his vice co-chairman, acted quickly to head off the tensions in authority that were bound to develop. On 10 March 1977 a letter from Vance to Fascell placed the commission's entire staff under the direction and subordinate to the secretary of state. Tensions were bound to develop on the congressional level as well because the House Committee on Foreign Affairs had created a Subcommittee on Human Rights and International Organizations in 1947. Unlike the new committee, its membership consisted solely of members of Congress, and Fascell himself had served as its chairman in the 86th, 88th, and 89th Congress when the United Nations served as the arena for human rights activity.[66]

But these overlapping administrative agencies did not interfere with the activities of the commission. In November 1976 a study mission had been sent to learn how the eighteen signatories of the Helsinki Final Act were implementing the human rights provisions. Vance was requested to upgrade the chairman of the delegation, Arthur Goldberg, to the title of assistant secretary of state for the forth-coming Belgrade follow-up conference.[67] The two contingents of the commission worked together if not in perfect harmony then without discord coming to public attention. U.S. policy for the CSCE came to the desk of the deputy secretary of state Warren Christopher, but the diplomatic correspondence was accessible to commission staffers, and weekly meetings between department officials of its Bureau of European Affairs and staff members became normal operating procedure, a rarity in Washington. It helped that Arthur Goldberg, chairman of the American delegation to Belgrade, was also not a department insider.[68] Over the opposition of the NATO delegations, the former Supreme Court judge and cabinet member employed a prosecuting attorney's confrontational approach using specific cases such as Sharansky's arrest to tackle the crucial implementation question. To the dismay of the Soviet delegation and the delight of Soviet dissidents Goldberg treated the Accords as almost contractual. He also called frequent press conferences to bring attention to the implementation issue.

Despite Goldberg's aggressive approach to the implementation question the general appraisal of the Belgrade follow-up conference was one of failure. By March 1978 as the conference drew to a close tempers were frayed. The concluding document contained no new ideas and made no mention of human rights.[69] Taking exception to the general opinion, Arthur Goldberg thought that a "breakthrough" had in fact occurred. The follow-up conference was on its way to becoming an instrument to check human rights performance. Small concessions to hasten the emigration procedures were being conceded by Moscow even while the crackdown on the Helsinki Watch groups proceeded. The Helsinki Watch and the idea of human rights were developing into an instrument for dissent in the Eastern bloc. Beginning as a sleeper event, it raised the hope of changing the existing oppressive Soviet system from within, a hope that became a reality in 1985.

At the next and longest follow-up conference in Madrid in November 1980, Max Kampelman, Goldberg's successor, aware that his predecessor had broken precedent by openly discussing Soviet depredations at an international forum, continued the tactic of open confrontation on specific cases. At an address before the NCSJ at the Roosevelt hotel in New York, Kampelman took note of the startling increase in arrests but also observed that in contrast to the Belgrade conference, when only the United States brought up the treatment of dissidents, at the Madrid conference eleven nations did so.[70] The signs that the Soviet authorities had bitten off more than they could chew were already visible before the Belgrade conference. Soviet strategy called for deemphasizing the review of implementation and shifting attention to the discussions on transport, energy, environment, economic cooperation, and above all disarmament, which Brezhnev had proposed for a series of pan-European conferences. The human rights argument was countered by citing racial injustices in America, including unemployment and lack of medical insurance. "American society has not been able to solve its domestic, racial and civil rights problems," stated one Soviet spokesman, "and for this reason only, American should hold their horses before rushing into human rights drives elsewhere."[71]

Fascell's connections in Congress proved useful to the department, but the commission's highest priority was to air the numerous failures to implement the Helsinki agreement. The American delegation had placed itself at the head of the implementation campaign only to discover at Belgrade that NATO members did not want a fuss made about the Soviet failure to implement. Fascell was aware of the difficulties the U.S. delegation was encountering to convince CSCE members to pay greater attention to the human rights question. Like Washington, which constantly heard about the unresolved race question, each CSCE delegation had its own difficulties with the implementation of human rights. Despite these inconsistencies, with the help of Fascell's influence, the Carter administration did project attention on the Helsinki process and brought the human rights enterprise to a higher level of reality.

The American investment in human rights was already inherent in the waiver provision of the Jackson amendment, but it was limited to anti-Jewish depredations. The Helsinki commission now broadened the American approach. Under Fascell's skilled guidance the commission served as a collecting point for all human rights failures. Interviews with almost a thousand recent emigrants in Israel revealed that 60 percent were subject to harassment and one-third were fired from their jobs. In August 1977 a 194-page volume detailing more than 3,500 Soviet violations was published and widely distributed by the commission.

More important, the moral high ground that some activists believed was lost by entering into negotiations over human rights with the Kremlin was partly restored by the monitoring groups who were not in the negotiating business but simply monitored implementation of rights already agreed to. Helsinki held out a broader, more hopeful approach to human rights, of which the right of emigration was part. It precipitated a foreseeable complication between Jewish activists in the Soviet Union whose interest was limited to emigration and those who held out hope that liberalization could yet be achieved and that Soviet governance could be humanized. The Helsinki process spoke more to the "liberalizers" than to the "refuseniks" who did not want to challenge the Soviet system, only to leave it. That fissure was bridged after Andrei Sakharov, the doyen of the dissenters, placed the right to leave one's country as requisite for all other human rights. We have noted that the Helsinki Final Act spoke only of the right of reunification of families, not general emigration. Still, human rights generally, as propounded in Basket III, became the center of gravity of those seeking to force changes in Soviet conduct. It also became a crossover juncture for all involved in the emigration movement. Legislators who were previously exclusively amendment advocates now broadened their interest in human rights. Gradually, as the impact of the Jackson-Vanik Amendment weakened after 1980, the vacuum was filled by the Helsinki process, which contained none of its quid pro quos. It worked on the more elevated principle that human rights belong to all and need not be bargained for.

From the outset the Belgrade conferees faced a difficult challenge. They were greeted by a message from Andrei Sakharov reminding the delegates of the universality of human rights, which meant that no one could be left behind. Sakharov's message was eloquent and righteous but left the delegates little "wiggle room" for reaching agreement with Moscow. The Soviet delegation was pressing for peace and security embodied in Baskets I and II of the Accords. Their rationale, which placed the need for peace ahead of human rights, most of which fell in the purview of domestic law, was compelling. Baskets I and II were in conflict with Basket III, which enumerated the human rights all humans were entitled to as a matter of natural law. In a word, Helsinki had little meaning if it was not universally implemented. Moscow's response in July 1978, the sentencing of Sakharov to silence in the closed city of Gorky and the arrest of key members of the Helsinki Watch group, was ominous.

Given the unexpectedly strong emphasis on the human rights aspect of the Helsinki Accords some Soviet leaders must have rued the day they introduced the CSCE idea in to the international relations arena. But in the months after the accords were signed Moscow continued to wax enthusiastic about Helsinki: "History has never yet witnessed a meeting of thirty-three nations that could produce a document like Helsinki." The Soviet leadership believed that the problem of Jewish emigration would solve itself slowly. Brezhnev declared to the congressional delegation led by Speaker Carl Albert. "The Third Basket (human rights provisions) will be settled by the process of life as time goes on. . . . You know Jewish applications are dropping. What am I to do? I cannot require them to leave."[72] But in the meantime they had unknowingly involved themselves in a process that threatened to further weaken their control system rather than propping up their security. The legitimacy of Soviet hegemony in Eastern Europe undersigned in Helsinki did not create the sense of permanent change. The first CSCE report noted that the Helsinki Accords "have stirred a remarkable response of hope and even action among the peoples of the Soviet Union and Eastern Europe."[73] A version of Finlandization, the neutralization of Western client states that had been a fear in the West in the early seventies, now seemed more likely to occur in Eastern Europe under the label of "Euro-communism." It was partly the adverse reaction to the Warsaw Pact invasion of Czechoslovakia in August 1968 that triggered Moscow's renewed peace offensive. The invasion proved that Moscow had the military power and the will to retain control of its satellites. But no military force could crush the growing sense of autonomy among the subject nations. It was especially apparent in the Communist Parties of the West.

The Helsinki process focused world attention on the freedom of movement idea. In that sense it helped move the movement for Soviet emigration forward. But the goals of the negotiators were limited, and there was no intention of bringing the Soviet regime down in a deluge of human rights. For Soviet Jewry the right to emigrate had not in fact changed. It remained limited to family reunification. Most other rights were considered aspirational rather than matters of law. Moscow's gradual compliance with the rights listed in Basket III with the advent of Gorbachev in 1985, though often done on its own terms, was unanticipated by the Soviet Jewry movement and distrusted when they became policy. They did not believe that the Soviet system of repression could dismantle itself without triggering cataclysmic change. That was the message also transmitted by activists in the Soviet Union.

■　What proved to be most nettlesome for the Soviets were the provisions of Basket IV that called for the monitoring of the Accord and evaluation conferences to be convened by the permanent secretariat of the CSCE. The Soviets viewed the enumerated rights as pronunciamentos with little need for implementation. But the monitoring groups, which everywhere in the Soviet bloc became focal points for dissidents, were based on the principle that these rights, while not law, embodied desirable universally agreed-upon standards. They served as a blueprint for what is entailed in developing a free democratic society. Compliance was based not on police powers but as noted, on a force related to "shame" or loss of reputation for failure to achieve a desired level of behavior. Few could have failed to notice that the level aspired to was based on a Western standard of value.[74] As it became clear that the Soviets were defaulting on the Helsinki spirit, the misgivings regarding Soviet ability to comply with human rights standards, even on the most minimal level, again surfaced.

Not only was there failure to implement the enumerated rights but the Soviet security agencies were actually moving in the opposite direction as if they did not recognize the commitment made by their foreign office. One might well ask, "Who rules in Moscow?" There had been a more than 60 percent increase in exit permits since the Belgrade conference in 1977, but at the same time the onslaught of the KGB against dissidents and the rejection of Basket III rights had also intensified.[75] The picture was confusing. The years after the signing of the Final Act witnessed a wave of suppression that was reminiscent of the darkest days of Stalin. On one hand, the treatment of refuseniks had grown more arbitrary and harsher. On the other hand, in 1978 and 1979 more applicants than ever before were being granted exit visas, at a faster rate. The Accords were "having a restraining effect on some repressive behavior in the East," according to a report of the CSCE.[76] But hopes of a mitigation of the harassment were dashed by the seeming inability to control the KGB. "We in the Interior Ministry," began General Vladimir Borisenkov of the KGB, "have not authorized anyone to make a statement about decisions coming within the competence of our ministry. No maximum period for refusing exit visas has been set. We will never set any."[77] At the time few realized that the generosity may have been temporarily spurred by the desire to sweeten the SALT II negotiations scheduled to take place in Vienna on 15 June 1978. We have noted that the Kremlin's pique at the fact that China had been granted the much-desired MFN status by Congress may also have played a role.

Within the Soviet Union the picture was complicated by the different attitudes taken toward the Accords by different sections of the dissident movement. We have previously noted that most activist Jews in the early seventies did not believe that they would ever be able to live full Jewish lives under Communist rule. Some went further to believe that anti-Semitism was so deeply ingrained in Russian culture that, even in the less suppressive society that might eventually succeed Communism, the development of a full Jewish communal life would not be possible. They therefore focused exclusively on emigration, usually to Israel. The separation from the Soviet "democratizers" also had resonance in the American movement. The older and more established NCSJ, which was beholden to the organized Jewish community, tended naturally to view the emigration and suppression issue as primarily a Jewish one. The strategic separation from the general democratizing movement of which human rights movement was part was a long established one. The right to emigrate, declared President Stanley Lowell at an NCSJ board of governors meeting on 18 February 1977, "remains separate and distinct from the campaign of Soviet Democratic dissidents."[78] The more civil rights-oriented UCSJ made the turn toward human rights more easily even while it clung stubbornly to the Jackson-Vanik Amendment.

Nevertheless, the relationship between the dissidents or democratizers and the Jewish activists or refuseniks was far from hostile. The importance of creating a connection with what Elena Bonner identified as "the international ideology of human rights" was understood by the democratization movement in the Soviet Union. It was the refuseniks who were able to provide the international connection and to create an awareness of the importance of public relations. At least 60 percent of the dissident groups were vaguely of "Jewish origin," and some, such as Sharansky, Orlov, and Alexeyeva, were equally comfortable in either camp. Mikhail Zand, Vadim Meneker, Vitaly Svechinsky, and Yuli Telesin were also active in both movements, and Boris Tsukerman, a self-taught legal expert in Soviet law, served as Andrei Sakharov's legal advisor. One observer noted that among the refuseniks "non-Jews are the most active members of the movement" and that *Exodus,* the information bulletin of the emigration movement, was started and edited by Victor Fedoseyev, a non-Jew.[79] There were many crossovers. Lydia Voronina, deeply involved in Moscow's Helsinki Watch group, was also active in the Jewish emigration movement, but feeling that Zionization and sometimes reversion to religiosity was attributable to the experience of suppression, she was unable to embrace either Judaism or Zionism. She was convinced that the refuseniks were using their Judaism to protest the Soviet system. When she expressed her reservations at one of the numerous secret discussions it caused an uproar.[80] On the other hand Alexandr Ginsberg, who worked closely with Sakharov, crossed over the other way and devoted much of his energy to helping the families of political prisoners. There was much back and forth between the two groups but there were also tensions within the separate camps. Because their sole objective was emigration, Zionists, who were often zealous recent converts, sometimes harbored hard feelings toward those who happily chose a less precarious course, though becoming a Soviet dissident was not without danger. In the Russian camp some nationalists such as Solzhenitsyn believed that the Jewish quest for emigration, which Sakharov supported, placed Jews outside the Russian struggle to throw off the Communist yoke. He also considered Helsinki a betrayal of those who remained entombed in the Gulag. But the picture was balanced when hundreds of Pentacostal Christians vowed to begin a hunger strike on behalf of imprisoned Jews.[81]

As in the United States, there developed a separate human rights movement whose tactical astuteness was revealed in an incredible demonstration on 5 December 1965 on Moscow's Pushkin Square using the slogan "Respect the Soviet Constitution." The movement's formal origins date back to May 1969 when Moscow's first human rights organization, Initiative Group to Defend Human Rights in the USSR, was founded. Five years before the Helsinki Accords were signed in August 1975 a Moscow Human Rights Committee, some of whose members later formed the core of Moscow's Helsinki Watch group, was already in existence. The same handful of activists also supported the Fund to Aid Political Prisoners in the USSR, founded in 1974. After the Helsinki Final Act became known new kinds of dissenting organizations based on religion came into existence in Russia. Foremost was the Christian Committee to Defend Believers' Rights that was founded by Russian Orthodox believers in 1978. These groups were not urban centered and emanated from all parts of the Soviet political spectrum. Their human rights advocacy emphasized the need to realize their own goals rather than a broad tolerance of others. Undoubtedly they were energized by the example of the Jews, thousands of whom had already been allowed to emigrate, and the fact that the Communist Party had after all allowed the full text of the Helsinki Final Accords to be published in September 1975.

Before his arrest on 10 February 1977, Yuri Orlov was among the first to grasp the need for a common ground to unite the broad spectrum of dissidents that included democrats such as Sakharov, Marxists such as Roy Medvedev, nationalist Ukrainians and Lithuanians and Russians such as Solzhenitsyn, Crimean Tatars, Zionists, Catholics, Baptists, Pentecostals, Seventh-Day Adventists as well as Volga German and Armenians.[82] It also included a nonpolitical cultural wing composed of writers and artists, many practicing self-publishing (samizdat). It was through this underground communications net that the human rights movement survived in the Soviet Union, but those who became the purveyors of its message courted danger. "I write it myself," stated Vladimir Bukovsky, "censor it myself, print and disseminate it myself, and then I do time in prison for it myself."[83]

Although reaching into many areas of Soviet life, the dissident movement in which the advocacy of human rights was anchored posed little threat to the established Soviet order, which was totally dominated by the Communist Party and its suppressive right hand, the KGB. The Soviet Jewry movement within Russia offered Soviet dissidents a crucial link to the outside world and an early awareness of how tenuous the hold of the Party was on Soviet life.

In contrast to the condition in the Soviet Union the atmosphere in the United States if not welcoming was benevolent. There prevailed an assumption in American public opinion much strengthened by the civil rights struggle that injustices ought to be ameliorated and that people who were denied human rights ought to be helped. The waning American civil rights movement would provide an ideal incubator for human rights. In September 1977 Bayard Rustin, then a sponsor for the newly formed National Conference on Human Rights and formerly a prominent leader in the American civil rights movement, invited the NCSJ to affiliate with the group and attend a forthcoming international conference. Rustin argued convincingly in his communication with Jerry Goodman that the developments on the human rights front was "one of the more significant and hopeful developments in American life since the Civil Rights movement of the early 1960's."[84] The civil rights orientation seemed to lead as a matter of course to an appreciation of the possibilities of human rights for the liberation of Soviet Jewry. But the activists in Moscow viewed it otherwise. Their closed society, they argued, was a far cry from the free society of America and therefore the first order of business should be not to beg for concessions, but to break the Soviet yoke.

But in America the human rights movement found support on either side of the political spectrum, by liberals for doing needed humanitarian work and by the political right for the cudgel it offered to beat the Communist regime. The Jackson-Vanik Amendment gained much support from the fact that it could be viewed in human rights or Cold War terms. But the amity toward the Helsinki process in which the support for human rights was anchored was not unanimous. Kissinger viewed the Helsinki process as an intrusion, and Jackson believed that it legitimated Soviet control of Eastern Europe. In the belief in the futility of the Helsinki Final Act Jackson and Kissinger saw eye to eye.

That is where the situation stood when Carter made human rights a priority issue at his inaugural and set high priorities for it thereafter. His position won the support of Jewish voters who had viewed the Soviet Jewry issue as one of human rights from the outset. But Carter's approach to human rights was nonpolitical, which in the heating up of the Cold War could not carry its weight. He experienced difficulty in achieving consistency in upholding the universality of human rights principles that were as applicable in Pinochet's Chile as they were in the Soviet Union. "Our people have now learned the folly of our trying to inject our power into the internal affairs of other nations," he told the Foreign Policy Association in June 1976.[85] But like his predecessors in the Oval Office he was compelled to use the trade weapon to buttress the American position in the Cold War. What was different is that in the Carter administration there was a conscious effort to infuse foreign policy with a moral content, which meant a focus on human rights.

Jewish leaders were assured that before SALT II would be signed the Soviet Jewry issue would be aired.[86] When Carter precipitously raised the issue with Brezhnev at the Vienna summit, Gromyko protested the fact that the Jewish question had been made "the touchstone of [Soviet] sincerity" on human rights and was allowed to interfere with crucial war and peace matters in Soviet-American relations.[87]

In fact, the human rights issue posed almost as many problems for the Carter administration as it did for Brezhnev. In the discussions of the Democratic platform committee in 1975 there were portents of the problem that broad support of human rights posed. Carter had inherited a particularly vexing situation in Argentina where the State Department had turned a deaf ear to the Dirty War.[88] Should the U.S. support "progressive" forces in Chile under the heel of General Pinochet, as the McGovern wing of the party insisted? Or was the administration's position intended to apply only to Communist dictatorships?[89] How does one prioritize the need for peace and disarmament and the need to raise the standards of human rights throughout the world?

Carter soon discovered that a policy of severing human rights from the need for arms reduction, proposed at his first news conference on 8 February 1977, entailed agonizing choices. Questioned about the relationship between the two goals, Carter later responded, "I don't want the two to be tied together."[90] But of course they were. It was far easier to respond to human rights abuses in Latin America where no nuclear threat existed than to abuses in the Soviet Union, where it did.[91] The conflict between preventing thermonuclear war and extending human rights led to a deep moral dilemma. Some of the nation's most eminent thinkers wrestled long and hard with the choice and concluded ultimately that the human rights question was less salient to human survival than disarmament. For Soviet leaders there was an additional paradox. Their support of the Helsinki Accords was motivated by their desire to enhance their legitimacy in Europe, yet it was precisely the human rights question that increasingly cast doubts on it.

When Carter placed human rights at the center of his foreign policy he unknowingly touched upon an exposed nerve in the Kremlin. Whether the Soviet leader's overreaction to the human rights issue was caused by what a noted Sovietologist Adam Ulam identified as their "power hypochondria" or it revealed a growing unease in the Soviet leadership, the impact on the activists of the resultant crackdown was drastic. That may also account for the paradox of the Kremlin pushing on one hand for the Helsinki agreement and on the other using every technique of suppression to prevent Basket III rights from being implemented. Carter stumbled onto this problem and failed to fathom that the strong human rights statement in his inaugural address threw down the gauntlet to the Soviet rulers, especially after he pledged to Sakharov that the United States would do its utmost to promote human rights in the Soviet Union. He was surprised at the sharpness of Brezhnev's response.[92] Yet when his secretary of state, Cyrus Vance, who preferred to put human rights on a backburner, visited Brezhnev in Moscow in April 1977, he refused to meet with dissidents, unlike George Shultz, who sought them out. Carter's proclivity for human rights was a highly personal one stemming from deep religious convictions. He was unable to integrate it fully into his foreign policy.

But in the first year of his tenure Carter waved the human rights banner despite his fear that the issue would subvert progress on disarmament. When the noted dissident Vladimir Bukovsky visited the White House no photographs were permitted. Carter openly supported Sakharov after a letter from him was delivered on 21 January 1977 by Martin Garbus, an American lawyer who at the behest of the NCSJ had previously defended a well-known Georgian refusenik.[93] The letter may have sharpened his inner conflict. He publicly intervened in Sharansky's trial to insist that the KGB charge that he was a CIA spy be stricken from the record. But Carter again fell between two chairs. The State Department and his close advisors believed that he had overextended himself in the Sharansky case, but on the other side of the political spectrum the executive committee of the NCSJ believed that he had not gone far enough.[94]

The exchange of letters with Sakharov may actually have energized the KGB effort to once and for all roll up the "nest of traitors." At the same time, Carter made concessions to the Kremlin. Kissinger's strategy of keeping the Kremlin out of the Middle East peace negotiations that had culminated in the Begin-Sadat talks at Camp David in November 1977 was abandoned, as were plans to produce a new B1 bomber. At the same time there were also plans to soften the waiver provision of the Jackson-Vanik Amendment.

Even before the Soviet invasion of Afghanistan, which triggered a mid-course correction in Carter's Cold War strategy, the SALT II disarmament talks showed little forward movement. The climax of seven years of disarmament negotiations, the June talks were viewed as the linchpin to finally move the superpowers away from the abyss of nuclear war. Despite the opposition of those in Washington who viewed the negotiations as a dangerous form of appeasement, Carter pushed the talks to a critical point. Years of effort were in danger of being undermined by the worsening of the Cold War atmosphere. For the moment the Soviet Union seemed to be in ascendancy, and many Soviet activists shared the feeling that

Carter's response was weak and inconsistent. But the reality may have been that it was the climate of the Cold War that most affected emigration and treatment of Soviet Jewry generally. Those who became convinced that Soviet policy toward its Jews was primarily conditioned by outside events pointed to the Sharansky treason trial and the general crackdown on dissidents and activists, followed by the sharp decline in emigration after 1979, as a direct reflection of the worsening relations between the two superpowers.

The Carter administration eventually became aware that the open and direct pursuit of human rights came at a price and that sometimes choices had to be made. By the third year of his administration his human rights endeavor was in ruins. Assuming the initiatives without Vance's approval, Brzezinski, Carter's National Security Advisor, sought to use the Madrid follow-up conference to focus pressure on Moscow. With the help of Max Kampelman, whose appointment to head the U.S. delegation he strongly supported, the Madrid conference gave considerable attention to airing the charges that Moscow was not implementing the rights enumerated in Basket III. Carter continued to oscillate between the soft and the hard position but after the Soviet invasion of Afghanistan his options vanished and he pursued the harder line. In January 1980 he withdrew consideration of the SALT treaty by the Senate and reimposed a partial embargo on grain sales. The boycott of the Moscow Olympics soon followed. The strong reaction and the debacle in Tehran after the seizure of the American embassy in November led to the resignation of Vance, leaving Brzezinski in virtual control of foreign policy. It also left the Soviet Jewry issue, which had become part of the Cold War transaction between the superpowers, dead in the water. In November 1979 Ronald Reagan, a staunch proponent of a "get tough" policy toward Moscow, easily won the election and with his victory the Soviet Jewry issue entered a new phase.

For the American Soviet Jewry movement the sharpening of the Cold War during the Carter years posed a dilemma. The Jewish emigration issue had initially been amplified through its association with the nation's Cold War goal of containing the Soviet threat. That was one of the reasons why political leaders as varied as Jackson and Brzezinski were drawn to the amendment whereas supporters of détente viewed it as a distraction. But as détente became almost a dead letter there was a shift in spirit. An aspect of the decline in relations between the superpowers was the Soviet leadership's reluctance to deal with the emigration problem at all. As Kissinger had cautioned, direct pressure on Moscow projected through the Jackson-Vanik and Stevenson amendments was having a negative effect.

But in the end something unforeseen by either side began to happen. What had been intended by Moscow as merely an ornamental footnote to the real purpose of the CSCE, to legitimize its postwar territorial and political arrangements, the human rights aspect became instead its core and contributed notably to the internal collapse of the pervasive control system of the Soviet bloc.

■ For those who seek logic in the flow of events the American approach to Helsinki remains enigmatic. Initially, there was little faith that the human rights movement or that the talks begun in Helsinki would amount to anything. The State Department was simply passive about what the protracted two-year negotiation was leading to. Neither Arthur Goldberg nor Max Kampelman, the two Jews who headed the American delegation, was a great favorite at Foggy Bottom. But when it was realized that the human rights rhetoric had a strong resonance among the people of Eastern Europe, Washington abandoned its passivity to become an active player in the movement. The U.S. backed into its leadership position largely unaware of what was happening. To some extent that was also true of the Soviet Jewry movement, which clung to the idea that the Soviet regime could be compelled to give up its Jews by a combination of seduction and coercion. Unlike the Nazi Reich during World War II, Moscow had no desire to be *Judenrein*. As it turned out, a good portion of the Jews of the Soviet Union also had no desire to leave before 1985 if resettlement in Israel was the only prospect.[95] That is an important reality during the Reagan years, the subject of the next chapter.

SEVEN The Soviet Jewry Question During the Reagan Years

On the face of it the fate of Soviet Jewry was primarily an issue in Jewish history. It concerned the wish of Jews to leave the Soviet Union, the need for American and other communities in the Jewish Diaspora to extricate them, and the desire of Israel to absorb them. But like most Jewish matters, the emigration problem was played out on the world historical stage. Its full meaning does not become clear until we understand the Cold War context in which it developed. The "freedom of movement" issue that so impassioned activists became a cudgel in the Cold War. By 1982 every summit conference and all the Helsinki follow-up conferences had human rights, in which the emigration of Soviet Jewry was embedded, on their agendas. But only when the fortunes of that war tilted decidedly toward the West during Reagan's second administration did the prospects for gaining the release of Soviet Jewry become fully realizable. It was a sudden change. The years immediately preceding were the leanest for emigration since the early seventies.

Although Cold War developments help account for the broad changes in the positioning of the Soviet Jewry issue, it is the change in perception of how to manage the Soviet threat initiated by the Reagan administration that created the actual momentum for change. The fate of Soviet Jewry, like the fate of all captive people in the Soviet sphere, awaited the victory of the West. From his manichaean view of the Soviet empire as unredeemably evil to his Star Wars initiative, the new president was determined to follow a tougher course in dealing with the Soviet Union.[1] Little remained of the policy of détente, which placed much faith in managing the Soviet juggernaut through trade and its need for credit. The sensibility that one could do business with Moscow that underlay Kissinger's Cold War strategy under Nixon and Ford was not totally abandoned, but the posture of "going along to get along" changed. During the Reagan years the discontinuance of practices such as

Ambassador Dobrynin's secret access to the State Department together with other niceties were signs of the new Reagan tone.

The disenchantment process was hastened by the Soviet moves into Angola with Cuban proxies in 1975 and the deployment a new generation of mid-range intermediate missiles aimed at Europe. The culmination came with the Soviet invasion of Afghanistan in December 1979 and its crackdown on Solidarity in 1981. Reagan believed that the extension of American power, as happened in postwar Germany and Japan, translated into the extension of the sphere of liberty and that an extension of Moscow's hegemony led inevitably to tyranny and stagnation. It followed that America was the world's best hope.[2] Never a great conceptualizer of policy, Reagan entered the White House with a few basic moral principles that he supported by a rhetoric honed sharp during his prior years as a well-paid promotional speaker on the Soviet threat. There was one group of influential intellectual supporters whose origins could be traced to a group of thinkers and publicists of Jewish origin. The neoconservatives (neocons) were a loosely knit diverse group of thinkers, most of whom came out of the Social Democratic strand of Jewish political culture. They were among the first to become aware of the murderous nature of the Stalinist regime and became committed to exposing it. A new voice in the conservative camp, they furnished the intellectual muscle to counteract the détente policy and to rationalize Reagan's hard anti-Soviet stand. Some were led into the Republican fold by Norman Podhoretz, editor of *Commentary Magazine,* and Irving Kristol, a founder of *Public Interest.* In 1976, sensing that the United States was falling behind in the arms race, they helped organize the Committee on the Present Danger to alert like-minded CEOs, academicians, and public officials to what they saw as a growing danger. In 1980 Podhoretz wrote *The Present Danger,* which outlined the Soviet threat in the direst terms. Though most had been registered Democrats, like most Jewish voters, the neocon connection with the Jewish voter was tenuous because Jews remained in the Democratic fold and opposed Reagan's enormous increases in military spending. The opposition of the Jewish electorate to the war in Vietnam developed earlier and more intensely than other ethnic voting blocks. Jeane Kirkpatrick, who became ambassador to the United Nations and was Reagan's favorite neocon, remained a Democrat who occasionally pulled down the Republican lever in the voting booth. For Richard Perle, the assistant secretary of defense for international security policy, the encounter with the Soviet Jewry movement was more sustained. He was instrumental in fashioning the strategy behind the Jackson-Vanik Amendment. As Scoop Jackson's assistant he remained in the Democratic column, and his liaison with the Reagan administration was indirect. Nor were neocon views on specific policy steps necessarily uniform. Concerning trade and disarmament policy, in some cases neocons thought that Reagan had not gone far enough to bring the Soviets to heel.[3] While most adherents did not express specific opposition to foreign policy measures, Norman Podhoretz believed that Reagan was not acting fast and consistently enough to counteract Soviet aggression in the Persian Gulf and the Caribbean.[4] Because the group represented no voting bloc, there was at first little formal political contact with the administration, only a shared mistrust of Soviet motives.

Walter Mondale, the Democratic candidate, remained the Jewish favorite in the election of 1984, but support for Reagan was slightly higher than support for Nixon or Ford. From the perspective of the Soviet Jewry movement, George Shultz, who became secretary of state in 1982, expressed such personal sympathy and emotional involvement with the refuseniks that it seemed to reach beyond established policy.[5] Unable to understand Shultz's ardor, Gromyko often complained that he was constantly bringing up this "third rate" question of Jewish emigration as a negotiating gambit. However, during the negotiations over Jackson-Vanik, Shultz had an instinctive distaste for bargaining for the release of the emigrants. He preferred to confront each issue separately without linkage and without prior conditions. The dispassionate problem-solving approach of a professional economist had first become apparent when he negotiated the Palestine Liberation Organization's exit from Lebanon. He considered that feat a career high point. It was well known that there were many Jewish friends and advisors in his circle, but men such as Irving Shapiro, president of DuPont; Larry Silberman, his general counsel in the labor department; Paul Wolfowitz, director of policy planning; and even Henry Kissinger were not advocates or spokesmen for Jewish causes.

■ There are those who are convinced that Reagan's huge defense expenditures hastened the internal collapse of the Soviet Union, whose response burdened its economy beyond its capacity.[6] But that leaves much unexplained regarding the Soviet response to the emigration issue. In many cases Reagan was no tougher than his predecessors concerning trade and credit and in some cases less so. During the period of intense hostility in the early eighties, Soviet-American trade actually reached a peak of $3.8 billion, more than matching the best years of détente.[7] More important, symptoms of economic weakness may have had long-range significance for strategists but in the short run Moscow still had its finger on the nuclear trigger. As was the case with the Carter administration, there was a gap between the Reagan administration's rhetoric and its policy. It too grew aware, as did the prior Carter and Ford administrations, that wielding the economic weapon was a double-edged sword. It was not clear whether it altered unacceptable Soviet behavior, but it clearly could have a drastic impact on the American economy, especially the agricultural sector.

There were those who continued to be convinced that of all the conditions shaping the Cold War it was the Soviet economy that held a key to the behavior in areas such as emigration policy. We have noted that in the early years of the seventies it was believed that Soviet need for trade and credit would, in some measure, determine its willingness to bargain about Jewish emigration. Presumably that need for trade and credit had not diminished in the eighties, but added to it was a growing concern regarding the possibility of remaining viable as a major power without finding some solution to its economic problems. Much of the leverage the Soviet Jewry movement could bring to bear on Moscow involved the ability to make available or withhold trade and credit granted through government fiat. The impact of that lever had been minimized by Moscow's rejection of the Soviet-American Trade Act of 1974. But during the Reagan period some again believed that with signs that the Soviet economy was failing the trade and credit weapon could be wielded with good effect. The instrument available for militants on both sides of the ocean continued to be the Jackson-Vanik Amendment, which they supported well beyond Gorbachev's liberalization.

Yet clearly such conviction was based as much on hope as on reality. The hope rested on an overestimation of Soviet economic vulnerability and the priority Soviet leaders were willing to give to the emigration question. The years when the malaise in the Soviet economy became most apparent in the early eighties corresponded to the most unyielding policy on emigration and harassment. That raises the question of whether the Kremlin could have been pressured into human rights compliance by economic pressure alone. We have noted that Soviet inability to keep pace with Western technology did not immediately translate into military vulnerability. From atomic submarines that ran silently to ICBMs with multiple warheads, the Soviets matched the West and in some areas outpaced it in weapons design and development. As cumbersome and inefficient as the Soviet economic system was it had the ability to concentrate resources on a single problem so that in some aspects of missile technology the Soviets were actually ahead of the United States[8] In the 1970s the Soviet Union outpaced the United States in the production of coal, steel, cement, and oil. Many of the effects of retardation in the development of technology were long term and could be partly deflected by purchasing and stealing the latest technology from the West. The Kremlin's strategic calculations also differed from those in the West because it could be fairly certain that their country would not be subject to a first-strike offensive attack.

Despite its failing agricultural sector and a chronic need for credit, between 1960 and 1972 some estimates measure the Soviet economy growing at a respectable rate of 5 percent annually. In 1972, when talk of exchanging trade and credit for Jewish emigration began, the Soviet economy boasted a gross national product of $710 billion, second only to the United States.

The pressure for trade was not a one-way street. Some of it strongest proponents in the United States, the East-West Trade Council, the National Association of Manufacturers (NAM), and industrialists such as Armand Hammer, sometimes appeared more anxious for trade than the Soviets.[9] The American wheat farmer generated considerable pressure to get in on the giant wheat sales to the Soviet Union in the sixties and seventies. Jackson was compelled to address their concerns by ensuring opponents of the proposed amendment that it would not affect the American economy because "as the enormity of the failure of the Soviet economy looms larger . . . we can expect that they will continue to make critical purchases in the U.S."[10] Soviet grain purchases were in fact increasing slowly by the autumn months of 1971. Like Lyndon Johnson before him, Nixon sent his secretary of commerce to Moscow in November 1971 to build a basis for increasing trade. It was to be more than a stimulant to the economy. Nixon considered it "an important and necessary element in strengthening relations."[11] Clearly, the need for trade was reciprocal, and a lobby composed of trade associations had been established to promote it.

In trade negotiation Soviet negotiators were not precisely supplicants. Credit and technology were available elsewhere. The German, Japanese, and French were becoming increasingly competitive in these areas and successfully absorbed 20 to 25 percent of trade in technology that might have gone to the United States so that in 1980 Soviet trade with the United States was only 5 percent of its total trade. Soon after Moscow leaders rejected the Trade Act of 1974 they concluded a $10 billion credit agreement with a consortium headed by Britain and Germany. The loss of trade in technology was not solely linked to Jackson-Vanik but also to self-imposed strategic export controls. It is difficult to avoid the conclusion that the need for trade and credit that went with the granting of most-favored-nation status did not play the major role in how Jackson-Vanik played itself out in Moscow. That is the reason why they were able to repudiate the agreement without looking back in the final months of 1974. The impact of the amendment was consistently overestimated in Washington and among Jewish activists. The real effect of Jackson-Vanik was not in the economic sphere but in its catapulting the emigration issue to the center of the Cold War stage.

The Soviets had much to worry about in the economic sphere but strangely that did not include a fear that they were sitting at the edge of a popular uprising. When the Soviet system collapsed, it was not overthrown by violence from below. There was a resiliency in the Russian people that did not show up on the economic models. In the seventies most Soviet consumers did not measure the economic system under which they lived by the high standards that prevailed in the West. They asked only for sufficiency—was there enough bread—not was there a car in every garage. The Soviet food distribution system was primitive compared to that of the West but superior to what it had been before Khrushchev made the first effort to improve the Soviet standard of living. Soviet leadership was aware that the economy must do better and in 1971 initiated a five-year plan to improve the quality and quantity of consumer goods. Meanwhile, 5 billion rubles would be set aside to purchase grain, meat, and butter abroad.

Food shortages stemming from the failure of the Soviet agricultural economy could not, of course, be concealed. It is one of the ironies of the economic situation against which the Soviet Jewry issue had to be projected that while surpluses in grain plagued the American economy, the Soviets experienced a sequence of seven poor harvests after 1978. Grain had to be purchased from the West, but here too the Soviets had a choice of several markets. The nation that once produced a wheat surplus was now one of the world's biggest grain importers. In the American farm belt it was the awareness that there was a Russian market hungry for their grain that generated opposition to using trade to win concessions for Jewish emigration. Throughout the eighties, using their leverage as the United States's biggest customer for surplus grain, the Soviets were able to strengthen their hand in the perennial negotiations over the Jackson-Vanik Amendment and ultimately to bypass it. The European need for Soviet gas and oil, which was finally coming on line, played a similar role.[12] But that did not halt the desperate need of the capital-starved Soviet economy for credit, which Gorbachev again requested on his first visit to Washington in 1985.

▪   In the economic arena Moscow was not without options. It could buy what was needed on the world market. But no such solution was in the offing that might help to extricate the regime from the growing debacle in Afghanistan or the rapid succession of aging leaders after the death of Brezhnev in November 1982.[13] Yet the Soviet regime probably could have continued to muddle along for years and perhaps even have found a solution to some of its economic problems. In the short run, the Soviet Union was secure at least in the military sense. Once mutual assured destruction had been attained it mattered much less whether the Soviets did or did not develop clean nuclear bombs or that their technology was on a lower level than that of the West.[14] The deterrent was still in place. Reagan's insistence on developing Star Wars and the disastrous accident at Chernobyl on 26 April 1986 and the subsequent eighteen days delay in making a public statement may have gone further to generate loss of confidence in its leadership than the weak economy.[15] Some emigrants cited Chernobyl as an important factor in their decision to emigrate.

The Soviet man-in-the-street was not yet fully removed from his rural roots, and although a taste for consumption had developed he was not yet completely immersed in a consumer economy. Twenty percent of citizens continued to live in communal apartments, and the Soviet living standard was below that of its satellite, the German Democratic Republic, yet it was still superior to what it had been during the Stalin years, and that was the comparison the Soviet citizen was prone to make. Life expectancy was falling and infant mortality rate was rising as was the perpetual problem of alcoholism. Yet many citizens were able to take a Sunday trip to a former home in the country where food and bread could be purchased or grown in lovingly cared-for vegetable gardens. Many were removed from the peasantry by only one generation. Millions of Russians grew or purchased much of their food in the gray economy or grew their own vegetables in country gardens. Twenty-five percent of produce consumed came from private plots.[16] The impulse so common in a democracy of holding the leadership to account was not developed in the Soviet system. Dissidence was rare and the regime faced little organized opposition. Before its collapse there were few signs of revolutionary ferment from below as in East Germany in 1953 or Hungary in 1956. What Soviet Jews were complaining about and especially their desire to leave was not well received by the stoic Soviet citizenry.

The average citizen involved in making ends meet cared little, and probably understood less, about the failure of the Soviet economy to produce capital or its low growth rate. During the war their factories had produced the T-34 tank, probably the best armored vehicle design on either side. There was an enormous pride regarding the successful orbiting of Sputnik on 4 October 1957. With the help of captured German scientists Soviet rocket design was ahead of the West. Could one believe that the economy was failing when one heard the beep of Sputnik circling the globe and the knowledge that one's country had achieved strategic parity with the United States?

The coercive state police powers gave Soviet leaders more leeway than leaders of the West to give higher priority to guns than butter. The period of greatest economic need between 1968 and 1978 corresponds roughly to the period of Soviet military expansionism when millions of rubles were spent arming Egypt, Syria, North Vietnam, and friendly nations located at other Cold War hot points. These were also the years when the emigration movement made its presence known. But the reaction to these systemic failings was not to sympathize with Jews or resort to the revolutionary barricades. At most there was among the elites a desire to see the outside world.[17]

When Reagan and Alexander Haig, his first secretary of state, began to speak of Soviet system as the close of a "bizarre chapter" of history in 1981, they were reminded by Sovietologists that although the system was dysfunctional, the Soviet economy was still the number one producer of oil, coal, steel, and concrete and in absolute terms the economy was still growing. Most important, the Russian masses, unlike their Polish counterparts, indicated little desire to challenge the system.[18] In the end, locating the reason for the change in Soviet self-confidence on the weakness of the economic performance of the system may serve as background but does not go far enough to explain the collapse of the political structure at that precise historical juncture. Rather, it is in the collective effect of a series of factors relating to maintaining its internal control, of which the Jewish emigration question was one, that the seeds of the implosion may be found.

Though predictions that the failure of the Soviet system was imminent it was mostly in the nature of a wish. There are few clues that Western policy makers knew of the imminence of collapse and were making their plans accordingly. There existed three areas in Soviet foreign relations that might have yielded some advance notice or at least some explanation of Soviet behavior. One concerned the general interest in disarmament and the relationship with the restless satellites. A second area was the deteriorating relationship with China, which after Nixon's opening created a new strategic problem for Moscow. This tension culminated in a serious border skirmish in 1979. The third was the relationship with Israel and the Middle East, generally where Moscow found itself in the costly role of arms supplier for the losing side even while facing an increasingly effective Islamic resistance in Afghanistan.

The picture of a growingly desperate regime facing enormous problems at home and abroad is the context in which the Soviet Jewry problem is best viewed in the eighties. But during Reagan's first administration signs that the Soviet government fathomed the direness of its situation came not in displaying more flexibility on the Jewish question but in greater rigidity. The attitude toward emigration was a barometer that might have foretold that changes were coming. But few in the Soviet Jewry movement read the signs of failure or foresaw that their goals would be realized with the imminent collapse of the regime.

■   In the 1980s the Soviet Jewry movement existed in the shadows of the realization that a thermonuclear holocaust was but a miscalculation away. After the United States placed intermediate-range missiles in the Federal Republic of Germany, the danger seemed even greater. Once the mainstay of the détente idea, the quest for a disarmed world did not magically disappear with the advent of the Reagan administration. It was the disarmament question that dominated the relationship between the two superpowers, so much so that Morris Abram, who succeeded Theodore (Ted) Mann as the chairman of the National Conference on Soviet Jewry (NCSJ) in 1982, pondered how the Soviet Jewry question might regain the high place it had won on the agenda during the heyday of the Jackson-Vanik negotiations.[19] "How could we hitch the Soviet Jewry claims to the meetings which were essentially designed to bring about . . . reduction in nuclear weapons."[20] For Jewish leaders to have attempted to hold the disarmament talks hostage to the release of Soviet Jewry would have caused a direct confrontation with the still powerful post-Vietnam peace movement. Rep. Dante Fascell, who had become chairman of the House Foreign Affairs Committee, also warned that the Soviet Jewry issue could lose the attention it had gained if the peace initiative, combined with the penchant of the administration for quiet diplomacy, prevailed.

For Morris Abram the answer, embodied in a one-page memorandum submitted to Reagan before the Geneva Conference on 9 September 1985, was to base the Jewish case on human rights as contained in the Helsinki Accords. Moscow should be reminded that no trust could be placed in disarmament provisions of any treaty as long as there were violations of the "humane provisions" of the Accords that the Soviets treat "as if they never happened." There was a concerted public relations effort to move the Soviet Jewry issue, which had been placed under regional conflicts / other issues on the provisional agenda, to a first-tier place.[21] Unaware that this reasoning had originated in an earlier letter from Sakharov to Carter, Reagan resorted to it at the summit conference. It availed little; the human rights issue received only two lines in the joint statement released at the end of the Geneva conference.

But in preparation for the Reykjavik summit the following year Reagan and Shultz again met with the Jewish leadership. Reagan displayed a copy of the

Helsinki Accords for the gathered press, showing Brezhnev's signature. At the meeting a memorandum prepared by the NCSJ showing the precipitous drop in emigration after 1979 was handed to Shevardnadze and a smiling Shultz said: "Now look, if you can do 51,000, you can continue to do it." [22] Gorbachev was informed that a productive relationship required Moscow to deal with the inescapable reality of the Soviet Jewry problem. The Soviet answer was to repeat the untruth that all the Jews who wanted to emigrate had already done so. Gromyko had difficulty understanding Shultz's concern for a handful of Jews, while the secretary found the Soviet refusal to let these Jews leave incomprehensible. Activists surmised that what worried the Russians was not the 11,000 outstanding visa applications but the 400,000 potential applicants who were ready to leave if the protracted months of having to live in limbo once the application had been submitted were shortened.

The Reykjavik summit was considered a failure on the human rights issue, but the Soviets agreed to form a joint working party to continue discussion. For the first two years of Gorbachev's tenure the emigration of Soviet Jewry was far from being a high priority issue, but the Soviets would now create a government bureau concerned exclusively with humanitarian issues and human rights. The joint communiqué at the close of the meeting announced that the human rights issue would be on the agenda at the next summit conference scheduled for December 1987. But suspicion of Soviet motives was far from dispelled. In his television address to the nation Reagan continued on his now-favorite rhetorical theme: Trust but verify. "When it comes to human rights and judging Soviet intentions," said the president, "We are all from Missouri. You have got to show us." [23] Gorbachev may have been following through when two months after Reykjavik, the Sakharovs, released from involuntary exile, returned triumphantly to Moscow's Yaroslavl station. News of the administration's victory was used by the State Department to mute the impact of Reagan's Star Wars proposal, which most Europeans greeted as being "looney."

In Soviet eyes the Reagan administration's support of Israel and the backing it gave to the emigration issue were cut from the same cloth. It was taken as additional evidence that Jews exercised a powerful influence in Washington. In a peculiar way the anti-Semitic fantasy that overestimated Jewish political influence helped the emigration cause. The Soviet authorities used it as a kind of safety valve. For example, the KGB was aware that the *vyzovs* sent from Israel were overwhelmingly bogus. They were accepted nevertheless because partly it provided a safety valve to get rid of undesirable activists and dissidents and allowed the potential emigrants to remain a useful gambit in the bargaining for trade credits. Moscow was not averse to using its captive Jews as a chip to strengthen its bargaining position on other matters.[24] At the same time it confined emigration to the single humanitarian ground of family reunification. The Soviet leadership was also aware of Israel's sustained efforts to build a bridge to Soviet Jewish communities with a view of one day reclaiming this "lost" Jewry. But from a geopolitical and ideological vantage, Israel was in a poor position to realize its claim of somehow representing the interest of Soviet Jewry. Israel was after all the home of the reviled world Zionist movement, which, aside from being a retrogressive throwback to bourgeois nationalism, interfered with the smooth integration of Russian Jewry into Soviet society and culture.

Most important, in Cold War terms Israel was a client state of the United States. In December 1983 Congress ratified a $2.6 billion package in military and economic aid, the most generous aid package granted to any American ally.[25] In the eyes of Soviet policy makers Israel's presence in the international arena went beyond the defeat of its Arab clients on the field of battle. On a day-to-day level Israel caused the Soviet Union endless public relations problems. Like Castro's Cuba was to America, Israel was a thorn in Russia's side. After the humiliating defeat of its Arab allies in 1967, the Soviet government broke all diplomatic ties with Israel and even after decades adamantly refused to restore them, though Israel made it abundantly clear that what it desired most was the normalization of relations. Israel's policy on Soviet Jewry often seemed to be subsidiary to this need. One of the many instances when a possible solution seemed within reach came in July 1985 when Yuli Vorontsov, the Soviet ambassador to France, met with Ovadia Sofer, his Israeli counterpart, at the home of Daniel Barenboim, the noted pianist. A package was agreed upon in which Israel would return most of the Golan Heights and put a stop to all anti-Soviet propaganda in turn for which Moscow would renew relations and direct Jewish emigrants exclusively to Israel. It never happened but demonstrates what Israel aspired to. Several times since 1967 the Kremlin had overreacted to Israel's mere existence. It threatened direct intervention in the Sinai War, the 1967 war, and in 1973. Its severance of diplomatic ties after the June war was considered an unprecedented reaction against a minor power. The formidable Soviet propaganda machine was thrown into high gear after Helsinki, spewing scurrilous propaganda about Zionism and the Jewish state. The caricatures and conspiratorial image of a world Jewish conspiracy linked it directly to the familiar Russian anti-Semitism that had produced the *Protocols*.

Withal, Israel's objective remained unchanged after 1976. It was to establish a direct emigration conduit to Israel through direct flights from Bucharest and if possible, Moscow. The liaison bureau was convinced that the mere existence of such an alternative would increase the flow of emigrants and also bypass the dropout problem. But as it stood the Dutch embassy, which after 10 June 1967 was handling the flow of emigrants, opposed any Israel suggestion that even implied that "freedom of choice" would be limited, as did Washington and the European Union.[26]

Strangely, Moscow seemed unconcerned that Soviet Jews represented a useful chip in the Arab-Israel conflict. They were, after all, in possession of the population stock Israel needed to shore up her demographic deficit. It was that circumstance that compelled Israel to seek out Soviet Jewry in the first place. In the early years of the eighties, when the emigration figures were kept at an all-time low, there was little for Arab leaders to complain about. An opportunity to reimmerse itself into the Middle East maelstrom after the disaster of the 1973 war seemed to materialize with Israel's invasion of Lebanon in June 1982. Fundamentalist Islamic wrath seemed to turn against Washington. A car bomb destroyed the U.S. Embassy in Beirut in April 1983, and in October a suicide car bomb attack on the Marine Corps headquarters killed 241 American Marines and wounded 70.

At the same time, the Soviets were getting their own taste of jihad in Afghanistan. Though not then fully understood in either Washington or Moscow, a new bloody variable had been introduced in the Middle East that pitted Islam against the West. Washington tried for its own Cold War ends to harness the Islamic resistance that had been mobilized in Afghanistan. There was little hint that the project would boomerang twenty-five years later. The Soviets tried at first to absorb its disaffected Islamic population. In the Khrushchev era they belatedly recognized that their failure to fully integrate its Islamic nationalities posed a serious threat of internal unrest. In some measure the denial of positions to Jews in the best universities and Communist Party schools, which began in earnest in those years, may be partly attributable to a need to make place for the candidates of its Islamic Asian republics. That limitation contributed notably to the emigration problem after 1975. The nettlesome nationalities question that Stalin had used to establish his bona fides as a Marxist thinker was no closer to a solution in the 1980s. The Tatars wanted to return to the Crimea. The Ukraine and Belarus argued constantly over linguistic and cultural issues, and Armenia and Azerbaijan would soon mount a bloody war.

One of the immediate effects of Israel's invasion of Lebanon was the postponement of the Israel-sponsored Third International Conference on Soviet

Jewry, scheduled to meet in Paris in October 1982. Moscow's Anti-Zionist Committee of the Soviet Public intensified activities, which signaled that Moscow was less than ever prepared to make concessions on the emigration question and recognition.[27] The lack of clarity in Israel's Soviet policy was also becoming a source of contention among activists outside of Israel. A Knesset debate in October 1984 on Israel's Soviet policy also reflected unhappiness with the Foreign Office's handling of the general relations with the Soviet Union over the emigration issue. Some Knesset members openly articulated their sense that the foreign office should assume an honest posture in support of the refuseniks and stop its unseemly pursuit of the hopeless goal of making some secret deal with Moscow. It could not continue to follow both policies at the same time, argued the opposition in Israel and the United States and especially the growing number of former Soviet emigrants who sensed the duality of Israel's policy.[28]

From the perspective of the Soviet Jewry movement elements of hope and despair seemed to live side by side during the early Reagan years. The Soviet authorities continued to be adamant regarding emigration so that in the years between 1980 and 1987 comparatively few Soviet Jews were able to emigrate. The reaction to the emphasis on the implementation of the rights enumerated in Basket III of the Helsinki Accords brought a serious KGB crackdown in its wake. That picture of despair was partly balanced by signs that the Soviet control system was weakening in the satellites, where the quest for human rights, including the right to emigrate and return, was upheld. But what might have generated more hope, the sense that the combination of economic failure of the system and loss of confidence in the leadership was raising the conditions for the internal collapse, was not yet present. It was that condition that would eventually lead to the release of Soviet Jewry. But only a handful, almost none in the Soviet Jewry movement, realized what was about to happen.

■   After Gorbachev came to power Soviet relations with Israel lost some of its bitter tone. Its rejection of reestablishing diplomatic ties with Israel had been partly outflanked by events after Egypt and Jordan showed indications of willingness to come to terms with Israel. Shimon Peres, who became Labor prime minister in September 1984, brought a new flexibility to the West Bank issue and also a willingness to mute Israel's anti-Soviet propaganda. To the dismay of Likud's Yitzhak Shamir, Peres hoped that by offering Moscow an opportunity to participate in the ongoing peace negotiations, the Soviets would become more flexible. Moscow too seemed to soften. In March 1985 *Izvestia* published a greeting from

Haim Herzog, the president of Israel, praising the Soviet Union for its heroic role in defeating the Nazi menace. Sharansky's release on 11 February 1986 became a high-profile public relations event that momentarily raised hopes in Israel. They were soon dashed when new wave of KGB arrests followed. Except to note that the Middle East was a possible "hotbed" of war, the Arab-Israeli dispute was not mentioned in Gorbachev's Twenty-seventh Party Congress speech. Soviet policy toward Israel continued to fluctuate widely, but beneath there was a bedrock of hostility. Ideologically, Zionism had always been the archenemy of the Communist Party of the Soviet Union (CPSU). Yet when Reagan confronted Libya, a potential Soviet client, with a direct air attack on 15 April 1986, the Soviet Union remained silent, perhaps fearing a similar response might be made against Syria. Clearly, the initiative in the Middle East was held by Washington while the Soviets, saddled with expensive client states that seemed unable to perform on the field of battle, remained the outsider in the Middle East, where Kissinger had skillfully maneuvered them a decade earlier.

Secret Israeli/Soviet talks had been going on in a desultory fashion since July 1985. The talks in Paris concerned not only the price of reestablishing diplomatic relations but such things as returning the Golan Heights, which Israel would not accept as a quid pro quo. The culmination of these back channel contacts occurred in Helsinki in 18 August 1986 when Soviet and Israeli delegations met to discuss outstanding problems, including the care of property belonging to the Russian Orthodox Church. The hope that the Soviets would be ready to make some concessions was raised after Chernobyl and after a drop in international oil prices had worsened its foreign exchange problem. But aside from a promised inventory of property belonging to the Russian Orthodox church the talks were ended precipitously. The Soviet Foreign Ministry announced that further meetings would not take place. An American diplomat suggested that Israel's anxiousness to restore diplomatic ties had led them into a tactical error of raising the Soviet Jewry issue before a low-level delegation.[29] Strangely, the sudden curtailment of the talks hardly put a dent on Israel's hopes to restore diplomatic relations with Moscow. An informal talk between Shimon Peres and Shevardnadze at the United Nations again raised hope that a less ideologically burdened leadership would prevail in Moscow, but on the ground Moscow's hands seemed tied. Syria, now Moscow's most loyal client state in the region, opposed any rapprochement until the Golan Heights was returned. There was speculation that Soviet strategists opposed regional stabilization because it would preclude the need for Soviet support in the Arab world. The question of recognition became more remote when the unity government brought Likud's Yitzhak Shamir to power. The recognition possibility and the related issue of emigration were again put on a back burner. Yet events were moving in a direction that would give the emigration issue a momentum of its own.

By 1981 more than a quarter million Soviet Jews had resettled in the United States and Israel. The flow of letters and phone calls to kin and friends that had been a trickle became a torrent. Some former emigrants had even been allowed to return for a visit. Not all the news they brought from the West was good, and the Soviets did much to publicize the real and unreal problems involved in resettlement and absorption. A negative image of Israel was continuously projected by the Soviet propaganda machine. It did not affect the desire to emigrate by the highly motivated Zionist-oriented emigrants of the first wave, but it contributed to the dropout phenomenon. That was balanced by the fact that it now became more difficult to isolate the refuseniks and activists without compromising the Soviet postal system that was, in some measure, bound by international postal agreements.[30] The initial failure to isolate Soviet Jews from other Jewish communities meant not only that the activists and refuseniks could continue to cultivate prominent outside contacts to make their case but news of Soviet repression could be communicated to the outside world almost instantly. It indicated a loss of control of information sources, a condition threatening to totalitarian systems. It also buttressed the public relations campaign, which had by 1980 become a primary activity of American Jewish activists. Now, when a hapless Soviet Jew was arrested for economic crimes or "hooliganism" his name was known to the outside world almost immediately, and often a bracelet with his name indicating a new "prisoner of Zion" was forged to be worn by an activist and displayed on placards on Solidarity Sunday. The repression within was more than ever used to feed the public relations campaign without.

Despite the prominent place human rights had been given on the Reykjavik agenda there were few signs in the early Gorbachev years that there would be a radical change in the way Moscow came to terms with its Jewish problem. The Cold War, which served as the international context of the Soviet Jewry movement, was in its twilight. But for the time being the strategy of isolating and intimidating the Jewish activists continued. That meant arrests of "speculators" and "parasites," inevitably with Jewish surnames, duly reported in the press. The virulent anti-Zionist and anti-Semitic campaign continued unabated. In some cities it even increased in virulence. Emigration remained at a virtual standstill in 1985 and 1986, but there was a positive consequence. By counteracting the KGB strategy of siphoning off potential leaders by emigration it stabilized and solidified the exist-ing leadership cadre.[31] At the same time the Soviet authorities worked on the premise that the majority of Soviet Jewry could be won over if they were granted more cultural freedom and the restoration of access to the universities and elite party institutions. In that way Jewish loyalty would again be ensured. That strat-egy was discussed at the Twenty-sixth Party Congress in 1981. But on the ground the growing enthusiasm for emigration could not be so easily reversed. By the time of Perestroika a good portion of Soviet Jewry could no longer be convinced that there would be a place for them in the new liberalized Soviet society. The con-ventional wisdom among the leadership of the NCSJ was that the pool of visa ap-plicants might reach as high as 380,000 if relaxation of regulations occurred. Not until 1987, two years after Gorbachev came to power, was the stage set for the So-viets to confront the emigration question directly.

▪   As in prior administrations, there was an element of opportunism in the trade policy implemented by the Reagan administration. Initially it followed the Nixon precedent and placed the human rights issue on a backburner.[32] But after George Shultz became secretary of state in 1982 the consistently high priority given to the plight of Soviet Jewry was clear to all. Shultz and Reagan were drawn to the prob-lem not merely through abstract notions of human rights but also through per-sonal contact. Meeting with refuseniks had a visceral impact on Shultz, and Reagan began to take an inordinate interest in the Pentecostals who had found refuge in the American embassy in Moscow on 27 June 1977. Thereafter, Shultz, at least in his face-to-face negotiations with the Soviets, linked the improvement of Soviet-American relations to the emigration question.[33] According to Elliot Abrams, the assistant secretary of state for human rights and humanitarian affairs, it was not brought up in a pro forma way by tagging it on at the end as a never-to-be-reached item on the agenda, but presented at the outset of a discussion so that the Soviet negotiators could not fail to note the priority it was given. In April 1987 a high point was reached when Shultz was invited to the annual Passover Seder or-ganized at Spasebo House in the U.S. compound to which leading refuseniks were also invited. These Seders were organized by Richard Schifter, a lawyer and son of a survivor who was appointed as an assistant secretary of state for human rights and humanitarian affairs on 1 November 1985. He soon became a crucial factor in linking the Soviet Jewry movement to the administration and working directly with Soviet officials on the emigration question. In the spring of 1986 the Soviet Foreign Ministry created a parallel Humanitarian Affairs Ministry under Yuri

Kashlev. There had been rumors that Soviet lawmakers were working on the emigration problem and that a new law was imminent. Only the problem of the refuseniks designated as possessing security information and certain other roadblocks such as the need to receive clearance from relatives stood in the way of a general release of the remaining refuseniks. Shultz accepted the invitation and in a moving moment in the evening, wearing a skull cap, he addressed the refuseniks, urging them "never to give up" and reassuring them that the United States would never do so. It was a surprising show of emotion from the usually stoic Shultz. Realizing that they were witnessing a special moment in their struggle, some of the forty leading refuseniks, including Ida Nudel, Victor Brailovsky, Yosef Begun, Ofer Neiman, Alexander Lerner, and Vladimir Feltsman, had tears in their eyes as they applauded Shultz.[34] The incident was duly reported in the press in the following days but few noted that Shultz's reaction was one of personal sympathy and had little to do with American policy. He realized that the refuseniks were made to pay a terrible price for the natural human right to emigrate. "They managed to keep it a human rights issue without getting involved in strategic arms issues," noted Nechemia Levanon, former head of Israel's secret Liaison office.[35]

The two Pentecostal families who crashed their way into the American embassy in June 1977 became relevant as a collateral issue that broadened the public sense of Soviet unreasonableness on the general emigration question. From the outside it seemed like a typical case of bureaucratic bungling from which there was no honorable way out for the Soviets. The "Siberian Seven" from Chernogorsk possessed Israeli visas, the only exit available, but the *vyzovs* proving close family connections were rejected for some reason. That made their fate a cause célèbre. To gain visibility in the media one of their number went on a protracted hunger strike. But unwilling to establish a precedent for leaving the Soviet Union in this way, not until 18 July 1983, six years later, did the Soviet authorities relent.[36]

The American government effort on behalf of Soviet Jewry reached a high point during the Reagan administration. But despite Max Fisher's efforts to bring the Jewish vote into the Republican column, it is unlikely that domestic politics had much to do with the effort. American Jewry continued to vote and financially support Democratic candidates.[37] Together with Richard Allen, Reagan's advisor, Fisher helped insert a strong pro-Israel and Soviet Jewry statement into the president's acceptance speech. But Reagan's remote leadership style was not compatible with Fisher's role, and his ready access to the Oval Office became more limited. The Soviet Jewry issue had gained some traction among Jewish voters, but an

American Jewish Congress (AJCong) exit poll on the eve of the election of 1984 showed that their primary interest remained focused on the security of Israel.[38] Paradoxically, it was the question of Israel's demographic security that now threatened its relationship with American Jewry. The issue that divided them concerned the disposition of the dropouts. It was not a new conflict, but as the Soviets slowly liberalized their emigration policy it once again came to the fore. The question of "choice" for the emigrants was becoming serious enough to threaten Israel's crucial relationship with American Jewry.

By 1980 the conflict went beyond the first signs of disharmony to the control of the flow of information, which we have seen was primarily in the hands of Israel in the early seventies. Behind the conflict was a factor indigenous to American Jews. As noted earlier, latent communal guilt regarding the American Jewish witness role during the Holocaust energized much of the Soviet Jewry movement, particularly the younger membership. These intense emotions surfaced in April 1985 when Reagan's pending visit to a military cemetery in Bitburg where 47 members of the Waffen SS were buried was announced and riled community sensibilities.[39] The strength of that Holocaust obsession was again in evidence in the budget priorities within the community where memorialization was the primary motivation of the survivors who had reestablished themselves in the United States. The survivors' influence could be noted in the fact that virtually every American Jewish community and congregation had either already built or had on the drawing board some kind of Holocaust memorial. The larger urban communities were planning museums focused on the Holocaust. At its apogee was the enormous fund-raising effort to build the Holocaust museum on the Mall in the nation's capital. The campaign also included an effort to get the government to assume a financial role in helping to maintain the museum, as if to compensate for government indifference during the Holocaust.

It is a small wonder in a communal atmosphere in which the memory of the Holocaust was so pervasive that many American activists assumed the threat faced by Soviet Jews was analogous. They believed that they too needed to be rescued. The travail of Soviet Jewry, especially during Stalin's final years, was seen as a kind of Holocaust coda. The advent of a more liberal Gorbachev regime, which removed the remaining signs of physical threat to Jewish dissenters and seemed ready to restore banned cultural institutions, had little impact. It was as if the Jewish world could not take "yes" for an answer. "Never again" remained the communal war cry and "rescuing" Soviet Jewry was its objective. Yet some were wary of the Holocaust analogy. Phil Baum, the executive director of the AJCong, dared to point out that after Gorbachev, Soviet Jewry did not require rescue any more than any other Soviet ethnic groups.[40] But that opinion ran against the stream.

The Bitburg incident cast light on a related factor in the Soviet Jewry story. It again brought the Jewish role as historical victim to the attention of the American public, though whether it generated public empathy for the plight of Soviet Jews remains an unknown. With the exception of those involved with the civil and human rights movements, together with certain liberal Protestant church officials, selected members of Congress, and certain government officials, the Soviet Jewish problem remained largely an intra-Jewish community concern. Not all American Jews were happy about the attention Jewish victimization was bringing to the community. Becoming a victim of history was not considered a positive factor in strengthening group identity. Better to be history's master than its victim, counseled the prevailing Zionist ideology.

■ It took two years after Gorbachev assumed the leadership role for the Kremlin to move on the emigration question.[41] When the new regulations were in finally put in place in January 1987, the *vyzov* requirement was limited to "first degree relatives" (siblings, parents and grandparents), the waiting period was limited to one month, and there would be a right of appeal in cases of rejection. The security provision that refused visas to anyone who had knowledge of state secrets was relaxed so that hundreds of the approximately 11,000 refuseniks who had been denied visas on the arbitrary use of this restriction could reapply.[42] With one blow four of the major items on the refusenik shopping list were granted. But would the authorities follow through? In May most "prisoners of conscience" were actually released and allowed to leave the country. Four months later OVIR began to accept applications even for non-close relative claimants desiring to immigrate to countries other than Israel. Gradually, Soviet emigration laws were beginning to resemble those of the West. But paradoxically, if the objective of the liberalization was to get rid of the nettlesome Jewish emigration problem, precisely the reverse occurred. Opening the gates partially stimulated new applications for emigration.

The stage was now set for an exodus, and both sides waited anxiously to see what would happen. The activists had insisted that if permitted to do so, hundreds of thousands of Soviet Jews would exercise their right to emigrate. The Soviet authorities had countered by insisting that most Jews were loyal citizens and that all who had wanted to emigrate had already done so. It did not take long to discover that the activists who had spoken of large numbers ready to emigrate were more realistic, but not for the reason they imagined. These potential new emigrants were not inclined toward Zionism, but many clung to the remnants of their Jewish identity and endured the pervasive anti-Semitism of Russian society, which was not confined to the daily taunts of their neighbors but also amplified by government policy that denied their children access to a better life. Moreover, even if Jews could find acceptance in the newly emerging society many foresaw years of chaos ahead.

The historical cookie thus crumbled in favor of the activists, and Israel hoped against hope that it would be able to "ingather" the new wave of emigrants. By 1987 and every year thereafter the emigration figures mounted so that even Israel, which was ready to tax its economic system to the limit to absorb the emigrants, was overwhelmed by the numbers. Jewish activists were not alone in watching the unexpected exodus. While they celebrated their success in finally opening the closed gates of the Soviet Union, immigration officials in Washington were concerned that access to the United States under the liberal refugee law of 1980 would entail an unforeseen expenditure of many millions of dollars.[43] Attorney General Edwin Meese had earlier written a memo stressing the urgent need to reinterpret "refugee status" so that the burden of proof rested on the would-be refugee.[44] It was estimated that 100,000 Soviet emigrants would have applied for visas to the United States in 1989 alone at an estimated cost of $5,000 per refugee to the Jewish welfare agencies.

Despite the fact that between 1980 and 1987 emigration figures were so low that there was little to argue about, the bitter conflict about the final disposition of the emigrants simmered throughout these lean years. The arguments had not appreciably changed in the later eighties. The promise of increased numbers of emigrants that would follow upon the liberalization of the emigration regulations was creating growing conflict within the organizational world of American Jewry and between Israel and American Jewry. A massive Jewish emigration was about to happen and the matter could no longer be muddled through.

The problem was that increasingly the Soviet emigrants, whom Israel viewed as the solution to its demographic problem, did not consider themselves exiles to be "gathered in" but ordinary refugees seeking a better life, which they believed was more available in the United States. Israel's distress at the rejection of the Jewish state was palpable. For Israel, the child of the Zionist movement, the failure to gather in the Soviet emigrants went beyond its demographic crisis. It was a moment of truth for the Zionist movement. The dropouts where a bold-faced negation of the idea that the Jewish people could reclaim their history in their ancient land after thousands of years of exile. That was the assumption on which Zionism was based. Israel had submitted all manner of diplomatic and administrative strategies to head off the increasing flow of emigrants to the United States and other Western countries. In Washington Israel's diplomats argued that as long as there was an Israel with its "law of return" the Soviet emigrants could not be considered to be "refugees." But such cries availed little. The generous American refugee law allowed little hope that the dropout phenomenon could be resolved in favor of Israel.

By 1985 the position on both sides had hardened. Most American Jews affiliated with organizations favored the idea of freedom of choice. We have noted that because they were immersed in a Holocaust-haunted communal culture, they viewed the Soviet emigration as a rescue operation, which meant that priority should be given to getting them out as quickly as possible. The destination was secondary. Until 1989 American administrations would not tamper with the politically sensitive issue of changing the refugee law. That is where the situation stood at the historical juncture when Russia was about to open its gates.

For Israel the goals were clear. Moscow must be convinced to relent on reestablishing diplomatic ties so that direct flights to the homeland could be established, and Washington must be persuaded to abandon its seductive refugee policy. With a little help from history, Israel succeeded in doing both. It is not a victory heralded in history books, but success in both endeavors had perhaps more to do with assuring Israel's long-term survival than its victories on the battlefield.[45]

■　We have noted that the decade after the signing of the Helsinki Final Act in August 1975 was not an auspicious one for emigration. It was as if somewhere in the inner recesses of the Kremlin a decision had been taken to halt the transaction that was in effect an exchange of captive Soviet Jews for credit and trade. The Helsinki follow-up conferences continually heard complaints of Moscow's failure to implement the agreement, but on the ground the conditions were in fact far worse. The danger faced by activists became more threatening as dozens were arrested. The worsening conditions led to cries of "dump Helsinki" especially among the Soviet activists. As one journalist put it: "Teaching civility to Moscow is like teaching golf to wolves."[46] In 1988 Sakharov feared that George Bush, the newly elected president, and his secretary of state, James Baker, would be taken in by the wily Gorbachev as he suspected that Reagan and Shultz had been, and there were the grand old foreign policy thinkers, such as George Kennan and Henry Kissinger, who found the human rights note introduced into international discourse by the Helsinki Accords to be too shrill and moralistic.

Nevertheless, the Helsinki movement overcame opposition and developed into a continuous process. During the eighties four follow-up conferences were convened, including Madrid (11 November 1980–9 September 1983), Vienna (1983–86) and Helsinki (1989). In addition, minor specialized and review meetings dealing with specific aspects of the Final Act were convened at various times in Budapest, Belgrade, Ottawa, and Copenhagen. The conferences were ongoing and were generally viewed as insignificant before 1985. But that did not take account what was developing beneath the surface in Eastern Europe. There is some evidence that by setting specific human rights goals to strive for the Helsinki process was one of the sources of pressure for liberalization in Eastern Europe and the Soviet Union. The continuous round of meetings was finally institutionalized in 1989 by furnishing the Conference on Security and Cooperation in Europe (CSCE) a permanent secretariat headquartered in Prague.

From the perspective of Soviet Jewry the Madrid follow-up conference, convened after the Soviet invasion of Afghanistan, is especially significant because it revealed at one stroke the Kremlin's expansionism. It also placed the Helsinki process, which depended on at least a modicum of international comity, in jeopardy. At the same time Jewish organizations had become more aware of the opportunity offered by the Helsinki process and descended on Madrid.[47] There were leaflets, rallies, and prepared reports to be distributed to the delegates. Avital Sharansky, who had become newsworthy in her own right, arrived in Madrid to publicize her plight. When word got around that direct pressure on the Soviets was possible the delegation to the Berne follow-up conference on human rights was inundated with appeals from refuseniks. A drumbeat of speeches and articles on the "systematic" Soviet violations of the Helsinki Accords were heard. The more raucous tactics of the Jewish Defense League also continued, to the dismay of the legitimate organizations. A tear gas bombing at the Metropolitan Opera where the Moiseyev dance company was performing on 2 September 1986 received much press attention.[48] There were also appeals from Germans, Lithuanians, and Pentecostals, all following the Jewish precedent for emigration on the basis of family reunification, which remained the only basis to leave the Soviet Union.

By the time of the Madrid conference the cumulative impact of the public relations campaign was evident. No longer limited to such activities as street protests and picketing within the community, the campaign was now amplified by repeated mention of Soviet violations in the media, including broadcasts on Radio Liberty and Radio Free Europe. It put the massive Soviet propaganda machine, busily defending the invasion of Afghanistan, on the defensive. How far the Soviet

Jewry movement had come was reflected in the rapturous reception given to the recently released Sharansky by the gathered legislators in the Rotunda under the Capitol dome where he would be granted the nation's Gold Medal of Freedom in 1989. In the Oval Office the following day, President Reagan stressed that his preference for "quiet diplomacy" could be effective only if strong public pressure and the free flow of information continued. The good opinion of the world was the thing the Soviet authorities were most anxious to obtain. That in turn related to their failing sense of legitimacy in Europe, which paradoxically was the original reason why Moscow initiated the Helsinki process.

The Madrid conference also focused attention on Max Kampelman, whose reputation as a cold warrior preceded his appointment to co-chair the U.S. delegation. Some questioned such an appointment to the CSCE, which was essentially detentist in origin and purpose. There was apprehension lest Kampelman, who like many cold warriors did not speak well of the Helsinki process when it came into existence in 1975, would employ the prosecutorial approach initiated by Arthur Goldberg in Belgrade, thereby endangering the growing friendliness between the NATO and Warsaw Pact members. By 1980, 35 percent of the Soviet Union's petroleum exports were earmarked for Western Europe, and West Germany was importing more than 40 percent of its natural gas from the Soviet Union.[49] Neither Griffin Bell, who replaced William Scranton as co-chairman, nor Max Kampelman, who also co-chaired the delegation, had prior diplomatic experience.[50] Bell's opening address tried to allay these fears. While declaring that the United States believed itself duty bound to fight for the release of those recently imprisoned, he also informed the delegates that "despite all that has happened" the issue of peace and disarmament would be given "absolute priority."[51] In contrast, Kampelman seemed hardly able to contain his strong anti-Soviet feelings. Like Reagan, he believed that he was dealing with an "evil empire" that should be given no quarter. In his opening address, which had not been checked with the State Department and bore no relation to the objectives of the Helsinki process, he denounced the Soviets for everything, from the invasion of Afghanistan to the arrest of Victor Brailovsky. Using his own funds when necessary, Kampelman made certain that his addresses received the widest dissemination.

A week before the conference was to convene the Democrats lost the election, which meant that the two co-chairmen would require reappointment from the incoming administration. Bell did not want the position, but Kampelman, who had received the title of ambassador, was delighted with it. He used all his influence to win a reappointment, overcoming the opposition of the *Wall Street Journal* and prominent dissidents such as Vladimir Bukovsky. According to one researcher, he then "puffed up" what was relatively minor post to a high profile "bully pulpit."[52] His credentials as a cold warrior now stood him in good stead in the new administration. Although he had little formal connection with the world of Jewish organizations, he was a founding member of the Jewish Institute for National Security affairs, whose program was directed to mobilizing Jewish communal leaders and legislators in support of a strong American defense posture. He was well connected with the Israel establishment but did not consider himself a Zionist. Predictably, Kampelman, as head of the delegation, became a confrontationist, which dismayed many European delegates. "I learned from that first experience with the Soviets," he wrote in his autobiography, "that they needed to be asked, to be prodded, to be confronted."[53] At the same time he was not averse to bargaining on the disposition of the Pentecostals holed up in the Moscow embassy and the possible early release of Sharansky.[54] With Kampelman at the helm, the Helsinki process developed into what it was perhaps always destined to be from Washington's view, a tool to wage the Cold War on the human rights front.

The conference might have drawn less attention from the Jewish press had it not been for René Panis, the Belgian delegate to the Basket I working group who raised the issue of intensified anti-Semitism in the Soviet Union. That led to an adamant denial by the Soviet delegate. But three months later there was ample evidence that the charge had found its mark when Brezhnev condemned anti-Semitism as a "national aberration" in a speech before the Twenty-sixth Congress of the CPSU and called for a new policy of "neither anti-Semitism nor Zionism." But with the demise of détente and Brezhnev's deteriorating health, Moscow's willingness to implement the long list of complaints regarding compliance that gave the Jewish emigration issue an especially high place weakened. After a paper detailing Soviet suppression of Jewish culture, which culminated in the arrest of Brailovsky, the status of Soviet Jewry took center stage in the proceedings. Kampelman turned out to be an astute and articulate diplomat on Soviet Jewry and other issues. Through his connections in Washington he was able to convert his original three-month temporary appointment into a three-year stint. He left an indelible impression on the Helsinki process.

The focus on the Soviet Jewry issue was a historic breakthrough. For the first time in an international forum the Soviet treatment of refuseniks was paired with a specific violation of the Helsinki Final Act. The sharp decline in exit permits was cited as a deliberate manipulation of emigration for political purposes by John Wilberforce, a prominent activist in the British Soviet Jewry movement. Under the direction of Stephen Roth, director of Britain's Institute of Jewish Affairs, and the International Council of the World Conference for Soviet Jewry, the European section of the movement had worked through the Helsinki process since its outset in 1975. But it awaited the Madrid conference to serve as the juncture where the Soviet Jewry movement joined forces with the worldwide human rights movement. Kampelman tried to allay fears that Moscow was getting too much out of Helsinki. "Instead of Helsinki becoming a tool for Soviet propaganda," he informed a mixed audience in at a meeting in New York, "it is now a tool for liberty and human rights." [55] He did not add that his leadership had made it so but he may have thought it. Two years later he had become much more circumspect in touting his success. Matters had again taken a turn for the worse.

The Madrid conference was the longest held by the CSCE. It was followed two years later by the general meeting in Vienna. Emphasizing the legitimacy of raising the human rights issue, Shultz spoke of the 380,000 Soviet Jews who wanted to emigrate. He noted that "Soviet leaders have shown increasing awareness of the public relations price they pay as a result of their conduct." [56] But confident that it had successfully set aside agitation on human rights issues, Moscow seemed unaware of such a price. It was now anxious to host a follow-up conference of foreign ministers to meet in Helsinki's Finlandia Hall for the occasion of celebrating the tenth anniversary of the signing of the Helsinki Final Act. It would be the first occasion for Shultz to meet Gorbachev's new team, especially Eduard Shevardnadze, his foreign minister.

More than ever convinced that Helsinki offered an opportunity to push the Soviets to comply with the protocol, Shultz delivered a stinging speech on Soviet dereliction on the human rights front. Shevardnadze complained about the toughness of the speech. "When I come to the U.S., should I talk about unemployment and blacks?" he queried smiling, to which Shultz replied, "Help yourself." [57] The two men went on to become fast friends, and Shultz later believed that American openness in pushing the human rights issue helped convince both Gorbachev and Shevardnadze of its centrality. When Gorbachev proposed that confrontation on the human rights issue be avoided and each side follow their own path to human rights and not try to impose their ideologies on the other, it led to a remarkable exchange on the basic differences between the two systems. But Gorbachev came to realize that the Western approach to rights held sway even on the streets of Moscow. The human rights issue could no longer be avoided.

Sufficient work had been done at the smaller specialized meetings in Berne and other minor follow-up conferences to call upon the general conference of the

CSCE to give the work its imprimatur. During the early years of negotiations on human rights the process was checked at every turn by Soviet counterargument and resistance, but with the advent of Gorbachev some light could be seen at the end of the tunnel. The Soviets had promised to consider allowing the free flow of information as required in the Final Act by ending the jamming of Western radio and television broadcasts and to consider the release of imprisoned dissidents on trumped-up psychiatric charges. When the Vienna conference ended its business with a ringing declaration of the work achieved and problems waiting to be solved, Shultz viewed it as a near fulfillment of the Helsinki mandate. Soviet delegates at the Vienna conference revealed some details of the impending reform of its emigration system that would eliminate bureaucratic impediments. But for the moment the question of priorities—which problem would receive the earliest attention—remained. Reagan personally insisted that agreements on the reduction of conventional arms could begin only when there were written guarantees on human rights. Finally, Shultz was able to convince a reluctant Reagan to agree to a forthcoming general conference in Moscow that the Soviets seemed particularly anxious to host.

Previously, in the gloomy atmosphere of Geneva in November 1985, Shultz had again spoken of the crucial need for the Soviets to come up to the Western standard on human rights. He cautioned that the Soviet Union would continue to fall hopelessly behind if it did not open its system to free movement and the free flow of information, both crucial to the Soviet Jewry movement. That address was among the steps taken by Shultz in the fulfillment of assurances made to Gerald Kraft, an NCSJ vice president and president of B'nai B'rith International.[58] The Soviet Jewry emigration issue had become a major item in Cold War diplomacy. Distrust of the Soviet intentions did not vanish all at once, and for some activists it would never do so. Morris Abram expressed concern that the declaration lacked "definite language on significant performance," which would enable the Soviet Union to wiggle out of its obligations.[59] Similarly, Richard Schifter feared that Shultz had been taken in by Moscow's subterfuge.[60] Sakharov, who like most dissenters distrusted the leaders in the Kremlin, also feared that Reagan and Shultz were too convinced that basic changes were actually taking place in the Soviet Union.[61] The changes in Moscow's behavior were inconsistent but gradually the perception was growing that liberalization would occur even in the delicate area of emigration. In 1988 the Kremlin announced its withdrawal from Afghanistan. A symptom of the changing times occurred when the Fascall congressional human rights committee, which coordinated and published the results of worldwide monitoring activities, was granted permission to meet with activists in Moscow in the spring of 1988. In 1976, its request to visit Moscow had been rejected. Things were changing on the ground and the end of the Cold War seemed at hand. Strangely, the Reagan administration was earlier than the dissidents and some Jewish organization in sensing that.

Some activists could not conceive that a breakthrough had occurred even when the facts stared them in the face. They saw that even after the Madrid conference there was no way to compel the Soviets to implement the dozens of recommendations for reform. Often they were dismissed as simply an attempt to interfere in Soviet internal affairs. Arrests of monitoring groups were still occurring and the number of visas allowed had only begun to rise slightly in the final months of 1987. But a closer look might have revealed a growing drumbeat for change within the Soviet empire. Even before the advent of Gorbachev the human rights idea, as embodied in the Helsinki Accords, was becoming the driving force of the liberalization that would eventually release Soviet Jewry. The Helsinki follow-up conferences and the rise of watch groups provided a comparative secure locale for liberalizers to meet and maintain communications with the outside. They alerted the CSCE to the dozens of instances of failure to implement already agreed upon reforms. It was that outside pressure, especially when it emanated from the People's Republics of Eastern Europe, that played an important role in generating a mood for reform. Eventually that continuous pressure led to new regulations for emigration first considered by the Soviet Councils of Ministers in August 1986. The regulations did not quite meet Basket III proposed standards but they were an improvement over the prior arbitrariness and set the stage for the massive emigration that began in earnest in 1989.

In years to come, historians may want to consider whether there was not something in the reform process itself, when undertaken by societies who exercise total control, which ultimately undermines their control system. It sets a momentum for change in motion that can be stopped only with severe suppression. That may be what actually was happening in the Soviet empire. It collapsed internally when the suppressive structure was dismantled. If that is a valid rendering of a largely internalized process, then the Soviet Jewry movement's weight in history may go beyond its efforts on behalf of its own clients, to its contribution in loosening the Soviet control system. It has a valence not only on the Jewish historical canvas but in the larger arena of Cold War and world history.

The Reagan administration did not realize the power of the human rights movement to change Soviet behavior all at once. As late as the Reykjavik summit there were still reservations that had to be overcome. On the American domestic political scene that point came when the Senate ratified and Reagan signed a prized item on the American Jewish wish list, after seven prior administrations had failed to do so, the Genocide Convention of 1988. It represented a congressional sensitivity to the necessity of guidelines for behavior in the international arena. For the Soviet Jewry movement the Madrid conference marks a similar turning point, a sense that an international consensus favoring human rights codes was developing. Strategists such as Henry Kissinger opposed what they viewed as the shrillness of the follow-up conferences, but they seemed gradually to be producing results. By the time the Copenhagen conference convened in June 1990, Moscow had converted from a confrontational position to one of cooperation. Forty-two years after the original human rights declaration was introduced, the conference produced with Moscow's support a new declaration of human rights that soon became known as the Magna Carta of Europe. By that year liberalization, too, was in full swing. The breakthrough was almost complete but an effort by Western nations to condemn anti-Semitism and anti-Zionism was held off by the Soviet delegation. It was popular anti-Semitism, released paradoxically by the liberalization itself, which would now pose the greatest threat to Soviet Jewry.

■   The Soviet Union's acceptance of human rights that had a "made in the West" label was a victory in the ideological Cold War. But the geopolitical aspect of that war in the Middle East, which would now be impacted by the release of thousands of Soviet Jews, had yet to be determined. Ironically, at the juncture when the emigration problem seemed to be on the road to solution, the dropout problem came to a head. In the early months of 1987, Israel's endeavors in Washington and Moscow, where the destination of the Soviet emigration would be decided, were intensified. Israel's political room for maneuver was limited. On the Right, the Soviet settlers had rapidly formed themselves into a political force led by Sharansky and others, which counseled that a hard line should be taken at the forthcoming conference, to be convened in Moscow in 1986. Aware that Moscow wanted to participate in the forthcoming Middle East peace negotiations, the Likud insisted that Cold War relations in the Middle East should not be linked to the emigration issue. "If the Soviet Union wants to improve its image and attain a different attitude from the West by changing its policy on Jewish emigration," declared Yitzhak Shamir in April 1987, "it must open its gates and allow hundreds of thousands of Jews out without imposing any restrictions and qualifications. We must not sell the Jewish cause cheaply." [62]

That change was imminent stemmed from Moscow's new emigration regulations, the first of which were issued in January 1987 limiting the "close relatives" provision to "first degree" relatives. It hardly seemed likely that the new strictures would halt the flow of emigrants to the United States and at the same time suggested that Moscow was finally tackling the emigration problem in earnest.[63] At the same time the informal agreement reached by Morris Abram and Edgar Bronfman in March 1987 hinted that there were new concessions in the wind concerning the situation of the refuseniks and the renewal of cultural activity. By the time of the Moscow summit in November 1986, neither Labor's soft nor Likud's hard approach had much to show for their efforts. The Soviets remained unwilling to use the emigration bargaining chip it had in its possession and continued to be seemingly unconcerned about the ultimate destination of the emigrants. From a strategic view the dropout phenomenon served Moscow's interest because it relieved Arab pressure regarding emigration to Israel and it humiliated the world Zionist movement.

Israel's strategy also called for reduction of the role of the helping agencies, the Hebrew Immigrant Aid Society (HIAS) and the American Jewisn Joint Distribution Committee (JDC), by placing its case directly before the Council of Jewish Federations and Welfare Funds (CJF), their major funding agency. Simultaneously, it would call on the American government to change the refugee law to restrict Soviet Jewish emigration. The first attempts to implement the strategy were not successful. The "direct flight" plan to bypass Rome and Vienna, which would have solved the problem in Israel's favor at one blow, was rejected by the Netherlands. At the same time the Reagan administration rejected any change in the refugee status of Soviet emigrants, and the CJF rejected Israel's appeal to limit funding. But in the following years the situation was reversed.

In February 1987 Yitzhak Shamir, Israel's new prime minister under the rotation arrangement of the unity government, visited Washington. His primary objective was to ensure passage of an aid package. But Shamir had an important secondary objective, to convince American political and Jewish communal leaders to allow a change in the definition of political refugee to exclude Soviet Jewish emigrants. That would remove a major roadblock impeding the flow of Soviet emigrants to Israel. The premier was particularly sensitive to the problem posed by the instability of Israel's population under the impact of both *yerida* and *Neshira*.[64] Morris Abram, who had been involved in negotiating an agreement with the Soviets, cautioned Shamir not to challenge the definition of refugees, which, if successful, would eliminate the highly valued freedom of choice by reducing the government funds made available under the refugee law. But the prime minister refused and as in 1976 when the CJF rejected the modified proposal of the Committee of Eight, ran into a wall of opposition from Jewish leaders. Stanley B. Horowitz, president of the United Jewish Appeal, the principle fund-raising agency, warned Shamir against a direct intervention with the U.S. government. Surprisingly, Sharansky, who had earned a major voice in Israel on the emigration question, did not support Shamir's effort to force a change in the definition of "refugee." "I have no doubt that the best place for a Jew to live is in Israel," he told an audience in Jerusalem, "but I don't want anyone brought here against his will." [65]

Despite disclaimers, Shamir did bring up the question of the refugees in his private conversation with Reagan in February, only to be rebuffed. Lobbyists for Jewish organizations made known their strong opposition to such a change in the halls of Congress and the State Department, which came out strongly for freedom of choice for the emigrants. But from February to September 1987 Israel mounted an unrelenting effort to bring Washington and the Jewish organization around to its way of thinking. The liaison office was mobilized to press congressional representatives and government officials on the interpretation of refugee status. In October Shamir approached Shultz on the possibility of substituting a "right of repatriation" for "freedom of choice" at the summit meeting scheduled for December in Moscow. The idea was precedented by the release of thousands Poles, several thousand Jews among them, who were repatriated in 1956. In the meantime the former prime minister broke the traditional caution regarding intrusion in the nation's political affairs by informing a group of congressional representatives that Israel favored waiving the Jackson amendment. [66] At the same time Israel's need for additional aid for absorption of the expected inflow of emigrants was made known. [67] Withal, it would take an additional two years until political and budgetary circumstances compelled the new Bush administration to abandon its support of the "freedom of choice" position, but the groundwork for such a change had been established.

Shamir's initial confrontation with the leadership of the Jewish organizations was also a standoff. The prime minister began his effort heavy handedly by characterizing the Abram/Bronfman agreement as a "sell out" of Jewish interest for a handful of Jews. That comment did not sit well with those activists who had lived through the lean years when few emigrants were granted visas and suppression was an everyday reality. His visit marked a low point in American Jewish–Israel relations. The consensus among liberal minded American Jews favored the position of the Labor party on the all-important basis for peace and its more sensitive approach to the dropout problem. A repeat of slanderous accusations against the JDC and HIAS did not help matters. Armed with the latest statistics indicating that aliyah was the choice of only a small minority, American activists, most affiliated with the UCSJ, remained determined to continue their fight for freedom of choice. The statistics were also devastating for Israel. Of the 18,963 emigrants in 1988, only 11 percent selected to settle in Israel. Clearly, if something was not done soon the pending flow of Jewish emigrants would settle elsewhere or remain in the Soviet Union.

It was at that juncture that Israel won a decisive round in its struggle to "ingather" Soviet Jewry. In May 1987 Israel finally received a hesitant Soviet signal that direct flights out of Bucharest would be permitted. Moscow was already considering a proposal that originated with the Committee of Eight that a visa based on family reunification, supported by an authentic *vyzov*, would make the emigrant eligible for an exit permit to the United States and other countries. The American limitation on immigration would act as a brake on the expected flood of applicants. If the proposal to normalize its procedures was accepted by Moscow, the Israeli visa would no longer be the only exit instrument out of the Soviet Union, and those wishing to settle elsewhere would be free to do so. Technically, the potential emigrant would be able to leave directly from Moscow to the United States. The emigrant would have "choice" but it would be made in Moscow. That would take the sting out the charge of Israeli coercion, which influenced federation leaders, but it would also rule out refugee status and the crucial government financial support that went with it. It also entailed an open immigration policy that Moscow was not yet ready to countenance in 1987.

The budget question was also crucial for federation leaders, who foresaw huge expenditures stemming from Moscow's granting of direct visas. The costly support of refugees in Vienna and Rome would be alleviated, but a totally dependent emigrant would then require support from the community, virtually without government help. On one hand they continued to strongly favor "freedom of choice," and on the other, they also supported "direct flight," which in effect eliminated choice. In the end it is difficult to avoid the conclusion that in the direct confrontation between the Jewish Agency (JAFI) and the CJF, the latter flinched first. Shoshanah Cardin, the president of the CJF, repeated the fiction previously suggested by the Netherlands. She argued that as a democratic society Israel did not force emigrants who were seduced by the prospect of direct flights to remain in Israel. They could apply for an emigration visa to leave Israel as thousands did every

year. Choice still existed, it had merely been delayed. Israel could consider such
emigrants as refugees rather than Israeli citizens, as required by the "law of return." But in truth, in terms of cost and the narrowed definition of "refugee" used
by the Immigration and Naturalization Service (INS), the possibility of retaining
one's refugee status in such cases was remote. For most emigrant families one
transplantation per lifetime was sufficient. For most, resettlement in America,
after a temporary stay in Israel, was not conceivable without refugee status.

The tables turned in Israel's favor when, after years of indifference, Moscow finally indicated some movement on the possibility of renewal of the diplomatic relations that had been broken in 1967. In March 1988 a six-person temporary
mission to look after Soviet interests in Israel, including Russian Orthodox Church
property, arrived. In exchange, an Israeli mission was permitted to set up shop in
Moscow. Fear of Arab reaction led to a prohibition against using the former Israeli
embassy. Instead, the five-member consular delegation moved into the Hotel
Ukraina. But the restoration of full diplomatic ties discussed at the Moscow summit conference in June ran into a roadblock when Gorbachev insisted that such ties
would be restored only after Moscow's full participation in the forthcoming Middle East peace conference was assured. By entering the negotiating arena by imposing terms on the belligerents, a position unacceptable to Israel, which favored
direct negotiations, the Soviets doomed the prospect of normalization to failure.
Israel's demographic needs continued to remain hostage to Moscow's realpolitik.
It would require another two years for Moscow to abandon its aspiration to remain a superpower with worldwide interests.

Formal diplomatic ties with Israel were not reestablished until 2002, but in the
interim direct flights out of Bucharest were implemented in August 1988. One
roadblock had been bypassed, but Israel's hopes of neutralizing the support activities of HIAS and the JDC by withholding the names of those who had been
granted Israeli visas, a threat frequently made by Leon Dulzin, could not be so easily realized. The Netherlands and other members of the European Union remained opposed to any arrangement, such as direct flights from Bucharest, that
they viewed as attempts by Israel to deprive the emigrants of freedom of choice.[68]
The embassy would issue visas only to Vienna or Rome. Never was the absence of
diplomatic ties with Moscow more keenly felt. On the eve of a deluge of humanity that Israel desperately wanted it discovered that Moscow held the key to its future, not only because Moscow served as arms supplier of its Arab foes but also
because Moscow controlled the population stock that could ensure its demographic viability.[69]

The gates of the Soviet Union were in the process of being opened. What Israel now required was for the gates of the United States to be closed to Soviet refugees. In the fall of 1988 that too began to appear possible. A budgetary shortfall caused partly by the unexpected number of Soviet refugees and also refugees from elsewhere brought the issue of refugee definition to a head. The INS would no longer automatically grant the status of refugee to Soviet emigrants; instead, visas would be granted on a case-by-case basis. By March 1989 6 to 7 percent of such applicants were being rejected, mostly on the basis that no coercion was discernable in Gorbachev's Russia. That meant that congestion would soon reach a critical point in Rome and Ladispoli, which housed about 1,000 Jewish families, about 4,000 people.[70]

Meanwhile, in response to the general "freedom of choice" sentiment among Jewish organizations, the State Department undertook efforts in September 1988 to induce Moscow to grant exit permits directly to the United States. A meeting in the Hague the following month, called at Israel's request, led to some concessions on the "freedom of choice" issue. It was decided to give the Bucharest direct flight alternative a six- to nine-month trial. But the agreement, to which the Dutch reluctantly consented, proved to be fragile. Moscow remained unwilling to widen the exit gates beyond specific national groups such as Jews and Germans, who could claim the right of repatriation. Applicants for exit visas to the United States could make no such claim. The final months of 1988 showed that Israel's effort to divert the emigrant stream were not fully effective. But with Washington's realizations of rising costs, a modification of its generous refugee policy was predictable. Historical circumstances as much as Israeli pressure caused the refugee stream to be directed toward resettlement in Israel.

▪ For those involved in the Soviet Jewry movement the six years between the Soviet invasion of Afghanistan and the advent of Gorbachev would prove to be the most disheartening in their long struggle. They witnessed their movement being rocked by forces stemming from the Cold War that were beyond their control. Many were haunted by doubt regarding the prospect of total success and became willing to settle for something less. Could it have been possible to forego the lean years between 1980 and 1987? In the years of 1978 and 1979, when the promise of revising the Trade Act of 1974 were high, the Kremlin responded to reestablishing the linkage of trade, credit, and emigration with the highest rate of emigration since the early seventies. Those who saw an opportunity missed argued that the hope of a small, privately funded movement wracked with internal dissent whose clients were in any case not anxious to resettle in Israel suffered from illusions if they thought they could change the emigration policy of a superpower. That illusion, they could argue, victimized the innocent and caused needless suffering. What did they have to show for their years of effort?

Some few activists understood that from its beginning of the movement in the early sixties there was nothing reasonable about the plan to extricate Soviet Jewry and to protect it in place. It was a dream. In the discussion that follows we learn how a conspiracy of events in Moscow and Washington turned that seemingly unrealizable dream into reality.

EIGHT Free at Last

So bleak had the prospects for Soviet Jewry become in the early eighties that some thought the future of the movement was in doubt. "If nothing is done soon," noted a Moscow activist, "the Jewish national movement may be crushed in the near future."[1] In 1984 only 522 exit visas had been granted. The harassment of activists had reached near epidemic proportions, with many arrested and imprisoned. Reagan's "evil empire" pejorative was the source of much humorous comment in the media, but for activists that had firsthand experience with the KGB crackdown, it was no fiction.[2] The much touted human rights spelled out in Basket III of the Helsinki Final Act were not being implemented. Israel's hope of gaining the diplomatic recognition requisite for negotiating direct flights out of Moscow remained unfulfilled. There were few clues in the years before 1985 that the situation was about to change radically in the months and years ahead.

Yet in 1987 the political stasis that had characterized the Soviet system for years was giving way to rapid change. It had now arrived at Russia's intractable nationalities question to which the emigration question was related in the Soviet mind-set. The process of opening the gates of the Soviet Union had begun hesitantly. The right of emigration, at least on the basis of family reunification, was recognized. Thousands of Jews were planning to emigrate. Activists were being released from prison. Refuseniks, who for years had been denied exit visas, were being granted the right to leave. Several Jewish cultural and religious institutions were allowed to open their doors. In short, the day when Soviet Jewry would be "free at last" was dawning in a most unexpected way. Under Gorbachev the Soviet system, thought to be immutable, seemed to be undergoing basic ideological and structural changes. The hasty movement to implement basic reforms related to a vision of internal collapse of the system that only a handful of dissidents such as Andrei Amalrik had dared to foretell.[3] Still unanswered is the precise relation of outside pressure to that collapse. The historical role of the Soviet Jewry movement, its protest rallies and innovative techniques for focusing world attention on its clients, are best judged not only in terms of the emigrants directly "rescued" but in terms of its role in generating that outside pressure. From the perspective of the Soviet Jewry movement the generating of outside pressure and the extrication of Soviet Jewry are interrelated. The preponderant majority of the almost two million Jews who ultimately left the Soviet Union did so either during or after the collapse of the Soviet system. They were able to leave because the grip of the system had weakened.

Paradoxically, as the gates of the Soviet Union were finally swinging open, America was closing its doors to the refugee dropouts who had risked much to realize the immigrant dream of starting a new life in America. The new Immigration and Naturalization Service (INS) regulations required emigrants to demonstrate an "immediate fear of persecution" or a "well founded" fear of it. Initially, the question of authenticating "persecution" was directed not against the Jewish emigrants, but the Armenians whom Moscow was voluntarily allowing to leave. The INS interpretation was challenged by the State Department, but until the courts would decide the matter, the gates of America were slowly closing for the dropouts. Between November 1988 and January 1989 the percentage of denials more than doubled, from 8.5 to 19 percent. By April it had risen to 40 percent, and the backup in Ladispoli and Rome reached critical proportions. Denial of refugee status did not mean return to Russia or an immediate choice of Israel for resettlement. The law allowed the rejected to appeal, which often meant months of additional upkeep at American Jewish Joint Distribution Committee (JDC) expense. The refugee sections of the U.S. consulates in Vienna and Rome expanded years earlier to help handle the dropout congestion were closed. Negotiations were pending to have emigrants who wanted to enter the United States apply directly to the American embassy in Moscow and pay for their flight in rubles.

The escalating increase in the number of visa applications and the appeals process created an administrative headache for the State Department. The change in the refugee regulations during the final months of the Reagan administration and the early months of the succeeding Bush administration did not go unchallenged. There was a move in the Senate to reverse the new regulations by means of new legislation. Most troublesome was the worsening backup in Ladispoli caused by the new definition of "persecution" now required to establish the bona fides of the refugee.[4] An INS directive issued on 8 December permitted 2,000 dropouts per month to enter as parolees, but they received no government support. It increased access from 18,000 to approximately 25,000 and was further increased to 43,000 in January 1989. But the cost would fall almost entirely on the helping agencies, the Hebrew Immigrant Aid Society (HIAS) and JDC.

In September 1988 the problem was worsened by the inability of the U.S. Embassy to process visas because the budget had been depleted.[5] Having inherited an administrative debacle, the incoming Bush administration experienced difficulties in setting a firm course on refugees. It at first extended the refugee slots allotted to the Soviet emigrants from 18,000 to 43,000 annually. James Baker, Bush's newly appointed secretary of state, created a coordinating committee to generate new guidelines to deal with the problem raised by the unexpected increase in the number of applicants. Reasoning that it was less costly for refugees to await the decision on their status in Russia, the department implemented its new procedures that it was hoped would solve the growing congestion in Vienna and Rome. Refugee admission would be strictly limited to those with American relatives who would assume some of the cost of resettlement once in the country. In addition an unspecified number would continue to gain admission under the attorney general's parole authority. But the great mass would be encouraged to seek resettlement elsewhere, including Israel, Canada, and Australia. The possibility of gaining access to the United States would be lessened, but technically "choice" would continue to exist. It was hoped that that subterfuge would allay the pressure from the "free choice" advocates. But it was a hope that would remain unfulfilled. The Bush administration sought to regain the political ground lost by the gradual whittling down of the strict implementation of the new INS regulations. The blow was also softened by the appropriation of an additional $85 million, of which $23.8 million was earmarked to help resettle Soviet refugees through the private agencies helping in the crisis in Ladispoli and other areas.

But when the American Embassy in Moscow ran out of money in June, forcing it to curtail its operations, the outcry from Jewish organizations, the National Conference on Soviet Jewry (NCSJ), HIAS, and a slew of non-Jewish agencies whose budgets depended on government matching funds was loud and clear. The shortage of government funds also threatened Israel's absorption and resettlement program. At the moment the State Department had temporarily discontinued the processing of applications in September 1989 Israel was in the process of requesting financial help from the United States to help absorb and resettle its growing number of emigrants.

One source of the problem was the unexpectedly large number of applicants. During the first surge of refugees in the final months of 1988 it appeared as if a good portion of Soviet Jewry was intent on leaving en masse. The unexpected surge stretched the department's refugee care budget of $346 million to the breaking point. In October the department advised the refugee settlement organizations that there would be a shortfall of $7 to $10 million in government matching that these agencies normally received for resettlement. For HIAS and JDC and non-Jewish agencies such as World Church Service, the inability to follow through had a special irony. The right to emigrate had earned a fairly high priority in concessions demanded of Moscow to "normalize" relations. The Soviet concessions on emigration marked a triumph for American Cold War diplomacy. Now at the brink of victory the American government could not fulfill its part of the transaction.[6]

By the spring of 1989 the Ladispoli situation had eased somewhat, but the moratorium on applications for visas caused chaos in Moscow as hundreds poured into the American embassy to pick up applications before the gates were entirely closed. That finally happened in November when the Vienna-Rome pipeline through which thousands of Soviet Jews sought refuge in the United States was closed. Now the Soviet exit visa could be exchanged for a visa allowing entrance only to Israel at the Dutch embassy. Many were caught midstream when, in response to the American policy change, the Dutch embassy reacted by limiting itself to issuing Israeli visas only to those intending to go to Israel. The headlines in Israeli newspapers heralded the victory and the *Daily Bulletin of the Jewish Telegraph Agency* reported sharply rising anti-Semitism and reports of pogroms in Soviet Asia.[7] The dropout problem was solved. In Israeli eyes it did not come a moment to soon.

But buffeted by strong political pressure, Washington's new stricter refugee policy was not yet firmly in place. Politically, the Reagan and Bush administrations had committed themselves to "freedom of choice," only to discover that the policy was irreconcilable with the budgetary limitations and foreign policy considerations concerning the Middle East. Shultz, who was passionate in his support of Soviet emigration, tried to bridge the gap by arguing that although the emigrants have a right to leave as assured by the Helsinki Accords, "There is no corollary right of immigrant entry into . . . the United States."[8] The American effort was aimed at extricating Soviet Jewry, not ensuring access to the United States.

Shultz's interpretation did little to stave off the direct pressure on the Democratic Congress from a primed Jewish community spearheaded by militant activists. There was reluctance in Congress to deny refugee status to the 27,000 applicants remaining in the pipeline. Soviet emigrants were simply granted presumptive refugee status together with Vietnamese, Cambodians, Laotians, and the thousands seeking to escape repression from the endless civil strife in Central America. Faced with the possibility of an influx of hundreds of thousands of refugees from Africa, the Caribbean, and Latin America, the Bush administration sought some solution to its dilemma when it met with representatives of the involved Jewish organizations during the summer of 1989.

In the interim Sen. Frank Lautenberg, acting with the advice of JDC and HIAS, sought to attack the new refugee policy at its source, the redefining of the assumption of "fear of persecution" on which refugee status was based. He reasoned that a restoration of the automatic granting of that status would cut down on the 50 percent appeal rejection rate that was at the heart of the Ladispoli chaos. His bill, which was combined with a similar measure introduced in the House, went far to stabilize the refugee situation. The Lautenberg Amendment of November 1989 exempted most Soviet emigrants from having to prove "well founded fear of persecution" to gain refugee status. The number of rejections was reduced to 20 percent. But it did not serve the interest of Israel and a growing number of federation leaders who now favored encouraging the flow of Soviet emigrants to Israel.[9] The result was that within a sixteen-month period between July 1988 and November 1989, U.S. immigration policy was in utter confusion. At the outset standing immigration regulations were changed by administrative fiat and then partially reversed by statute. We shall see that in the end the restriction proposed by the INS became U.S. law. That seemingly insignificant shift in American refugee policy had an enormous impact on our story.

■ By the final months of 1988 a shift in the positions of American Jewish organizations involved with Soviet Jewry was also perceptible. Though little was said openly at the administration's meeting with Jewish organizational leaders, an astute observer might have noted that budgetary considerations had dampened the enthusiasm for absorbing an estimated additional 115,000 Soviet Jews, which could increase to as many as 500,000 over a five-year period.[10] "The crunch is coming," warned Ira Eisenstein in an editorial in the *Reconstructionist*, "American Jewry must now put our money where our mouths have been in our support of Soviet Jewry."[11] Even if it were possible for the federations to pick up the estimated $114 million required merely to resettle the emigrants there would still be a budgetary shortfall of many millions. The 1989 United Jewish Appeal (UJA) "Passage to Freedom" campaign failed to achieve its goal of $145 million. By the following year the estimate of the cost of resettlement more than tripled. The General Assembly of the Council of Jewish Federations and Welfare Funds (CJF), meeting in Miami in February 1990, planned a special fund-raising appeal, "Operation Exodus," to raise $420 million to help resettle Soviet emigrants in Israel. But it was estimated that barely a third of that sum would be raised. By the final months of 1989 it was clear that the organized effort to maintain "freedom of choice" was foundering. As always, much of American Jewish organizational life was shaped by budget politics in which the welfare of Israel played a prominent role. Now, however, a new factor was discernable. Israel's financial needs still had a high priority determined by formula, but they were far from being an exclusive consideration. Some federation leaders questioned Israel's motives and tactics employed in finally winning a major portion of the emigrant pool. In September 1991 Israel turned to the Bush administration with a request for a $10 billion credit line to help finance the Soviet resettlement, among other things. But Bush was reluctant to make such a commitment, and the threat of congressional action to proceed with the loan and a deluge of American Jewish communal leaders descending on the capital to lobby for it could not change his mind.

We have noted that in June 1988 the Soviet government finally agreed to consider Israel's wishes for direct flights by adopting a two-track system agreed upon by all the involved American organizations. There would be direct flights to Israel from Bucharest for those choosing to settle in Israel and visas to other countries for those wanting to settle elsewhere. Considered together with Moscow's new *vyzov* regulations that strictly enforced the close relatives provision, Israel's victory was almost complete. Since technically Soviet Jews would still be able to enter the United States as normal immigrants, the freedom of choice imperative was technically still in play. Some already in the pipeline as special status refugees would gain access to the United States as a result of special provision made by the Lautenberg Amendment and the INS. But in practice the new refugee policy meant that far fewer Soviet emigrants would be able to gain access to the United States. Between January 1989 and January 1996 approximately 264,000 Soviet Jews settled in the United States, compared to the more than 400,000 who settled in Israel.

For the moment Israel's victory threatened the crucial ties it maintained with Jewish communities in the diaspora, especially American Jewry. The militant Jewish activists associated with the Union of Councils for Soviet Jewry (UCSJ) were dismayed at Israel's open and direct exercise of its sovereign power. Many of the idealized notions that the Jewish state was somehow exempt from normal *raison d'état* considerations had to be abandoned. But the agents of the liaison bureau from the outset were more likely to believe that, incomplete as it was, Israel's success in winning the Soviet emigrants was merely "reconfirm(ing) its seniority (in the) partnership." [12] Others may have wished that the policies of glasnost and perestroika, which signaled the liberalization in Soviet policy, had never happened because reform of the Soviet system tended to neutralize the Cold War mind-set that served as one of the major energizers of the Soviet Jewry movement. As the Soviet system began to disintegrate the UCSJ and the NCSJ faced a dilemma. Should they continue the struggle and against whom? Strongly influenced by the Soviet activists, the UCSJ at first insisted that glasnost was a ruse that exaggerated the Soviet interest in human rights and raised false expectations. Announcing that emigration depended more on government policy than on administrative regulations, the State Department also counseled caution. Richard Schifter observed that the new regulations were actually "scaring off" prospective applicants and that the Kremlin's real goal remained to close down emigration completely after 10,000 refuseniks were allowed to leave.[13] The UCSJ response was to mount yet a new public relations campaign based on the theme that glasnost was a sham and that conditions were worst under Gorbachev than his predecessors. The object was to keep the pressure on Moscow. Rabbi Herschel Schacter, former chairman of the Conference of Presidents, revealed an almost missionary attitude when he cautioned the Soviet Jewry movement not to disband as long as there were more than two million Jews in the Soviet Union "who have to be made aware of their Jewishness and develop a measure of Jewish commitment."[14] Usually more political in its approach, the NCSJ cautiously favored a new move to soften the Jackson-Vanik Amendment in exchange for getting something from the Kremlin: an exodus of those refuseniks who were still in the pipeline and the immediate halting of KGB harassment.

Coincidentally, at the juncture when Soviet opposition to emigration seemed finally to be softening, the movement's skills in protest and public relations had become more organized and effective than ever.[15] More legislators were approached for support, more lists prepared for presentation to Soviet authorities, more rallies organized, and more bracelets with the name of imprisoned refuseniks worn. By the mid-eighties the Soviet Jewry movement had become the most far-reaching mobilization of Jewish communal resources since the campaign for the recognition of Israel in 1948. As if heeding Sharansky's continuous urging to apply ever more pressure on the Kremlin, in December 1986 major Jewish organizations mounted new programs to showcase the plight of Soviet Jewry.[16] Despite its divisions and strife it had succeeded in placing the fate of Soviet Jews high on the international agenda. In 1986, organizational skills honed sharp by years of experience, their activity had grown more intense than ever. The range of the movement was broad but its divisions were also deep. Between 1967 and 1989 less than a half million had been released but now it was payoff time. Moscow seemed ready to make real concessions. Two events illustrate the range of its activity and the continuing drift toward division within its ranks. The first concerns the mission of Morris Abram and Edgar Bronfman to Moscow in March 1987, and the second was the giant rally in Washington on 6 December 1987.

■   The genesis of the Abram and Bronfman mission to Moscow is related to the personal desire of both leaders to demonstrate organizational initiative in the Soviet Jewry arena. Because it boasted a worldwide network and had previous experience in negotiating directly with Moscow, the World Jewish Congress (WJC) was able if it so desired to preempt the role organizations such as the NCSJ, the UCSJ, or any of the dozens of Israeli and other organizations active in the Soviet Jewry area. It had become almost a personal fief of Edgar Bronfman, its funder and president. The pairing of Bronfman and Abram, two seemingly incompatible negotiators, for a mission to Moscow was a choice of the lesser of two evils. Matters would have been worse should it have proved impossible to solve the turf battle between the NCSJ and the WJC.

Both the American Jewish Committee (AJC) with which Morris Abram was long affiliated and the WJC claimed long continuous contact with the Soviet government over Jewish issues. From its establishment in 1936 the WJC considered itself the closest thing the amorphous Jewish world had to a governing agency. Nahum Goldmann, its founder and first president, thought of himself as a diplomat for the Jewish people. Both organizations considered Jewish foreign affairs to be their bailiwick. In the throes of its organizational culture and heedless of the warnings of Morris Abram, Bronfman visited Moscow in April 1985 to "negotiate" with "high level" Soviet policy makers on the Soviet Jewry problem. Abram, who held the joint leadership of the Conference of Presidents and the NCSJ, was reluctant to embark on the venture: "The World Jewish Congress cannot possibly have any effect in the United States on the one party which the Soviet Union is trying to court and that is the U.S. government."[17] The WJC, a nominally autonomous agency, loosely affiliated with the world Zionist movement, was not part of the American Jewish organizational world, but it had a strong representation in American Jewry, which gave it a major portion of its financial backing. The non-Zionist Abram could not have been unaware that, though autonomous and not subject to a Zionist mandate, the WJC, like the American Jewish Congress (AJCong) maintained a Zionist orientation. Nahum Goldmann, its founder, had once been approached to play a founding role in the governing establishment of Israel and was not convinced that Soviet Jewry was ready to be transplanted to Israel. He did not believe that the confrontational tactics favored by the UCSJ and its affiliates were effective. Several times he cautioned that they endangered Soviet Jewry. The WJC could serve as a back channel for Israel, which had no formal diplomatic contact with Moscow, to be represented in any negotiations regarding the disposition of Soviet Jewry. As it was there was little likelihood of Soviet policy makers negotiating with the heads of two nongovernmental organizations regarding the disposition of its Jews.[18] But the mission could serve as a sounding board for the outlines of a future agreement.

The announcement of the mission was not warmly greeted. For some activists the joint mission was reminiscent of *Shtadlanut,* which in former historic epochs attracted Jews of wealth and station to represent communal interest before governments. The democratization of communal governance was begun by the AJCong in 1918. Paradoxically, the WJC was an offspring of that movement. Neither Abram nor Bronfman had bothered to contact the Soviet Jewish activists themselves, who now formed a separate interest group outside the Soviet Union. Abram, a former president of the non-Zionist AJC and vice chairman of the U.S. Commission on Civil Rights, naturally was concerned about freedom of choice for the emigrants, but the opposition of the passionately Zionist-oriented refuseniks did not faze him. "I learned one thing, " observed Abram, "and that is that there are as many divisions and points of view in Soviet Jewry as there is in American Jewry and you can't talk to one without the other being very unhappy about it."[19] What might have been the NCSJ's moment in the sun became instead a source of continuing controversy, especially over the question of whether the Soviets would adhere to any agreement made at the level of nongovernmental organizations negotiating with governments. Ominously, once the delegation arrived in Moscow the scheduled meeting directly with Gorbachev at the highest level never materialized.

Considering the circumstances of their mission and the lack of a common vision the chances for a successful negotiation were poor. Nevertheless, with Dobrynin, now head of the international department of the Communist Party of the Soviet Union (CPSU), acting as midwife and the breakthrough created by the release of Sharansky, the two embarked for Moscow full of hope. In turn for long-sought concessions on the refuseniks, some of whom were categorized as "never to be released," and on the direct travel to Israel issue, the Soviets would receive assurances of Jewish organizational support for a favorable change in the waiver authority at the heart of the Jackson amendment and a relaxation of the credit restrictions of the Stevenson Amendment, a complete reversal of the Jewish position in 1979. Bronfman had long favored such a move and Abram too believed that something had to be done to make Jackson-Vanik useful. The possibility of Soviet access to the forthcoming Middle East peace negotiations was also held out. That was the gist of the report Abram and Bronfman delivered upon their return to 150 communal leaders convened by the NCSJ on 1 April. Bronfman refused to say with whom the agreement had been reached. It seemed to be an agreement based on a wish rather than reality.

Not included in the negotiations, Israel simultaneously released a report of the pending arrival of large numbers of emigrants and an invitation for Shimon Peres to Moscow. But clearly Israel did not want the Abram and Bronfman mission to be interpreted as a loss of its initiative on the Soviet Jewry issue. Israel need not have worried. The Soviet Foreign Ministry denied that a formal meeting had taken place.

The organizations did not welcome the presumptuousness of "self-appointed" leaders preempting the negotiating role and were skeptical about the Soviet intention to implement the nine points of the informal agreement. Pamela Cohen, the president of the UCSJ, the major American Jewish grassroots organization concerned with Soviet Jewry, was never informed of the trip and was especially incensed about talk of changing the waiver provision of the Jackson amendment when no clear move was yet perceptible from Moscow.[20] As if to deemphasize the importance of the Abram and Bronfman mission, Rabbi Arthur Schneier of the Park East Synagogue and president of the Appeal of Conscience Foundation, reported to the press that he had successfully negotiated in Moscow and Bucharest a new transit procedure that would eliminate the dropout problem.

Concealed behind the contretemps was the fact that the purported agreements disregarded the freedom of choice principle, which was close to the heart of the UCSJ. Yet it contained something to satisfy all parties. Israel was assured the direct flights through Bucharest and the possibility of teaching Hebrew in the reopened communal schools. There would be a more liberal interpretation of the first-degree relatives rule by allowing those emigrants already settled in Israel and the United States to vouch for relatives yet to come. The Soviet activists received assurances that there would be a review of "never to be released" refusenik cases, with the exception of those exposed to classified material. Religious Jews were ensured unrestricted access to Jewish religious literature published abroad, the reopening of synagogues where there was a clear need, access to rabbinical training overseas, and the possible practice of religious slaughter (*shechita*) and the opening of a kosher restaurant in Moscow. In exchange Moscow would receive Jewish support for a change in the Stevenson Amendment and annual waiver of the trade restrictions in the Jackson amendment based on measured progress in the emigration process.

But aside from establishing the parameters of a future agreement, the Abram and Bronfman mission came to naught. The negotiators on the Soviet side were connected to the International Department of the Central Committee of the CPSU who, in the chaos of Soviet political life in 1987, could not ensure government adherence to any agreement. Another sticking point was that there was no precise report on how many Jews would be allowed to leave annually. Moreover, the idea that a sovereign nation would reveal such figures to two agents of Jewish organizations or a well-known rabbi was not credible. That is what the State Department had counseled at the outset. The Soviet settlers in Israel, now organized and active, were convinced that failing a guarantee of rights, the Soviet authorities would renege after releasing 12,000 applicants, leaving the remaining 380,000 seeking to leave in limbo. In February 1988 the State Department registered a complaint at the international human rights conference in Venice regarding Soviet backsliding on the acceptance of *vyzovs*. Nothing less than a total change liberalizing Soviet law on emigration in compliance with the Helsinki Accord was acceptable. But in the meantime OVIR acted as though it was unaware of agreements made and assurances given.

Predictably, in Israel where the issue of freedom of movement was overshadowed by the imperatives of the national security question and the tenets of Zionist ideology, the emigration issue played itself out differently. On the assumption that the emigration was an absolute right that should not be bargained for, the Likud party wanted to keep the emigration issue separate from the question of whether Moscow should have a role in the peace negotiations. However, Labor gave emigration the highest priority and was willing to forego formal diplomatic ties for the release of all Soviet Jews who wanted to leave. Haunting both parties were the dropouts, whose numbers had reached astronomic proportions in 1988. What mattered the pending exodus of thousands if they chose not to settle in Israel?

But the Abram and Bronfman agreement did offer a hope that a change was pending in Moscow. Paradoxically, the contentiousness of Jewish organizational life revealed by the mission seemed to have reached a high point precisely at the juncture when the goal of gaining the freedom of Soviet Jewry showed some possibility of realization. A new low was struck during a giant Solidarity Sunday mass rally held in May 1987 in which a renowned refusenik, Iosef Mendelevitch, broke into the proceedings to express his anger at the Abram and Bronfman negotiation.

What the mission left in its wake was the unresolved issue of who speaks for Soviet Jewry.

■   Although the Abram and Bronfman effort to negotiate directly with Moscow spluttered, the massive rally held in Washington in December 1987 showed clearly where the real strength of American Jewish organization existed, and it was not in negotiating with sovereign powers that gave no assurance that they would implement what might be agreed to. The giant Washington rally of 6 December 1987 demonstrated that public relations techniques to focus attention on the plight of Soviet Jewry had become a formidable skill developed by the American Soviet Jewry movement. Washingtonians might at first have thought that it was another march for civil rights or for ending the Vietnam War. The crowds generated a familiar spirit of celebration. But the thousands of milling, singing, and dancing protesters who gathered on the Washington mall as if called by an ancient shofar were a decade too late for that.[21] They were calling attention to a cause most Americans had never heard of. The huge crowds who traveled to the capital from almost every state in the union were there to demonstrate for the redemption of Soviet Jewry but also to display the formidable power of organized American Jewry to make its voice heard.

The mass mobilization was brilliantly orchestrated. Demonstrators at a preliminary meeting where Gorbachev was scheduled to speak were told to tone down their passion in deference to the changes in emigration policy already implemented. Before the Sunday demonstration there were a congressional prayer and a fast vigil held in tandem with the testimony of five prominent refuseniks before the Helsinki commission. A news conference was scheduled for the Friday before the demonstration and two dinners at its conclusion, at which Sharansky was awarded the AJC's "courageous fighter for Jewish Dignity" award, followed by the National Campaign Committee dinner of the UJA to honor former refuseniks Yuri Edelshtein and Vladimir Slepak. The rally marked a high point of the Soviet Jewry movement in America and in American Jewish history.

The preplanning for the rally began as early as April 1986 with a series of regional conferences conducted through the National Jewish Community Relations Advisory Council (NJCRAC) network in cooperation with the NCSJ to mount an intensive public campaign in preparation for Gorbachev's first visit. Timed to take place twenty-four hours before Gorbachev was scheduled to arrive in Washington for a two-day summit conference on disarmament, there were some who thought that for precisely that reason the timing for the demonstration was wrong. Gorbachev, after all, was the Soviet leader most sensitive to the price Soviet society was paying for its Judeophobia. Moreover, it was clear that things were already loosening up in the Soviet Union. But the organizers, David Harris, who headed the Washington office of the AJC, Jerry Goodman (NCSJ), and Al Chernin (NJCRAC), seeing light at the end of the tunnel, pushed ahead. As 6 December approached the organizers were taken by surprise by the overwhelming response. It was December and the weather would be unpredictable. It was estimated that 150,000 at most would come to rally in the capital. That was the average crowd for the Solidarity Sunday gatherings. But on that Sunday more than twice that number gathered in Washington. No one knows the precise reason for the huge turnout aside from the intense prerally publicity. After a decade and a half of protest activity communal enthusiasm for Soviet Jewry had actually begun to wane. The outpouring many have been triggered by the opportunity to show Gorbachev personally that American Jewry was mobilized. Malcolm Hoenlein, the energetic executive director of the Greater New York Conference on Soviet Jewry, believed that it was precisely the fact that the Soviet Jewry movement was not fully "institutionalized" that permitted full mobilization at the grass roots.[22] But that should also have played a role in prior rallies. It may be that this largest, best-organized protest rally in American Jewish history served for many as a kind of victory rally, a celebration of their successful effort to "free" Soviet Jewry before the movement disbanded.

After Morris Abram, who chaired the proceedings, read a message from the president reassuring the audience that human rights was on the agenda for the summit meeting, there was a wave of applause. George Bush, the favored candidate for the Republican presidential nomination, assured the assembly that he would personally raise the issue with Gorbachev, adding "I will not be satisfied until the promise of Helsinki is a reality."[23] Then with perfect staging the shofar was sounded, followed by Pearl Bailey singing "Let My People Go." Another high point of the rally occurred as a group of recently released refuseniks, Ida Nudel, Yosef Begun, Felix Abramovich, Vladimir and Masha Slepak, Misha and Ilana Kholmyansky, Yuri Edelshtein and Natan Sharansky took their place on the stage to light "freedom candles." The audience was on an emotional high and barely felt the cold December breezes. The haunting shadow of the Holocaust was omnipresent as Elie Wiesel reminded the audience that had there been such rallies in the forties, "millions of Jews would have been saved . . . too many were silent then. We are not silent today."[24] It was exactly the note the audience wanted to hear.

The giant rally was an illustration of what the organizers had learned to do so well. The summit was supposed to deal with arms reduction, but Reagan, much to the annoyance of Gorbachev, harped on the rally. "Have you heard about the rally on the mall last Sunday?" he asked Gorbachev, coming back to the emigration issue repeatedly. The impact was confirmed when Abram met with Shultz after the demonstration. He noted that the secretary had stopped talking of individual cases and revealed that Gorbachev understood, perhaps for the first time, the enormous pressure that that been generated in Washington for the case of Soviet Jewry. By 1987 the movement within the Soviet Union had a fairly good view of outside activities on their behalf triggered by the broadcasting of the proceedings by the VOA and was able to plan their own "sympathy" demonstrations. The massive September rally thus also marked a high point in presenting the image of a worldwide coordinated movement to the media.

At the same time the long-awaited release of thousands of Soviet Jews came as something of a letdown for some activists. The passion generated by being part of the movement and becoming involved in the making history was enormously seductive. Some who stemmed originally from the civil rights movement spoke with conviction of their need to make a difference, and they had done that in the Jewish arena. But now the problem was happily on the road to solution and the movement through which they had for their most formative years invented themselves had fulfilled its mission or was clearly on the way to doing so. At the historical juncture when the largest emigration began it seemed as if a movement was no longer needed. "It is a big problem," observed Yehoshua Pratt, who managed the liaison bureau in 1987. "We established a 'Golem' which did wonders. It's not just a 'Golem,' we established an organization and Jews got involved." Now "they don't like to die. Yes . . . like old soldiers don't die." [25]

The post-Gorbachev years ushered in a new problem and with it new faces on the board of the NCSJ. Jerry Goodman, its executive director, had occupied what Richard Maass called the "hot seat" for fifteen years. When he left the position in February 1988 the organization, which was really a creature of many other organizations, had somehow survived and mobilized disparate organizations to do what they would have had little inclination to do acting alone. Some believed that without Goodman's political skills the organization would not have achieved what it did.[26] The fact that the NCSJ held together at all may in the future be considered something of a miracle.

■ We come finally to the point of tying the multiple strands of the Soviet Jewry story together. This study ends with a great paradox. An overheated historic imagination might find the situation in 1989 analogous to the years of 1921 and 1924 when the newly enacted American immigration laws turned sharply in the direction of restrictionism. In those years too, just as the need to leave Eastern Europe reached its zenith, the "golden" gates of the United States were closed. In 1989 just as the gates of the Soviet Union opened the gates of America again closed. But that is where the comparison ends for in the 1920s, led by Louis Marshall, there were few Jews who did not advocate keeping the doors of the nation open. That, we shall see, was not the case six decades later, especially after it became clear that the Soviet migration required heavy financial outlays, and a Jewish state anxious to receive the emigrants was in existence.

It was also on the eve of their long-awaited victory that the simmering conflict between the two competing organizations, the NCSJ and the UCSJ, came to a head. Perhaps the sharpening of tensions was caused by the sense that finally there was something concrete to argue about, such as strategy and, most seductive of all in Jewish communal life, moral principles. In its simplest terms the conflict involved two related questions, one strategic and the other ideological. The first questioned asked again whether the time was now propitious to negotiate the release of Soviet Jewry by making concessions on the Jackson-Vanik and Stevenson amendments. The second involved the tricky question of freedom of choice. Should the soviet Jewish emigrants have it or should circumstances be arranged to compel them to settle in Israel? We have noted previously the factors involved and the complex arguments on both sides. It remains now to relate how the final round of that conflict between American activists associated with the UCSJ and those who largely remained loyal adherents of the Israel/Zionist interest worked itself out.

Gorbachev's accession to power created a new opportunity to consider the Jackson-Vanik Amendment. For the leadership of the AJCong and others who counseled that the leverage afforded by the amendment would count for nothing if it was not used to gain concessions, the continued Jewish support of the amendment in 1979 without prospect of transaction with Moscow seemed futile. Looking back from the vantage of 1985 it seemed that the proponents for keeping the amendment in place without change had miscalculated and brought the movement to its knees while causing six years of needless suffering. The amendment had served its purpose, argued Marshall Goldman. With Gorbachev's liberalization an opportunity had once again materialized and should be taken.[27] In May the Senate Majority Leader, Robert Dole, a Republican from Kansas, a grain-producing farm state, joined others to suggest that the waiving of the amendment's restrictions might be more effective in bringing the release of emigrants.

The organization most reluctant to turn the corner on Jackson-Vanik was the UCSJ that, under the influence of activists in the Soviet Union, adhered strictly to the "barometer" theory, which held that the ups and downs of Soviet emigration policy correspond to periods of intense outside pressure and economic need as well as the rhythm of the Cold War. The Jackson-Vanik Amendment was considered as being ideally suited to sustain such pressure. As late as 1988 when the Kremlin made its crucial decision to withdraw from Afghanistan, which served for most as a sign that the troublesome Brezhnev Doctrine was being abandoned, there was little change in the attitude of the UCSJ. Supporters of keeping the amendment in place awaited more solid evidence of change in Moscow.

In 1979 the NCSJ's board had also voted to continue its support of the amendment in place, but some of its constituent members had become convinced that bargaining would yield higher dividends. By 1986, after six lean years, that inclination had grown stronger. Though it supported the Joint Statement signed by all organizations concerned with Soviet Jewry on 30 May 1986 that pledged continued support for the amendment, behind the scenes something was stirring. A more flexible posture was hinted in the NCSJ press release that assured "there is no new policy" merely a "modification" that "could occur in non-strategic items . . . under appropriate circumstances."[28] The NCSJ would try to bridge the gap between the two positions and in a cautious "step by step" manner try to win concessions from Moscow. The Abram and Bronfman mission to Moscow in March 1987 was one such effort. Two months later, on 11 May 1987, the NCSJ joined with the Center for Foreign Policy Options to again consider the amendment in the general context of a full reexamination of American policy toward Soviet Jewry.

But for the Reagan administration the amendment continued to be a political hot potato. On 14 July, testifying before House Foreign Affairs Sub-Committee on European Affairs, Thomas Simons Jr., deputy assistant secretary of state for European affairs, assured the committee that the administration had no plans to dilute the amendment, which remained the law of the land. It was no longer possible to avoid the fact that Gorbachev was in fact a serious reformer and that the Soviet Jewry movement was again in danger of missing an opportunity to extricate those Jews who wanted to emigrate. Conditions in the Soviet Union were marked by uncertainty and the gates, now partially opened, might at any moment be closed again. Rumor had it that the Soviets were prepared to guarantee as many as 20,000 to leave annually in turn for trade and credit. Schifter, who had previously complained to Shultz that getting Soviets to release refuseniks was like "pulling one tooth . . . at any one time," was now requested by Soviet government officials to submit names for exit visas. "With that statement, I knew the back of our re-fusenik problem was broken," he writes in 1987.[29] Most of the remaining prisoners of conscience were being released. The number of refuseniks had been reduced from 11,000 to about 2,000. In preparation for the summit conference scheduled to begin on 29 May, the Kremlin had dramatically increased the number of exit visas issued. At the same time Israel, sensing that Soviet recognition was imminent, abandoned its reluctance to openly "interfere" in American domestic policy and use its considerable influence with the American Jewish leadership to gain sup-port of a more flexible position on the amendment. That was the thrust of Yoram Dinstein's address at the annual convention dinner of NCJRAC on 22 February 1987.

Noting that most Jewish organizations had never supported a boycott of U.S. companies that do business with the Soviet Union, the NCSJ now contemplated a "corporate involvement strategy." In contrast, taking its cues from the effective disinvestments movement for South Africa, the UCSJ had previously considered using such a strategy for generating pressure. Little came of it, and their opposi-tion to any plan that would soften the waiver provision of the Jackson amendment remained in place. Apprehensive about the increase of private bank loans to the Soviets totaling billions annually, the UCSJ and its affiliates remained opposed to increased business contacts, which might lead to bypassing the Jackson-Vanik Amendment.[30] Pamela Cohen, national president of the UCSJ, did not think that the United States owed the Kremlin anything for the release of the refuseniks. In-stead, she counseled for a "wait and see" policy. Cohen believed that more conces-sions could have been won in exchange for agreeing that Moscow would be the host of the human rights conference in 1991, something that the Soviet leadership very much wanted.[31] The new plan of the NCSJ was to enlist these corporations in the "struggle." "We are for business," declared Myrna Sheinbaum, associate exec-utive director of the NCSJ, in support of a visit to Moscow of U.S. business leaders in April led by Secretary of Commerce William Verity.[32] But the NCSJ remained cautious and did not fully approve the Abram and Bronfman trip until it received assurances from Verity that no breech of Jackson-Vanik was planned.

The decade-long conflict over the disposition of the amendment was finally coming to a head. On 10 January 1989, Mark Levin, the director of the NCSJ's Washington Office, announced that it was reexamining its position on U.S.-Soviet trade relations in light of "recent positive changes" in the treatment of Soviet Jews.[33] The NCSJ's announcement followed meetings between Jewish leaders and Verity and members of the U.S. Soviet Trade and Economic Council. After a meet-

ing with the secretary of commerce, Morris Abram proposed such a rapprochement with the business community. By mid-1988 the NCSJ leadership, which represented a cross-section of Jewish organizations, recognized that a profound
change in the situation of Soviet Jewry was underway and that a concomitant
change in its position on Jackson-Vanik was in order. But such a change threatened
to leave stranded the Soviet Jewish activists and their closest allies in the United
States, who for good reasons could never trust the Soviet leadership.

The congressional response to the changed Jewish mood was perceptible. Rep.
Vanik and Sen. Stevenson had reconsidered their position in 1979. Now they were
joined by other legislators who supported relaxation of the waiver provision of
the amendment. For the legislators who had voted for the administration's expensive defense budget, Reagan's strong support of export restrictions on high technology products that might have possible military uses dwarfed those of the
Jackson amendment. But for the moment the NCSJ had gotten out in front of the
Reagan administration. Before the Moscow summit in June 1988 the administration again made clear its opposition to extending most-favored-nation (MFN) status to the Soviet Union. It may have increased American leverage at the summit.
Openly interested in undoing the amendment, Gorbachev quizzically inquired, referring to Jackson and Vanik: "Why should the dead hold on to the coat tails of the
living? One of them's already physically dead. The other's politically dead," he
quipped to the gathered reporters while complaining that the Soviets receive "un-
favored-nation treatment" from Washington.[34] Congress too was slow in abandoning the Cold War spirit that was behind the Jackson amendment. The idea of
wringing acceptable behavior by withholding trade gained a new momentum
with an amendment by Sen. James McClure to the military budget bill that went
further than the Jackson-Vanik amendment. Passed by voice vote in the Senate on
13 May, the McClure amendment required that the president certify that the Soviet
Union and other countries are "in substantial compliance" with the human rights
provisions of the Helsinki Accords. That put the trade restriction far beyond the
Jackson-Vanik Amendment, which sought only to withhold MFN based on compliance with the right to emigrate.

The final touch was presented by the NCSJ when in June 1989 its board of governors announced that if appropriate assurances of "significant progress" were received from the Soviet authorities, it would then support a softer waiver process.
At the Malta Conference, the UCSJ insisted that any trade and credit concessions
await the actual passage of new immigration laws. It was a difficult pill for the
once-proud Soviet leaders to swallow. Eventually the negotiators accepted Gor-

bachev's promise that there would be such a law "not as concession to the Americans but as a logical consequence of our *perestroika*."[35] True to his word the Congress of People's Deputies passed a new immigration law in November 1989 that met most of the requirements laid down at the Conference on Security and Cooperation in Europe follow-up conference in Vienna in January 1989. Four months later in May, the Bush administration declared that it would await a "strong consensus" before agreeing to a waiver. Clearly it would take some additional years to close the books, but the amendment's contribution to catapulting the emigration issue onto the Cold War agenda was drawing to a close, as was the Cold War of which it was part.

Predictably, the approval of Moscow's new emigration law in November did not appease those activists who saw the amendment as a crucial lever. Pamela Cohen, president of the UCSJ, declared that there would be no approval of a waiver until the "final enactment" of the law and its "fair implementation."[36] But repeal of the amendment was no longer an issue because the law allowed the president to recommend an eighteen-month waiver to Congress that may then be followed by annual renewals. That was the course the Bush administration chose. Preparing for his shipboard summit off the coast of Malta, Bush planned to offer Gorbachev the one-year waver option that was part of the amendment as a first step to allow the Soviet Union to "graduate" fully from the provisions of the amendment. The UCSJ held out for full implementation of the new Soviet emigration law, but the NCSJ came out in support of the waiver on 13 June even as its former chairman, Morris Abram, continued to oppose it. Most Jewish organizations followed the lead of the NCSJ and the WJC to support Bush's gesture. The amendment as part of the Trade Act of 1974 remained in place until 2002 but it had lost its teeth.

■ Because it concerned the security of Israel, which has the highest priority among American Jews, the problem of the dropouts continued to cause much dissension. Again it was the UCSJ, which was most closely aligned with the Soviet activists, that adopted an "odd man out" position. We have seen that in the dropout phenomenon there was a demographic imperative that Israel could ignore only at its own risk. As Jews began to leave the Soviet Union in larger numbers, the Jackson-Vanik Amendment, which had played such a crucial role in generating pressure on the Soviet authorities, was less in the picture. Its place, we have noted, was partly taken by the broader human rights movement that sought to correct the injustices in Soviet life, one of which was the denial of the right to emigrate. Sensitive to the fact that the Soviet Jewish population pool held one of the keys to its survival, Israel had muted its voice of opposition in the hope that eventually diplomatic relations would be reestablished. That was requisite for direct flights that would bypass the seductive help agencies and once and for all solve the problem in Israel's favor.

A week after Shamir's visit to the Oval Office in February 1987 the Knesset passed a supporting motion for his position suggesting that the working definition of "refugee" used by the administration should be changed to comply with reality. That threw down the gauntlet for American Jews who, sensitive to the human rights issue, continued their support of "choice" and made known their opposition to the Israel's interference. Like so many activists Glenn Richter, the fiery leader of SSSJ, sought to find a bridge to the advocates of choice by noting that the right of Soviet emigrants to leave Israel for the United States, carrying like other *yordim* an Israeli visa, still existed. The freedom of choice position, which he vaguely favored, had not been discarded. A committed Zionist, he also recognized the demographic needs of the Jewish state. But legally and practically the position that conceived of Israel as a way station en route to the United States could not be maintained. A similar suggestion had been made previously by Shoshana Cardin, chairperson of the NCSJ. But under Israel's Law of Return an emigrant automatically becomes a citizen of Israel upon landing in Israel and therefore cannot claim to be a refugee. Moreover, on 27 July the State Department announced that it had no plans to change the immigration laws so that refugee status could be maintained when the emigrant had settled in Israel.

After his discussions in Moscow Morris Abram became convinced that the agreement that he and Bronfman had reached with the Soviets for direct flights that the emigrant could choose or reject was the solution that would satisfy all sides. But by the end of 1987, diplomatic ties with Russia seemed as elusive as ever and the figures for dropouts had reached astronomical proportions. Israel was losing the battle for biological supplementation and in frustration its political leaders broke their own policy of silence regarding American Jewish politics to vent their passions in the media. In April, using the only leverage it had left in its arsenal, Israel decided to act unilaterally. Pointing out that the integrity of its visa was involved, the country would grant it only to those who intended to settle there. At the same time, the Foreign Office made known the new possibility of voluntary direct flights to Israel through Bucharest. But the hope that such direct action would finally bring an end to the dropout phenomenon did not materialize. Each month saw an increase in the dropout rate. The irony of Israel's policy could not have escaped the activists. Israel was in effect now proposing to limit the right of movement while human rights activists stressed that very right in their campaign to extricate Soviet Jewry.

By the time of the convening of the International Council Meeting of the World Conference of Soviet Jewry on 30 November 1988, Israel's two-pronged strategy, which called for the restoration of diplomatic relations with the Soviet Union combined with an effort to convince Washington to view Soviet dropouts as nonrefugees, was in full play. To heal the breach with Moscow Israel had prepared what it believed to be an irresistible package. It included using its influence with American Jewry to encourage the president to use the eighteen-month waiver provision of the amendment to finally grant Moscow the MFN it sought. Israel now proposed to support Moscow's participation in the forthcoming Middle East peace talks and its request to convene the Helsinki follow-up conference scheduled for 1991 in Moscow. It also promised to cease anti-Soviet agitation and propaganda at international forums. In return Israel's needs would remain the same: restoration of diplomatic ties and direct flights out of Moscow. Informally that meant the restoration of Israel's access to potential emigrants in the Soviet Union.

If that package was accepted then all the talk of freedom of choice would be bypassed since the new Soviet emigration regulations of 1987 were not based on a total acceptance of the "freedom of movement" idea. Emigration was allowed only for "national repatriation," as in the case of the Poles in 1956, and for "reunification of families," which was the legal rationale for allowing Jews to leave. Israel could argue for emigration on the basis of either, but family reunification was preferable because it did not suggest fulfillment of the Zionist "ingathering" ideology that was anathema to Moscow. Once diplomatic relations were reestablished, Israel could bypass the resistant Dutch Embassy in Moscow that handled emigration matters for Israel. Processing would be done directly at the United States or Israeli embassy depending on the destination of the emigrant. The exchange of low-level diplomatic and trade missions made Israel hopeful that the strategy would eventually bear fruit. In July there was an agreement to exchange consular delegations and a meeting between Shimon Peres and Shevardnadze at the United Nations was friendly and raised more hope.

In Moscow indications that Gorbachev's reforms were taking hold were everywhere. Synagogues and schools were again beginning to function, some with the help of JDC funds. In February 1989 the Mikhoels Jewish Cultural Center opened its doors followed in December by the Congress of a Union of Jewish Organizations in the Soviet Union. Gradually the best universities and schools abandoned their limitations on Jewish enrollment. In New York Samuil Zivs, co-chairman of the Anti-Zionist Committee of the Soviet Public, which had been a Communist Party instrument in denouncing Jews who chose to emigrate, now denounced the committee as a "mistake." Some took these changes as a sign that contrary to Zionist insistence that emigration was the only answer, there was a possibility of restoring some form of Russian Jewish communal life for those who would not or could not resettle in Israel. Alex Goldfarb, a well-known refusenik, revisited Moscow in October 1987 and reported that fewer than 10 percent of Jews now had plans to emigrate and that most were choosing to remain in the Soviet Union and rebuild some form of Jewish life there. But it was difficult to judge whether the decision to remain was related to the benevolent impact of the liberalization or the knowledge that the United States had grown far less accessible.

Liberalization could become a two-edged sword. There were also troubling signs of ethnic conflict and nationalism within the Soviet republics accompanied by a shrill, threatening anti-Semitism. Food shortages in the cities caused partly by the collapse of the infrastructure were now chronic. At the same time the remaining roadblocks to Jewish emigration were being removed. By 1988 it was possible to apply for exit permits for Romania or Sofia where exit visas exclusively for Israel would be issued. The waiting period for visas was shortened and with it the dreaded state of economic limbo. It is probably going too far to suggest, as one historian does, that the new emigration policy was accompanied by the realization of "the value of Jewish goodwill and the price of forfeiting it," among the Soviet leadership.[37] But that feeling of regret and loss could not be discerned among the Soviet people who were more likely to view the Jewish exodus with resentment and perhaps among a certain few, with envy.

Finally, on 18 October 1990, Israel's efforts to restore diplomatic relations were rewarded with success.[38] It did not happen a moment too soon as Israel was about to be inundated with thousands of emigrants. How much the situation had tilted in favor of Israel is indicated by the latent fear that if access to the United States were not available the Soviet Jews would choose to remain where they were. But to the surprise of the Soviet authorities and many activists as well, thousands of visa applicants appeared at the Netherlands consular section on Bolshaya-Ordinka Street beginning in January 1990 selected to risk leaving the security of life they knew for the uncertainty of settling in Israel. Unlike the emigration of the early seventies these applicants were not Zionists. They were being pushed to emigrate by forebodings that Soviet society would descend into social and economic chaos for which Jews would pay the price. The new liberalization allowed the venting of the folk anti-Semitism that was beneath the surface of Soviet life and which for the CPSU represented one of the available strands of consensus that it could find in a rapidly declining situation.

By the summer of 1988 few could still deny that a cataclysmic change was underway. The year began with Gorbachev's speech before the UN General Assembly announcing a 54 percent cut in the Soviet Union's military budget. For a moment it seemed that the entire Socialist camp was imploding. In China's Tiananmen Square the students who were massacred that dark day on 4 June 1989 had but a day before carried the familiar Western icons of freedom, including a likeness of the Statue of Liberty artfully made of paper-mache. In December Angola and Cuba signed an agreement for the removal of Cuban troops. In January 1989 Vietnam, which had defeated the United States in a bloody war, was forced to withdraw from Cambodia. With the pending Soviet-China rapprochement Vietnam would be diplomatically and economically isolated and eventually be compelled to seek investment capital from its former American enemy. That month too the Soviet Union began to destroy its poison gas stockpile. America's dominance in world affairs was symbolized by its unilateral action against Manuel Noriega in Panama in December 1989 and its action against Iraq a year later. Both were undertaken with little protest from the states of the former "peace camp."

Finally, in his address before the UN General Assembly, Gorbachev declared triumphantly that the Gulag had been emptied of those imprisoned because of religious or political beliefs and that the unresolved aspect of the refusenik problem would be solved by restructuring state security regulations. The long-awaited breakthrough in introducing a new Soviet emigration code came in November 1989. It addressed most concerns of the refuseniks including the nettling security problem. The law contained a five-year limit on the amount of time a prospective emigrant could be barred from leaving after exposure to classified material. Those refused had the right of appeal to an administrative commission of the Supreme Soviet. Requirement of waivers of financial liability from parents and relatives and the *vyzov* requirement were either eliminated or lightened. Prospective emigrants could now apply directly to the country to which they wanted to immigrate. Every month thereafter witnessed an increase in emigration figures. The victory of the West in the Cold War seemed complete, and some of the fruits of that victory were won by Soviet Jewry. All that remained for Israel was to convince Washington to change its definition of refugee. That would help channel the expected mass emigration to Israel. We have noted that the process was already well under way before Israel's efforts came into play.

■   In the American Jewish political arena the conflict continued unabated. Freedom of choice had become the mantra of the grassroots activists, many of whom were associated with the UCSJ. Mark Talisman, who before he became a lobbyist for CJF was part of the original Bunker group, informed a House committee that to reject freedom of choice would undermine support of immigration of any sort. Representatives of HIAS, testifying before the same congressional committee hearings, believed simply that human beings ought to have the right to live in the country of their choice.[39]

The voices in favor of resettlement in Israel with American government and philanthropic help were now often heard as well. The comparative higher cost of resettlement in the United States was a primary consideration that added credence to the argument of the Zionist-oriented activists that resettlement in Israel was more feasible. But to absorb the thousands of *olim* expected Israel would require the financial and political support of American Jewry. The former Ambassador Simcha Dinitz, now chairman of the WZO and the Jewish Agency for Israel (JAFI) executive, had previously spoken out against the allocation of funds for HIAS. Now at a meeting of JAFI officials in New York in January he again apprised the CJF/UJA fund-raising apparatus of the enormous absorption costs Israel faces. He feared that the 50 percent allocation normally given to Israel as part of the distribution formula would be diverted for domestic American use to cover their expected absorption costs because under the pending INS regulations these emigrants would not automatically be granted refugee status. Cost of maintenance and transportation would fall on JDC alone. He reminded UJA officials that the agency was originally created "to build and sustain the Jewish homeland."[40] The prospect of having to support the 30,000 to 40,0000 dropouts was indeed a sobering one for the American Jewish fund-raising apparatus, especially when the Bush administration was rapidly withdrawing the prospect of American financial support for resettlement. It cooled the ardor of the most ardent freedom of choice advocates among the federation leaders, especially when Israel wanted and needed the emigrants. Even then the $145 million that would be required to partly defray the cost of the absorption was clearly beyond the ability of the UJA's "Passage to Freedom" campaign. When it was announced that the proceeds of the campaign would be split between America and Israel on a fifty/fifty basis, Dinitz was again up in arms. The allocation of funds would cut into funds earmarked for

Israel, especially when the support of HIAS would come out of the 50 percent allocated to Israel. "Unity cannot be based on the disparagement of Israel," exhorted Dinitz.[41]

In the end Dinitz won his case but not because of the logic of his position. By 1989 many Jewish leaders had come to think that American Jewry should not compete with Israel on a matter so crucial to the survival of the Jewish homeland. To the Zionists among them, despite the talk of their human rights to settle where they pleased, the move of Jews from one diaspora community to another made no sense. Uri Gordon, later the official in charge of JAFI's absorption operation, argued that there were moments in history when the need of a beleaguered people had to be given precedence over individual human rights. Morris Abram would not go that far but insisted that the post-1987 emigrants were not refugees and that the Soviet Jewry movement always considered itself as an immigration, not a human rights movement. That is the reason it separated itself from the Russian democratizers and dissidents in the first place. But the candidates for emigration, the urbanized secularized Soviet Jews who made up the bulk of the dropouts, did not agree and neither did the human rights activists associated with the UCSJ.[42] For them there was a sense of satisfaction when a month before the election the Reagan administration announced that it was holding to its freedom of choice commitment.[43] Amazingly, when the outgoing Reagan administration raised the number of places for Soviet emigrants from 18,000 to 25,000 by taking slots allocated to the near East and Southeast Asia, it brought protest from the UCSJ, HIAS, and the AJC, who thought that the increase was politically motivated and taken at the expense of other deserving refugee groups.[44] But less than a year after George Bush's inauguration, a new less-generous refugee policy would be announced that would mark the final victory of Israel's two-pronged strategy. The change in policy was not a political payback for the Jewish support of Dukakis in the election. Bush received an above-normal 28 to 35 percent of the Jewish vote, and Jewish representation in Congress continued on its high post-1967 plateau. Thirty-one Jews were elected to the House and eight to the Senate, roughly the same as in the election of 1984.

In August there were rumors that the State and Justice departments intended to radically limit Soviet Jewish emigration by restricting entry only to those with immediate family in the United States. The Bush administration hoped to get Jewish organizational consent to the new limits. David Harris, who saw the change in policy coming, estimated that Jewish organizational consent to such a change was now "delicate but possible." Jewish communal leaders had become aware of the logic of the Israel solution.[45] Despite persistent rumors that the plan had been abandoned, the INS discontinued processing applications for refugee status from Soviet Jews on 30 September 1989. Visa applicants could now apply at the American Embassy in Moscow as normal immigrants. For Israel that meant that the dropout problem had been virtually solved.

But whether the change of policy was based on a calculation of the cost and the fear that other worthy refugees were being crowded out by the Soviet emigrants or Israel's behind-the-scenes pressure to deny the emigrants refugee status is not yet fully known. The change in American refugee policy may have been caused by a combination of several factors, but the influence of Israel and the Zionist movement in America played a considerable role.[46] According to the testimony of Roger Winter, executive director of the U.S. Committee for Refugees, it was a "highly political process" in which "foreign policy considerations have been the prime determinant of which refugees would be resettled in the United States."[47]

In the Gorbachev era the problem of defining "refugee" posed a special problem for the State Department. Israel's contention that the existence of a Jewish state willing to absorb the emigrants meant they were not refugees by any stretch of the imagination was difficult to refute. We have previously noted how problematic it became after 1985 to interpret the "greater persecution" clause favorably. Surely Cuban, Laotian, and Salvadoran refugees had a better claim for the 85,000 places set aside for refugees. That in turn brought the simmering budget crisis within the administration concerning refugees to a head. One estimate had it that the transportation of a single Soviet emigrant costs $7,000, far beyond the budget of the INS.[48] The granting of automatic refugee status to Soviet emigrants was ended in December 1988, though appeals for status would be handled after that date on a case-by-case basis. Israel had made its opposition to the refugee policy clear, and there continued to exist sufficient domestic opposition from the still sizeable and influential American Zionist movement to make Israel's position a political reality to consider. It was estimated that at least 50,000 would enter the emigration stream by the end of the fiscal year in October 1989. But unexpectedly the estimates for 1990 and the years to follow were twice and three times that figure. Like everyone else, the Bush administration had dismissed the figures announced by the activists as exaggerations submitted for political purposes. They may also have given some credibility to the Soviet counterargument that all those that had wanted to leave had, with the exception of a handful, already done so. They were certainly aware that most people now filing for visas would have dropped out in order to come to the United States. The situation was untenable; even with the generous increase of 40,000 slots for Soviet emigrants arranged with the help of Max Fisher, in June there were only 10,000 slots left for all refugees, including those from Southeast Asia and the Caribbean. In a word, the "free choice" policy advocated by the UCSJ, if it ever was a possibility, could not now be sustained. The prospect of thousands of Soviet emigrants turned away from the nation's doors after years of struggle to get them out was too much to contemplate for most activists. Israel had become the practical alternative.

The response of the Jewish organizations in effect accepting Israel's dual track solution to the crisis was made in a joint statement on 6 June 1988.[49] There would be direct flights from Moscow to Israel, which the Soviet Union finally permitted in February 1990, and those wishing to settle in the United States would be able to apply directly to the American Embassy in Moscow for a visa. The exit permit needed to leave the Soviet Union would still be subject to the stricter requirements of a legitimate *vyzov* attesting to close family connections. There were persistent rumors that the *vyzov* requirement of the Soviet emigration code would be abandoned or modified in the forthcoming proposed reforms. Those now wishing to emigrate had the choice of either applying to the American embassy, which had a quota of 50,000, all but 10,000 of which would be assigned to legitimate refugees. Under the new Soviet regulations the remainder could apply to leave as ordinary emigrants wanting to join their families. Some of these might eventually win refugee status under the attorney general's parole authority. By 1990 Soviet emigrants could either leave for Israel almost immediately or brave the growing uncertainties of life in Russia to perhaps gain access to the United States at a later date. In effect, the new policy meant that those who still wanted to emigrate would likely end up in Israel by default. Two weeks later, despite the fact that thousands of dropouts in Rome and Vienna could still not be forced to emigrate, Israel's cabinet approved the agreement.

Israel's victory seemed complete but it did not come without a price. There was apprehension regarding not only the economic cost of absorption but the social one as well. The memory of the debacle that occurred during the absorption of the Jews of North Africa had not been forgotten. As had been the experience of prior waves, many emigrants actually experienced a decline in status. The renowned "mother of refuseniks" Ida Nudel, who fought for sixteen years to be allowed to emigrate, was not happy at what she saw in Israel. "Israel and Israelis are indifferent to immigration from the Soviet Union," she noted. Better to drive a taxi in New York then to drive one in Israel and "engage in self degradation."[50] Steeled by years of struggle, the voice of the Soviet emigrants would make itself heard in Israel.[51] Three years previously Sharansky, who had come to personify the struggle of Soviet Jewry, castigated members of the Israeli Knesset for the weakness of its effort. It was necessary for Israel to speak out clearly and directly "so that . . . the American press will write more about the anti-Soviet demonstrations and less on the dress of Mrs. Gorbachev."[52]

■   Remaining was the problem of how to finance the expected mass emigration that would now flow largely to Israel. Israel's projections were that a minimum of 100,000 emigrants would arrive in 1990. The cost for housing, employment, and infrastructure would come to $3 billion, of which $500 million would be born by American philanthropic agencies. Israel would contribute $2 billion. When leaders of the major philanthropies convened in New York on 27 September the cost estimates and funding strategy received a mixed reception. The cost estimates seemed high and beyond the abilities of the agencies to meet. In February 1990 the General Assembly of the CJF meeting in Miami kicked off its "Operation Exodus" campaign to fund the expected massive emigration. The solution of the dropout problem did not magically bring harmony to Jewish organizational life. Federations in Cleveland and Chicago continued to favor "choice" but they were now balanced by others who for ideological and fiscal reasons favored a solution that kept the idea of "choice" in place but only hypothetically. They were also aware that to vote otherwise would put an enormous budgetary burden on the federations.

It was a difficult decision for Zionists who disagreed among themselves on the right course. Carmi Schwartz, CJF's outgoing executive vice president, differed with his successor Martin Kraar. No one could say with certainty whether the thousands of dropouts in the pipeline would heed the command of the American Jewish organizations or whether agencies such as HIAS, would stand by to witness the deprivation of their former clients still living in limbo in Ladispoli and other areas. Its moral dilemma was solved only when the remaining dropouts in the pipeline were granted American visas. The actual change in the Bush administration's refugee regulations on 30 September 1989 that restricted the number who could claim refugee status settled the matter. In the banner year of 1990, of the 212,000 who emigrated 184,849 received visas for Israel and 182,000 Soviet emigrants actually settled there, and only 27,717 dropouts were granted refugee status in the United States and elsewhere. Israel's victory on the dropout issue was not total but by 1995 it was sufficient to increase its population by almost 20 percent.[53]

Left unanswered was the question of how many emigrants were needed to stabilize Israel's population. Much depended on the central question that divided Israel's polity: Should Israel include the West Bank and Gaza, called Greater Israel, by the Likud party? The Soviet emigration could ensure a demographically stable Jewish state for the foreseeable future but absorbing a sufficient number of emigrants to settle Greater Israel probably could not be achieved by Soviet emigration alone.[54] But that improbability did not prevent Yitzhak Shamir, in a speech on 14 January 1990, calling for the settlement of Judea and Samaria because "big immigration requires Israel to be big as well."[55] When Congress appropriated an additional $400 million for resettlement in November 1990 it followed Bush's requirement laid down in October 1989 that there be assurances that the money would be used only for settlement in the pre-1967 borders.

The Cold War was waning, but the intractable Arab-Israeli conflict went on as if it had a life of its own. There was a clamor in the Arab press when U.S. aid for resettlement became known. The resort to violence, which Palestinians called Intifada, again brought the issue of the relationship of the Soviet emigration to the West Bank settlements to the fore. Palestinian spokesmen argued that Israel was using the emigrants to strengthen its claim to the area. It was an issue that further complicated American refugee policy, one which could not be easily dismissed. Israel's publication of statistics showing that the argument that Soviet emigrants were being used to solidify its hold on the West Bank were false hardly lessened the frequency with which the charge was made by Palestinian spokesmen.[56] In 1989 few foresaw that the Arab-Israel conflict would endure beyond the Cold War. Even fewer fathomed that the conflict was a portent of a bitter war between Islamic fundamentalism and the West that would shape the history of the early decades of the twenty-first century.

■   For American Jews involved in the Soviet Jewry movement there was the satisfaction of knowing that they had played a role in shaping Jewish history. They had made a difference. The release of Soviet Jewry for which they had struggled did not happen in quite the way they expected, through the collapse of the Soviet state. Activists probably would have dismissed the notion that their real contribution related as much to that collapse of that tyrannical Soviet system as to the "direct" rescue of Soviet Jews. But when the history of the Cold War is written it may well stake such a claim. Its historical weight may be determined not merely by the thousands whom it helped extricate in the seventies but also the hole that the movement punched in the iron curtain and its talent for calling attention to the human failings of the Soviet system. The instances in American Jewish history when an organization announces "mission accomplished" and closes shop could probably be counted on the fingers of one hand. By the end of 1989 all indications pointed to the fact that the long hoped for moment was rapidly arriving.

A certain sign that the struggle was winding down was the abandonment of a venerable institution of the traditional Solidarity Sunday activities scheduled for 13 March 1989.[57] The sometimes noisy demonstrations before the United Nations and the Soviet embassy were rarely seen now. A high-level Soviet official, Deputy Foreign Minister Anatoly Adamishin, paid an unprecedented visit to the offices of the NCSJ on 26 July for a three-hour luncheon during which all outstanding problems of Soviet emigration were discussed without rancor. What further proof was needed that the Russian wolf was becoming a lamb? Those activists who devoted themselves fully to the cause may have felt an emptiness in their lives when the struggle ended. Aware that the next phase of history was upon them, the NJCRAC, which had provided the grassroots connection for the NCSJ, convened thirty-five local directors of community relations councils to plan for the new phase. The local councils, which often provided the volunteers for the "struggle," were all dressed up with nowhere to go. They would begin the task of culturally rebuilding the Soviet Jewish community. Al Chernin, the executive vice chairman of NJCRAC, envisaged a "pied piper" role for Soviet Jews who had remained uninvolved. But that role promised little of the excitement of the struggle to get there. They had been young, idealistic, and Jewishly committed when they joined the movement in the seventies. Now victory hade come suddenly and for some too soon. "It's not yet 'Dayenu'," declared Jacob Birnbaum, national director of the Center for Soviet Jewry. "When the history of the Soviet Jewry movement is written," declared a frustrated but still passionate Rabbi Avi Weiss, SSSJ chairman, "historians will ask how it is possible that, in only a few months, the infrastructure of the movement has disintegrated."[58]

We have previously noted that despite the practiced sharpness of the public relations tactics and the brilliant orchestration of rallies and demonstrations, the movement had actually begun to show signs of disintegration during the lean years of the eighties. In a sense the victory was too long in coming. For leaders such as Jacob Birnbaum, who had conceived, nurtured, and then virtually invented themselves through the movement, there were no other causes on the horizon that offered at once the possibility of building ethnic identity, of tasting power and at the same time the certainty of moral rightness. Such clear-cut victorious moments are rare in history. He and the hundreds of activists sensed that they had taken on a Moloch, a monstrously powerful tyrannical regime, and brought it to its knees, with a little help from their friends, to paraphrase a popular ballad.

For Israel the emigration victory was no less sweet for its lateness in coming. "We may have to reach the point of winding up our campaign, declaring victory [and] sending the troops back home," crowed Yoram Dinstein, the outspoken Israeli representative of the liaison office.[59] True, the victory was preceded by a slugfest whose weapons were political not martial. At the decade's beginning Israel's dual objectives, to convince the Kremlin to release its Jews and Washington and American Jewry to help resettle them in Israel, still seemed impossible to realize. By 1989 it was possible to see that its objectives had been largely attained. A judgment regarding Israel's path must await the emergence of the full history of those years but no matter what new revelations are found in the archives generations hence, Israel's victory in its protracted political struggle to bring Soviet Jews to the Jewish state may count for more than those fought on the field of battle.

■   The Soviet Jewry movement operated within the context of the Cold War. We have noted how first the Jackson-Vanik Amendment and then the question of human rights helped create leverage that compelled Moscow to react. It was only when the Cold War tilted decisively to the West that it became possible to foresee the release of Soviet Jewry. The long-range signals of Soviet decline could be noted in the restlessness in the Soviet satellites. More apparent in the short run were Gorbachev's last-minute desperate attempts to reform the system, which included new regulations that eased the painful emigration process. This first phase of the Soviet emigration movement ended symbolically with the collapse of the Berlin Wall in November 1989, which signaled the collapse of the Soviet empire. It was the collapse of the Berlin Wall that allowed thousands of East Germans to exercise precisely that freedom of movement that lay behind the efforts of the activists. That event was precipitated not by armed resistance but by the exercise of the "freedom of movement" first heralded by the Soviet Jewry movement in its "Let My People Go" slogan.

The citizens of the German Democratic Republic were permitted to travel freely to other states in the "socialist camp." Hungary was a favorite destination not only because of its mild "Goulash Communism" under Janos Kadar but also because it was possible to circumvent the wall blocking travel to West Germany by crossing the now-open border between Hungary and Austria. That state became a kind of depot for escaping Soviet Jews and East Germans, a strange historic coupling. By August 1989 it was estimated that 120,000 East Germans had fled to the German Federal Republic in that way. The world witnessed the hemorrhaging of a Soviet satellite that thousands of armed soldiers did not seem able to stop. That was acknowledged when Egon Krenz, Erich Honecker's successor as chancellor of the German Democratic Republic, announced the opening of the Berlin Wall. The rest is history.

Sometimes history's verdict seems strange indeed. The "freedom of movement" was a relatively minor human right that was granted to Jews in modified form in the Helsinki Final Act. Few realized that it provided the nail in the coffin for the Soviet control system. The Helsinki Accords granted only a partial right limited to those who could claim reunification with families, but it set an example. The familiar rights such as freedom of religion, speech, and others included in the panoply of human rights remained internal affairs subject to implementation by the very power that had denied them. The right to leave and return to one's country at will was different because it permitted subjects to vote with their feet, to remove themselves from its control. Moscow understood that better than the West. That was one of the reasons it resisted the release of its Jews. It is in that sense that the emigration of Soviet Jewry, which was the sine qua non of the Soviet Jewry movement, posed a standing threat to the Soviet system of control. The refuseniks came in contact with the sharp cutting edge of that resistance, which was embodied in administrative decree, spoken and unspoken because their desire to leave hit at the very heart of the system.

Some historians would begin their research the year that I lay down my pen. In 1989 the scene of thousands of Soviet Jews debarking from planes, many carrying cherished musical instruments, became more prominent than ever before. It is such images that give the reader a glimpse of the drama of hundreds of thousands of people uprooting themselves from the land whose culture they drank from thirstily for centuries. But I find that scene merely the closing episode of a long and sometimes frustrating voyage. For the historian the real story is to discover how that unlikely exodus was made to happen and how in the process of seeking its liberation, Soviet Jewry helped bring a tyrannical power to its knees. The rest is commentary. Yet the release of Soviet Jewry barely registered on the historical equivalent of the Richter scale. From a general historical perspective it takes its place with the series of events and processes that led to the demise of the Soviet empire. In the larger Cold War arena the rescue role of the Soviet Jewry movement may seem dwarfed. But on the post-Holocaust Jewish historical canvas it has a redemptive quality. It marks the juncture when its players, Soviet Jewry, American and diaspora Jewry, and Israel, brought a crucial and often troubled episode of their joint history to a successful conclusion.

NINE Afterthoughts

The improbable story of how a small divided movement composed of voluntary organizations and activists succeeded in bending a superpower to release its Jews, something it resisted doing for decades, is best understood in the context of the Cold War and American Jewish history. The Cold War produced a confluence of interest between the movement's objectives and American policy. The history of American Jewry is replete with instances when it came to the aid of beleaguered kindred Jewish communities abroad. We noted in the early chapters that the desire to protect the Jews of Russia was in fact a well-known datum in American Jewish history. The Holocaust served to again bring these earlier involvements with Russian Jewry to mind.

Though the exodus of Soviet Jewry occurred largely during the 1990s, this study ends in 1989. In that year it became clear that the freedom of movement idea that was the key to the Soviet emigration struggle would prevail. It was the flight in East Germany that presented an early sign that the Soviet system was especially vulnerable to the idea of freedom of movement, the last-listed of the human rights in the Helsinki Final Accords signed in 1975. The fall of the Berlin Wall in 1989, which signaled the imminent collapse of the Soviet system, was related directly to East Germans exercising the right to leave by making their way to the German Federal Republic by way of Hungary and Austria. Less well known is the parallel exodus of Jews from the Soviet Union, which became a demographic hemorrhage after 1989. Between 1967 and 1995 about 1.2 million Soviet Jews left, leaving the once-sizable community with less than a million professing Jews. How that unlikely exodus was made to happen is the core of story here told.

■ Most researchers dealing with the Cold War barely mention the Soviet Jewry movement and would question the weight this study grants its activities as a factor in the collapse of the Soviet system. It is a role difficult to assess because it deployed no battalions and divisions but rather expended its resources in building and maintaining a communications link to a world Jewish movement created for the express purpose of gaining the release of Soviet Jews. Closed systems cannot abide that kind of connection. The Soviet Jewry movement was not alone in punching a hole in the iron curtain but it was different in that it connected an aggrieved group with a related outside community experienced in projecting political influence in Washington and well practiced in public relations. Soviet dissidents did occasionally get a hearing in the West, but the media attention given to the refuseniks and the Soviet Jewry movement generally was more continuous and of a higher order of magnitude. The movement insistently called the world's attention to a problem that most Western political leaders considered a distraction from the crucial issue of disarmament. Yet within a decade the world learned about the desire of Soviet Jews to emigrate and the terrible price they were made to pay for wanting to do so. The emigration of Soviet Jewry and the movement devoted to making it happen became not only a harbinger of the crisis in the Soviet system but in a sense also a factor in it.

Unlike Israel, American Jewry was not a sovereign player in the international arena. It makes its mark through the host culture that acts in its behalf. The Kremlin's reluctance to permit the emigration of Soviet Jewry became a natural part of the general Cold War indictment of Soviet domestic policy. In the United States the emigration issue was packaged as a human rights issue. But that could create problems of separating Cold War from human rights motives. The overlap is best illustrated in the person of Sen. "Scoop" Jackson, the amendment's staunchest defender on human rights grounds. But the view of Jackson as a cold warrior was popular currency in the media. From the perspective of this study, it is clear that without the Cold War to amplify the Jewish interest, the plea for Soviet Jewry might well have remained a cry in the wilderness. It helped move a relatively minor issue to near the center of the historical stage. But a conspiracy of additional factors, which includes a new factor in Jewish history that was not present in prior crisis and sorely missed during the Holocaust, was the role of a sovereign Jewish state. The eventual unlikely mass emigration of Soviet Jewry cannot be explained without understanding the role played by Israel.

The Cold War has passed into history, but the Middle East has remained a troubled area. This study ponders the problem posed by the potential resettlement of more than a million Soviet Jews in Israel. That possibility injected a "politics of demography" into the intractable conflict between Arabs and Jews in which Moscow held an important chip. It strengthened a latent appetite in both of Israel's major parties for settling the West Bank, and it placed Washington, whose financial support helped settle the emigrants in the United States as well as Israel, in a quandary.

The emigration of Soviet Jewry became not simply an interest of American Jewry in which the support of the American government was enlisted. In a larger sense the emigration problem impinged directly on the right of freedom of movement that went to the heart of the ideology that separated the two superpowers. The strategy developed involved denial of credit to a huge capital-starved economy with concomitant denial of markets to the American economy, a population infusion for Israel to head off a demographic deficit, and an allaying of the deep feelings of guilt of American Jewry regarding its inadequacy during the Holocaust. The quest for the release of a handful of refuseniks, which is how the movement began, turned out to be only the tip of the iceberg.

The American Soviet Jewry movement was hardly exempt from the organizational conflict that is a given in American Jewish communal life, but its intensity and persistence while focused on the same goal is difficult to explain. Matters of organizational turf may have played a role in the lesser tensions, such the conflict between the National Conference on Soviet Jewry (NCSJ) and the National Jewish Community Relations Advisory Council (NJCRAC). Had there been no rewards or power at stake there would have been little to fight about. But the tensions between the two major organizations involved in the struggle, the NCSJ and UCSJ, were of a different order of magnitude. Strangely, their conflict was not over goals, but means, and not about ideology, but how much ideology should count in operations. They disagreed about principles and estimates of the character of the Soviet regime and the nature of the restraints within which the movement was compelled to operate. In some sense the activities of the two primary organizations complemented each other. Both played important roles in convincing legislators that the emigration issue served the American national interest, both mounted effective public relations campaigns, and both mobilized communal and political support on all levels. But unlike the UCSJ, the NCSJ kept its ideological sword in its sheath and realized earlier that the approaching victory of the West in the Cold War changed the terms of the struggle to extricate Soviet Jewry.

We have taken special note of the deep differences between the UCSJ and the NCSJ concerning the Jackson-Vanik Amendment and the dropout phenomenon. Both organizations were expressions of the American Jewish enterprise but positioned the Zionist ideal of homeland differently. The organizations under the NCSJ umbrella in some measure remained under the influence of the post-Holocaust sensibility that gave the highest priority to the security of Israel. Because of its passion to rescue Soviet Jews, the UCSJ and its affiliates were in a strange way less able to enter into political transactions. It had strongly supported the Jackson amendment, which was in effect a highly political instrument designed to compel Moscow to transact business on emigration. Yet, when there was clear evidence that the Soviet empire was coming apart, the UCSJ continued to oppose using the lever given by the waiver clause that might achieve that goal. As late as 1990 it was still waiting for implementation, even after Sharansky announced his willingness to deal. So deep was its commitment that it could not take "yes" for an answer.

Like individuals, movements pay a price for the failure to perceive reality. In some measure the organizational conflict within American Jewry and between the American Jewish movement and Israel is anchored in that difference of perception regarding the nature of the crisis and the way it might be resolved. It partly accounts for the post-1979 insistence by American activists that the dropouts be allowed "freedom of choice." Their conflict with Israel was based partly on the assumption of the urgency of "rescue." The idea was to get them out as quickly as possible. The would-be rescuers became aware that Israel was as much interested in "rescuing" Israel from its demographic shortfall as it was in rescuing Soviet Jewry. Of course, for Israel the two rationales were not in conflict. The need for Soviet Jewry to leave the Soviet Union and the existence of a Jewish homeland to absorb and resettle them was the fulfillment of a Zionist dream. It was evidence that the Zionist Weltanschauung remained valid.

Supporters of the grassroots UCSJ took to referring to the NCSJ as the "establishment," meaning no doubt that its positions were determined by a consortium of mainline organizations represented on its executive board. It is true that the NCSJ had many masters, but it also developed considerable leeway in taking initiatives. Despite its cumbersome command apparatus it proved more able to handle the nongrassroots political activities that were essential to winning the support of five administrations. The source of the dilemma goes back to the nature of Jewish power in the world arena, which I call "proxy power." Bereft of the instruments of sovereignty, American Jewry was compelled to persuade the American government to act in its stead on the basis of confluence of interest. That transaction often requires political wheeling and dealing and settling for half a loaf when a full one was not available. No matter how insistently a private interest group presses its interest, its ability to pull foreign policy out of its national interest grooves in the direction it favored is limited.

Acting politically also meant the meshing of many different opinions within the movement in order to speak to power holders with one voice. It was not an easy task and was never fully achieved. Sometimes it seemed as if behind the heated language separating the different wings of the American movement there was a clash between those who operated on the political level by finding tactics that would work and those who were ideological devotees who found it difficult to abide even a single additional day of injustice. Pressing the Soviet Jewry case in the halls of Congress they discovered the disheartening fact that what was a matter of life and death for them was for the power holders merely one of several aggrieved voices calling for help. We have noted that within the Cold War context in which it operated the Soviet Jewry movement was comparatively effective in catapulting what might easily have remained a minor issue to a comparatively high place on the political agenda.

There is also much that can be distilled about the character and viability of American Jewry from its response to the plight of Soviet Jewry. There were divisions that separated those committed to "rescuing" Soviet Jewry. But a good portion of American Jewry, perhaps a majority, remained unaware and passive regarding the fate of their Soviet brethren. But unlike the communal experience during the years of the Holocaust, there remained sufficient group cohesiveness to speak to the administrations in power with one fairly coherent voice. Sometimes that voice took a long time to decide what it wanted to say and there were times when it seemed inaudible. But a voice there was despite the fact that Jewish communalism had entered into a period of decline in the 1960s. The defense organizations such as the American Jewish Committee (AJC), American Jewish Congress (AJCong), and the Anti-Defamation League (ADL) were all in the process of contracting their budgets and activity. Fraternal organizations such as Hadassah and B'nai B'rith, once the glory of Jewish communal life, were generally less attractive to the baby boomers. But if there was a general loss of what one researcher calls "social capital in the community" in the case of Soviet Jewry movement it was not noticeable in the dedication of the rank and file who found social purpose in belonging to it.[1] The effectiveness of the Soviet Jewry movement was an indication that American Jewry retained more communal vitality than generally imagined. One historian may have been on to something when he observed that the movement itself provided American Jewry with a "new focus of communal purpose."[2]

What we observe in these pages is a picture of Jewish political influence at once innocently wielded and yet formidable. Rather than being conspiratorial, as Soviet leaders imagined, there was conflict regarding the most effective strategy for doing business with the Soviet authorities that triggered family quarrels within the Soviet Jewry movement. The most militant activists were believers rather than clever tacticians. They possessed none of the conventional accoutrements of power. Aside from Israel there was no other sovereign state that could plead the emigration case before the United Nations and at the outset there was little unified communal support. They were basically powerless in the face of the awesome power of a lawless totalitarian society. It is that circumstance that makes their ultimate victory so intriguing.

■   We have noted Israel's founding role for the movement in the Soviet Union and the part it played in awakening an interest and establishing and shaping the movement in the Jewish Diaspora. The Soviet Jewry movement was born out of Israel's biological and ideological need for immigrants and nurtured in an Israeli incubator. It was Israel that early began to rebuild the all-but-forgotten ties to the Jews of Russia. Given Moscow's implacable hostility to the Jewish state, the leverage of the United States and its influential Jewry would somehow have to be brought to bear to extricate the potential emigrants. American Jewry alone possessed the financial resources and the political clout to play the necessary advocacy role before the American government. Israel played a crucial role in alerting American Jewry to its responsibility. By the early seventies, with the help of the liaison bureau, organizations had been alerted to the problem, and a group of activists and publicists such as Moshe Decter had been enlisted. Undoubtedly some will argue that Israel should have withdrawn from the field at that juncture, but in terms of goals it risked losing everything by total withdrawal. Israel remained in the background and tried to guide the American movement in the "right" direction. The story of how American Jewry assumed a primary role is fascinating. It reveals for all to see that the basic assumptions informing the political behavior of Jews in America and Israel are quite different. For most American Jews the prospect of a *Zwungsaliyah* such as was ultimately favored by Israel was not acceptable. It was the tensions that developed over the question of "choice" for the emigrants that provide new insight to a perennial problem that generates much anxiety among Jewish survivalists. It concerns the strength and permanence of the bond between the Jews of America and Israel.

The free atmosphere of Vienna and later Rome where the emigrants were bound for processing became a scene of great disappointment for the representatives of the Jewish Agency. There were always a sprinkling of emigrants who changed their minds once out of the country, but the full dimension of the problem did not become clear until after 1975 when a new less Zionized and Judaized emigrant began to arrive. The bitter conflict over their disposition that followed exposed a yawning gap between those who gave the highest priority to the freedom of movement and those who gave precedence to Israel's need for a biological supplement. No incident in contemporary Jewish history better reveals how "reasons of state" have sometimes acted to divide American Jewry and Israel.

The conflict that developed between Israel and American Jewish organizations was particularly troubling because Israel's security was important to all Jews but so too were the rights of those who chose to dropout. The rift between American activists and Israel, many of whom were associated with some affiliate of the UCSJ, cannot entirely be accounted for by differences in organizational culture. There were also near irreconcilable differences in values and interests. Beyond the question of the rights of the individual emigrant there existed the question of communal survival. Some believed that Israel had entered upon a zero sum game whereby its population gain was directly related to Soviet Jewry's population loss, which would diminish the possibility of post-Soviet rebuilding of Jewish communal life. From a non-Zionist perspective it seemed as if Israel's motives were related to national interest rather than rescue per se. When emigration became the preferred solution to the Soviet Jewish problem in the 1960s, Leonard Shapiro, recognized as an outstanding expert on Soviet Jewry, cautioned that the emigration solution did not address the problem of those Jews who would remain in Russia. "Israel in particular will not, it must be hoped, in its zeal to acquire new immigrants, forget the plight of those Soviet Jews who do not wish to emigrate."[3] Much depended on the attitudes of Zionist-oriented activists who generally negated Jewish life in the diaspora and were therefore convinced that restoring some kind of Jewish communal life in the Soviet Union, even in its liberalized incarnation, was not feasible or desirable.[4] That was not an uncommon position among Zionist ideologues. In survivalist terms, Israel offered a much better chance for Jewish communal survival than investing scarce human and financial resources in the dubious enterprise of restoring Jewish life in the Soviet Union.

Some ardent Zionists carried a similar assumption into the conflict over the dropouts by arguing that settling the emigrants in the United States was putting them on a sinking ship. The feeling among Zionist activists that the restoration of Jewish communal life was a hopeless endeavor persisted even after the establishment of the Council of Jewish Cultural Associations in December 1989 that saw approximately 700 Jewish delegates representing 175 Jewish organizations from 75 cities and outside observers convene in Moscow. It was the first open conference of Jews in seventy years. Three years later the organization of a formal communal structure, the Va'ad, allowed some hope that some form of communal rebuilding on a small scale was possible. But twelve years later even that slim hope seems forlorn in the face of continued shrinkage. In 2002 there were approximately a quarter of a million Jews remaining in the Russian Federation, only 24 percent of whom were professing Jews.[5] Still, the Zionist assumption that emigration to Israel was the best solution for all concerned was not shared by all American Jews. "Our exclusive focus on refuseniks and emigration must be altered," counseled the *Reconstructionist,* "what is needed now is generous support for Jewish life in the Soviet Union."[6] That sentiment was shared by Chabad, which maintained a sizable representation in the former Soviet Union. Surprisingly, Edgar Bronfman, president of the Zionist-oriented WJC, also declared in 1989 that the emphasis must be communal revival rather than emigration to Israel.[7]

For Israel the Soviet emigration in extremis was an example of the very reason for its existence. There could be no conflict in doing everything to resettle the Soviet emigrants in Israel. It was that ideological zeal that led to the sometimes risky enterprise of reestablished contact with the "lost" Jews of Russia. The proprietary attitude toward the Soviet Jewish enterprise that many have noted was based on the fact that in the initial stage the movement was in fact undertaken exclusively by Israel. The crucial network through which communications with the outside was maintained was established first by the hard and dangerous work of Israeli consular personnel. There would have been no formal Soviet Jewry movement without Israel's initial investment of resources and people willing to brave the danger of making the contacts.

By the eighties Israel witnessed its hope of a Soviet aliyah fading away and with it the best chance of stabilizing its population. Yet in the midst of its dilemma, which was seen as involving the very survival of the state, and its outrage at the role of the Hebrew Immigrant Aid Society (HIAS) and the American Jewish Joint Distribution Committee (JDC), Israel never took the extreme step of instructing the Dutch embassy not to issue visas to potential dropouts, which would have presented the potential emigrant the alternative of either settling in Israel or remaining in the Soviet Union. That would have been the most direct solution to the dropout problem. After America's generous refugee policy was finally discontinued in the fall of 1989 and the Soviet Union agreed to direct flights, that became the de facto choice faced by the emigrants. Remaining unanswered is the question raised by Uri Gordon, head of the absorption and resettlement department of the Jewish Agency, who asked whether there is a point where the collective welfare of the Jewish people as represented by Israel should be given priority over the individual choices of a newly liberated people, many of whom no longer identified as Jews.

The ardor with which many American activists held to "freedom of choice" serves as evidence of how profoundly American the Soviet Jewry movement was. To this day the expressions such as "choice" conjure memories of the civil rights struggle and its rhetoric of freedom. It made the idea of a *Zwungsaliyah* to Israel, which denied the "freeness" of the newly liberated emigrants, difficult to accept. They had after all become emigrants on the basis of the human rights principle of freedom of movement. Some of Israel's disappointment in the dropout phenomenon stemmed from the fact that they viewed the world through ideological glasses that made them unable to accept the reality that there were Jews who would not come "home." That, they argued, is what Israel's "law of return," which gave the refugee Israeli citizenship the moment the Israeli visa was accepted, signified. For a committed Zionist who witnessed Soviet emigrants, using the visas from the state that Zionism established precisely as a place where Jews could be at home to settle elsewhere smacked of betrayal. Many American Zionists shared Israel's disappointment and became strong advocates of using budget priorities to direct the emigration flow to Israel.

Zionist disappointment might have been allayed had they had a more realistic picture of the composition of the emigrant stream and the Soviet Jewry from which it stemmed. It was in fact composed of several distinct cohorts. The emigrants of the early seventies on which the refugee image was based were Zionized and highly urban. It included surviving elements of a once strong Zionist movement in the Baltic States that amalgamated with Russian Zionists, many of whom possessed the passion of the newly converted. It was this minority that aspired to resettle in Israel and confronted the system to do so. They desired not merely to escape the Soviet Union but to rejoin the Jewish people. Many were rejected by OVIR and assumed the limbo status of the refusenik. Historians will, I suspect, ultimately recognize that this group, more than any other in the Soviet Jewry movement, made history happen and did so with great courage.

The second and much larger group more typical of Soviet Jewry entered the emigration stream in numbers in the post-1976 years and grew in size thereafter.[8] They were less ideological and in motivation much like normal emigrants desiring to improve the material condition of their lives. They were not Zionists, not passionately anti-Soviet, and not searching for Jewish identity and sometimes not Jewish at all, at least according to Jewish law. Nor were they inclined to place their lives in jeopardy for a cause. Once there is an awareness of who the dropouts were, their choice not to settle in Israel becomes understandable. It was the same choice made by the grandparents of many American Jews. But deeply imbued with the imperative of "ingathering," Zionists could not accept that the urbanized Soviet emigrants, the end-products of a russification and modernization process that deprived them of much of what was identifiably Jewish, would not choose to return to the Jewish homeland. Some have suggested that their rejection of Israel was partly rooted in the feeling that they would not fit. Paradoxically, Israel seemed too Jewish for them.

Living side by side with its demographic crisis, Israel's attitude toward the dropout also possessed a missionary aspect. They felt an obligation to restore their lost Jewish identity to the emigrants and were convinced that they were the only ones in a position to do so. A contemporary view of how they fared in Israel suggests that they may have been partly right. In the end, resettlement in Israel seemed to work even for the reluctant emigrants. Though it was not always apparent on the grassroots level, Israel needed them and to feel needed, we are informed, is in itself rehabilitative. Israel emerged as the winner in the struggle for the Soviet Jewish emigrants. It increased the size of its population with a well-educated wave of immigrants. But from a contemporary perspective it has become apparent that the victory was not decisive. The Soviet emigration has strengthened its ability to sustain itself in a troubled region, but it has not disarmed the implacable opposition of the Islamic world.

■ In a sense everything linked to the struggle to free Soviet Jewry, from the Jackson-Vanik Amendment to chaining oneself to a UN fence to make known the plight of Soviet Jewry, is encompassed in the human rights movement. The campaign for Soviet Jewry was quintessentially a struggle for human rights.

While separating themselves from the democratizers for strategic reasons, the Soviet activists focused their activities on a single human right, the freedom of movement. Strangely, the Soviet Union, which took credit for initiating the Helsinki process, also claimed to favor human rights but was never convinced that such rights were inalienable. They were considered internal matters that could be granted or denied by government. That may account for the Soviet ease in entering informally into arrangements to allow its Jews to emigrate in exchange for trade and access to credit. Moscow could also apply it selectively, as when it repatriated Poles living in the Soviet Union in 1956 or later the Germans and Armenians. But in the case of Soviet Jewry there was no such largess, even after the Soviet Union became a signatory to the Helsinki Final Act, which specifically assured the right to emigrate on the basis of family reunion. The complaints stemming from the Helsinki follow-up conferences regarding the failure to implement this right were simply ignored and the activists gathered around the watch groups were harassed and arrested.

Like the Soviet approach to human rights, the American approach was also infused with Cold War motives. The Jackson amendment and the Helsinki process that together form the axis on which the American human rights policy was based were quite different. Though the amendment did not mention Soviet Jewry or any other group and Jackson insisted it encompassed all suppressed groups behind the iron curtain, in reality it was focused on emigration rights for Soviet Jewry. Together with the Volga Germans they were the only applicants for emigration who had a homeland anxious to receive them. Basket III of the Helsinki Final Act, which at the outset gained only hesitant support from Washington, was more broadly conceived. It aimed at extending human rights, including the right to emigrate to anyone who wanted to exercise it. Like the Jackson amendment it was used as a cudgel to put the Soviet Union under pressure to change its conduct.

The high priority demanded for human rights by activists and dissenters posed problems for American policy makers because it impinged on the détente policy. Supporters of that policy assumed that life and death matters such as steps to prevent a nuclear confrontation through disarmament needed to be given precedence over human rights. What mattered rights when life on earth was threatened with destruction? Like Moscow, Washington too considered immigration policy an internal matter, and some of its staunchest Cold War allies, such as the Pinochet regime in Chile, were human rights trespassers. Although the rhetoric of human rights heated the atmosphere it could not by itself convince sovereign governments to change their behavior. In response to the drumbeat of charges against them the Soviets countered with publicizing shortcomings in the United States, especially in the area of race relations. Clearly, the human rights cudgel was not easily wielded. Rather than having an immediate impact, its effects were cumulative and long range. It had the greatest impact when demanded by an aroused public opinion.

One way of making sense of Gorbachev's perestroika is to view it as the long awaited "kicking in" of the human rights effort that was, in effect, a listing of Western ideas of what had to be done for the Soviet Union to catch up to the elevated standards of the West. In the end it was not the pressure of the Jackson-Vanik Amendment or the cajoling of American diplomats that opened the gates of that closed society. Something more was required to change a system that thought it needed to hold its subjects captive. No matter how tight their controls all governments require some consensus to govern. The insistence on human rights placed Moscow in a difficult position because from its perspective, human rights, as advocated by the West, had inherent in it a potential for subverting the Soviet control system. Some rights, such as freedom of speech and religion, had gained universal acceptance. Societies that thwarted their spirit lost support, at least among the intelligentsia that acted as opinion leaders. Evidence of human trespasses could cause grave problems in a world where even tyrannical powers had somehow to garner the good will of their subjects. The Soviet authorities fashioned a propaganda apparatus specifically designed to engineer such good will. But it did not work well when the consensus regarding human rights has hardened as it had in Czechoslovakia and other nations. Just as human slavery had earned opprobrium in the nineteenth century, so human rights had won a special place in the post-Holocaust world of the twentieth. In that world persecution of Jews had, at least for the moment, become the sine qua non of such a trespass.

The Soviet system especially craved the legitimacy that could be derived from a concern about human rights and geared its formidable propaganda machine to convince the world that it was genuine. The "peaceful coexistence" campaign of the fifties and sixties, a kind of Soviet version of détente, went far to establish the image of a peace-loving, caring society. But especially after Khrushchev's revealing address before the Twentieth Party Congress in 1956 confirmed much that had been suspected and disheartened true believers, few could still believe that Moscow was a benevolent force in the world. A society that had as part of its control system a Gulag into which millions had disappeared stood little chance of convincing public opinion of its interest in human rights, even its own definition of rights, which emphasized economic equality and security. Its military presence in Cuba, Angola, the Horn of Africa, and Afghanistan and its suppression of resistance in Hungary (1956) and especially in Czechoslovakia in 1968 reinforced the image of an expansionist suppressive social order. It was the Communist parties of the West who bore the brunt of the anti-Communist animus. They subsequently played an important role in informing the Soviet power holders of their negative popular image in the West.

The failure to develop a control system based on popular support was well known to the "new men" like Gorbachev and Shevardnadze who came to power in 1985. Speaking before a meeting of officials of his Foreign Affairs Ministry in July 1988, Shevardnadze mentioned that part of the legacy he had inherited was the need to restore the good reputation of the Soviet Union that had been compromised by previous regimes: "We cannot exhibit indifference to what others are saying and thinking about us for our self-respect, our well being, our position in the world hinges largely on the attitude of others towards us."[9] That was the desired self-image that created a new receptivity to the human rights embodied in Basket III of the Helsinki Final Act. It was the beginning of hope that the rights of Soviet

Jewry, including the right to emigrate and return, would receive favorable consideration. In the end it was not divisions and missiles that brought change to the Soviet Union but the power of the idea of human progress. It may have been as much Moscow's concern about the negative image generated by the emigration issue as its supposedly dire economic situation that convinced Soviet power holders to make concessions. From that perspective it was the ability of the Soviet Jewry movement to make its case known that proved to be its most important weapon.

The Soviet Jewry movement did what Jewish leaders had always needed to do; it convinced world public opinion that the treatment of Jews warranted concern. In the human rights context the travail of the refuseniks no longer stood alone. It positioned the Soviet Jewry problem beyond yet another case of victimization that historically had not yielded great concern. The Helsinki Accords provided an instrument for the entrée of the case for Soviet Jewry into a larger worldwide framework. For some, gaining a place on the "to be ameliorated" list was a negative form of recognition. But within Gorbachev's domain it promised improvement of the Jewish condition.

While the Jackson amendment may have propelled the Soviet Jewry problem to prominence, it was the activism on human rights centered in the Helsinki follow-up conferences that proved to be a powerful reinforcement for the right of Soviet Jewry to emigrate. The idea that Communist regimes would do better if they practiced a Socialism "with a human face," as existed for a brief moment in Czechoslovakia in 1968, was in some sense recognition that a human rights ingredient had become requisite for governing in the client states. The liberalization that finally came during the Gorbachev era that brought with it the freedom of movement, albeit incomplete, was cut from the same cloth. When Soviet Jewry finally became free to emigrate it was wrought by the same historic forces that liberated other captive communities in the Soviet sphere.

■   We come finally to the role of American Jewry and its movement for Soviet Jewry. Had it not been for the radical unpredicted way the Holocaust reshaped Jewish history, the Soviet treatment of its Jews might have become the most important historic preoccupation of American Jewry.[10] We have seen, aside from fear, that the supposed "Jewish" character of the Bolshevik revolution was becoming part of the anti-Semitic imaginings; the role of JDC in resettlement schemes in the Ukraine during the twenties suggested a growing Jewish entanglement with events in the Soviet Union. To the extent that historians can find a core to American Jewish political interests in the 1920s it concerned the question of "free immigration," which Jews of all stripes, including those of the AJC, favored. The goals of the Soviet Jewry movement that started in the early 1960s were hardly a new concern for American Jewry but rather a return to an old one.

But such a return is not the entire story. In retrospect the reason the American branch of the Soviet Jewry movement was able to sustain itself for more than three decades finds much of its roots in its witness role during the Holocaust. It was an important movement for American Jewry because of the opportunity it offered for some kind of redemption from the guilt felt regarding its imagined failure during those years. It is not necessary here to ponder the question of whether that sense of guilt was justified. But we need to be aware of the fact of its existence and the many forms it assumed, from the proliferation of museums, memorials, books, and research projects to the impact of the Jewish Defense League's (JDL's) "Never Again" slogan, to conclude that in the years of this study the American Jewish preoccupation with the Holocaust had become near obsessional.[11] An emotional state is not precisely a historical datum but in the case of Soviet Jewry the historian cannot ignore it.

It should not come as a surprise that American Jewry's view of the Soviet Jewry problem was conditioned by its recent experience with what was thought to be an analogous crises. Undoubtedly some imagined that history was repeating itself and might end in genocide as it was rumored Stalin planned before his timely death in 1953. So pervasive was the analogy that the profound difference between the National Socialist and Communists case was swept aside. The murder of European Jewry during World War II, in which Soviet Jewry suffered disproportionate losses, became part of a single continuous process, as if a totalitarian power of similar ilk was continuing the Final Solution. It invested the American activists with an urgency to act. They saw the Soviet Jews as victims of a vicious regime only to discover that many Soviet Jews did not muster the same high level of survival anxiety.

That may also account for the difficulty in distinguishing between the heroic refuseniks of the earliest emigration wave and the dropouts who came later and were more representative of average Soviet Jews. Their reasons for wanting to emigrate did not notably differ from those that had pushed Jews out of Russia since 1870. Unlike the refuseniks, they were not candidates for "rescue" but rather candidates for a better life. Also overlooked by those who saw themselves as rescuers was another startling difference between the Communist persecution of the Jews and that of the National Socialist. The Communist regime wanted to prevent Jews from emigrating whereas Berlin wanted to rid the Reich of its Jews first by immigration, then by deportation, and finally by extermination. Also unlike the case of Soviet Jewry, with the exception of an occasional neutral observer, there was little contact possible with European Jewry after the outbreak of war in September 1939. Berlin's ability to conceal the operation of the final solution stands in sharp contrast to the Soviet case where the anti-Jewish depredations and later the refusal to implement the Helsinki Final Act were not only known in the West, but they served as grist for the public relations mill that kept the plight of Soviet Jewry in the news.

Although it is clear that Soviet Jewry had experienced a massive assault on its culture, approximating a kind of "cultural genocide," after the death of Stalin and certainly after the advent of Gorbachev, imagining that biological genocide was imminent was not part of the reality. Threats and harassment, withdrawal of opportunity and the hope that accompanies it surely were for Russia's Jews. But the danger they faced in the seventies and eighties is not comparable in its lethality to that faced by the Jews of Europe during the Holocaust. It was of a different order and rationale. The urgency attached to the "rescue" of Soviet Jewry, as heartfelt as it was, was not based on an accurate gauge of reality, especially after 1985.

▪   To interest the American government in the need for intercession for Soviet Jewry an aroused public opinion had to be generated through a public relations campaign. The urgent need to bring out the Jews of Russia had to be marketed and sold. Moscow's trespasses were known, but an awareness of the Jewish aspect, particularly its anti-Semitism parading as anti-Zionism, had first to be created. The sustained public relations campaign to create such awareness, first among American Jews and then the general public, is the movement's finest hour. Its effectiveness in this area, the rallies and continual rounds of protests, had the cumulative effect of distinguishing the Jewish crucible from the numerous other aggrieved groups Soviet misrule was heir to.

Little sense can be made of the Soviet Jewry movement without first understanding the role the Jackson-Vanik and the Stevenson amendments played in generating such awareness. Their significance lies not in the economic threat they posed for the Kremlin. More than anything else the Jackson-Vanik Amendment catapulted the issue of Jewish emigration to the top of the Cold War agenda. The surprise lies in the origin of the amendment with a group of Jewish congressional assistants and the behind-the-scenes support of Israel's liaison bureau. Few had foreseen that the so called Bunker group could be a source for amplifying Jewish influence on the Hill. The involvement of Jewish legislators, such as Sen. Javits and Sen. Ribicoff, the Bunker group, and Israel's liaison bureau is well known. Even today the boldness of their strategy and its implementation seems breathtaking.

Less attention had been paid to the non-Jewish sources of the legislation. Henry Jackson, Charles Vanik, Adlai Stevenson III, and the dozens of other legislators mentioned in these pages were not Jewish, nor were they necessarily serving a Jewish constituency. Sometimes it seemed as though both the NCSJ and the UCSJ were faced with a fait accompli hatched in Congress by the Bunker group. It is likely that in the context of the Cold War a feeling of helping captive people carried with it a certain "psychic income." If in addition one could do well, garner some political support and IOUs, while doing good, helping an oppressed people, all the better. Human rights advocacy, we note, had a sizeable constituency in Congress that went beyond the Jewish interest.

For this study the most significant fact is that the critical lever that brought the Soviet Jewry issue to the fore in the international arena originated not with the formally organized Soviet Jewry movement but in the halls of Congress. But without the drumbeat of attention-getting activity generated by the organizations that called attention to the problem little action would have been forthcoming from Congress. It was the strong support of the Soviet Jewry issue in Congress that encouraged and sometimes pressured the administrations in power to repeatedly question Soviet authorities regarding the treatment of its Jews.

The politics behind the amendment are intriguing, but after Moscow's formal repudiation of the new trade law in 1975 the role it played in actually gaining the release of refuseniks was minimal. It had done its job merely by raising the question. It also littered the historical landscape with practical and moral dilemmas. Granting most-favored-nation (MFN) status and access to credit to Moscow was not unlike the payment of ransom. The back-channel bargaining Kissinger undertook in 1974 meant dealing with a Soviet regime that was in effect selling rights that in the free world belonged to every citizen. Was it worth surrendering the moral high ground to save lives and lighten the burden of the refuseniks? For observant Jews the problem was even more complex. Though the ransom of prisoners (*pidyon shivuim*) has the highest priority in Jewish law, there was some question whether Soviet emigrants could actually be defined as prisoners.

The practical dilemmas were equally daunting. For example, by failing to soften the waiver provision of the amendment in 1979, was an opportunity missed to bring many emigrants out by a phased emigration, thereby avoiding the lean years between 1980 and 1987? It is possible to conclude that the amendment worked more as a public relations tactic than wringing concessions by withholding MFN. The underlying assumption that the Soviet economy was so pressed for credit that Soviet leaders would be induced to make concessions on Jewish emigration in order to get MFN and the credit line that came with it does not hold up well in retrospect. From the outset the assumption that Soviet domestic policies such as emigration were extrinsically driven, known as the barometer theory, was questionable. Moscow refused almost entirely to deal with the emigration question in the teeth of a severe economic crisis during the early Reagan years between 1980 and 1987. Clearly, when matters of prestige or ideology were concerned, the barometer thesis was not operative. It appeared as if Soviet emigration policy was primarily driven by internal factors that had little to do with trade and credit, which was also available from other nations as often were the high technology items embargoed by law. The picture was complicated by the inconsistency of American economic pressure, especially when it came to the export of grain. During the Nixon, Carter, and Reagan administrations it sometimes seemed as if America was more anxious to sell its surplus grain than the Soviets were to buy it.

The Soviet emigration problem became one of several instruments in the hands of those opposed to détente. The amendment aroused the ire of Sen. Fulbright and others who became convinced that American Jews were exercising too much influence in shaping American foreign policy. Their conviction was reinforced by the fact that Sen. Henry Jackson was able to hold Henry Kissinger's détente policy hostage over the Soviet Union's immigration policy. Without intention American Jewry found itself in the middle of a bitter struggle over the tenets of Cold War strategy embodied in the policy of détente. The weakened Nixon presidency deepened the problem by adding another dimension to the problem. The political campaign to pass the amendment became in effect a struggle over who should control foreign policy, Congress or the president. But little could be done to allay the image of a Jewish-sponsored "hijacking" of America's Soviet policy held by some legislators. A half century after the Holocaust American Jewish discomfort at occupying the center of the historical stage was balanced by its need to this time play its advocacy role fully, something it was thought Jewish leaders failed to do during the Roosevelt years.

While the Jackson Amendment remained in play until 1992, evaluating its contribution to the successful resolution of the emigration problem is difficult. We have noted that it was not the major source of economic pressure on the Soviets and that after Moscow's repudiation of Kissinger's back-channel agreement that would have bypassed its effects, the Soviets simply refused to do emigration business under the threat of the amendment. The amendment remained in the background but the emigration struggle was then spearheaded by the human rights movement and the Helsinki follow-up conferences. Emigration could now be advocated, not as a reward for victimization, but as an inalienable human right. Some had argued all along that that is where the emigration issue belonged.

The impact of the Soviet Jewry movement in America rested in some measure on its ability to mobilize American public opinion. Once it was established as an issue that could draw the Jewish and American public, there developed a possibility of placing it on the Cold War agenda. How that was achieved is detailed in the preceding chapters. I have grouped the manifold tactics developed to gain the attention of the Jewish and general public under the rubric of public relations, but the term does not fully encompass the many techniques used to "Let My People Know."

The ongoing imaginative public relations campaign that culminated in the giant mass rally in Washington in December 1987 is perhaps the movement's greatest contribution. The impassioned demonstrations, the rallies, the bracelets, the brilliant slogans, may not always have had an immediate impact in Moscow, but they projected a sense of an organized effort, a movement at the grassroots level. There seems to have been no central authority to orchestrate activities, and that may have been the source of the abundance of techniques developed. But the openness also had its drawbacks. Most activists opposed the confrontational tactics used by the JDL. Yet the "Never Again" slogan, which linked the "rescue" of Soviet Jewry to the Holocaust, had high resonance that was heard in all corners of the community.

Whether the public relations campaign focused on demanding the release of specific refuseniks or organized a speaking trip for Avital Sharansky, there was a common denominator. It fed the pervasive image of the Soviet Union as human rights trespasser. Its persona as a denier of god-given rights became so pervasive, even among its own people, that ultimately it undermined confidence in the regime. The Sharansky trial and imprisonment might well have remained one of countless unsung cases of injustice had it not been for the ability to use Avital to publicize the cruelty of keeping a loving couple apart. It was a situation with which the entire world could sympathize. What is puzzling is how a government so well practiced in agitprop (agitational propaganda) could repeatedly subvert its own public image. As happened in the case of the Berlin airlift, the Soviets allowed themselves to become the heavies in the case of emigration. Like the penchant for show trials during the thirties, the arrest and trial of refuseniks as in the Leningrad hijacking and the education head tax became grist for the public relations mill. The effectiveness of that public relations effort was in its ability to take an egregious incident and make it a worldwide concern, much the way the Soviets did with the Rosenberg espionage case.

In the calculus of power the cumulative impact of public relations tends to be underestimated. Regimes such as the Soviet Union are thought to be resistant to moral suasion. If it was moral, after all, it would not be involved in depredations. Yet slogans such as "Let My People Go" or "Prisoners of Zion" had a biblical ring that enhanced their resonance in the West and the East. The movement's talent for conceiving slogans that had almost immediate mass appeal and could awaken sympathy among non-Jews had an impact. It became apparent after the advent of Gorbachev when there was a Soviet desire to legitimate itself by adopting Western standards of human rights.

Answers for the remaining unsolved problems regarding the impact of the Soviet Jewry movement might be found if we understood more about what caused the collapse of the Soviet system. At the moment of its collapse the Soviet regime lacked few of the military accoutrements that normally figure in the power calculus. It had the largest army in the world and a nuclear arsenal that could destroy civilization, if it so willed. From the Kremlin's perspective, its confrontation with the Soviet Jewry movement on the public relations front might initially have seemed less foreboding than the popular uprisings in Berlin (1953), Hungary (1956), or Czechoslovakia (1968). Yet these were as easily lanced by military force as a boil and allowed to heal. The Jewish confrontation, however, was self-generating and sustained. It could not be made to disappear by military action. Strangely, although a direct military threat to its security had priority, the Soviet authorities were also inordinately concerned about the loss of the good opinion of the world. The public relations of the Soviet Jewry movement made a disproportionate contribution to that negativity and did so with no expenditures needed from Washington.

In the last analysis, it was the energetic effort to keep the story in the news through the efforts of the hundreds of activist and volunteers that marks one of the major contributions of the movement. Whether it was achieved through protest rallies or any one of the imaginative tactics often copied from the civil rights or antiwar movement, public relations became an essential movement activity. Rabbi Israel Miller, an early founder of the movement, concluded that without the protests and rallies and demonstrations before Soviet consulates, without international conferences in Brussels and other cities, the movement would have come to nothing. It was that visibility that allowed the right of emigration to become a priority item on the Cold War agenda. Without it the story of the Soviet Jews might never have surfaced. Yet, lest we misstate its role, although public relations was crucial for getting the problem known and sometimes, as in the case of the education head tax in 1972, could cause the Soviets to back off a particularly onerous policy, by itself it was insufficient to change basic Soviet policy. It was only after reform was underway that the cumulative impact of the human rights movement as embodied in the Helsinki follow-up conferences became apparent.

■ Organizations such as the NCSJ and the UCSJ represented the community's voice that speaks to power holders. But that voice would not be audible if the promise of political rewards in the form of votes, campaign funding, and other forms of support were not part of a political transaction. Many worthy causes are never heard in the corridors of power because of the inability of its advocates to amplify it beyond their immediate circle. The campaign for Soviet Jewry was an early instance in American Jewish history where the full utilization of its new sources of power was based no longer only on numbers, but on its ability to amplify its influence through fund-raising and its strong representation as communicators, political pundits, speech writers, poll takers, campaign managers, and all kinds of specialized policy "wonks." American Jewry came close to projecting such political pressure only in 1948 when the recognition of Israel was at stake and the Democratic Party was in desperate need of their votes. But in the decades that followed its proportion of the electorate declined, and these supplementary ways of amplifying influence developed in their place. That growth in confidence and quickening of the Jewish political metabolism can be traced to the 1967 war. After Israel's victory American Jewry went beyond being merely a small but influential ethnic voting bloc. Though compared to other ethnic voting blocs such as the Hispanic, the number of votes it could deliver decreased its representation in Congress as well as the state and municipal level grew. That expansion as an important factor in American politics must also be factored in to account for the success of its Soviet Jewry movement.

■ It would be surprising if the story of three separate streams of history compelled to interact in the context of the Cold War would leave the reader with a satisfactory feeling of closure. As is often the case in reconstructing the past this study raises as many questions as it answers. Among the most persistent is the question of historical weight. In the context of the Cold War how important was the movement's role in winning the release of the Jews and their protection in place?

In making that judgment much depends on the prism through which the event is viewed. We noted at the outset that the Soviet Jewry question overlaps several strands of history. That the emigration of Soviet Jewry loomed large on the American Jewish and Israeli historical canvas is a given. Less well known is that the Soviet Jewry issue played an important role in shaping the course of American foreign policy. Henry Kissinger often rued the fact that the immigration policy of a sovereign state, which international and American law considers to be an internal matter, was being used by his opponents to undermine the mainstay of his approach to foreign relations with the Soviet Union. His view that the accommodation of a lethally armed superpower had to take precedence over the welfare of a comparative handful of Soviet Jews was not easily countered. But the acceptance of the notion that the treatment of its Jews was an "internal matter" was also not acceptable and did not rule out the possibility of convincing the Kremlin to change its policy. That is what the Soviet Jewry movement tried to do, and the enlisting of the American government to realize their goals was a legitimate part of that. The possibility of realizing their goals without the full support of the American government was very remote. The success of the movement in involving a reluctant American government was an important achievement. Once it was involved the historical weight of the issue was enhanced. That too might be attributed to the Jackson-Vanik Amendment.

What motivated and sustained activists in a seemingly hopeless struggle is a source of wonderment. What we see, after all, is an outside agency, composed of several disparate organizations, seeking to shape the public policy of the Soviet superpower notorious for disregarding the will of its own citizenry. The movement could protest, cajole, and in any way possible try to influence political decision makers, but by its own efforts it could not produce a new historical datum. Governments do not customarily negotiate with foreign voluntary organizations. That was the role of the American government through whom it was compelled to act. Although the five administrations often pressed the case of emigrants informally, for various reasons the executive branch was less able and willing to play the advocate role. Congress had no such problems and could act as the governments gadfly.

The better part of wisdom in determining whose history has the strongest claim on these events might have been to simply treat the Soviet Jewry movement as part of Jewish history and let it go at that. But once the American government was involved even in a minimal way it became difficult to determine to whose history the movement belongs. One soon discovers that the fate of the Soviet Jews was not in Jewish hands. For their own interests governments outside the Jewish arena became involved. The Soviet Jewry movement was called upon to influence these others to act on behalf of a beleaguered Jewry. The Jackson-Vanik Amendment that catapulted the Soviet Jewry problem onto the world stage was not passed by a Jewish parliament. Yet the players in the movement, the activists, the refuseniks, the organizers of the conferences and Solidarity Sundays, were acting as Jews, on behalf of other Jews. The Soviet Jewry problem and the movement to which it gave birth remind us again of how anomalous is the Jewish position in history. It is a minor player on the historical stage yet the role it is compelled to play brings it to the center of the drama.

Measuring the importance of the role each component of the Soviet Jewry movement played is a thankless task because no branch, Israel's liaison bureau, Soviet Jewish activists, the American movement, could have achieved it alone. Nechemia Levanon, who played a crucial role for Israel, acknowledged as much when he called it a "concerted effort" even while crediting Israel with finding Soviet Jewry and building the movement to extricate them.[12] There are undoubtedly others who would grant the major credit to the American movement or the heroic role played by activists in the Soviet Union. A simple formula might credit Soviet refuseniks with the daring task of challenging the Soviet control system and raising the issue, Israel with finding the "lost" Jews of Russia and building the network that allowed the movement to sustain itself, and American Jews with mobilizing the public relations and political advocacy skills to get them out. But such a simple division of labor does not encompass the full complex historical picture. As incompatible as the relationship often seemed it was the synergy between them that made the total effort greater than the sum of its parts and set the stage for success.

The focus of this study is on the American movement, so perhaps it warrants a more precise measuring of its contribution. That is what this study tries to do by examining the role of the advocates and those officials who listened to their message. Once the data are in hand it becomes possible to pose the most fearsome question of all. How did the way American Jewry fulfill its responsibilities in relation to the Roosevelt administration compare with the way it met its responsibility toward Soviet Jewry. It includes its advocacy before the American government, particularly the Congress, which submitted dozens of legislative proposals aside from the Jackson-Vanik Amendment to the five administrations who were often less than happy with the constant agitation about Soviet Jewry. (The roles of Sen. Jackson and George Shultz would be excluded from the list of government officials who wished the problem would go away.) The role of the numerous communal leaders and "activists" in the American Jewish community whose names appear in these pages would have to be acknowledged. Credit would also have to be given to the American human rights movement, particularly Rep. Dante Fascell and Rep. Millicent Fenwick who established and then managed the American Helsinki monitoring operation. Finally, to all that must be added the circumstance of the Cold War, which amplified the Jewish case against Moscow and without which the Soviet Jewry movement would have been far less effective.

In the American Jewish response to the Holocaust, which we have noted haunted its Soviet Jewry movement, researchers have a standard of comparison to judge, however hesitatingly, its performance. We do so in the face of our prior insistence that the analogy between the two crises is in some ways misleading. The results are surprising. A generation of continued assimilation after the Holocaust, the leadership cohort that held the reins of communal power was more confident, more knowledgeable, and keener to find the levers of power and to pull them than were its predecessors. The figure of Nahum Goldmann, whose leadership spanned both events, also allows for some interesting conclusions regarding "quiet diplomacy," which he counseled would be a more effective alternative in both instances, especially if he were the diplomat. Admittedly, the chances for amelioration sometimes appeared to be better in dealing with Moscow than Berlin. But concerning the use of "quiet diplomacy," when dealing with dictatorial regimes that target Jews with a special animus, the judgment of history seems fairly clear. It failed miserably during the Holocaust and was little more effective between 1967 and 1989. Something more is required to compel such governments to cease their depredations.

■ Our story ends with a flood of emigrants poised to leave the Soviet Union. The struggle for Soviet emigration is over. David has beaten Goliath. The challenge of extricating Soviet Jewry now gives way to another problem. Will the Jews who chose to remain in the chaotic sometimes dangerous world of post-Communist Russia be able to restore some semblance of Jewish communal life and culture? Much of the answer depends on the vantage of the viewer. Israel, as a matter of course, continues to welcome the emigrants and despite grave absorption problems remains convinced that the place for Soviet Jewry, for that matter of all Jewry, is in the Jewish homeland. American Jews, though still professing to favor "choice," have like Shoshana Cardin, the last chairwoman of the NCSJ, come to view Israel as the choice that had to be given precedence.[13] The reluctance of russified Jews to believe in the promise of emigration also persisted. One former emigrant visiting Moscow was chagrined at the drive to get all the Soviet Jews out.

"Why are you in the West only talking about emigration? Our major problem is anti-Semitism. I want my grandchild to be admitted to Moscow University, not to drive a cab in New York."[14] That Jewish drive for place rather than identity was especially noted in the post-1989 emigration. Under Gorbachev's perestroika there was a last-minute effort to restore accessibility for Jews, but the realization that it was a crucial factor in motivating the Jewish emigration came too late. In a strange twist of history and as if aware of the enormous loss Russia has sustained as a result of the emigration of 90 percent of its Jews, President Vladimir Putin expressed a desire for their return to Russia.[15] There was no reported crush for visas at Soviet consulates, yet from the beginning of the exodus there was a trickle of returnees to Moscow and Leningrad. Like the Jews of Germany of the thirties, Russian Jews loved "mother" Russia, only to discover that it was unrequited. Whether the long and troubled course of Russian Jewish life comes to an end with the emigration has yet to be revealed by history.

In contrast, the performance of the American Soviet Jewry movement dispels such doubts about the American Jewish future, at least for the moment. It had to do many things in mobilizing itself, but its most difficult task was to provide the "noise" so that ears that did not want to hear were compelled to listen. It broke through the curtain of silence as Jewish leaders were unable to do during the years of the Holocaust, which needs to be considered by the survey researchers who project that we are in the final chapter of Jewish experience in America. Whatever weaknesses the American Soviet Jewry movement may have had, and there were many, it was not the performance of a moribund community.

Abbreviations
Notes
Glossary
Index

Abbreviations ■

AFC	Anti-Fascist Committee
AIPAC	American Israel Public Affairs Committee
AJC	American Jewish Committee
AJCong	American Jewish Congress
AJCSJ	American Jewish Conference on Soviet Jewry
CCSA	Committee on Soviet Anti-Semitism
CJC	Congress For Jewish Culture
CJF	Council of Jewish Federations and Welfare Funds
CPSU	Communist Party of the Soviet Union
CSCE	Commission on Security and Cooperation in Europe
FRUS	U.S. State Department's *Foreign Relations of the United States* series
GNYCSJ	Greater New York Conference on Soviet Jewry
HIAS	Hebrew Immigrant Aid Society
INS	Immigration and Naturalization Service
JAFI	Jewish Agency for Israel
JDC	American Jewish Joint Distribution Committee
JDL	Jewish Defense League
JLC	Jewish Labor Committee
JLM	Jewish Labor Movement
JTA	*Jewish Telegraph Agency Daily News Bulletin*
KOMZET	Soviet Government Agency for Crimean Resettlement
MFN	most-favored-nation status granted to U.S. trading partners
NCSJ	National Conference on Soviet Jewry
NGO	nongovernmental organization
NJCRAC	National Jewish Community Relations Advisory Council
NYPL	New York Public Library
OVIR	Office of Visas and Registration, the Soviet bureau for processing visa requests
SALT	Strategic Arms Limitation Talks
SSSJ	Student Struggle for Soviet Jewry

UJA   United Jewish Appeal
UCSJ   Union of Councils for Soviet Jewry
WJC   World Jewish Congress
WZO   World Zionist Organization

Notes ■

1. Historic Seeds

1. Samuel Joseph, *Jewish Immigration to the United States from 1881 to 1910* (New York: Arno Press, 1969), 93.

2. Cyrus Adler and Aaron Margalith, *With Firmness in the Right: American Diplomatic Action Affecting Jews, 1840–1945* (New York: Arno Press, 1977), 172.

3. J. J. Goldberg, "Kishinev 1903, The Birth of a Century," *Forward,* 4 Apr. 2003, 14.

4. Gary D. Best, *To Free a People: American Jewish Leaders and the Jewish Problem in Eastern Europe, 1890–1914* (Westport, Conn.: Greenwood Press, 1982), 30–31.

5. S. Ettinger, "The Jews in Russia at the Outbreak of the Revolution," in *The Jews in Soviet Russia Since 1917,* 3rd. ed., edited by Lionel Kochan (Oxford: Oxford Univ. Press, 1978), 22.

6. Cyrus Adler, *Jacob H. Schiff: His Life and Letters* (Garden City: Doubleday, Doran, 1928), vol. 1, Schiff to T. Roosevelt, 8 Dec. 1905, 137.

7. Kenton J. Clymer, "Anti-Semitism in the Late Nineteenth Century, The Case of John Hay," *Publications of the American Jewish Historical Society* 60 (June 1971): 351.

8. Philip E. Schoenberg, "The American Reaction to the Kishinev Pogrom of 1903," *American Jewish Historical Quarterly* 63 (Mar. 1974): 262–83.

9. Taylor Stults, "Roosevelt, Russian Persecution of Jews, and American Public Opinion," *Jewish Social Studies* 33, no. 1 (Jan. 1971): 13–22.

10. See Louis L. Gerson, *The Hyphenate in Recent American Politics and Diplomacy* (Lawrence: Univ. of Kansas Press, 1964), and William Korey, *The Promises We Keep: Human Rights, the Helsinki Process and American Foreign Policy* (New York: St. Martin's, 1993), 5ff.

11. J. William Fulbright, *The Crippled Giant: American Foreign Policy and Its Domestic Consequences* (New York: Random House, 1972), 109.

12. U.S. Congress, House, Committee on Immigration and Naturalization, *Hearings on Restriction of Immigration,* HR 5616, 8th Cong., 1st sess., 3 Jan. 1924, 388–89. The response of the committee chairman was that Jews should have taken care to be born in Scotland.

13. The one-third refers to the vision projected by Konstantin Pobedonostsev, an advisor to Alexander III, which saw the solution to Russia's Jewish problem as requiring one-third of Russian Jewry to perish, one-third to become totally assimilated, and one-third to emigrate.

14. Naomi W. Cohen, *Jacob H. Schiff: A Study in American Jewish Leadership* (Hanover, N.H.: Brandeis Univ. Press, 1999), 138.

15. Decter's seminal role in the Soviet Jewry movement is examined in chapter 3.

16. Cohen, *Schiff,* 130.

17. Louis Marshall (LM) to Laueterbach, 9 July 1912. *American Jewish Archives,* L. Marshall MS, box 1581. Interestingly, the Leningrad hijacking trial and the numerous other trials between 1967 and 1989 posed no such problems for activists.

18. William Korey, "Rescuing Russian Jewry: Two Episodes Compared," *Soviet Jewish Affairs* 5, no. 1 (1975): 3–19.

19. See Naomi W. Cohen, "The Abrogation of the Russo-American Treaty of 1832," *Jewish Social Studies,* 25 (Jan. 1963): 3–41. The bypassing of Goldfogle in favor of the non-Jewish Parsons went beyond strategy. Marshall's dislike of Goldfogle's tactics was involved. See LM to Goldfogle, L. Marshall MS, box 1580, 11 Mar. 1911.

20. Cohen, *Schiff,* 144–45.

21. The transportation problem and other logistical problems proved so difficult to overcome that by 1918 when things were already changing in Russia the unit had not yet left the United States. See LM to Lansing, 9 Apr. 1917, and LM to J. Schiff, 13 Nov. 1917, L. Marshall MS, box 1587.

22. LM to S. S. Ochs, 25 Apr. 1917, L. Marshall MS, box 1587.

23. Marshall particularly foresaw the danger this linkage between Bolshevism and Judaism posed for Jews. See LM to Julian Mack, 12 Dec. 1918, L. Marshall MS. box 1588.

24. Best, *To Free a People,* 214.

25. LM to editor, *The Jerseyman,* 10 Feb. 1919, L. Marshall MS, box 1589.

26. Jacob Schiff passed away in 1920, Simon Wolf and Mayer Sulzberger in 1922, Oscar Strauss in 1926, and Louis Marshall in 1929.

27. LM to Reuben Fink, 4 Sept. 1919, L. Marshall MS, box 1589.

28. See Baila Shargel, *Practical Dreamer: Israel Friedlander and the Shaping of American Judaism* (New York: Jewish Theological Seminary of America, 1985).

29. By 1970, even after a sharp decline in university enrollment, Soviet Jewry remained the most highly educated national group in the Soviet Union with four times as many university graduates as the Georgians, the next highest group. V. Zaslavsky and R. J. Brym, *Soviet-Jewish Emigration and Soviet Nationality Policy* (New York: St. Martin's, 1983), 14–15.

30. Annelise Orleck, *The Soviet Jewish Americans* (Westport, Conn.: Greenwood, 1999), 17ff.

31. Jews remained the largest ethnic group in the Communist Party of the Soviet Union between 1967 and 1989. Rita Simon, *In the Golden Land: A Century of Russian and Soviet Jewish Immigration in America* (Westport, Conn.: Praeger, 1997), 49–50.

32. Leon Shapiro, introduction to Kochan, *Jews in Soviet Russia,* 1–14.

33. Between 1917 and 1925 there were 250 Jewish schools in the Ukraine and a number of Jewish theatrical companies, and as late as 1935, years after the sovietization effort had been abandoned, there still were ten Yiddish newspapers in the Ukraine and hundreds of Yiddish writers and artists. As late as 1959 almost a half million Soviet Jews listed Yiddish as their mother tongue. S. Levenberg, "Soviet Jewry: Some Problems and Perspectives," in Kochan, *Jews in Soviet Russia,* 39–40.

34. Socialist Zionism was a real contender for Soviet Jewish loyalties. In October 1917 Russian Zionist organizations had a membership of about 300,000 organized in 1,200 units. That may have been a factor in Moscow's anti-Zionist fixation.

35. The full story is best told in Melech Epstein, *The Jew and Communism: The Story of Early Communist Victories and Ultimate Defeats in the Jewish Community, U.S.A., 1919–1941* (New York: Trade

Union Sponsoring Committee, 1959), 126–50, and David Dubinsky and A. H. Raskin, *David Dubinsky: A Life with Labor* (New York: Simon and Schuster, 1977).

36. Editorial, *American Hebrew*, 11 Mar. 1921.

37. Allan L. Kagedan, *Soviet Zion: The Quest for a Russian Jewish Homeland* (New York: St. Martin's 1994). C. Abramsky, "The Biro-Bidzhan Project, 1927–1959," in Kochan, *Jews in Soviet Russia*, 64–77.

38. Levenberg, "Soviet Jewry," 34–36.

39. Yehuda Bauer, *My Brother's Keeper: A History of the American Jewish Joint Distribution Committee, 1929–1939* (Philadelphia: Jewish Publication Society of America, 1974), 57–62.

40. Quoted in Israel S. Wechsler, *Modern Judaism* 13, no. 4 (Aug. 1927): 392.

41. Lawrence Bachmann, "Julius Rosenwald," *American Jewish Historical Quarterly*, 66, no. 1, Sept. 1976, 103.

42. For a summary of the arguments, see Henry L. Feingold, *A Time for Searching: Entering the Mainstream, 1920–1945* (Baltimore: Johns Hopkins Univ. Press, 1992), 177–82.

43. C. Adler to H. J. Rubin, 26 Nov. 1934, and C. Adler to L. Finkelstein, 27 Dec. 1934. Adler, *Jacob H. Schiff*, vol. 2, 288–89.

44. One estimate puts the percentage of Jews in the Lincoln Brigade, the American contingent of the International Brigade, at 30 percent of the 2,800 recruits. Ten to 18 percent of the 18,000 men in the brigade are estimated to have been Jewish. Haim Avni, *Spain, the Jews, and Franco*, translated by Emanuel Shimoni (Philadelphia: Jewish Publication Society of America, 1982), and Albert Prago, "Fifty Long Years Later: Commemorating The Spanish Civil War," *Jewish Currents*, Mar. 1987. Two Soviet Jewish generals, Grigory Shtern and Kleber, served as advisors to the Republican army.

45. Mel Scult, ed., *Communings of the Spirit: The Journals of Mordecai Kaplan, Volume 1: 1913–1934* (Detroit, 2001), 137.

46. Earl Browder, *The Jewish People and the War*, Worker's Library, May 1940, 7 (mimeographed). Found in American Jewish Committee Wiener Library in a folder entitled "Communist, Jews, and Communist Party Propaganda."

47. Sidney Hook, "Promise Without Dogma: A Sound Philosophy for Jews," *Modern Judaism* 25, no. 3 (Oct.–Dec. 1937): 274–75.

48. A full description of that role is contained in Zvi Gitelman, "The Soviet Union," in *The World Reacts to the Holocaust*, edited by David Wyman (Baltimore: Johns Hopkins Univ. Press, 1996), 295–324.

49. Ibid., 304. Gitelman estimates that if the 200,000 Jewish combat casualties are included as many as 1.7 million of the pre-1939 Jewish population did not survive the war. One estimate of the losses rates it as from 2.5 to 3 million. Petrus Buwalda, *They Did Not Dwell Alone: Jewish Emigration from the Soviet Union, 1967–1997* (Washington, D.C.: Woodrow Wilson Center Press, 1997), 15ff. Orleck, *Soviet Jewish Americans*, 25ff, and R. Ainsztain, "Soviet Jewry in the Second World War," in Kochan, *Jews in Soviet Russia*, 281–99. Both place Jewish losses at 1.5 million.

50. See Gitelman, "Soviet Union," 309, and Orleck, *Soviet Jewish Americans*, 25.

51. Gitelman, "Soviet Union,", 306–15. See also William Korey, "Down History's Memory Hole: Soviet Treatment of the Holocaust," *Present Tense*, no. 10 (winter 1983): 53.

52. Quoted in *Modern Judaism* 3 (Oct.–Dec. 1943): 296–99.

2. Setting the Stage

1. That trend first became apparent with the accessibility of Soviet archives and the publication of Arno J. Mayer, *Why Did the Heavens Not Darken?: The "Final Solution" in History,* (New York: Pantheon, 1988).

2. Folk humor suggesting that Jews fought on the front lines of Tashkent, a favorite resort city far removed from fighting, continued to be popular currency long after the war. Yaakov Ro'i, *The Struggle for Soviet Jewish Emigration, 1948–1967* (Cambridge: Cambridge Univ. Press, 1991), 17.

3. The recognition was portrayed in the Soviet press as Jews waging "armed struggle" against British imperialism. That opened a way for Soviet Jews to become interested in Zionism as a "Progressive" force. Ibid., 21. See also Robert Freedman, "Soviet Jewry as a Factor in Soviet-Israeli Relations," in *Soviet Jewry in the 1980s: The Politics of Anti-Semitism and Emigration and the Dynamics of Resettlement,* edited by Robert Freedman (Durham: Duke Univ. Press, 1989), 64–65.

4. The sale of arms was not based on ideology or altruism. The revenue-starved Czech republic, which Moscow had forbidden to accept Marshall Plan aid, was also selling its surplus arms to Syria in April 1948. One such ship, the *Lino,* was intercepted and sunk by the Hagana. Arnold Krammer, *The Forgotten Friendship: Israel and the Soviet Bloc, 1947–1953* (Urbana: Univ. of Illinois Press, 1974), 69, 81.

5. The reaction of some Soviet Jews was a heady optimism. See Yehoshua Gilboa, "The 1948 Zionist Wave in Moscow," *Soviet Jewish Affairs* 1, no. 2 (Nov. 1971): 35–39.

6. Such assurances were again given by Soviet officials in 1947. Boris Morozov, *Documents on Soviet Jewish Emigration* (London: Frank Cass, 1999), 8.

7. Hungarian Jews could obtain exit visas for Israel until the end of 1948. By February 1949, of Hungary's 150,000 surviving Jews, only those older than fifty could obtain such visas. In that year 6,830 Hungarian Jews settled in Israel. By the end of 1949 Poland had released 47,343 Jews to Israel and Romania, with the largest Jewish community of 350,000, released 13,596. But Romania would prove to be a special case. Before 1989 it boasted the largest aliyah to Israel. Krammer, *Forgotten Friendship,* 153ff.

8. The best description of these events is contained in Yehoshua Gilboa, *The Black Years of Soviet Jewry, 1939–1953,* translated by Yosef Shachter and Dov BenAbba (Boston: Little, Brown, 1971), 226–27. It includes an account of the strange twist that the Crimean resettlement project took in Stalin's mind. He saw it as an attempt to detach the Crimea and use it as a military base aimed at the Soviet Union.

9. Mapam received only 14.5 percent of the vote, and the largely Arab Communist Party of Israel received 3.44 percent.

10. Aside from the crush of well-wishers before the synagogue, Meir was also well received by government officials. Reading Meir's description reinforced Ben-Gurion's notion that Russia's Jewish millions might yet be claimed for Israel. Golda Meir, *My Life* (London: G. P. Putnam, 1975), 238–52.

11. The warning was contained in an article in *Pravda* and was also presented to Mordecai Namir, the legal counselor of Israel's Moscow legation, on 2 Dec. 1948. Krammer, *Forgotten Friendship,* 126. A consular inquiry concerning the possibility of emigration of certain Soviet Jews may also have contributed to Stalin's suspicion.

12. Meir, *My Life,* 254.

13. Recent researchers question whether there ever was a plan for mass deportation. See Samson Madievski, "The Doctor's Plot," *Midstream* 49, no. 6 (Sept.–Oct. 2003): 12.

14. In 1935 Jewish students accounted for 13 percent of university enrollment. By the 1960s it had declined to 2.5 percent. Jewish representation remained disproportionately high, especially in the theater arts. By 1976–77 the figure was down to 1.4 percent. Orleck, *Soviet Jewish Americans,* 39–41. Another rationale relates the exclusion to Soviet concern about restlessness in the Asian Islamic Republics of the Federation. It would be counteracted by inviting their elites into Soviet universities. See also Zaslavsky and Brym, *Soviet-Jewish Emigration,* 18–19.

15. In a sense belonging to the intelligentsia or the professional strata was a Soviet version of the "good life." It was comparatively well paid for shorter hours, and day care, often organizational cars, and dachas were available. It was the Soviet equivalent of the upper middle class in the West.

16. Three days later the Soviet mission was recalled and Israel was asked to do the same. Diplomatic relations were renewed on 20 July 1953.

17. Between 1956 and 1963 most surviving synagogues were closed. In the Ukraine most of those convicted for economic crimes such as embezzlement were Jews, and so were almost 50 percent of the more than 200 "criminals" executed. Freedman, "Soviet Jewry as a Factor," 64.

18. Quoted in William Korey, *The Soviet Cage: Anti-Semitism in Russia* (New York: Viking, 1973), 35. It is likely that the same sensitivity to opinion abroad was behind the reinstitution of *Sovietish Heimland* as a bimonthly under the editorship of Aron Vergelis in 1962. Much of its 25,000 circulation was distributed abroad.

19. Memoranda from D. Shevliagin and A. Beliakov to the CPSU Central Committee, 17 May 1966 and 3 Oct. 1966. Both memoranda concern inquiries from the Communist Party of Great Britain and the Italian Communist Party requesting information on Soviet Jewry to respond to "Bourgeois propaganda about discrimination against the Jewish population of the USSR." Morozov, *Documents,* 58–61.

20. The best analysis of the "shoot in the foot" phenomenon is contained in the dispatches of Ambassador Kohler. See Kohler to Rusk, 26 Feb. 1966, U.S. State Department, *Foreign Relations of the United States,* vol. 14, 1964–1968. See also Fred Coleman, *The Decline and Fall of the Soviet Empire: Forty Years That Shook the World, from Stalin to Yeltsin* (New York: St. Martin's, 1996), 113.

21. Laurie P. Salitan, *Politics and Nationality in Contemporary Soviet Jewish Emigration, 1968–89* (New York: St. Martin's, 1992), 174. In the summer of 1957 Eleanor Roosevelt made a similar inquiry to Khrushchev and was given a similar encouraging response: "The time will come when everyone who wants to go will be able to go." Quoted in Korey, *Soviet Cage,* 1–93.

22. An observation also made by Albert D. Chernin, "Making Soviet Jews an Issue: A History," in *A Second Exodus: The American Movement to Free Soviet Jews,* edited by Murray Friedman and Albert D. Chernin (Hanover, N.H.: Brandeis Univ. Press, 1999), 28–29.

23. A series of publications alerting the Jewish reading public to what was happening to Jewish communities behind the iron curtain was produced by these agencies. See, for example, "A Decade of Destruction: Jewish Culture in the USSR, 1948–1958," published by the Congress for Jewish Culture, and "Jews Behind the Iron Curtain," published by the Jewish Labor Committee (Feb. 1949).

24. But Leon Uris's *Exodus* (New York: Bantam Books, 1966), which told the story of hapless Jewish refugees pitting themselves against the British blockade, went on to become the most popu-

lar single book in Jewish samizdat and went far to awaken a sense of connectedness with world Jewry.

25. The hope that thousands would stampede to Israel after the establishment of the state was unfulfilled, especially after Israel's ability to absorb large numbers was found wanting. By 1949 only 24,500 displaced persons had arrived in Israel. Aware of the *Yishuv's* limited ability to absorb large numbers, Ben-Gurion and Arthur Ruppin favored a selective migration during the war. Dvora Ha-Cohen, *Immigrants in Turmoil: Mass Immigration to Israel in the 1950s and After* (Syracuse: Syracuse Univ. Press, 2003), 1–11, and Arieh Kochavi,*Post-Holocaust Politics: Britain, the United States, and Jewish Refugees, 1945–1948* (Chapel Hill: Univ. Of North Carolina Press, 2001), 105–10.

26. Several Israelis were falsely implicated and sentenced. Mordecai Oren was arrested in May 1951 and sentenced to fifteen years. He was released in 1956. But the indictment was never set aside by the Dubcek government's Commission of Inquiry of 1968.

27. This KGB report describes in detail the contact activities of the Israeli embassy staff and suggests ways to counteract them. Ivashutin was chairman of state security. Memorandum, P. Ivashutin to CPSU Central Committee, 3 Nov. 1959, Morozov, *Documents*, 45.

28. The Dutch provided the administrative help free of charge. The Netherlands considered itself Israel's "best friend" after the United States. There was "an element of repentance" in it, according to the Dutch ambassador in Moscow. Petrus Bewalda, *They Did Not Dwell Alone: Jewish Emigration from the Soviet Union, 1967–1990* (Baltimore: Johns Hopkins Univ. Press, 1997), 23.

29. The liaison bureau was referred to simply as Lishka, the Hebrew word for office.

30. Some of the credit for helping make these contacts is claimed by Max Kampleman, who went on to become a key advocate of the Helsinki Accords on human rights at the Madrid follow-up conference. Max M. Kampelman, *Entering New Worlds: The Memoirs of a Private Man in Public Life* (New York: Harper Collins, 1991), 195.

31. Interview with Yoram Dinstein, New York Public Library, Dorot Jewish Division, Wiener Oral History Project, 8 Nov. 1989. Hereafter the collection is abbreviated as NYPL, Wiener Oral History.

32. That exposure is a major theme in Deborah D. Moore, *To the Golden Cities: Pursuing the American Jewish Dream in Miami and L.A.* (Cambridge, Mass.: Harvard Univ. Press, 1996).

33. Edward S. Shapiro, *A Time for Healing: American Jewry since World War II* (Baltimore: Johns Hopkins Univ. Press, 1992), 125.

34. See Henry L. Feingold, "From Class Struggle to Struggle for Class," in *A Time for Searching: Entering the Mainstream, 1920–1945* (Baltimore: Johns Hopkins Univ. Press, 1992), 125 ff.

35. Jews gave 15 percent of their vote to Wallace, higher than any other ethnic voting block. Few seemed aware that an overwhelming 75 percent of the Jewish vote went to Truman.

36. The Rosenberg case was followed by two other "Jewish spy" cases: Judith Coplan was a secretary at the United Nations who was indicted for spying for the Soviet Union, and Colonel Rudolf Abel was a Soviet agent who operated out of Greenwich Village.

37. Raul Hilberg, *The Destruction of the European Jews* (Chicago: Quadrangle Books, 1961). A controversial description of the pervasive influence of the Holocaust on American Jewry and the misuses to which it was often put is contained in Peter Novick, *The Holocaust in American Life* (Boston: Houghton Mifflin, 1999). The publication of Arthur Morse's *While Six Million Died: A*

Chronicle of American Apathy (New York: Random House, 1968), followed by my own *The Politics of Rescue: The Roosevelt Administration and the Holocaust, 1938–1945* (New Brunswick, N.J.: Rutgers Univ. Press, 1970), had a considerable impact on the younger generation.

38. Quoted in Eli Lederhendler, *New York Jews and the Decline of Urban Ethnicity, 1950–1970* (Syracuse: Syracuse Univ. Press, 2001), 188.

39. Zvi Gitelman, "Soviet Jews: Creating a Cause and a Movement," in Friedman and Chernin, *Second Exodus*, 91–92.

40. William W. Orbach, *The American Movement to Aid Soviet Jews* (Amherst: Univ. of Massachusetts 1979), 23–24.

41. Interview with David Geller, NYPL, Wiener Oral History, 30 Apr. 1990.

42. The first formal contact was made by a group of five well-known rabbis who felt that the spring of 1956 might be a "propitious" time for contact. Surprisingly, they were granted visas and were everywhere well received and allowed to preach during their month-long stay. They did notice that many Jews, thinking that they were part of the government group represented by Rabbi Schliefer, the chief rabbi of Moscow, would not speak to them. Interview with Rabbi Herschel Schacter, NYPL, Wiener Oral History, 20 Sept. 1989.

43. The well-known letter written by Bertrand Russell to Khrushchev and other Soviet leaders on 25 Feb. 1963 was published and responded to in *Pravda* and *Izvestia*.

44. The matzoh protest was effective and was partly resolved in July 1963 after Rabbi Yehuda Levin, the chief Rabbi of Moscow, led a delegation of Soviet Rabbis to visit the United States. The New York Board of Rabbis then offered to supply matzohs to Soviet Jewry. A year after the imaginative "Matzoh of Oppression" campaign in 1966 the authorities permitted temporary matzoh bakeries to operate in certain cities. The Orthodox community in general, fearing that Jews would be endangered, counseled against militant protest and favored "quiet" diplomacy or negotiations.

45. Between 12 January and 29 July 1953, eighteen congressional resolutions were introduced in the House concerning religious persecution in the Soviet Union. Such notes, written in general terms, were sent by Averell Harriman, undersecretary of state, on 27 Oct. 1963, Richard Gardner (deputy assistant secretary) December 1963, Dean Rusk, secretary of state, April 1964. Upon solicitation, messages of support were sent to sundry rallies as low as the congregational level throughout 1964 to 1966. They became stronger and more frequent after the 1967 war. I have described them as part of a "politics of gesture" that garnered political points for the administration at no cost. See Feingold, *Politics of Rescue*. The early resolutions did not speak of emigration but confined themselves mostly to religious persecution.

46. For a description of this "fierce" pressure from other ethnic groups, see Cathal J. Nolan, *Principled Diplomacy: Security and Rights in U.S. Foreign Policy* (Westport, Conn.: Greenwood, 1993), 5.

47. Despite Yoram Dinstein's poor prognosis for the new organization, it succeeded in getting a resolution concerning Soviet Jewry in two both party platforms. But when it came to congressional resolutions, which passed overwhelmingly in the House on 23 Sept. 1964 and in the Senate on 14 May 1965, it was soon learned that they were watered down in an effort to make them interdenominational. In the context of the Cold War, separating a Jewish issue from general religious persecution was problematic in political terms.

48. The Soviet Jewry issue appeared in the budget of the CJF only in the mid-seventies when ab-

sorption and resettlement in local communities and the funding of agencies such as the Hebrew Immigrant Aid Society (HIAS) and New York Association for New Americans (NYANA) became urgent.

49. The best critique of the Jewish organizational malaise is contained in the MacIver report commissioned by the National Jewish Community Relations Advisory Council (NJCRAC) in 1951. The report's suggestion that Jewish communal life needed to be more centralized and coordinated was generally ignored.

50. Lederhendler, *New York Jews,* 187ff.

51. It was thought that Moscow would dismiss them as cold war initiatives. However, the department encouraged efforts of private American citizens and organizations "especially when joined in by leaders of all religious faiths and made on an international basis." William B. Mcomber Jr. (assistant secretary of state for congressional relations) to Rep. Clark MacGregor, 5 Dec. 1967, American Jewish Historical Society. National Conference on Soviet Jewry I, 181, box 30, State Department file, 1965–69.

52. The best firsthand description of the early development of the American Jewish response is written by Albert Chernin, who was himself deeply involved. See Chernin, "Making Soviet Jews an Issue," 59ff.

53. When Morris Abram was appointed to the UN Human Rights Commission, Meir Rosenne prevailed upon him to speak out against Soviet anti-Semitism. Abram was reluctant, but after the Kitchko incident he did so without instructions from the state department. Interview with Morris Abram, NYPL, Wiener Oral History, 6 Mar. 1989.

54. Interview with Yoram Dinstein, NYPL, Wiener Oral History Project, 8 Nov. 1989.

55. The Cleveland Federation was one of the first core groups to challenge the Israeli role. It went on to help form the UCSJ.

56. Dinstein traces the rebellion against Israel's authority in the movement to this incident, which had no relation to the Soviet Jewry issue. Interview with Yoram Dinstein, NYPL, Wiener Oral History Project, 8 Nov. 1989.

57. Ibid. Dinstein traces the decline to a conciliatory approach imposed on his successor Yehoshua Pratt with the result that there was "total chaos and total disintegration of Israeli authority in the field."

58. For example, when the newly formed AJCSJ organized its first protest rally at Madison Square Garden on 3 June 1965, Nahum Goldmann denounced the plan and particularly Phil Baum of the AJCong who had helped organize the rally. The difference between the SSSJ and the "establishment" AJCSJ also involved money and budget. When Jacob Birnbaum, a founder of the SSSJ, requested financial support from George Maislin, the head of the AJCSJ, he was turned down on the grounds that budgetary support required adherence to organizational ground rules. The real issue was the militancy of the new groups who insisted on the value of such tactics as picketing the Soviet consulate and UN mission.

59. In 1966 there were 2,027 visas issued, and before emigration was discontinued in June 1967 an additional 1,416 became available.

60. "Negro Leader Charges Soviet Embassy with Evasion on Jewish issue," *Jewish Telegraph Agency Daily News Bulletin* (hereafter *JTA*), 20 Mar. 1967.

61. The inclusion on the agenda was probably attributable to the efforts of Morris Abram, the

head of the U.S. delegation to the United Nations, and Arthur Goldberg. See Rabbi Israel Miller to Goldberg, NCSJ, box 30, State Department file, 1966–69, 23 Mar. 1967.

62. The appeal was a breakthrough in another respect. Heretofore Congress insisted on making such resolutions interdenominational, including discrimination in East European countries, and on diluting the specific animus against Jews. See Theodore Comet to Rep. Edna Kelly, NCSJ, box 31, House of Representatives file, 1965–70, n.d.

63. Memorandum of conversation, Dobrynin-Thompson, 16 June 1967, *FRUS,* 492–94.

64. Eli Lederhendler, ed., *The Six Day War and World Jewry* (Bethesda: Univ. Press of Maryland, 2000), 2. The fullest account of the events leading to war and the international reaction is contained in Michael Oren, *The Six Day War: June 1967 and the Making of the Modern Middle East* (New York: Ballantine, 2003).

65. See Peter Grose, *Israel in the Mind of America* (New York: Schocken Books, 1984), 309.

66. HaCohen, *Immigrants,* 253–57.

67. Gitelman, "Soviet Jews," 86–87.

68. Others pointed out that continued Arab dependency on Moscow required Israel to continue to exist. See Freedman, "Soviet Jewry as a Factor," 69–71. See also Zev Katz, "After the Six Day War," in Friedman and Chernin, *Second Exodus,* 133.

69. It was an extensive campaign. In 1969, ten books attacking Israel and Zionism were published. Between 1970 and 1974 the writing and publication of such books and pamphlets became a small industry. In that period there were seventy-four anti-Zionist publications, usually emphasizing the theme that Zionism was a species of racism. The campaign reached its zenith on 9 Nov. 1973 when the UN General Assembly passed its "Zionism Is Racism" resolution.

70. Ludmilla Alexeyeva, *Soviet Dissent: Contemporary Movements for National, Religious, and Human Rights,* translated by Carol Pearce and John Glad (Middletown, Conn.: Wesleyan Univ. Press 1985), 181.

71. Thomas Sawyer, *The Jewish Minority in the Soviet Union* (Boulder: Westview Press, 1979), 100, fn 75.

72. Clearly there was a latent national consciousness before the 1967 war that was released by the remarkable victory. It had an enormous emotional impact. See Zvi Gitelman, "The Psychological and Political Consequences of the Six-Day War in the U.S.S.R.," in Lederhendler, *Six Day War,* 249.

73. Memorandum from Iu. Andropov and A. Gromyko to the CPSU Central Committee and Draft Resolution of the CPSU Central Committee, Moscow, 10 June 1968. That plan dovetailed with Kosygin's "free to go" statement in Paris in 1966. Morozov, *Documents,* 65–66.

74. In some cases more than one-third of the names on the petitions were those of prominent Jewish intellectuals. Katz, "After the Six Day War," 333–40.

75. The rupture of diplomatic relations on 10 June 1967 was related to the activities of Israel's diplomatic staff in developing its contacts and communications network with Soviet Jewry. The war served as an opportunity by the KGB to finally put a stop to these activities. See Ro'i, *Struggle for Soviet Jewish Emigration,* 337.

76. Summary of discussion with U.S. ambassador to United Nations, Charles Yost, NCSJ, box 30, State Department folder, 1965–69, 22 Apr. 1969. Present were Richard Maass, Phil Baum, and Rabbi Israel Miller.

77. James W. Moore, "Immigration and the Demographic Balance in Israel and the Occupied Territories," *Middle East Policy* 1, no. 3 (1992): 99–103. Aryeh Pincus, chairman of the Jewish Agency Executive, called for at least 40,000 immigrants annually to cope with Israel's growing demographic problem. *JTA,* 9 Aug. 9 1967, 2.

78. In a get-acquainted meeting between the new Nixon administration State Department team and a Jewish delegation on 17 Mar. 1969, Elliot Richardson, the undersecretary of state, asked point blank about the demographic implications of the 1967 war and emigration. Thereafter, the question often came up. See "Summary of Discussion," NCSJ, box 30, State Department folder, 1965–69, 17 Mar. 1969.

79. Quoted in Edward Rothstein's review of Michael Oren's *Six Days of War,* in *New York Times,* 6 Jan. 2002, 15, book review section.

80. A State Department intelligence memorandum calls the decision "a most fateful one." "The USSR International Position after Czechoslovakia," 19 Sept. 1968, *FRUS,* 717–18.

81. Andrei Sakharov, *Memoirs,* translated by Richard Lourie (New York: Knopf, 1990), 290.

3. The Curtain Rises

1. After the war Israel switched from France to the United States as its arms supplier. The continued unwillingness of the Arab nations to accept the existence of Israel was expressed in the Khartoum declaration of August 1967.

2. In March 1970 Harry S. Dent, special counsel to the president, assured some Jewish leaders who feared the weak Jewish voter support would redound badly for Israel that the administration would not abandon its pledge of security for Israel and that it had not "given up" on the Jewish vote. *JTA,* 11 Mar. 1970, 3.

3. Dwight L. Chapin to Lewis Weinstein, NCSJ, box 30, Nixon Administration folder, 2 May 1969. "Official demands on [the president's] calendar" made it necessary to track the request to Henry Kissinger. After several new requests the pair finally was able to see Helmut Sonnenfeld to receive the customary assurances of concern.

4. "McGovern Accuses Nixon of Silence," *JTA,* 31 Aug. 1972.

5. Richard M. Nixon, *RN: The Memoirs of Richard Nixon* (New York: Grosset and Dunlap, 1978), 484–85.

6. Milton Shapp and Frank Licht, the Jewish governors of Pennsylvania and Rhode Island, both Democrats, threw their votes to McGovern at the tight convention and campaigned for him.

7. Usually Leonard Garment, Nixon's former law partner and liaison with the Jewish community, served as the primary conduit. For the Democrats, whose funding came primarily from Jewish sources, the Oval Office was much more accessible and distributed over many personages such as Max Kampelman, a Washington insider who was close to the Humphrey camp and who smoothed the path for Nechemia Levanon to visit Humphrey before his meeting with Kosygin in 1971.

8. "NCSJ Says Rockefeller Statement Confirms Soviet Jewry Discussed at Moscow Conference," *JTA,* 15 Aug. 1972; "Roger Emphatic in Confirming Soviet Jews Discussed in Moscow," *JTA,* 15 Aug. 1972.

9. When the Nixon tapes were opened in March 2002, the most revealing incident, which oc-

curred on 1 Feb. 1972, became public. His personal friend and source of moral support, the evangelist Billy Graham, cautioned that "Satanic Jews" have "total . . . domination of the media." *New York Times,* 17 Mar. 2002, 29.

10. See Henry Kissinger, *Years of Upheaval* (Boston: Little, Brown, 1982), 20–23, 212. He considered Jews predominantly liberal, controlling the media and forming a powerful cohesive group, unwilling to make necessary concessions to the Palestinians. But his support was, he claimed, "based on broader issues than just Israel's survival."

11. Nixon, *RN,* 477. Kissinger states that Nixon simply did not fully trust him in the making of Middle East policy. See Henry Kissinger, *White House Years* (Boston: Little, Brown, 1979), 559.

12. Kissinger was mistaken in his assumption that all immigration was based on internal law and therefore not subject to outside intervention. In 1972 Moscow abandoned its diploma tax because of strong outside intervention. The tax was not law but imposed by administrative decree.

13. At a Party congress address in February 1976 Brezhnev said, "Détente does not . . . abolish, nor can it alter the laws of the class struggle." Coral Bell, *The Reagan Paradox: American Foreign Policy in the 1980s* (New Brunswick, N.J.: Rutgers Univ. Press, 1989), 4. See also Frederick C. Barghoorn, *The Soviet Cultural Offensive: The Role of Cultural Diplomacy in Soviet Foreign Policy* (Princeton, N.J.: Princeton Univ. Press, 1960), 126.

14. Excerpts from the Minutes of the CPSU Central Committee Secretariat, 22 June 1973, top secret, in response to inquiry from the Communist Party of Jordan. "In comparison with the emigration of Jews to Israel from other countries, including Arab countries, these figures appear quite insignificant." Morozov, *Documents,* 181.

15. The "Bunker" group was not formally organized and its membership varied. At its heart were Jackson's assistant Richard Perle and Morris Amitay, who played a similar role in Sen. Ribicoff's office, and Mark Talisman, Sen. Vanik's assistant. Included also were Kenneth Gunther and Roy Millenson, who worked for Sen. Javits; Jayson Berman, Sen. Bayh's administrative assistant; and Richard Gilmore and Judith Davison, Sen. Humphrey's and Sen. Mondale's foreign policy advisors, respectively. Their informants from the Jewish organizations varied greatly in membership and interest. Included were I. L. Kenen of the American Israel Public Affairs Committee (AIPAC), Jerry Goodman of NCSJ, and occasionally Yehuda Hellman of the Conference of Presidents of Major American Jewish Organizations. For Perle's background and his relationship to Jackson and also to Albert Wohlstetter, the leading theoretician on nuclear war, see Jay Winik, *On the Brink: The Dramatic, Behind-the-Scenes Saga of the Reagan Era and the Men and Women Who Won the Cold War* (New York: Simon and Schuster, 1996), 35–50.

16. Quoted in Stephen D. Isaacs, *Jews and American Politics* (Garden City, N.Y.: Doubleday, 1974), 174.

17. Nechemia Levanon, "Israel's Role in the Campaign," in Friedman and Chernin, *Second Exodus,* 74–76. In 1970 Goldmann, in an effort to head off the "hotheads," volunteered to preside over a Paris conference of leading European intellectuals, organized by Saul Friedlander and Meir Rosenne, to slowly bring the Soviet Jewish problem to world attention.

18. Interview with Nechemia Levanon, NYPL, Wiener Oral History, 3 Dec. 1989.

19. Interview with Phil Baum, NYPL, Wiener Oral History, 1989, n.d.

20. Interview with Yoram Dinstein, NYPL, Wiener Oral History Project, 8 Nov. 1989. During

the years of this study American Jewry was left without representation on the Court for the first time since the appointment of Frankfurter by Roosevelt in 1935. Abe Fortas, who was appointed to the Supreme Court by Lyndon Johnson in 1965, was forced to resign in May 1968, and Arthur Goldberg yielded his seat that year to become U.S. ambassador to the United Nations. A National Association of Jewish Legislators founded in 1978 included Jewish lawmakers on all levels of government but was a social-fraternal grouping rather than a caucus.

21. Jonathan Frankel, "The Anti-Zionist Press Campaign in the USSR: An Internal Dialogue," *Soviet Jewish Affairs* 2, no. 1 (May 1972): 23–26. There was a division of thinking between neo-Stalinists and Leninists. The campaign itself was an ad hoc response to the emigration campaign.

22. As early as 1959 King Ahmad of Yemen cautioned Khrushchev that Jewish emigration would be an "immense danger" for the Arab world. Secret memorandum from R. Ulianovskii the to CPSU Central Committee, 21 Feb. 1972, Morozov, *Documents,* 135–36. The memorandum mentioned diplomatic opposition to the prospect of mass immigration to Israel was expressed by Z. Ismail, the Syrian deputy minister of foreign affairs; Astir Arafat, chairman of the executive council of the Palestine Liberation Organization; and other Arab leaders. According to this report the Soviet emigration was apparently a frequent topic of discussion among students, especially in Egypt.

23. There are researchers who are convinced that outside pressure and the Middle East situation played no role in Soviet emigration policy, which was subject to a deeply ingrained historical opposition to emigration. The policy was intrinsic. Lukasz Hirszowicz, "The Soviet-Jewish Problem: Internal and International Developments 1972–1976," in Kochan, *Jews in Soviet Russia,* 368.

24. "Soviet Brain Drain Fears Seen One Reason for Huge Increases in Exit Costs by Jewish Experts," *JTA,* 18 Aug. 1972. The tax had an impact on academics, which composed 40 percent of the refugee stream to Israel. *JTA,* 28 Aug. 1972.

25. Excerpts from the Minutes of a Politburo Meeting, 20 Mar. 1973, top secret, Mozorov, *Documents,* 170–74. "Soviet Clarification of Head Tax Welcomed but Still Unacceptable," *JTA,* 3 Jan. 1971.

26. It is estimated that between 1968 and 1983, 20,000 to 35,000 out of a possible 300,000 visa applicants were refused. Rejection was a minority phenomenon no less than applying for a visa itself. George Perkovich, "Soviet Jewry and American Foreign Policy," *World Policy Journal* 5 (1988): 443.

27. Sidney Heitman, "Jewish, German and Armenian Emigration from the USSR: Parallels and Differences," in Freedman, *Soviet Jewry in the 1980s,* 115–34.

28. Just a random handful gives us some idea that these were not Tevyes. Vladimir Slepak was an electronic engineer of considerable reputation. At the time of his arrest Sharansky already had a reputation in physics and mathematics. Viktor Polsky was a physical engineer, Alexander Lerner had a worldwide reputation in cybernetics, and Roman Rutman specialized in automation controls, Herman Branover in hydrodynamics, Ilyal Glazer in brain morphology, Yevgeny Ratner in plant physiology, Victor Yakhot in solid state physics, and Pavel Abramovich in radio engineering. The names of refuseniks in medicine, art, and music and other fields of scholarship would read like a "Who's Who" in the Soviet Union.

29. The only possible exceptions to that rule are the activities of the Jewish Defense League (JDL), which, try as it might, never became part of the Soviet Jewry movement. The blowing up of

the Soviet mission house in Tel Aviv in 1948 as a response to the Doctors' Plot was not related to an organized movement for Soviet Jews.

30. "Nine on Trial in USSR on Charges of 'Banditry and Treason,' " *JTA*, 16 Dec. 1970. Of the eleven defendants on trial between Dec. 15 and 24, only nine were refuseniks who planned to settle in Israel.

31. Sakharov, *Memoirs*, 321–23. Since it was not a human rights case, Sakharov kept out of it but his wife, Elena Bonner, was instrumental in getting the story out.

32. Rather than charging the eleven defendants with "illegal departure abroad," which carried only prison sentences, they were charged with "betrayal of the fatherland," which was the Soviet equivalent of treason and carried a possible death sentence. Indeed, two of the plotters, Mark Dymshits and Eduard Kuznetsov, were sentenced to death and the remainder to long prison terms.

33. The role of the Christian churches was especially important because they too had a stake in religious freedom. In 1942 they had made their opposition known to shipping lend-lease equipment to the Soviet Union. They were mollified only when Roosevelt made a dubious claim, based on Stalin's reopening of the churches, that the prospects for religious toleration in Russia were good. See Nolan, *Principled Diplomacy*, 4–5.

34. The full extent of the massive protest in the United States is contained in NCSJ, box 31, House of Representatives folder, 1971; "Christian Reaction to Leningrad Trial of Soviet Jews," *Congressional Record* 117, no. 79 (26 May 1971).

35. Colgate Prentice (acting assistant secretary for congressional relations) to Hon. Frank Horton, NCSJ, box 30, Nixon Administration folder, 2 Jan. 1970. See also "State Department Concerned about Soviet Jews but Fears to Intercede Openly," *JTA*, 25 Nov. 1970.

36. The call for such a conference was preceded by a general heightening of international interest. A separate international conference had already been convened in London on 15 June 1969. In April 1970 Rep. Leonard Farbstein, chairman of the subcommittee on Europe of the House foreign affairs committee, convened hearings in New York that called for a "international inquiry" under UN auspices to investigate "Soviet action against the Jewish population." The primary thrust for internationalization is claimed by Rabbi Israel Miller, who suggested the need for an international conference to Shaul Avigur of the Israeli Lishka. Thereafter, the Conference of Presidents played a key role in helping Avigur to organize the conference. Interview with Rabbi Israel Miller, NYPL, Wiener Oral History, 15 Feb. 1990.

37. Seven hundred sixty delegates from thirty-eight countries actually attended.

38. The Soviet counterpropaganda plans were extensive. They included a media campaign, a reprinting of the pamphlet *Soviet Jews: Myths and Reality*, special news briefs for television prepared in several languages, and the film *We Were Born Here*, prepared for distribution in Belgium and also broadcast on NBC and West German television. Novosti, the Soviet official press agency, sent its best political commentator to interact with the USSR-Belgium Friendship Society. Memorandum from A. Iakovlev to the CPSU Central Committee, 31 Mar. 1971, Mazorov, *Documents*, 107–8.

39. Micah H. Naftalin, "The Activist Movement," in Friedman and Chernin, *Second Exodus*, 231.

40. Quoted in Orbach, *American Movement*, 62.

41. Interview with Nechemia Levanon, NYPL, Wiener Oral History, 3 Dec. 1989.

42. Lewis H. Weinstein, "Soviet Jewry and the American Jewish Community, 1963–1987,"

American Jewish History 77, no. 4: 609. Weinstein is convinced that the Brussels conference would have been buried in the back pages if the Soviet authorities had not mounted a campaign to denounce the conference, which included an "open letter" to the government of Belgium from "Soviet citizens of Jewish identity" denouncing the conference as an "anti-Soviet provocation." A similar message was delivered in person by Colonel General Dragunsky, a well-known Soviet Jewish war hero.

43. The required invitation from family relatives *(vyzov)* usually from Israel frequently was "lost" in the mail. Only when it was safely in hand did official registration and processing at the OVIR begin. In 20 percent of the cases the dreaded wait ended with rejection. The submission of numerous forms was required, including the *Kharakteristika,* a clearance report card signed by your superiors in the work place and trade union representatives. Once submitted, the reward was usually the loss of position, medical benefits, pension rights, and in some cases, habitat. A filing fee of about forty rubles was required. The applicant was then first informed of his "eligibility" status. Later, a rejection could be appealed but except for a rejection on the grounds of security, no precise reason needed to be given. In some regions a letter attesting that the applicant had voluntarily resigned his position and that his children no longer attended a Soviet school was required. Even before the education tax was imposed there were steep fees for each separate family member and an additional fee upon actual receipt of the exit visa and the passport.

44. To exacerbate the problem there was also considerable variation in the amount of tax levied. It went from 4,500 rubles for humanities degrees to 19,400 rubles for a doctorate in science.

45. Bewalda, *Dwell Alone,* 91.

46. It was rumored that Romania received about $3,000 from the Jewish Agency for each Jew released. Between 1961 and 1975 approximately 160,000 Jews were "ransomed" in this way.

47. Feingold, *Politics of Rescue,* 50–59. It was labeled that by Dorothy Parker. The Schacht plan called for issuing bonds using sequestered Jewish property as collateral.

48. Joseph Polakoff, "The Future of the Soviet Tax 'Suspension' Pending Hearings," *JTA,* 24 Apr. 1973, 3.

49. Excerpts from the Minutes of a Politburo Meeting, 20 Mar. 1973, top secret, Morozov, *Documents,* 175.

50. If local organizations, religious congregations, and professional associations are included that network of organizations is extensive. The *American Jewish Yearbook* divides them into eight categories but this study limits itself to three: cultural community relations, overseas aid, and Zionist and pro-Israel. Of the 350 Jewish national organizations usually presented as major national organizations in these categories this study deals with twelve. (See the abbreviations list.) The estimate of the American Jewish population in 1981, which does not include non-Jewish family members, is 5.69 million. See *American Jewish Yearbook,* vol. 82 (New York: American Jewish Committee, 1982), for population, 283, 165; for organizations, 293–337.

51. Interview with Yoram Dinstein, NYPL, Wiener Oral History Project, 8 Nov. 1989.

52. Interview with Moshe Decter, NYPL, Wiener Oral History, 22 Feb. 1990.

53. Quoted in Orbach, *American Movement,* 24–25. Simcha Dinitz was Israel's fiery ambassador in Washington.

54. The degree of commitment differed with each Jewish community and within each community. Sometimes, as in Cleveland and the Bay Area, it was a matter of leadership. In Philadelphia,

which was early and fully involved in the Soviet Jewry issue, it may be that the original Jewish immigrants who were overwhelmingly from Eastern Europe with a strong labor tradition felt viscerally closer to Soviet Jewry.

55. Hellman was totally opposed to the reorganization plan for the AJCSJ and agreed to go along only when assurances were given that the conference would be invited to attend all meetings in the Oval Office. The NCSJ thus never possessed clear control of its relationship with the Oval Office and Congress. Interview with Yoram Dinstein, NYPL, Wiener Oral History Project, 8 Nov. 1989.

56. Ibid.; interview with Rabbi Herschel Schacter, NYPL, Wiener Oral History, 20 Sept. 1989.

57. Interview with Nechemia Levanon, NYPL, Wiener Oral History, 3 Dec. 1989.

58. Interview with Yehoshua Pratt, NYPL, Wiener Oral History, 1989.

59. The GNYCSJ, which shared quarters with the NCSJ, was the umbrella organization for local New York organizations involved in grassroots activity. Chernin's subordinate in Philadelphia's NJCRAC, Malcolm Hoenlein, became its effective director. Pratt claims to have been the behind-the-scenes organizer.

60. Memorandum from Richard Maass to Executive Committee, NCSJ, box 8, Executive Committee folder, 21 June 1972.

61. Interview with Yoram Dinstein, NYPL, Wiener Oral History Project, 8 Nov. 1989; interview with Yehoshua Pratt, NYPL, Wiener Oral History, 1989.

62. Naftalin, "Activist Movement," 229.

63. The five were the Bay Area, Northern California, Southern California, Cleveland, and Washington, D.C. In September 1971 councils from Norfolk, San Diego, Toronto, and Long Island were added at the first UCSJ national convention in Philadelphia.

64. Quoted in Orbach, *American Movement,* 29.

65. The members of the SSSJ and similar student groups represented an interesting amalgam of Americanism and Judaism from which they stemmed. Fifty-one percent were involved in the antiwar movement, 28 percent were involved in the civil rights movement, 26 percent were campus activists, but 65 percent were also graduates of Jewish day schools. The majority had visited Israel and at one point in their lives may have considered making aliyah. Ibid., 4, 28.

66. Memorandum, Richard Maass and J. Goodman, NCSJ, box 8, Executive Committee Correspondence folder, 15 Feb. 1972.

67. Dinstein describes the incident in somewhat different terms in his interview. But there is little doubt that by 1970 there was a full-scale confrontation between representatives of the liaison bureau in the United States and the UCSJ and its affiliate the SSSJ. Interview with Yoram Dinstein, NYPL, Wiener Oral History Project, 8 Nov. 1989.

68. Ibid. See also Naftalin, "Activist Movement," 230, and Freedman, "Soviet Jewry as a Factor," 78.

69. Naftalin, "Activist Movement," 235.

70. The program was very successful, generating twenty stories in the local press and spots on four local radio and television stations. The campaign culminated with a public program attended by more than 700 Jews and Christians and the creation of an ongoing coalition that had plans for a letter-writing campaign to political leaders.

71. Kosygin, who had spoken of the release of some in 1966, was particularly concerned about

the public relations fallout from the developing emigration issue. He observed to his Politburo colleagues that "we are creating the Jewish problem for ourselves." Excerpts from the Minutes of a Politburo Meeting, 20 Mar. 1973, Morozov, *Documents,* 175.

72. That sensitivity was fully confirmed in the documents published by Morozov. They contain evidence that the Soviet leadership sought "to avoid unnecessary conflict" during the Leningrad hijacking trial and sometimes released "worthy" refuseniks in response to requests from Western leaders or at strategic moments in disarmament negotiations. Ibid., 18–19.

73. Interview with Malcolm Hoenlein, NYPL, Wiener Oral History, 14 June 1989.

74. Ibid.

75. Orbach, *American Movement,* 103.

76. A large-scale meeting scheduled for Madison Square Garden in New York on 13 Dec. 1971, packaged as "Freedom Lights for Soviet Jewry," to which Gerald Ford, then Speaker of the House, and many Broadway stars were invited, was disrupted by black activists.

77. On 26 Jan. 1972 a band of seven members of the JDL rolled small bottles of household ammonia down the aisles during a performance of the Osian Balalaika Orchestra in Torrington, Connecticut, disrupting the performance. The incident was covered in all local newspapers and on radio and television newscasts.

78. Anatoliy Dobrynin, *In Confidence: Moscow's Ambassador to America's Six Cold War Presidents* (New York: Times Books, 1995), 270ff.

79. Newsletter, Congressman Benjamin Rosenthal, 6 Oct. 1971, NCSJ, box 43, Human Rights folder.

80. U.S. Congress, House, Committee on Foreign Affairs, Subcommittee on Europe, *Hearings, Soviet Jewry,* 92nd Cong., 1st sess., 9 Nov. 1971, 49–50. Testimony of Richard T. Davies.

81. Ibid. Morgenthau statement, 133–36. See also Bernard Gwertzman, "U.S. Asserts Soviet Jews Are Not Living in Terror," *New York Times,* 10 Nov. 1971, 1.

82. *New York Times,* 11 Nov. 1971, 12.

83. Hearings, *Soviet Jewry,* 47. "A Reply to Mr. Davies," *New York Times,* 6 Dec. 1971, 13.

84. Decter to Davies, NCSJ, box 43, State Department folder, 1970–1976, 19 Nov. 1971. Decter was wary of the Holocaust analogy but hesitated when Davies requested to use his letter to defend himself.

85. Interview with Phil Baum, NYPL, Wiener Oral History, 1989.

86. Nahum Goldmann, *The Jewish Paradox,* translated by Steve Cox (London: Weidenfeld and Nicolson, 1978), 173.

87. Levanon, "Israel's Role," 74.

88. Interview with Glenn Richter, NYPL, Wiener Oral History, 16 Feb. 1990.

89. Mentioned in Albert Axelbank, *Soviet Dissent: Intellectuals, Jews, and Détente* (New York: F. Watts, 1975), 44.

4. Jackson-Vanik: The Elusive Search for an Economic Lever

1. There were diplomatic intercessions with Tsarist Russia in relation to treatment of Jews in 1869, 1879, 1881–82, 1891. Uncannily similar to the Jackson-Vanik campaign was the successful ef-

fort to abrogate the Commercial Treaty of 1832, organized by Louis Marshall, that came to a head in 1911. (See chapter 1.)

2. Peter Y. Medding, "The Transformation of American Jewish Politics: Integrating the Jewish and American Political Agendas," in *Jewish Political Studies* (American Jewish Committee, 1989), 8–9.

3. As early as 1949 and 1951 export control laws restricted the export of "strategic materials" to the Soviet bloc, and MFN was withdrawn for human rights violations. In 1962 Congress withdrew MFN from Yugoslavia and Poland as part of the Export Control and Trade Expansion Act. When the Johnson administration desired to increase trade with the Soviet block by granting MFN in 1966, the proposal was blocked by Rep. Wilbur Mills, chairman of the Ways and Means Committee. By the mid-sixties the idea of wringing greater sensitivity to human rights from Moscow supplemented the normal strategic goals for controlling trade.

4. Koch may have been unaware of Israel's proprietary interest in all Soviet Jews who might emigrate. The resolution was withdrawn at the behest of AIPAC, Israel's major lobbying agency in Washington.

5. Quoted in Perkovich, "Soviet Jewry," 456.

6. Bruce Parrott, ed., introduction to *Trade, Technology and Soviet-American Relations* (Bloomington: Indiana Univ. Press, 1985), xiii.

7. Quoted in Carl Gersham, "Selling Them the Rope: Business and the Soviets," *Commentary*, Apr. 1979, 39–45.

8. Ibid.

9. Karl Radek to Lenin: " 'Vladimir Ilyich, but where are we going to get enough rope to hang the whole bourgeoisie?' Lenin effortlessly replied: 'They'll supply us with it.' " Ibid., 39–45.

10. Parrott, *Trade, Technology*, 354.

11. The lend-lease debt had been scaled down radically from the original outstanding $11 billion to $2.6. The first impulse of the Perle group, before the head tax offered the needed leverage, was that the Soviets would abandon the tax in return for lend-lease forgiveness and support in the forthcoming talks between Kissinger and Le Duc Tho, scheduled for Paris. Paula Stern, *Water's Edge: Domestic Politics and the Making of American Foreign Policy* (Westport, Conn.: Greenwood Press, 1979), 19. The final figure to be paid by the Soviet Union was $722 million.

12. Yitzhak Rabin, *The Rabin Memoirs* (Boston: Little, Brown, 1979), 229–31. Alternatively, the linkage to emigration originated in the United States. As early as October 1963 there was a suggestion made to the Kennedy administration of linking trade to freedom. The idea of such a quid pro quo was again brought up on 5 Sept. 1971, when the first great wheat deal was in the offing. Then Louis Rosenblum included the idea that wheat for the baking of matzohs, the unleavened bread used during Passover, should be included in the deal, which was packaged in a "freedom of immigration" bill. Stern, *Water's Edge*, 21.

13. Sometimes also called "the Bunker" or the "Perle group," the informal interest group was unusual in Washington in that its leadership core was composed of congressional aides and representatives of outside pressure groups, including the top leadership of the NCSJ and AIPAC. Stern, *Water's Edge*, 4, 18.

14. A Jackson aid speaks of the Jewish leaders having "cold feet" in the early weeks of the

amendment process. Interview of Dorothy Fosdick, NYPL, Wiener Oral History, 16ff, 22 Feb. 1990; NCSJ, box 63, Trade USSR folder, MFN Status, Jackson to Chaim Drori, 12 July 1974.

15. Whether Nixon raised the emigration question at the May summit meeting in Moscow came up repeatedly. Kissinger insisted that it was raised but Ambassador Dobrynin revealed a pre-summit agreement that there would be no appeal for "Jewish/Zionist organizations." Dobrynin, *In Confidence*, 273.

16. Max Fisher had counseled that the Soviet Jewry issue should be showcased, but its incompatibility with détente made that problematic. Fisher did succeed in getting Rabbi Herschel Schacter, chairman of the NCSJ and president of the Religious Zionists of America, to deliver the convention's opening prayer.

17. States with large Jewish voting blocks, especially California, favored McGovern over Jackson despite a Jackson-sponsored amendment in the platform to support Israel against Soviet pressures. Jews worked closely in the McGovern campaign and in the Democratic Party's administrative machinery. See Joseph Poliakoff, "Jews Played Major Role in McGovern Triumph at Democratic Convention," *JTA*, 14 July 1972.

18. Quoted in J. J. Goldberg, *Jewish Power: Inside the American Jewish Establishment* (Reading, Mass.: Addison-Wesley, 1996), 168. See also *JTA*, 17 Sept. 1972, 2.

19. Javits did not abandon his reservations regarding Jackson-Vanik until he was convinced that the amendment's momentum made it unbeatable. When the Perle group finally had the amendment ready to be submitted, Javits made several corrections "to remove some of the needlessly provocative provisions originally proposed." Jacob Javits, *The Autobiography of a Public Man* (Boston: Houghton Mifflin, 1981), 473. Similarly, a series of congressional resolutions featuring emigration as a quid pro quo for trade or credit were in circulation. In May, Rep. Thomas M. Rees proposed an amendment to the Export Administration Act of 1969 that authorized the president to prohibit commodity exports to violators of freedom of religion and emigration. But little came of it. William Korey, "The Story of the Jackson Amendment, 1973–74," *American Jewish Yearbook*, 1974, 200–210. A proposal by Rep. Bertram Podell, a two-time elected Democrat from Brooklyn, drew up a bill in the summer of 1972 but was discouraged by Isaiah Kenen, director of AIPAC, who did not then support the amendment. In addition, once the ice was broken similar proposals came from Sen. James Buckley and Sen. Ribicoff. Similar interest could be noted in the offices of Sen. Mondale and Sen. Humphrey.

20. The resolutions on religious toleration were tied up by Sen. Fulbright in the Senate's Foreign Relations Committee. Two separate resolutions proposing financial help for resettlement proposed by Muskie and Schweiker, Javits and Ribicoff, and Jackson were consolidated into a proposal for $50 million but never made it into the budget submitted in October.

21. Joseph Polakoff, "What the American Jews Expect of the Party Platforms," *JTA*, 23 June 1972.

22. Excerpts from the Minutes of a Politburo Meeting, 20 Mar. 1973, Morozov, *Documents*, 173, 175. See also "Jewish Leaders Meeting With Nixon Express Confidence in President's Handling of Soviet Jewish Emigration," *JTA*, 28 Sept. 1972.

23. By 4 October Jackson had sixty-six cosigners but not the key names he needed, Senate Majority Leader Mike Mansfield and Minority Leader Hugh Scott. Jackson introduced the measure

shortly before Congress was scheduled to adjourn on 15 October. It would be reintroduced when Congress reconvened in January after the election.

24. That percentage seems nothing to boast about until one realizes that it was three times as high as the percentage of the Jewish vote Nixon received in 1968. But in the House two new "fiery" Jewish Democratic congresswomen, Bella Abzug and Elizabeth Holtzman, a Harvard-trained lawyer who would make her voice heard during the Watergate hearings, raised the Jewish profile. Unlike the situation during the New Deal when the issue was the rescue of European Jewry, the three major committees were chaired by Jews concerned with immigration and foreign policy. There were no Jewish chairs of relevant committees in the 93rd Congress. See Connie McNeely and Susan Tulchin, "On the Hill: Jews in the U.S. Congress," in *Jews in American Politics,* edited by L. Sandy Maisel and Ira N. Forman (Lanham, Md.: Rowman and Littlefield, 2001), 54–56.

25. Howard M. Sachar, *A History of the Jews in America* (New York: Knopf, 1992), 913.

26. Kissinger, *Upheaval,* 990.

27. Quoted in Rabin, *Memoirs,* 230–31. White House pressure was also reported by Washington columnists Rowland Evans and Robert Novak and promptly denied by Israel. "Israel Denies Pressure from U.S. to Disown Jackson Amendment," *JTA,* 20 Mar. 1973.

28. Kissinger, *Upheaval,* 203–4. But in their pragmatic nonideological approach to foreign policy Nixon and Kissinger were able to find common ground.

29. William Mehlman, "A Case of Bad Faith: Jackson-Vanik-Mills and the Jewish Establishment," *The Times of Israel,* Aug. 1974, 26–31.

30. *JTA,* 28 Feb. and 27 Mar. 1973. Kenneth Rush, a former deputy secretary of state, also foresaw "grave danger" for Soviet Jewry for the same reason.

31. "Jackson Scores Soviet Lobbying," *JTA,* 23 Mar. 1973.

32. Present were Mark Talisman, Sen. Ribicoff and his assistant Morris Amitay, Elihu Bergman (consultant for the NCSJ's Washington office), David Blumberg and Herman Edelsberg of B'nai B'rith, Richard Perle and Tina Silber of Jackson's staff, Jacob Stein, Charlotte Jacobson, Richard Maass, and Jerry Goodman.

33. "Remember the history of our people," wrote the activists, "Your smallest hesitation may cause irreparable tragic results. . . . Can you retreat at such a moment?" This well-conceived letter can serve as evidence that in some measure Soviet activists had gained considerable input in communal decision making. Much of the energy for the movement emanated from Soviet Jewish activists.

34. Kissinger speculates that the attack might have been a planned diversion by the KGB since Czechoslovakia, where the attack occurred, was a tightly policed satellite. Kissinger, *Upheaval,* 469. Prime minister Bruno Kreisky's response to the attack, the closing of the Schoenau transit center, was particularly disturbing to the activist community who were convinced that the prime minister would support a freer flow of emigration. But Kreisky, a Jew and a socialist, argued that his first duty was to protect the interests and security of Austria.

35. During the 1973 war the United States did have a contingency plan to seize the oil fields in Saudi Arabia, Kuwait, and Abu Dhabi, and American forces were placed on a global nuclear alert after it was learned that the Soviets were planning to send troops to the Middle East after Israel crossed the canal.

36. Fulbright pointed out that MFN is not a special privilege but merely a promise not to dis-

criminate. Jackson was misusing the MFN, which was never intended as a sanction to promote favorable behavior.

37. *JTA*, 18 Sept. 1972, 2.

38. Transcript of press conference, 29 June 1974. NCSJ, box 30, State Department folder, 1970–76.

39. Kissinger insisted that Watergate did not affect his crisis management. He was less concerned about the outcome of the Middle East crisis or Watergate than he was about the systematic "dismantling" of East-West relations. Kissinger, *Upheaval,* 979. Similarly, Nixon was convinced that liberal and conservative anti-détente forces had converged and "reached almost a fever pitch" on the emigration issue that they were using for their own purposes. Nixon, *RN,* 1023–24.

40. Henry Kissinger, *Years of Renewal* (New York: Simon and Schuster, 1999), 131.

41. Steve Bryan, an economist in the Department of Commerce, discovered and revealed to Sen. Case a number of secret commercial agreements concealed from Congress, including an extension of a $3 billion credit. The administration denied the transaction. Winik, *On the Brink,* 146–48.

42. Case discovered that the Export-Import Bank had been extending low-interest credit on a case-by-case basis beyond the $500 million legal limit. What disturbed him was that the arrangements for Soviet trade were not less favorable than those extended to other purchasers and that Occidental Petroleum, the company most strongly committed to increasing Soviet-American trade, was scheduled to receive a loan of $180 million and $49 million more for gas exploration in the Soviet Union. "Case to Ask Kissinger for 'Full Airing' on US-USSR Trade Pact," *JTA,* 8 Feb. 1974.

43. Among others there was Kissinger, George Shultz, (commerce), William D. Eberle (White House representative for trade negotiations), Peter Flanigan, executive director for the White House Council on International Economic Policy, and other notables in the administration.

44. Under pressure generated by the NCSJ, Corman dropped the waiver compromise the following day, and the amendment linking the waiver directly to emigration was restored.

45. U.S. Congress, House, Committee on Foreign Affairs, Subcommittee on Europe, *Hearings, Soviet Jewry,* 92nd Cong., 1st sess., 91–1, Nov. 1971, 134. Testimony of Professor Hans Morgenthau.

46. The question of numbers was also crucial in the Kremlin, as recent documents reveal. The Soviet authorities were particularly annoyed that the emigration movement was being described as a mass movement. When Arab diplomats complained about the emigrants they were informed that it was a selective small emigration of old people. They also pointed out that, contrary to Zionist propaganda "hostile to the Soviet Union and to Soviet-Arab friendship," OVIR was receiving few requests for visas and many visas granted were never used. They also spoke of many requests to return to the Soviet Union. Excerpts from the Minutes of the CPSU Central Committee Secretariat, appendix, 1 Mar. 1973, Morozov, *Documents,* 165–66.

47. The NCSJ found it particularly challenging to refute this story, which was echoed in major newspapers. The actual case was that since the beginning of 1974, despite harassment there were at least 4,000 applications for visas per month. We shall note later that the initial number of Zionist visa applicants may have reached its apogee by 1973, but there was still a sufficient number in the pipeline, now increased by a greater number who simply wanted to leave the Soviet Union but not necessarily to settle in Israel.

48. *JTA,* 11 and 18 July 1974.

49. Transcript of Press Conference, Office of the White House Press Secretary, 15 Aug. 1974, NCSJ, box 63, MFN folder.

50. *JTA,* 1 Oct. 1974.

51. Kissinger, *Renewal,* 132–33. Kissinger later argued that had Jackson worked with the administration, "respectable" improvements in the emigration figures could easily have been achieved.

52. Joseph Albright, "The Pact of the Two Henrys: How the Deal to Buy Jews from Russia Grew from a Moral Impulse into the Unwanted Policy of Two Superpowers," *New York Times Magazine,* 5 Jan. 1975, 20.

53. That would help circumvent the penchant of OVIR for favoring pensioners, dependents, and the unskilled for exit visas.

54. Kissinger, *Renewal,* 256. The agreement also prohibited punitive reprisals such as conscription, bringing criminal charges, and requiring parental permission for visa applications.

55. U.S. Congress, Senate, Hearings, *Emigration Amendment to the Trade Reform Act of 1974,* 93rd Cong, 2nd sess., Exchange of Letters Between Secretary of State Henry A. Kissinger and Sen. Henry M. Jackson of Washington, 18 Oct. 1974.

56. Christopher S. Wren, "Jews in Soviet Hopeful but Skeptical on Exit," *New York Times,* 6 Sept. 1974.

57. The change of the administration's course occurred when Democratic Majority Leader Mike Mansfield discovered that Kissinger had no assurances regarding the 60,000 figure and informed his colleagues that acting as if it did was bound to backfire.

58. Dobrynin, *In Confidence,* 340. Jackson's initial demand to be guaranteed in writing was 100,000. Kissinger was chagrined when this "outlandish" demand was leaked to the press on 15 Mar. 1974. Kissinger, *Renewal,* 132.

59. Israel had special reason to celebrate the breakthrough and confirmed that it had been told that the figure agreed to was 60,000 visas annually. "Dinitz Says Accord of Immigration Is of Revolutionary Importance," *JTA,* 25 Oct. 1974. Jackson had lowered his figure to a midpoint between Gromyko's proposed 45,000 and Jackson's original 100,000. But after offering the senators full credit for the agreement and requesting intervention from Rabin, the letter was still not ready in time for a Ford-Gromyko meeting scheduled for 20 Sept. 1974. Gromyko refused to mention any target figure. The finishing blow occurred when, after agreement had finally been reached on 18 October, Jackson spoke of a great victory for human rights from the White House briefing room, as if he were speaking for the president, and mentioned specific figures to the press. That accounts for Ford's statement that the agreement contains no specific numbers. It came too late.

60. Quoted in Marshall I. Goldman, "Jackson-Vanik: A Dissent," in Friedman and Chernin, *Second Exodus,* 119.

61. Ford to Russell, 27 June 1975, NCSJ, box 63, Trade, MFN Status folder.

62. U.S. Department of State, Bureau of Public Affairs, Kissinger statement, press conference, 14 Jan. 1975.

63. Interview with Fosdick, NYPL, Wiener Oral History, 22 February 1990.

64. Lowell to Kissinger, 5 Mar. 1975, NCSJ, box 63, Trade, MFN Status folder. The full reason for the Soviet repudiation remained unclear. Christopher Wren, a columnist for the *New York Times,*

blamed Arab concern about emigration, as illustrated by Egypt's earlier proposal that Israel restrict all further immigration. *New York Times,* 19 Dec. 1974, 52.

65. Sheila Woods to Jerry Goodman, 27 Dec. 1974, NCSJ, box 63, Trade, MFN Status folder. The tensions may have had their roots in the suspicion among some Jewish leaders that Kissinger was responsible for the resupply problem during the 1973 war.

66. Sponsored by Sen. Adlai Stevenson III. The amendment kept the waiver provision of the Jackson amendment intact. The president could lift the credit ceiling with congressional approval, which in turn would take into account Soviet behavior in the areas of emigration, arms control, and the Middle East. The amendment proposed to extend one-fourth less credit than what was available to the Soviet Union without MFN status. Nixon had promised to veto the Stevenson Amendment. But after Nixon's resignation the activities on the floor of Congress were neglected. Stevenson later regretted having submitted the amendment.

67. Quoted in Goldberg, *Jewish Power,* 172.

68. Stevenson did give public credit for the amendment to Jackson. Kissinger, *Renewal,* 134.

69. The Democratic Party's change in the rules for nomination spawned thirty state primaries for committed delegates. Jackson ran primaries in six states with a heavy Jewish voting block (New York, New Jersey, Massachusetts, Florida, Pennsylvania, and California.) New York's 274 votes were particularly important to win the 1,505 delegates necessary to win the nomination. Jackson won 104 delegates (61 percent) but only 36 percent of the delegates in the remainder of the states. See Stern, *Water's Edge,* xv.

70. See Peter Golden, *Quiet Diplomat: A Biography of Max M. Fisher* (New York: Cornwall Books, 1992).

71. *Shtadlanut* is the Hebrew term used to describe the court Jew pattern of Jewish leadership during the Middle Ages, remnants of which persisted to the modern age when wealthy connected Jews, such as Jacob Schiff or Oscar Straus, spoke to power for the Jewish community.

72. Peter J. Ognibene, *Scoop: The Life and Politics of Henry M. Jackson* (New York: Stein and Day, 1975), 187–90. Ognibene concludes that Jackson tailored much of his biography, including the Buchenwald story, to enhance his political appeal. He was publicly the most philosemitic of all the senators yet he was a member of Seattle's University Club and Maryland's Chevy Chase Club, both with a history of restricted membership. In his fund-raising for the 1976 campaign, almost two-thirds of the money raised came from Jewish sources. That largess stemmed from his reputation as Israel's staunchest supporter in the Senate.

73. Kissinger, *Upheaval,* 992.

74. Jackson supposedly admitted at a dinner in July 1975 that he may have pressed the emigration issue too hard under the impression that the Soviets would cave in. Dobrynin, *In Confidence,* 338.

75. Lowell to Kissinger, 28 Feb. 1975, NCSJ, box 30, State Department folder, 1970–76.

76. Donald Kendall, who had beaten out Coca-Cola to sign a lucrative agreement for Russian vodka that would be marketed in the United States in return for exclusive access to the Russian market, was the administration's point man for the effort of mobilizing the business community against the amendments.

77. Walter LaFeber, *America, Russia and the Cold War, 1945–1996* (New York: McGraw-Hill,

1997), 284. Kissinger recognized the challenge to détente under Ford. He attributed the mounting opposition to the efforts of the neoconservatives and remained convinced that the Soviet system would eventually implode. Kissinger, *Renewal,* 92–93.

78. Maass to Rush, 30 Nov. 1973, NCSJ, box 63, Trade, MFN Status folder.

79. The joint congressional resolution (HJ Res. 1145) passed on 7 Aug. 1965 gave Johnson the right to "take all necessary steps" to wage the war in Vietnam. It was the closest thing to an actual declaration of war against North Vietnam.

80. Kissinger, *Renewal,* 1–11.

81. Natan Sharansky, *Fear No Evil* (New York: Random House, 1988), 83.

82. Originally Perle wanted to consider the lend-lease forgiveness itself as compensating the Soviets for abandoning the head tax.

83. Goldman, "Jackson-Vanik," 115.

84. U.S, Congress, House, *Hearings,* Senate Finance Committee, 3 Dec. 1974, 58.

85. Interview with Phil Baum, NYPL, Wiener Oral History, 1989, n.d.

86. Unedited transcript of remarks made at Paramount Hotel , Liberty, N.Y., 25 Dec. 1973, NCSJ, box 63, Trade, MFN Status folder.

87. The fear was not without foundation. Despite his election victory, which raised the Jewish vote as compared to the election of 1968 by almost 10 percent, Nixon continued to feel that he owed nothing to the American Jewish voter. Kissinger describes how during fits of exasperation against Israel, Nixon would order all aid to be halted. Kissinger, *Upheaval,* 202.

5. Dropping Out

1. In 2003 the amendment was still officially on the books though suspended on a yearly basis. In 1977 Carter requested that the amendment, now section 4 of the trade act, be softened to allow him simply to extend MFN treatment if emigration levels were adequate. It was not honored. Neither was a similar proposal submitted by Sen. Stevenson in 1979. The AJCong strengthened its opposition to the amendment but, fearing the loss of leverage would endanger Soviet activists, most Jewish organizations continued to support it.

2. Some were convinced that the Soviet rejection of the treaty was not based on the credit limitation of the Stevenson Amendment but on the fear that the arrangement would have allowed anyone who was so inclined to emigrate.

3. There are considerable variations in the statistics presented by the Netherlands embassy that handled the issuances of visas for Israel, and the figures emanated from the Jewish Agency, HIAS and JDC. The number of *vyzovs* issued between 1968 and 1976 was about 318,914 but far fewer were received and even fewer used. Generally we can state that between 1968 and 1974 the dropout rate was about 10 percent; of the 132,500 Jews who emigrated, 114,800 settled in Israel. Thereafter, the percentage of dropouts rose steadily until it reached to well over 50 percent in the period after 1979. In 1977, 8,347 of 16,736 emigrants dropped out (50 percent); in 1978, 16,672 of 28,864 (58 percent); 1979, 33,706 of 51,320 (65 percent). By 1980, 81 percent of the emigrants chose to drop out. About sixty emigrants per month arrived in the United States directly, without Israeli

visas. In 1976 such emigrants totaled less than 900. "Emigration of Soviet Jews: Current Problems," Confidential Draft, (mimeographed), n.d., probably Jan. 1977, NCSSJ, box 40, Emigration Dropouts folder (2).

4. The most notable case was that of Andrei Amalrik, author of *Will the Soviet Union Survive Until 1984?* revised and expanded, edited by Hilary Sternberg (New York: Penguin, 1980).

5. The full story is told in Feingold, *Politics of Rescue*; Sharon R. Lowenstein, *Token Refuge: The Story of the Jewish Refugee Shelter at Oswego, 1944–1946* (Bloomington: Indiana Univ. Press, 1986). Ruth Gruber, *Haven: The Unknown Story of 1,000 World War II Refugees and How They Came to America* (New York: Coward-McCann, 1983).

6. The strengthening of the parole privilege provision in 1971 is largely attributable to Rep. Edward Koch. On 30 Sept. 1971 Attorney General John Mitchell assured Rep. Emanuel Celler, chairman of the House Judiciary Committee, that he would exercise his discretion in favor of admitting Soviet Jews. It supplemented Koch's proposal in March (HR5606) to provide 30,000 nonquota visas exclusively for Soviet Jews. After opposition from Zionist leaders, Koch withdrew the resolution. As early as June 1974 Sen. Javits, aware that loans for higher education were made available to Cuban refugees, asked the same for Soviet Jews in the United States. The normal student loan procedure was not available to emigrants.

7. In 1972, 251 emigrants declared themselves to be "political refugees" and were duly paroled by Attorney General John Mitchell. Many dropouts between 1978 and 1980 entered the United States as parolees under the immigration act, which meant that they had to wait longer to become a permanent resident and received less financial assistance. The sponsoring agency had to ensure support. In 1980 a new amendment to the law eliminated the refugee status entirely as a preference category. Generally, Soviet emigrants did better under the parole system. In 1989 the financial support system was eliminated.

8. Congress passed a block grant of $20 million for refugees not covered by existing aid programs. HIAS and JDC received $16 million for resettlement, shared with refugees from Cuba and Indochina. It rose to $21 million in 1976. Included were medical and dental care, language and civics instruction, the paperwork to establish their refugee status for the American consul, and a search for "first degree" relatives in the United States who might "sponsor" the emigrant. After the Palestine Liberation Organization attack in June 1973 the operation was transferred to Rome, where HIAS maintained a staff of eighty and JDC about thirty.

9. Though Charles Jordan, who headed the JDC operation in Austria, noted as early as March 1966 that some emigrants were requesting a change in destination, the dropout phenomenon is best divided into two phases. The first and much lighter phase between 1971 and 1981 introduces all the problems. It is examined in this chapter. The second phase, 1987–1989, witnesses heavy migration when the seeds of all the problems planted in the first phase come to fruition. It is examined in chapter 7.

10. "The Emigration of Soviet Jews: Current Problems," Jan. 1977, Confidential Draft (mimeographed), NCSJ, box 40, Emigration Dropouts folder (2). This group may have been enabled to leave by intercession or the ability to exit as a member of a delegation.

11. It is difficult to estimate the percentage of Soviet Jews who were disaffected. In the sixties Soviet Jewry still boasted the highest membership of any ethnic group in the CPSU. Many Soviet

Jews did not welcome the attention-getting protests of the activists. Theodore H. Friedgut, "Soviet Jewry: The Silent Majority," *Soviet Jewish Affairs* 10, no. 2 (1980), 8.

12. In 1975 Moscow claimed 72 percent; Leningrad, 73 percent; Odessa, 90 percent; Kiev, 16 percent; all of Georgia, 2 percent. See Sawyer, *Jewish Minority in the Soviet Union,* 210, 213.

13. Jews had four times the number of university graduates as the general population and were the most highly formally educated group in the Soviet Union. About 9 percent of its scientists and 14 percent of scientists who were also PhDs were Jews. In 1970, 5.6 percent of Soviet Jews qualified as professionals. Zaslavsky and Brym, *Soviet-Jewish Emigration,* 14–15.

14. William Korey, "The Future of Soviet Jewry: Emigration and Assimilation," *Foreign Affairs* 58, no. 1 (fall 1979): 72–73.

15. Even the possibility of identity enhancement through the memory of the Holocaust was less experienced by this urbanized group. It was the less educated small-town Jews of the Ukraine and Belarus who experienced the brunt of the Holocaust in Russia. Memorialization meetings became an early source of members for the movement within the Soviet Union. Alexeyeva, *Soviet Dissent,* 175–91.

16. Zaslavsky and Brym, *Soviet-Jewish Emigration,* 52.

17. Alexeyeva, *Soviet Dissent,* 180; Bewalda, *Dwell Alone,* 179. Some activists were convinced that the Soviet authorities deliberately favored "core" Jews for exit permits to lessen the emigration to Israel and to weaken the movement within European Russia.

18. The rise of the dropout rate directly reflects the rise of emigrants from the Soviet heartland. Between 1976 and 1981 when the dropout rate rose from 49 to 80 percent, over two-thirds of the emigrant stream was composed of heartlanders. Zaslavsky and Brym, *Soviet-Jewish Emigration,* 131.

19. Marcus Hansen, *The Atlantic Migration, 1607–1860: A History of the Continuing Settlement of the United States* (Cambridge, Mass.: Harvard Univ Press, 1940). The letters also contained information on the housing situation, unemployment, and sometimes comments on the climate, which assumed great importance as the situation for potential applicants worsened. The decline of applications in 1973 could be traced directly to the October war.

20. The Soviets were fully aware that the *vyzovs* did not emanate from "close relatives." They became convinced that the *vyzovs* were being sent to specialists and workers in high-security enterprises. To counter this the KGB screened the delivery, allowing applicants with little formal education, pensioners, and invalids to receive them. Andropov reported that applications for *vyzovs* declined by half in 1981 and then added "no claims from the Israel postal service for undelivered *vyzovs* have been received." But the NCSJ did register a complaint with the International Postal Service. Memorandum from Iu. Andropov to the CPSU Central Committee (secret), 6 Apr. 1981, Morozov, *Documents,* 236–37. The situation changed in June 1980 when Soviet authorities demanded affidavits from an immediate relative. "Jewish Leader Says Stiffer Soviet Rules Cut Emigration," *New York Times,* 8 June 1980, 3.

21. Report, Conference of Presidents of Major American Jewish Organizations, 31 Mar. 1976 (mimeographed), NCSJ, box 60, Scientists (Soviet) folder.

22. The dropout occupational profile was very high: 46 percent boasted some higher education, 25 percent were professional (scientists, medical doctors, engineers), 9 percent were techni-

cians, and 16 percent were white collar workers or former bureaucrats. The estimated per capita resettlement and absorption cost was $10,000 annually. The total package was priced at $150 million, which the local federations would have to take off the top of their budgets, often at the expense of the yearly allocation to Israel.

23. In 1972 the cost of resettling 35,000 Soviet emigrants was estimated at $390 million. That estimate became crucial in 1988 when additional thousands entered the refugee stream. The high cost became the principle factor behind the U.S. change in refugee policy. There are little reliable data on the comparative per capita cost of resettlement between Israel and the United States. Report, July 1973 (mimeographed), NCSJ, box 63, Trade, MFN folder.

24. Quoted in Sachar, *History of the Jews,* 927.

25. Goodman to Rabbi Lookstein, 13 Oct. 1978, NCSJ, box 6, Goodman folder, 1977.

26. Soviet authorities had difficulty in deciding on Sharansky's sentence but rejected the death sentence. As in the Orlov case, much depended on how the defendant behaved in court. Orlov and Sharansky behaved, according to Andropov, "indecently" and therefore received a heavy sentence, thirteen years of deprivation of freedom, including three years in prison. Piqued at the Soviet insistence on linking Sharansky to the CIA, Carter requested that all mention of the supposed connection be omitted from the trial records. Excerpts from the Minutes of a Politburo Session, 22 June 1978, top secret, Morozov, *Documents,* 228–29.

27. Chernin to Paul Kulick, Savannah Jewish Council, 7 Apr. 1977; Raab to Chernin, Aug. 15, 1978; Chernin to Raab, Sept. 14, 1978; NCSJ, box 7, correspondence folder, Sheinbaum, Myrna.

28. Lowell to Sidney Leiwant, 3 June 1976. NCSJ, Box 8, Executive Committee folder, 1976–78. The shortage of operating funds led to the firing of the editor of the *News Bulletin,* the major instrument of keeping the local groups informed. An office manager who became ill was not replaced. The NCSJ also received annual stipends from its affiliate organizations, especially the AJC, but finding themselves in financial trouble, the allotments were often late or missed or fulfilled in service.

29. Goodman to Marina Wallach, 1 Dec. 1976, NCSJ, box 8, Executive Committee folder, 1976–78.

30. Quoted in Orbach, *American Movement,* 73.

31. *Zwungsaliyah* is a German term that distinguishes between Jews compelled to settle in Israel because they could not find a haven elsewhere and immigrants who settled in the Jewish state voluntarily for ideological or religious reasons.

32. Henry L. Feingold, "Could Mass Resettlement Have Saved European Jewry?" in *Bearing Witness: How America and Its Jews Responded to the Holocaust* (Syracuse: Syracuse Univ. Press, 1995), 94–140.

33. *Bricha* refers to the movement to bring survivors to the American zone. *Ha'apala* is the movement to bring "illegal" Jews to Israel. Both were organized by the Zionist movement.

34. Leon Uris, *Exodus* (New York: Bantam, 1966; original publication, 1958).

35. Quoted in Bewalda, *Dwell Alone,* 163.

36. Kochavi, *Post-Holocaust Politics,* ix-xiii, 267–84.

37. Quoted from interview with Yehoshua Pratt, NYPL, Wiener Oral History, 1989.

38. Interview with Nechemia Levanon, NYPL, Wiener Oral History, 3 Dec. 1989.

39. Interview with David Geller, NYPL, Wiener Oral History, 30 Apr. 1990.

40. Press release, Israel Embassy, 10 Nov. 1974, NCSJ, box 63, Trade, MFN Status folder, July–Dec. 1974.

41. Action Committee on Soviet Jewry, Rehovot. "The Drop Out Problem," 10 Nov. 1976 (mimeographed), NCSJ, box 40, Emigration, Dropouts folder.

42. Interview with Yoram Dinstein, NYPL, Wiener Oral History Project, 8 Nov. 1989.

43. In October a group of returnees housed in Ostia petitioned President Ford requesting help and complaining that they had been lured to Israel by misinformation. NCSJ, box 40, Emigration, Dropouts folder, 23 Apr. 1976.

44. Interview with Nechemia Levanon, NYPL, Wiener Oral History, 3 Dec. 1989.

45. Report: "Quo Vadis? Policy on Russian Jewish Emigration." National Jewish Conference Center, Nov. 1976. NCSJ, box 40, Dropouts folder.

46. *The Jewish Week,* 4 Dec. 1976. "Letters from Our Readers," Dr. Stanley Birenbaum quoting Morris Brafman. A similar argument about "misuse" of the Israeli visa was frequently featured in the *Jerusalem Post.* See, for example, "A Threat to Aliyah" and editorial on 22 Sept. 1976.

47. "Behind the Headlines." *JTA,* 11 July 1979.

48. "View Point," *Jerusalem Post,* 23 Sept. 1976. See also H. D. S. Greenway, "Soviet Emigrants Who Drop Out to US Stir Dispute in Israel," *Washington Post,* 27 Sept. 1976, A20.

49. Survey research indicates that their prediction was well founded. Before 1985, if aid for re-settlement in North America were limited and emigration to Israel were the only option for potential emigrants, 33 percent would have chosen to remain in the Soviet Union. After 1985 the situation again changed. Zaslavsky and Brym, *Soviet-Jewish Emigration,* 129.

50. Robert Adelstein and Peter Pershan to Jerry Goodman, 2 Feb. 1977, NCSJ, box 40, Emigration, Dropouts folder.

51. Interview with David Geller, NYPL, Wiener Oral History, 1990.

52. Interview with Moshe Decter, NYPL, Wiener Oral History, 22 Feb. 1990.

53. Levanon, "Israel's Role," 81–82.

54. Interview with David Harris, NYPL, Wiener Oral History, Oct. 7, 1991.

55. Bewalda, *Dwell Alone,* 170.

56. Included among such groups were the Church World Service, the International Commit-tee of the Red Cross, and Rav Tov, which represented Satmar, a Hasidic group.

57. Max Fisher became the unoffical spokesman for the Interorganizational Committee (IOC). The IOC was composed of the heads of all major organizations involved in the Soviet emigration. The Committee of Eight was a subgroup of the IOC. The American side was represented by Ralph Goldman (JDC), Gaynor Jacobson (HIAS), Phil Bernstein (CJF), Irving Kessler (UJA). Israel was rep-resented by Leon Dulzin and Josef Almogi (JAFI), Nehemia Levanon (foreign office), Yehuda Anner (prime minister's office).

58. Added in October were two Americans, Jerry Goodman and Albert Chernin (NJCRAC). Both were involved with the Soviet Jewry movement from the outset.

59. "Jewish Agency Seeks Ways to Win Over the Soviet Drop Outs," *JTA,* 6 July 1979.

60. Seymour Lauretz to Jerry Goodman, 1 Nov. 1976, NCSJ, box 40, Emigration, Dropout folder.

61. Bertram Gold to Phil Bernstein (CJF), 28 Oct. 1976. The "Jewish Immigrant Aid Society of Canada" affiliated with HIAS expressed similar sentiments. J. Cage to Gaynor I. Jacobson, 24 Oct. 1976, NCSJ, box 40, Emigration, Dropout folder.

62. Goodman to Gold, 20 Oct. 1978, NCSJ, box 40, Emigration, Dropout folder.

63. The direct flight idea persisted as late as June 1988, this time supported by a joint statement of all the involved agencies, NCSJ, UCSJ, HIAS, JDC, AJComm, and AJCong. The plan was simple. All those who wanted to settle in Israel would take the flight directly from Moscow or Bucharest. The remainder would have "freedom of choice." On 18 June the Israeli cabinet again brought up the idea of direct flight via Bucharest. But the strategy, which from Israel's perspective was so practical, could not be implemented because Moscow opposed widening the channel of emigration and because the "freedom of choice" idea had gained support in the European Union.

64. "The Jews of Ostia: Waiting for a Miracle," *Time,* 14 Feb. 1977.

65. Interview with Phil Baum, NYPL, Wiener Oral History, 1989, n.d.

66. David K. Shipler, "Soviet Jews Choosing U.S. Put Israelis in a Quandary," *New York Times,* 13 Sept. 1981, E5.

67. David Landau, "Israel and US Jewish Leaders Reach No Conclusions on Dropout Issue," *JTA,* 29 June 1979, 1.

68. Chaired by Leon Dulzin (JAFI), the committee included Howard Squadron (chairman of the Conference of Presidents), Theodore Mann (past chairman), Seymour Lachman (chairman of GNYCSJ), Charlotte Jacobson (chairman WZO, American section), Edgar Bronfman (president, World Jewish Congress), Jack Spitzer (president, B'nai B'rith International), Claude Kelman (chairman, French Committee for Soviet Jewry), Raphael Kotlowitz (chairman of WZO's aliyah department), and sundry other members of the world Soviet Jewry Movement.

69. *JTA,* 26 Aug. 1981, 3.

70. "Dulzin Wants Refugee Status Denied Soviet Jewish Emigres with Visas for Israel But Who Go Elsewhere," *JTA,* 11 June 1985.

71. Between 1981 and 1987 the Netherlands embassy in Moscow issued 24,540 visas for Israel, compared to 101,382 issued between 1978 and 1980. Many were never used.

72. A similar conclusion is reached by Gideon Rafael, "Detergents and Convergence of American-Soviet Interests in the Middle East: An Israeli Viewpoint," *Political Science Quarterly* 100, no. 4 (winter 1985–86): 566–68.

73. The year 1984 saw approximately 890 visas issued by the Netherlands embassy. In 1985 the number rose to 1,153 but fell again to 902 in 1986. The breakthrough did not come until three years later. In 1988 and 1989 the embassy issued 109,849 visas, a record total for two sequential years. In 1990, 141,572 visas were issued for the first eight months. Bewalda, *Dwell Alone,* 221.

74. "Gorbachev Asks France to Fly Several Thousand Jews from the USSR to Israel on Special Airlift," *JTA,* 28 Oct. 1985.

6. Of Human Rights

1. The earliest UN study of the freedom of movement by Jose Ingles in 1963 did not mention Soviet Jewry's right to emigrate. Not until the number of deaths at the Berlin Wall began to mount did popular awareness grow regarding the centrality of the freedom of movement idea.

2. U.S., *Congressional Record,* 94th Cong., 2nd sess., 1976, 22, no. 84, 3 June 1976. On Jackson's staff, Fosdick describes Jackson as less interested in ethnic politics than he was in the human rights issue. Interview with Dorothy Fosdick, NYPL, Wiener Oral History, 1990.

3. Goldman, "Jackson-Vanik," 116.

4. The unspoken consensus is discussed in Daniel P. Moynihan, "The Politics of Human Rights," *Commentary,* Aug. 1977, 19–26.

5. In the case of the German Federal Republic negotiating for the emigration of Volga Germans the transaction was based on actual money per capita. The negotiation for the emigration of 125,000 Germans living in Poland over a four-year period in exchange for credits from Bonn amounting to nearly $1 billion dollars stemmed from an agreement reached between the Polish foreign secretary Gierek and Chancellor Schmidt in fall 1975. Soviet Germans and Jews resembled each other in their retention of a strong ethnic consciousness fed by a sense of persecution and also in their dispersion. That was not true of the Armenians. See Heitman, "Jewish, German, and Armenian," 115–38.

6. During the Holocaust Jewish leaders faced a similar dilemma. The first occurred in 1938 when George Rublee, Roosevelt's agent, negotiated what Dorothy Parker labeled a ransom offer for German Jewry, and the second time was in 1944 when Adolf Eichmann offered the "blood for trucks" deal. See Feingold, *Politics of Rescue,* 50–71, 270–77.

7. James K. Libbey, *Russian-American Economic Relations, 1763–1999* (Claremont: Regina Books, 1989), 111.

8. U.S., House of Representatives, Committee on International Relations, Subcommittee on International Economic Policy and Trade, *Hearings, Statement by Eugene Gold, Chairman of the NCSJ,* 20 Apr. 1978.

9. Eugene Gold to Howard Squadron, 28 June 1978, NCSJ, box 7 (correspondence), Executive Committee folder, 1967–68.

10. Interview with Rabbi Israel Miller, NYPL, Wiener Oral History, 15 Feb. 1990.

11. Don Oberdorfer, "Soviet Trade Minister Denounces U.S. Policy," *Washington Post,* 15 June 1977.

12. Wallach to Goodman, 1 Dec. 1976, NCSJ, box 8, Executive Committee folder, 1976.

13. Richard Burt, "Trade and Foreign Policy: Will Export Controls Influence Moscow?" *New York Times,* 24 July 1978.

14. In February 1978 Soviet banks successfully negotiated a $400 million credit line at the low rate of 0.75 above London rates from the Deutsch and Lloyds bank consortium. *Wall Street Journal,* 15 Mar. 1938, 36.

15. By 1976 trade volume stood at $2.3 billion. The net worth of exports was predictably ten times as high as imports. The sale of grains made up about 60 percent of sales, and the sale of industrial equipment, especially in advanced oil technology, was rising. The projected rise in these sales was $1 billion per year to 1980. Richard Burt, "Trade and Foreign Policy," *New York Times,* 24 July 1978.

16. The Soviet Jewry issue was not the only nonstrategic case for imposing of economic sanctions. The United States also restricted trade with Cuba, North Korea, Vietnam, and Rhodesia.

17. Quoted in *Business Week,* 24 July 1978, 181.

18. That was the gist of a memorandum to the NCSJ Executive Committee. "Memo-Update: Technology Transfer Legislation," NCSJ, box 8, Executive Committee folder, 1977–78.

19. Korey, *Promises,* 61.

20. Carter's decency and his success at Camp David later won the grudging respect of the Jewish electorate despite the role of George Ball, a presidential advisor, whom Jews viewed as anti-Israel and perhaps anti-Semitic as well. See John Ehrman, *The Rise of Neoconservatism: Intellectuals and Foreign Affairs, 1945–1994* (New Haven: Yale Univ. Press, 1995), 122–23.

21. Milton Himmelfarb, quoted in ibid., 123.

22. U.S. Congress, Senate, Senate Finance Committee, Subcommittee on International Trade, *Jackson-Vanik Waiver Authority Extension—China, Romania, Hungary,* Testimony of Sen. Henry M. Jackson, 21 July 1980.

23. Goldberg, *Jewish Power,* 180.

24. *JTA,* 14 Feb. 1979, 4.

25. Jackson continued to counsel against softening the "waiver authority" of the Trade Act of 1974, sec. 402(d)(5) until shortly before his death. Jackson reminded Reagan of his promise made in October 1980, in the heat of the presidential election campaign, to support the amendment under all circumstances.

26. *JTA,* 25 May 1979, 4.

27. Goodman to Wallach, Dec. 15, 1978, NCSJ, box 7, Goodman 1978 folder. Goodman suggested that "a succinct summary of the bill, with the appropriate amendments," would go far in clearing the air.

28. That was also true of some scholars examining the issue years later. See, for example, Robert Cullen, "Soviet Jewry," *Foreign Affairs* 65, no. 2 (winter 1986–87): 252–65.

29. NCSJ, box 8, Minutes of the Executive Committee folder, 26 June 1978. The committee authorized a request to the AJCong to reverse its stand on the Findlay bill. Squadron also suggested a one-year trial on the presidential waiver procedure. If the Soviets complied they would then be granted MFN.

30. Testimony before Committee on Banking, 10 Nov. 1978 (mimeographed), NCSJ, box 7, Goodman 1978 folder. On 13 June, three days before the scheduled Carter-Brezhnev meeting in Vienna where emigration and trade would be discussed, the NCSJ proposed "minimal criteria" for the lifting of trade and credit restrictions. Translated it meant no change but the possibility of reconsideration in the future.

31. Wallach to Goodman, 1 Dec. 1976, NCSJ, box 8, Executive Committee folder, 1976. She also counseled silence should repeal of the amendment become imminent.

32. Morris B. Abram, "Letter to the Editor," *New York Times,* 5 July 1983.

33. Laurie P. Salitan, "Domestic Pressures and the Politics of Exit: Trends in Soviet Emigration Policy," *Political Science Quarterly* 104, no.4 (winter 1989–1990): 671–87.

34. Goldman, "Jackson-Vanik," 122. See also his "Soviet Trade and Jewish Emigration: Should a Policy Change Be Made by the American Jewish Community?" in Freedman, *Soviet Jewry in the 1980s,* 141–59.

35. "Report on Leadership Assembly" (mimeographed), NCSJ, box 8, Executive Committee folder, 1974–75.

36. Basket IV contained four sections: human contacts, information flow, cultural cooperation, and educational cooperation. The Soviet Jewry issue came under human contacts that concerned governmental policies regarding status of citizens. The now-customary menu of rights was listed in a series of paragraphs, the most important of which was the eighth paragraph that repeated the right of free movement contained in articles 27 and 13(2) of the Universal Declaration of Human Rights.

37. Joseph Loconte, "Morality for Sale." *New York Times,* 1 Apr. 1904, A23.

38. Considering the number of people of Jewish origin who served in various capacities in the human rights area for the State Department (Morris Abram, Rita Hauser, Arthur Goldberg, Max Kampelman, Warren Zimmerman, Michael Novak, Elliot Abrams, Richard Schifter), one might conclude that it was considered a "Jewish" area of activity.

39. Hauser's revelations did not come as news to Jerry Goodman, who had received a report of a study for the AJC delivered on 21 Oct. 1963 telling of the enormous roadblocks that were developing in the United Nations regarding consideration of specific human rights complaints. Sidney Liskofsky to Goodman, 10 Apr. 1970, NCSJ, box 63, UN file.

40. Sheila Woods was made aware of the UN Commission's forthcoming meeting in Geneva in February 1973, but she too was pessimistic of the possibilities of working through a third world–dominated General Assembly. Memo, Sheila Woods to Jerry Goodman, 17 Jan. 1973, NCSJ, box 43, Human Rights folder. Two years later the UN General Assembly passed its "Zionism Is Racism" resolution.

41. Press release, US/UN-33(70), 34(70), 17 Mar. 1970, NCSJ, box 30, State Department folder.

42. News release, 14 Dec. 1972, NCSJ, box 63, UN folder.

43. See, for example, Robert Osgood's classic work, *Ideals and Self-Interest in American Foreign Relations: The Great Transformation of the Twentieth Century* (Chicago: Univ. of Chicago Press, 1953).

44. The restriction was precedented by a prior identical clause in title IX, section 116, of the Foreign Assistance Act of 1961. It was extended to the Food for Peace program in 1982.

45. U.S., *Congressional Record,* House of Representatives, 10 Sept. 1975, 8610. The measure surprisingly passed in the House by 74 votes but was defeated in the Senate.

46. The right of expatriation, the freedom of movement, or the right to leave and return to one's country is one of the rights embodied in natural law, the Magna Carta (1215), the French Constitution (1791), and an act of the U.S. Congress in 1868, which stated that "the Right of expatriation is a natural and inherent right of all people." It finally found its way into the Universal Declaration of Human Rights (article 29) adopted by the U.N. General Assembly on 10 Dec. 1948. From there the right to emigrate and return was included in most subsequent codifications concerning human rights, the Declaration on Granting Independence to Colonial Counties and Peoples (Dec. 1960), and the International Covenant on Civil and Political Rights (6 Dec. 1966), both adopted by the General Assembly of the United Nations. It was also included in a second body of international law concerning racialism. The International Convention on the Elimination of All Forms of Racial Discrimination was adopted by the General Assembly on 21 Dec. 1965, and the International Covenant on Economic, Social and Cultural Rights also passed unanimously on 16 Dec. 1966.

47. The Final Act, which was in effect a summary and refinement of all prior human rights statements, was signed by thirty-five nations, including the entire Soviet block.

48. Kampelman, *New World,* 218.

49. "The Congress of Helsinki," *Newsweek,* 16 July 1973, 38.

50. *An Evaluation of the Influence of the Helsinki Agreements as They Relate to Human Rights in the USSR,* 1 Aug. 1975–1 Aug. 1976, NCSJ, box 43, Helsinki-HR folder.

51. One of the earliest complaints regarding implementation was a complaint of the disruption of a scheduled symposium on Jewish culture in Moscow submitted by the Western Regional Conference on Soviet Jewry. The commission responded strongly on 12 Dec. 1976. A new way to amplify protest had been established. R. Spencer Oliver (staff director) to Robert M. Shafton, 10 Jan. 1976, NCSJ, box 83, Helsinki-HR folder.

52. The follow-up conferences lasted longer and longer, acting as a kind of permanent activator for the Organization for Security and Cooperation in Europe. They were convened in Belgrade (1977–78), Madrid (1980–83), Vienna (1986–89), Paris (1989) for a special subconference, Copenhagen (1990), Moscow (1991).

53. Quoted in World Jewish Congress, *Institute of Jewish Affairs,* Jan. 1973, 6.

54. They were Christopher Wren *(New York Times)*, Alfred Friendly Jr. *(Newsweek)*, and Krimsky (Associated Press). The operation was a typical KGB setup replete with evidence from Soviet citizens. The strategy called for breaking the link between Western reporters and the dissident movement. Four days before the Belgrade follow-up meeting, Robert Toth *(Los Angeles Times)*, who was writing on refusenik scientists, was also arrested and charged with espionage.

55. Altogether the KGB sweep led to over ninety arrests in fifteen cities. The charge of "crimes against the state" instead of the usual "slandering the Soviet state" was far more severe and reminiscent of the Stalin era.

56. That was the interpretation given to the events. See "The Sakharov Challenge" in the *Wall Street Journal,* 25 Mar. 1977.

57. David Prital (secretary general, Israel Public Council for Soviet Jewry) to Jerry Goodman, 22 June 1978, Goodman to Prital, 7 Aug. 1978, NCSJ, box 7, J. Goodman folder, 1978.

58. Margaret Galley, "Congress, Foreign Policy and Human Rights," *Human Rights Quarterly,* Aug. 1985, 344–53, contains tables cataloging all human rights details of all such legislation. The majority of proposals in the 95th Congress (1977) dealt with emigration from and harassment in the Soviet Union. Of the more than one hundred resolutions related to Helsinki, only three were adopted. Although only eight Helsinki-related resolutions were passed between 1977 and 1978, twenty-four were passed between 1981 and 1982.

59. U.S., *Congressional Record,* 94th Cong., 1st sess., 121, no. 182, 10 Dec. 1975.

60. See Amy Schapiro, *Millicent Fenwick: Her Way* (New Brunswick, N.J.: Rutgers Univ. Press, 2003).

61. According to information available to the NCSJ, the State Department tried hard to "pocket veto" HR15813, the bill to amend existing legislation to allow the establishment of the Helsinki commission as a standing committee. But Rep. Fenwick got wind of the plan. Ford signed the bill on 18 Oct. 1976.

62. The monitoring committees were quickly closed down in Eastern Europe, but in the West virtually every Jewish organization formed such a committee and communicated with the Fascell commission. Finally, in 1982 an International Helsinki Federation for Human Rights was founded by ten member groups, including watch committees in the United States and Canada.

63. In the case of Yuri Orlov, the founder of the Moscow Helsinki watch group, Fascell's reply to Orlov acknowledging the receipt of reports about the situation in the Soviet Union was used by the KGB when it tried Orlov and Sharansky.

64. A special place was reserved for the NCSJ to whom Fascell felt indebted for all the help it gave in getting the commission established. He expressed his thanks in person at the NCSJ board of governors meeting on 26 Oct. 1976.

65. As finally agreed to, Basket III contained three provisions relating to emigration: Signatories should deal "in a positive and humanitarian spirit with persons who wish to be reunited with members of their family." They must do so "as expeditiously as possible," and visa applicants should be treated in a way that does "not modify the rights and obligations of the applicant or of members of his family."

66. An additional office, Coordinator for Human Rights and Humanitarian Affairs, was established during the Carter administration in 1977. Richard Schifter, who succeeded Elliot Abrams in 1985 as coordinator with the rank of assistant secretary of state, then became the ranking government official on Soviet Jewish affairs.

67. He was given the rank of ambassador. Sen. Robert Dole shared the chairmanship of the commission with Goldberg. The two deputies were Spencer Oliver, who was eloquent in defense of human rights but had little support in the State Department, and Warren Zimmerman of the State Department Foreign Service. It was Max Kampelman, who succeeded Arthur Goldberg as delegation head, who ultimately shaped the commission into a formidable diplomatic instrument.

68. The appointment of Arthur Goldberg, who was to play a pivotal role in the success of the conference, was "accidental." He was pushed on Carter as a Middle East expert and negotiator by Hubert Humphrey. But the appointment ran into staunch opposition from Vance and Brzezinski. Goldberg's shift to an appointment to chair the delegation with the rank of ambassador was a "face saving" device. Kampelman, *Memoirs,* 220–21.

69. See Albert W. Sherer Jr., "Helsinki's Child: Goldberg's Variation," *Foreign Policy,* summer 1980, 155. See also Malcom W. Browne, "Little Gain Since Helsinki Accords, Eastern and Western Aides Agree," *New York Times,* 12 Sept. 1976.

70. The arrests continued unabated. In 1980 alone there were 242 arrests of Jews and non-Jews, the highest number of arrests in fifteen years. *JTA,* 31 June 1981, 2.

71. Quoted in Karl Helicher, "The Response of the Soviet Government and Press to Carter's Human Rights Policies," *Presidential Quarterly,* spring 1983, 296–304. When Andrew Young, Carter's UN ambassador, spoke of thousands of political prisoners in the United States, the statement was fully exploited in the Soviet media.

72. Quoted in Newsletter no. 94–8, Rep. Sidney R. Yates, 21 Aug. 1975, NCSJ, box 31, House of Representatives folder.

73. Report CSCE, 2 Dec. 1976, NCSJ, box 43, Human Rights–Helsinki folder.

74. A similar observation is made by Sherer, "Helsinki's Child," 155. See also Thomas Buergental, *International Human Rights in a Nutshell,* 2nd ed. (St. Paul, Minn.: West Publishing, 1995), 167ff.

75. The arrest of the Helsinki Watch group in Moscow, for example, occurred a few days before the Belgrade follow-up conference called to evaluate compliance with Helsinki's Final Act.

76. "Report of the Study Mission to Europe of the Commission on Security and Cooperation in Europe," 2 Dec. 1976.

77. Quoted in *Soviet Jewish Action Newsletter* 11, no. 3 (mid-June 1979); "Waiting, Watching," NCSJ, box 43, Human Rights—Helsinki folder.

78. NCSJ, box 8, Board of Governors Meetings folder (1), 18 Feb. 1977. He urged that the administration be commended when it defends human rights "even when Soviet Jews are not mentioned."

79. Alexeyeva, *Soviet Dissent,* 180. See also Gitelman, "Soviet Jews," 88–89.

80. Paul Goldberg, *The Final Act: The Dramatic, Revealing Story of the Moscow Helsinki Watch Group* (New York: Morrow, 1988), 143.

81. NJCRAC Report, 22 Mar. 1977, NCSJ, box 8, Board of Governors folder.

82. The broad range of different religious, ethnic, ideological, and national groups in the dissident movement are best described in Alexeyeva, *Soviet Dissent,* 3–15.

83. Ibid., 12.

84. Rustin to Goodman, Sept. 9, 1977, NCSJ, box 43, Human Rights folder. Most significant was Goodman's observation of the consensus of the conferees that "Soviet Union *wants* but doesn't *need* economic benefits from this country"; therefore, the use of the human rights instrument was called for. Goodman to Gold, Oct. 25, 1977, NCSJ, box 43, Human Rights folder.

85. Quoted in Jeane J. Kirkpatrick, "Establishing a Viable Human Rights Policy," *World Affairs,* spring 1981, 324.

86. The signing was in fact delayed until 18 June 1979, shortly before Carter's term expired.

87. Gromyko, *Memoirs,* 292–94.

88. See revelations in James Dao, "Argentine Junta Felt Safe from U.S." in *New York Times,* 22 Aug. 2002. See also Winik, *On the Brink,* 433.

89. Carter never solved the problem but on the intellectual level Jeane Kirkpatrick drew the distinction between "our" tyrants, who were authoritarian and not permanent, and "theirs," who moved to ever more total control and were impossible to remove once they gained power.

90. U.S. Department of State, *American Foreign Policy: Basic Documents, 1977–1980* (Washington, D.C.: Department of State), doc. 234, 558–59; doc. 163, 418. News conference, 8 Feb. 1977. See also *Public Papers of the Presidents: Jimmy Carter, 1977–1981* (Washington, D.C.: Federal Register Division, 1978–1982), vol. 1, 99–100.

91. Section 502B of the Foreign Assistance Act of 1961, which prohibited security assistance to human rights violators, was applied primarily against twelve Latin American Republics during the Carter administration. See David P. Forsythe, "Congress and Human Rights in U.S. Foreign Policy: The Fate of General Legislation," *Human Rights Quarterly* 9 (1987): 383.

92. Jimmy Carter, *Keeping Faith: Memoirs of a President* (New York: Bantam, 1982), 142.

93. The letter delivered to Philip Habib may have steered Carter away from the human rights issue. There was also the influence of Cyrus Vance, who pointed out that "one shot" affairs do not a foreign policy make. See Martin Garbus, *Traitors and Heroes: A Lawyer's Memoir* (New York: Atheneum, 1987), 179–92.

94. Minutes 26 July 1978, NCSJ, box 8, Executive Committee folder, 1976–78.

95. Soviet census figures are not fully reliable, but enough can be estimated to conclude that up to 1980 emigration was still a minority movement in Soviet Jewry. Of the 2.1 million Jews given by the Soviet census of 1970 only approximately 180,000 emigrated. Even if one estimates that the emigration pool was double that number, emigration remains a distinct minority movement. The Jew-

ish population study for 1979 projected a loss of more than a quarter of a million Soviet Jews since the 1970 census, but the majority of the 270,000 were lost to natural attrition and change in national identity declaration. The picture changed again by 1989. See Maurice Samuelson, "New National Soviet Census May Show Decline of Jewish Population," *JTA*, 18 Jan. 1989, 4.

7. The Soviet Jewry Question During the Reagan Years

1. Lest the manichaean element in Reagan's thought be carried too far, his "evil empire" reference came from George Lucas's 1977 *Star Wars* film, and his Star Wars proposal (Strategic Defense Initiative) resembles a theme in *The Empire Strikes Back,* its profitable 1980 sequel.

2. A good explanation of this approach can be found in Samuel Huntington, "Human Rights and American Power," *Commentary,* Sept. 1981, 37–43.

3. The neocon affiliation was not formal or organizational. Only two of the founders of the movement, Norman Podhoretz and Irving Kristol, accept the classification. The third, Daniel Bell, does not. Daniel Moynihan preferred to be known as a neoliberal. Aside from Kirkpatrick, who is not precisely in the neocon camp, there was also Elliot Abrams, Daniel Moynihan's former congressional assistant who eventually became assistant secretary of state for international organization affairs before he headed the department's human rights division. Max Kampelman would probably not consider himself a neoconservative though he shared their apprehension about Soviet intentions.

4. Norman Podhoretz, "The Neo-Conservative Anguish Over Reagan's Foreign Policy," *New York Times Sunday Magazine,* 2 May 1982, 30.

5. Shultz traced his commitment to Avital Sharansky's visit, which left him "wrung out" and frustrated at his inability to provide assurances about her husband's release. George P. Shultz, *Turmoil and Triumph: My Years as Secretary of State* (New York: Scribner's, 1993), 121.

6. Beginning in 1980 defense spending rose from $135 billion to $234 billion in 1984.

7. That can be partly attributed to the lifting of Carter's grain embargo on 25 Apr. 1981. Clearly Reagan's rhetoric was not allowed to interfere with business. The grain agreement was placed on a guaranteed annual basis by the Agricultural and Food Act of 1981, which compelled the Soviets to buy 9 million metric tons yearly. Grain was considered a nonstrategic item. See also Libbey, *Economic Relations,* 123, and Gary K. Bertsch, "American Politics and Trade with the USSR," in Bruce Parrott, ed., *Trade, Technology and Soviet-American Relations* (Bloomington: Indiana Univ. Press, 1985), 258.

8. Goldman, "Soviet American Trade and Soviet Jewish Emigration: Should a Policy Change Be Made by the American Jewish Community?" in Freedman, *Soviet Jewry in the 1908s,* 11. There is no agreement on the status of Soviet arms development except that it was appreciably upgraded during the Reagan administration. According to defense analyst Edward Luttwak, the Soviets had developed armaments of such destructive power that no equivalent existed in the West. Arnold Ages, "Behind the Headlines Soviet and American Military Might: The Jewish Factor," *JTA*, 12, 13 Sept. 1983.

9. After the NAM convened a conference February 1973 entitled "The New Realities and Opportunities in Expanding U.S.-Soviet Commercial Relations," it was target centered by the NCSJ and

the SSSJ for special attention, including a petition from forty-four Soviet Jews to E. Douglas Kenna, president of the NAM. See Goodman to Kenna, 14 Mar. 1973, NCSJ, box 63, Trade North America folder. See also Interview with Richard Maass, NYPL, Wiener Oral History, 1989, for NCSJ pressure on chief executive officers who did business with the Soviet Union.

10. U.S., *Congressional Record*, 93rd Cong., 1st sess., vol. 119, no. 56, 10 Apr. 1973.

11. Quoted in Bertsch, "Politics and Trade," in Parrott, *Trade, Technology*, 243.

12. The U.S. embargo of pipeline and oil drilling technology to the Soviets was based partly on the fear that Europe would become dependent on the Soviets for fuel. See Shultz, *Turmoil and Triumph*, 124.

13. His successor, Yuri Andropov, governed for less than two years when he died in February 1984, and his successor Konstantin Chernenko was in power less than a year when he was succeeded by Mikhail Gorbachev in March 1985. The rapid turnover of leadership in a society where the *Vozhd* (leader) plays a crucial role in governance surely contributed to the sense of instability.

14. The Reagan administration's export controls concentrated mostly on denying the Soviets advanced technology that could enhance its military capabilities rather than grain and consumer goods. See Libbey, *Economic Relations*, 135.

15. Some believe that Chernobyl and the sinking of the passenger ship *Nakhimov* in August, followed by the loss of a missile-carrying submarine off Bermuda in October, did much to shake Soviet self-confidence. It dimmed the hope of catching up and surpassing the West. Marshall I. Goldman, *Gorbachev's Challenge: Economic Reform in the Age of High Technology* (New York: Norton, 1987), 4–5.

16. One estimate places the meats and produce grown in privately owned gardens as high as 40 percent. LaFeber, *America, Russia and the Cold War*, 245.

17. Theodore H. Friedgut, "Passing Eclipse: The Exodus Movement in the 1980s," in Freedman, *Soviet Jewry in 1980s*, 7.

18. F. Stephen Larrabee and Dimitri K. Simes, "Don't Underestimate the Soviet Union," *Alert* 6, no. 1 (13 July 1981): 7.

19. Disarmament negotiations were almost continuous, and when some agreement seemed possible it resulted in a summit meeting. In June 1979 a second SALT agreement was signed but not submitted for Senate ratification because of the invasion of Afghanistan in December. It was followed by the Reagan Star Wars proposal in March 1983. The Geneva Summit (Nov. 1985) proposed a 50 percent reduction of nuclear weapons and was followed in October 1986 by the Reykjavik summit, which proposed to place human rights on a par with disarmament. Reagan proposed the need for verification, "trust but verify," which was put into place in December 1987 by a treaty to dismantle all medium- and short-range missiles in Europe and to establish a verification system.

20. Interview with Morris Abram, NYPL, Wiener Oral History, 6 Mar. 1989.

21. Ibid. See also "Jewish Groups Launch Campaign to Put Soviet Jewry Issue on Summit Agenda," *JTA*, 19 Nov. 1985.

22. The statement referred to the high number of exit visas granted in 1979. At the same time the well-known Washington law firm of White and Case prepared pro bono a study that compared Soviet emigration practices to international norms. It concluded that Soviet practices flouted all international norms concerning standards of emigration. Submitted to the Soviet foreign office it hit

on a sore point, the question of whether given its current emigration policy the Soviet Union matched the "civilized" standards of the West.

23. Quoted in "Failure of Summit Meeting May Diminish Possibilities for Improvement of Soviet Human Rights Practices," *JTA*, 15 Oct. 1986.

24. The accusation was standard fare among activists in the Soviet Union and the United States. See, for example, "Two Congressmen Say Soviet Jews Are Being Held Hostage for Future Deals with the U.S.," *JTA*, 25 Jan. 1982.

25. The Reagan administration cultivated close ties with Israel and valued its military strength. When it destroyed Iraq's Osirak nuclear reactor in June 1981, the American protest was pro forma. But the support was not across the board. Alexander Haig, Shultz's predecessor as secretary of state, was a strong supporter of Israel, but the secretary of defense, Caspar Weinberger, was more reserved and later revealed an animus at the espionage trial of Jonathan Pollard.

26. The reasons for their sustained opposition were twofold: It violated the principle of freedom of movement, and it undermined the moral force of the international human rights movement. Naftalin, "Activist Movement," 236–37. A later suggestion by the Dutch that dropouts be temporarily settled in Israel for one year was rejected by the State Department on the grounds that such emigrants would then automatically lose their status as refugees.

27. The Anti-Zionist Committee of the Soviet Public was established after the second Brussels Conference and reached its peak activity between 1983 and 1985. Promoted by Jewish Party members such as David Dragunsky and Samuil Zivs, its primary task was to dissuade Jews from immigrating to Israel. But it did so by promoting the party line, which spoke of the parallel between Nazism and Zionism. Despite its access to the media few Soviet Jews took the organization seriously.

28. "Mendelevich Criticizes Israel for Paying Scant Attention to Prisoners of Zion, "*JTA*, 23 Feb. 1981.

29. "Soviet Israeli Talks in Helsinki End After 90 Minutes: Meeting Is Described as 'Frank and Correct,'"*JTA*, 19 Aug. 1986.

30. There were numerous reports of Soviet efforts to cut the crucial contact with the outside by interfering with mail delivery and person-to-person contact. The high point of such interference came in July 1984 with a new regulation prohibiting citizens from transporting, housing, or providing "other services" to "foreigners" privately. "Report USSR Intensifies Campaign to Curtail Informal Contacts," *JTA*, 30 July 1984.

31. The observation belongs to Friedgut, "Passing Eclipse," 13.

32. There was a "systematic disregard of congressional intent" on the human rights question in Reagan's first administration and, according to Elliot Abrams, reluctance to use economic aid in support of a human rights policy. Forsyth, "Congress and Human Rights," 382, 387.

33. That this was actual policy was confirmed by Michael Gale, Reagan's liaison with the Jewish community. David Friedman, "Administration to Raise Soviet Jewry Emigration Issue at all Top Level U.S.-USSR Meetings," *JTA*, 22 July 1982.

34. Witnesses attribute the liberalization of Soviet emigration policy largely to the "unrelenting pressure" exercised by American leaders such as Shultz. Direct intervention didn't always work. When in May 1988 Reagan proposed to visit Yuri and Talyana Zieman, a family of refuseniks for ten years, he was forced to cancel when the family received KGB threats. A few months later the Zie-

mans received their exit permits. Gorbachev objected to Shultz's Seder activities and claimed that the refuseniks were not representative of the millions of patriotic Russian Jews who were loyal to the system, to which Shultz replied, "if you don't want them we'll take them." He later recounted that Ida Nudel's call from Jerusalem stating "I'm home" was "one of my most moving moments in my years as Secretary of State." Shultz, *Turmoil and Triumph,* 886–87, 894, 990. See also Schifter, "American Diplomacy," in Friedman and Chernin, *Second Exodus,* 155; Bewalda, *Dwell Alone,* 155–58. Don Oberdorfer, *The Turn: From the Cold War to the New Era: The United States and the Soviet Union, 1983–1990* (New York: Poseidon Press, 1991), 226.

35. Interview with Nechemia Levanon, NYPL, Wiener Oral History, 3 Dec. 1989, 74.

36. The case is all the more confusing since by 1989 the number of Pentecostals in the emigration stream may have been as high as 18.2 percent. See Bewalda, *Dwell Alone,* 183.

37. The Jewish vote for Republican candidates in the elections of 1980, 1984, and 1988 hovered between 32 and 35 percent, but in the election of 1980 John Anderson, the third-party candidate, siphoned off 14 percent of the Jewish vote. That was the first time since the election of 1924 that the majority of the Jewish vote did not go to the Democratic presidential candidate. Thirty Jewish members of the Coalition for Reagan-Bush, which included Max Fisher, George Klein, and Laurence Tisch, occasionally met with Reagan and members of the administration on specific issues such as the AWACS deal with Saudi Arabia. Noteworthy too is the emergence of Jewish candidates to Congress after 1967. In the election of 1988, thirty-one Jewish representatives (many from California) won seats in the House. There were eight Jewish senators elected, most on the Democratic ticket. Jewish office holding increased at the juncture when the Jewish proportion of the population was decreasing from 2.3 percent. Jews were winning elections in districts where there was no Jewish constituency.

38. The exit poll showed the traditional 70/30 split between Democrats and Republicans continued and the welfare of Israel remained the primary issue for the Jewish voter. Jewish representation in Congress increased slightly. "Two Jewish Senators Running for Reelection Win: The Number of Jewish Congressmen Stands at 30," *JTA,* 8 Nov. 1984.

39. Days before Elie Wiesel's plea at the White House Medal of Achievement award ceremony it was clear that a public relations disaster was in the making. But once scheduled it was staunchly supported by Pat Buchanan, a right-wing speech writer for Reagan who was considered a Holocaust denier by some Jewish leaders. Strangely, the Bitburg incident did not thereafter noticeably change the amicable relationship of the American Jewish electorate with the Reagan administration.

40. Interview with Phil Baum, NYPL, Wiener Oral History, 1989, n.d.

41. The actual reform process began earlier. In August 1986 a new chapter was added to the official "Statute on Entering and Leaving the Soviet Union" (1970).

42. By 1990 about 1,500 refusenik cases were still outstanding. Most were based on contact with security matters. In some cases the security factor was contrived, and personal pique might have played a role.

43. Though the law originated because of a desire to restrict refugee status, the Refugee Act of 1980 not only contained a broad definition of refugee but also continued the provisions to provide housing, medical care, employment, or retraining once such status had been granted. The major cost for the care of Soviet Jewish emigrants in Rome and Vienna was provided under this law. But ac-

cess was limited to 85,000 for all refugees (Cubans, Haitians, and Vietnamese) so that even a special increase in the Soviet refugee quota through the attorney general's parole authority would only have provided access for only 43,500. The shortfall came to a head in the first year of the Bush administration in 1989 and triggered the writing of new refugee regulations that made it far more difficult for Soviet emigrants to enter as refugees.

44. But at the same time Reagan expanded the parolee category so that a refugee could enter providing support was assured by guarantors.

45. Almost all Israeli political leaders acknowledged the centrality of immigration to Israel's survival. But few went as far as Yitzhak Rabin who was convinced that Israel would have been able to avoid its perpetual war with its Arab neighbors had there been 6 or 7 million Jews in Israel instead of 3.5 million.

46. Winik quoting George Wills, *On The Brink,* 272.

47. Included was the leadership of the NCSJ, the UCSJ, and the World Conference for Soviet Jewry. Conspicuous by their absence were representatives of Israel who had not been invited to join the CSCE.

48. The result was that members of the SSSJ, which was also picketing the performance, were assaulted by several of the evacuated audience who assumed that the SSSJ was involved.

49. David Andelman, "The Road to Madrid," *Foreign Policy,* summer 1980, 167–82.

50. The Bronx-born Kampelman boasted a solid Jewish background and would have passed as an ordinary Jackson Democrat but for his pacifism during World War II. He was passed over by Carter who appointed Governor William Scranton to the Helsinki post. Kampelman later became co-chair at the urging of Vice President Mondale who recognized Kampelman as an associate of his fellow Minnesotan, Hubert Humphrey, who died in 1978. Bell resigned after Carter's defeat in 1980. Kampelman was the only Democrat to be reappointed by Reagan and was later also appointed to head the American negotiating team for the upcoming arms talks in 1985.

51. U.S. Department of State, *American Foreign Policy,* doc. 176, 456, "Human Rights vs. Peace," 13 Nov. 1980, Madrid. A month earlier former Sen. Muskie of Maine sounded a similar note as if to assure the European members that the United States would not use Madrid as a propaganda platform. But it could not ignore recent violations. "Address of Secretary of State Muskie, Oct. 21, 1980, University of Wisconsin, Madison," doc. 172, 443–46.

52. Winik, *On the Brink,* 134–36.

53. Kampelman, *Memoirs,* 190. Kampelman was a member of the Coalition for a Democratic Majority, a group formed after the nomination of McGovern, who sought to bring the party back to its antitotalitarian position. Included were Lane Kirkland, Richard Schifter, Ben Wattenberg, Jeane Kirkpatrick, Hubert Humphrey, Scoop Jackson, Gene Rostow, Paul Nitze, Henry Fowler, James Schlesinger, and Elmo Zumwalt. Members of the Reagan administration such as George Shultz were honorary members.

54. When the Soviets seemed anxious to convene another conference, Kampelman asked for gestures of good faith and the release of political and religious prisoners, including Sharansky. The deal fell through when Sharansky rejected the idea of requesting release on the grounds of poor health.

55. "Diplomat Says Western Unity Was Achieved at Madrid Conference, "*JTA,* 21 Jan. 1981.

56. "Shultz to Emphasize USSR Human Rights Violations When He Goes to Vienna," *JTA*, 3 Nov. 1986.

57. Shultz, *Turmoil and Triumph*, 574–75.

58. The pledge to confront the Soviets with the human rights issue was fully realized in the fourth and final of the Reagan summit conferences in May–June 1988 in Moscow. Abram observed that the use of summit conferences to advance the human rights cause in which the emigration issue was embedded had become "absolutely institutionalized" during the Reagan administration. "Reagan Pledges to Push Moscow On Soviet Jews and Human Rights," *JTA*, May 13, 1988.

59. Warren Zimmerman, Kampelman's successor, assured him that he was aware that the Soviets ignored "textual commitments" when it suited them. See Korey, *Promises*, 239–40.

60. Schifter, "American Diplomacy," 152–53.

61. Shultz, *Turmoil and Triumph*, 1138.

62. Quoted in Freedman, "Soviet Jewry as a Factor," 93.

63. The implementation of the new regulations did not mean that emigration was unhampered. As late as February 1988 there was evidence that OVIR was now strictly interpreting the "close relatives" provision of the regulations and were also enforcing the "poor relative" and male conscription requirement. Applications not supported by legitimate affidavits from first-degree relatives were not accepted for processing. Shultz met with fifty such rejectees during his Moscow meeting with Shevardnadze on 22 Feb. 1987.

64. Shamir offered Israeli immigrants in the United States the services of Israel's absorption ministry to attract them to return to Israel. "Shamir's U.S. Agenda Also Included Yordim," *JTA*, 25 Feb. 1987.

65. "Sharansky Proposes That the West Offer the USSR Quid Pro Quo," *JTA*, 27 Mar. 1987.

66. Wolf Blitzer, "Israel Doesn't Oppose U.S. Aiding Soviets, *"Jerusalem Post*, 30 Nov. 1987.

67. Israel was not alone in advocating a softening of the waiver provision of the amendment. A meeting between the American Jewish leadership and American business leaders held at the Bronfman suite in Manhattan on 9 Jan. 1989 finally convinced many that the Jackson amendment had outlived its usefulness.

68. Bewalda, *Dwell Alone*, 160–63. The offer to give the franchise for these flights to KLM was rejected.

69. Reliable figures on *yerida* are difficult to come by partly because many of those leaving Israel did not consider themselves permanent immigrants. A conservative estimate of 400,000 made in 1990 assumed that most would be permanent. Another estimate is that at any point 10 percent of Israel's population lives outside the country and most will not return. Even with the statistics published by Israel's Ministry of Labor and Social Welfare, which estimates that between 1969 and 1979, 510,528 Israelis left the country and 384,000 Soviet emigrants settled there, Israel's population was not stabilized. It appeared more like a revolving door with Soviet and other emigrants entering the front door while Israelis were leaving through the back door.

70. A campaign to revert to the former policy of classifying as refugees all dropouts was led in Congress by Rep. Charles Schumer. But the problem of cost, especially those entering under the parole authority, was high because HIAS would have to foot the entire bill. HIAS advised emigrants in Italy not to choose the parole option. It cost the JDC $10 per diem for each emigrant. "Lawmakers Urge Refugee Status Be Given to All Jews," *JTA*, 12 Dec. 1988.

8. Free at Last

1. Quoted in Heitman, "Jewish, German and Armenian," 136.

2. While Reagan often referred to "evil" in his speeches he only used the term "evil empire" once on 8 Mar. 1983 when he spoke before the annual convention of Evangelics in Orlando. He never repeated it and may later have regretted using it.

3. Amalrik, *Will The Soviet Union Survive Until 1984?*

4. Michael Gordon, "U.S. to Ease Backlog in Soviet Emigration, But Draws Criticism," *New York Times,* 9 Dec. 1988, A1.

5. The budget debacle brought a Jewish delegation to Washington to discuss the matter with Shultz who was again told that American Jewry favors "freedom of choice" but with a new twist: the choice should be exercised in the Soviet Union, not in Italy. A few days later the House appropriated $24 million for refugee absorption, $6 million of which was earmarked for Soviet emigrants.

6. Kathleen Teltsch, "Groups Are Bracing to Help More Refugees on Slim Funds," *New York Times,* 11 Jan. 1988, A9.

7. "Israel Is Preparing to Receive Up to 1,000 Jews a Day," *JTA,* 13 Dec. 1989.

8. Quoted in Gregg A. Beyer, "The Evolving United States Response to Soviet Jewish Emigration," *Journal of Palestinian Studies* 21, no. 1 (autumn 1991): 143.

9. Clyde Haberman, "For Stranded Jews 'When' Is Now 'If'," *New York Times,* 11 Dec. 1988.

10. The estimate was similar to the State Department's and was based on the fact that the annual trickle of about 1,000 between 1980 and 1986 rose to 11,500 in 1987 and then to over 30,000 in 1988. The rise after that was so rapid that it quickly outpaced the ability of the INS to manage it.

11. *Reconstructionist,* Apr.–May 1989, 6.

12. Sachar, *History of the Jews,* 933.

13. "Government Policy, Not Written Law Most Important for Jewish Emigration: State Department," *JTA,* 9 June 1987. See also "Soviet Emigration Policy Meant to Satisfy U.S., Discourages Most Jews," *JTA,* 12 June 1987.

14. Interview with Rabbi Herschel Schacter, NYPL, Wiener Oral History, 1989.

15. Aside from the massive Washington rally in December, the organizations had gathered in Helsinki to greet Reagan before the fourth Summit Conference to be held in Moscow beginning on 29 May. The NCSJ held public hearings on Moscow's compliance with Helsinki Final Act, and there were Friday night services at Helsinki's main synagogue, to be followed by a dinner during which Shultz repeated his "we will never give up" theme. On the Sabbath there was a silent vigil in the center of the city. The Israeli embassy held a reception for human rights groups. The carefully orchestrated activities were covered in the press.

16. For example, in January 1988 the UCSJ convened a Commission of Inquiry to hear testimony from former refuseniks. B'nai B'rith international planned to stage a series of giant rallies to read the names of 12,000 refuseniks, and the SSSJ and other student groups spent days lobbying individuals in Congress.

17. Interview with Morris Abram, NYPL, Wiener Oral History, 6 Mar. 1989. The WJC was not a member of the NCSJ and as a world organization preferred to work on its own. Its well-publicized success in gaining the release of Iosif Mendelevich, imprisoned for his role in the Leningrad hijacking, was arranged privately through Bronfman's personal relationship with Dobrynin. *JTA,* 19 Feb.

1981, 1. In April 1985 he headed a delegation opposed to the Jackson-Vanik amendment to Moscow for talks in his dual capacity as a business leader and the leader of the World Jewish Congress.

18. In recent Jewish experience government negotiations with private Jewish organizations about the disposition of its Jewry is not unprecedented. Berlin did so in 1938–39 in the negotiations that grew out of the Rublee-Schacht-Wohlthat negotiations that produced a "Statement of Agreement" with outside Jews about the disposition of German Jewry. See Feingold, *Politics of Rescue,* 47–89.

19. Interview with Morris Abram, NYPL, Wiener Oral History, 6 Mar. 1989.

20. "Behind the Headlines: A Simmering Dispute." *JTA,* 3 Apr. 1987.

21. A ram's horn customarily sounded in the Judaic liturgy during the high holy days. The shofar was blown during the ceremonies.

22. Interview with Malcolm Hoenlein, NYPL, Wiener Oral History, 14 June 1989.

23. *JTA,* 7 Dec. 1987, 1.

24. Ibid.

25. Interview with Yehoshua Pratt, NYPL, Wiener Oral History, 1989.

26. Interview with Richard Maass, NYPL, Wiener Oral History, 1989. Goodman resigned after a heated meeting of the NCSJ's board of governors on 11 January. At the same time the board appointed him as a life member of the executive committee. Goodman himself recognized that after glasnost and "Freedom Sunday" the movement was entering its final phase.

27. Goldman, "Jackson-Vanik," 21.

28. "U.S. Jewish Group Shifts on Soviet," *New York Times,* 25 May 1986, A15.

29. Schifter, "American Diplomacy," 155.

30. In 1986, from $19 to $24 billion untied general purpose loans at low cost were made available, mostly from Japanese and some European banking houses. It was a source of concern for the Reagan administration, which called for an economic summit to fashion a uniform policy on private loans to the Soviet Union.

31. "Union of Councils Is Reluctant to Give Soviets a Quid Pro Quo," *JTA,* 12 Jan. 1989.

32. Howard Rosenberg, "Higher Jewish Emigration Rates May Continue, Shultz Indicates," *JTA,* 4 May 1988.

33. Susan Birnbaum, "Soviet Jewry Movement To Reexamine Stance on U.S.-Soviet Trade Relations," *JTA,* 11 Jan. 1989. According to the *JTA* correspondent the change followed hard upon a "secret" meeting of top Jewish leadership in Bronfman's penthouse apartment.

34. "Gorbachev Speaks of Ties with Israel, Differs with U.S. on Human Rights," *JTA,* 2 June 1988.

35. Quoted by Bewalda, *Dwell Alone,* 214.

36. "Soviets OK New Emigration Law: Jackson-Vanik Would Be Waived," *JTA,* 17 Nov. 1989.

37. Howard M. Sachar, *Israel and Europe: An Appraisal in History* (New York: Knopf, 1999), 332.

38. That event occurred after Israel sent a medical team to Armenia after the earthquake in December 1988 and followed with the construction of a children's rehabilitation center. Several probes later an Israeli delegation led by Yitzhak Moda'i met with Gorbachev in September 1990, shortly after Iraq's invasion of Kuwait. Consular relationships were reestablished on 5 October, to be followed by full-scale diplomatic relations. In turn the Soviet Union became a co-host of the next CSCE follow-up conference.

39. U.S., House of Representatives, Subcommittee on Immigration, *Report of the Hearings on Soviet Refugees, Refugees and International Law,* 6 Apr. 1989. Testimony of Mark Talisman and Ben Zion Leuchter, 247ff.

40. David Landau, "Agency Chairman Heads for U.S. Showdown Over Soviet Aid," *JTA,* 10 Apr. 1989.

41. Ibid.

42. Micah H. Naftalin, "Give Soviet Jews a Choice," *New York Times,* 18 June 1987, op. ed. page.

43. John M. Goshko, "Israel Fails in Plan to Divert Soviet Jews," *Washington Post,* 23 Oct. 1988, 33. Undoubtedly the Reagan administration was aware of the growing cost of its generous refugee policy, but it would have been politically unwise to change it a month before the election.

44. The Morrison bill would give Vietnamese, Pentecostals, and Soviet Jews equal presumption of eligibility for the 1990 fiscal year. The bill softened the "well founded fear of persecution" clause but did not eliminate it. By July 1989, 3,000 Soviet Jews had been denied a visa and an additional 400 had their appeal application rejected. The rejections triggered a hunger strike outside the U.S. Embassy in Rome.

45. "Jewish Groups May Not Fight Plan to Cut Immigration to U.S," *JTA,* 5 Sept. 1989.

46. Researchers take different positions on Israel's role and whether American Jewry finally reacted to an imagined threat to Israel. Orleck, *Soviet Jewish Americans,* and Bewalda, *Dwell Alone,* see it as primarily the former. A recent study by Prof. Fred Lazin attributes much of the change to Israel back-channel diplomacy. *The Struggle for Soviet Jewry in American Politics: Israel versus the American Jewish Establishment* (Lanham, Md.: Lexington Books, 2005).

47. Quoted in Beyer, "The Evolving United States Response," 143.

48. Before the Refugee Act of 1980 was changed in August 1988, the U.S. government assumed subsistence expenses during refugee processing under the law's "care and maintenance" provision.

49. Signers were the UCSJ, NCSJ, HIAS, AJC, and AJCong.

50. *JTA,* 6 Sept. 1989, 3.

51. The emigrants had organized themselves into the Tehiya Party and a new organization calling itself "Israel Action" whose purpose was to purge Israel's policy of its duality. As the time of the Helsinki meeting approached demonstrators blocked a traffic artery in Jerusalem and caused a mammoth traffic tie-up.

52. "Sharansky Critical of Israel's Policy Regarding Soviet Jewry," *JTA,* 10 July 1986.

53. Precise statistics vary with the agency giving them but in round numbers the total relationship between American and Israeli absorption between 1967 and 1995 comes to about 786,000 to Israel and 430,000 to the United States. Of these, 235,000 arrived after the Lautenberg Amendment passed in fall 1989, which included about 15,000 non-Jews, most of which came to United States.

54. The figure usually given to stabilize existing Israel's population is an influx of 750,000 immigrants to maintain a 60:40 Palestinian/Israeli ratio. For the absorption of the territories while remaining a Jewish state, an emigration of 8 million would have been required. In a word, well over 50 percent of the Jewish population of the diaspora was required to create a population of 12.7 million Jews as compared to 3.2 million Arabs. See Clive Jones, *Soviet Jewish Aliyah, 1989–1992: Impact and Implications for Israel and the Middle East* (London: Frank Cass, 1996), 66–67.

55. Quoted in ibid., 57. In a similar vein, when the absorption of 20,000 expected *Olim* was being planned for, housing minister David Levy suggested an "ideological call" for West Bank set-

tlers to "adopt" immigrants upon arrival. "All Want to Aid Absorption Effort, But Few Agree Who Will Pay for It," *JTA,* 3 July 1989.

56. Precise statistics are hard to come by. One estimate for the 1987–88 year is as high as 10 to 12 percent. A more precise statistic between April 1989 and June 1990 shows only 285 Soviet emigrants settled on the West Bank. Jones, *Soviet Jewish Aliyah,* 160.

57. Actually the traditional Solidarity Sunday rally, which began in 1972, was also cancelled the prior year, in 1988. A small token demonstration was staged before the Soviet UN Mission by SSSJ and the Long Island Committee for Soviet Jewry.

58. "A More Modest 'Solidarity' Rally for Soviet Jews Staged This Year," *JTA,* 8 May 1989.

59. Interview with Yoram Dinstein, NYPL, Wiener Oral History Project, 8 Nov. 1989.

9. Afterthoughts

1. The term is used in Robert Putnam, *Bowling Alone: The Collapse and Revival of American Community* (New York: Simon and Schuster, 2000), to describe the effect of the decline of social organizations. There have been prior organizations in the American Jewish experience that focused on a particular problem but not as formal and extensive as the NCSJ and the UCSJ.

2. Sachar, *History of the Jews,* 906.

3. Shapiro, introduction to Kochan, *Jews in Soviet Russia,* 13. See also Henry L. Feingold, "The Russian Aliyah: Communal Rescue or Plunder?" *Jewish Frontier* 64, no. 3 (May–June 1997).

4. The argument that Soviet Jewry was in sharp decline is supported by the census of 1979 that showed a loss from 2.1 million in 1970 to 1.9 million in 1979, a decline of 270,000. The major portion is attributable to change in national identity declaration. The greater internal loss would in any case have led to the irreversible decline of Soviet Jewry. See "Decline in Jewish Population in SU," *JTA,* 17 Jan. 1979.

5. The downward thrust continued. It is estimated that by 2000 fewer than a million Jews, 0.5 percent of the population, remained in Russia, 39 percent of whom were classified as atheists or agnostics.

6. Editorial, *Reconstructionist,* Apr.–May 1989, 6. The "Joint," which may have been familiar to some Soviet Jews from its activities in the 1920s, made a huge investment in that restoration and relief enterprise, detailed in Anita Weiner, *Renewal: Reconnecting Soviet Jewry to the Jewish People; A Decade of American Jewish Joint Distribution Committee (AJJDC) Activities in the Former Soviet Union, 1988–1998* (New York: University Press of America, 2003).

7. "Reviving Jewish Life in USSR Is Top Priority, Says Bronfman," *JTA,* 29 Mar. 1989.

8. The first year dropouts outnumbered *Olim* was 1977. By 1979, 65.8 percent (33,933 out of 51,547) of the emigrants chose not to settle in Israel. After that year the percentage opting for the West rose every year.

9. Quoted in Oberdorfer, *The Turn,* 372.

10. There is some evidence, drawn from the twenties, that it was on the way to becoming such a preoccupation. Morris Abram expressed wonderment that a Soviet Jewry movement did not form in the United States in 1919 when the Leninist policy of closing synagogues and cultural decapitation was first implemented. Interview with Morris Abram, NYPL, Wiener Oral History, 1989.

11. Historians have not ignored it. See again Novick, *The Holocaust in American Life.*

12. Interview with Nechemia Levanon, NYPL, Wiener Oral History, 3 Dec. 1989.

13. Address before the annual convention of the Rabbinical Assembly. *JTA,* 29 Mar. 1989, 2.

14. Alex Goldfarb, "Testing Glasnost: An Exile Visits His Homeland," *New York Times Magazine,* 6 Dec. 1987, 42.

15. Vladimir Yedidovich, "Forced Allegiance to Motherland Russia," *Forward,* 16 Aug. 2002, 11. Putin was speaking before the government-organized World Congress of Russian Speaking Jews in Moscow in August 2002. See also Perkovich, "Soviet Jewry," 452ff, for efforts after 1987 to restore Jewish institutions.

Glossary ∎

aliyah: immigration to Israel, Hebrew

Aliyah Bet: illegal immigration to Palestine

brenindiger: impassioned believer in a cause (Yiddish)

Bricha: operation to bring Holocaust survivors to American zone

Chabad: an alternate name for the Lubavitch Hassidic sect

Comintern: Communist International

dropouts: Soviet emigrants who chose not to settle in Israel

Evsektsya: Jewish section of the CPSU

Glasnost: policy of liberalization initiated by Mikhail Gorbachev

Ha'apala: operation to bring *Bricha* illegals to Palestine

Habonim: Zionist youth movement affiliated with Labor Party

Halacha: religious law in Judaism

Hasbara: educational propaganda

Kharakteristika: good character reference required by visa applicants

Kol Israel: Radio Israel

Kristallnacht: pogrom in Germany, 9 November 1938

Lishkat Hakesher: Israel's secret liaison bureau

Noshrim: Hebrew term for dropouts

perestroika: reconstruction aspect of Gorbachev's reform movement

pidyon shivuim: Talmudic law for the ransoming of prisoners

refusenik: Soviet Jew whose visa application was rejected

samizdat: self-publication of unsanctioned work in the Soviet Union

Sherit Hapleta: remnant of European Jewry that survived the Holocaust

olim: immigrants to Israel, ascenders

Verband: Yiddish name for Labor Zionist organization in U.S.

vyzov: required invitation from a host family to emigrate

Yevrei: used on Soviet internal passport to identify Jews

Yishuv: Hebrew term for Jewish settlement in Palestine

yordim: emigrants from Israel, descenders *(yerida)*

Zapadniki: Zionized Jews from Baltic

Zwungsaliyah: immigration of those who had no alternative but to settle in Israel

Index ■

Abram, Morris: agreement with Soviets, 255, 256, 270–71, 280; as American Jewish Committee president, 63; on disarmament and Soviet Jewry question, 235; on dropouts, 285; on freedom of choice for immigrants, 269; on Jackson-Vanik Amendment, 269–70, 279; mission to Moscow with Bronfman, 268–72, 276; on rapprochement with business community, 278; on refugee status of Soviet emigrants, 255–56; on Shultz's human rights declaration, 252; on Soviet Jewry in 1919, 364n. 10; at UN Commission on Human Rights, 5, 63, 64, 89, 90, 92, 197, 199, 328n. 53; and Washington rally of December 1987, 273, 274

Abramovich, Felix, 273

Abramovich, Pavel, 332n. 28

Abrams, Bob, 101

Abrams, Elliot, 242, 355n. 3, 357n. 32

Abzug, Bella, 339n. 24

accommodationists, 90–91

Adamishin, Anatoly, 290

Adee, Alvey, 3, 4, 5

Adler, Cyrus, 12, 26–27

AFC (Anti-Fascist Committee), 21, 32–33, 36, 41

Afghanistan: Soviet invasion of, 147, 156, 158, 182, 191, 224, 225, 228, 232, 234, 238, 248, 249, 304; Soviets announce withdrawal from, 252, 276

agricultural colonies, 23

Agro-Joint, 24, 26, 32

Agudath Israel, 61, 91

AJC. *See* American Jewish Committee (AJC)

AJCong. *See* American Jewish Congress (AJCong)

AJCSJ. *See* American Jewish Conference on Soviet Jewry (AJCSJ)

Albert, Carl, 211, 212, 217

Alert (journal), 96

Aliyeh Bet, 49–50

Allen, Richard, 243

Alter, Viktor, 32

Amalrik, Andrei, 261, 344n. 4

American Committee for Concerned Scientists, 100

American Hebrew (journal), 4, 6, 22

American Israel Political Action Committee (AIPAC), 122, 161

American Jewish Committee (AJC): as agency apart, 60; in commercial treaty abrogation campaign, 7, 11; in Conference of Presidents, 60–61, 90, 91; confrontational tactics opposed by, 93; "courageous fighter for Jewish dignity" award to Sharansky, 272; and Crimean resettlement project, 25; as declining in 1960s, 296; and democratization of American Jewry, 7, 9, 11; and dropouts, 176, 178; in early Soviet Jewry movement, 58–59, 63; on free immigration, 306; interest in Soviet Jewry promoted by, 46; and Jackson-Vanik Amendment, 196; and Judeobolshevik